Cape Town Harmonies

Memory, Humour and Resilience

Armelle Gaulier & Denis-Constant Martin

Published in 2017 by
African Minds
4 Eccleston Place, Somerset West, 7130, Cape Town, South Africa
info@africanminds.org.za
www.africanminds.org.za

© 2017
All contents of this document, unless specified otherwise, are licensed under a
Creative Commons Attribution 4.0 International License.

All photographs by Denis-Constant Martin unless otherwise noted.

ISBNs
978-1-928331-50-6 PRINT
978-1-928331-51-3 e-Book
978-1-928331-52-0 e-Pub

Copies of this book are available for free download at
www.africanminds.org.za

ORDERS
For orders from Africa:
African Minds
Email: info@africanminds.org.za

For orders from outside Africa:
African Books Collective
PO Box 721, Oxford OX1 9EN, UK
Email: orders@africanbookscollective.com

Published with the support of:

*Dedicated to
Anwar Gambeno & Melvyn Matthews
whose support and assistance contributed decisively
to our research on Kaapse Klopse and Malay Choirs*

Anwar Gambeno (left) and Melvyn Matthews (right)

Contents

Acknowledgements vii
Foreword xiii
Prologue xvii

INTRODUCTION *1*

Part One:
Memory and Processes of Musical Appropriation

CHAPTER 1
Music behind the music: Appropriation as the engine of creation   *39*

CHAPTER 2
In the footsteps of the future: Musical memory and reconciliation in South Africa   *59*

Part Two:
Nederlandsliedjies *and Notions of Blending*

CHAPTER 3
The *nederlandsliedjies*' "uniqueness"   *77*

CHAPTER 4
The meanings of blending   *107*

Part Three
Moppies: *Humour and Survival*

CHAPTER 5
Assembling comic songs   *135*

CHAPTER 6
Behind the comic   *179*

CONCLUSION
Memory, resilience, identity and creolisation   *219*

Appendix 1 – Nederlandsliedjies *lyrics*   *237*
Appendix 2 – *Cape Malay Choir Board adjudication reports*   *247*
Appendix 3 – Moppie *lyrics*   *253*
References   *321*
Interviews with musicians, judges and experts   *335*

Acknowledgements

ARMELLE GAULIER

I FIRST WENT to Cape Town from July to October 2006 to study *moppies* or comic songs. When I began my investigations, my interlocutors sometimes found it difficult to answer questions about what they called the "tradition". However, because I was a young French woman and had decided to come to Cape Town and stay in the Cape Flats in order to conduct fieldwork on the *Kaapse Klopse Karnival*, the New Year festivals in general and the musical repertoires associated with these events, I received a very warm welcome from Carnival organisers and leaders of *Klopse* and Malay Choirs. They not only made every effort to answer my questions, even when they sounded strange to them, but also allowed me to attend practices and facilitated my contacts in the world of the New Year festivals. My first interest was in the *moppies*, but they told me that in fact they considered the most important repertoire to be the *nederlandsliedjies*. I therefore decided to come back from January to March 2008, in time for the Malay Choir competitions, in order to prepare another study focusing on *nederlandsliedjies*. I was again granted a wonderful welcome. The material collected during these two fieldworks provided the basis for two masters dissertations in ethnomusicology.

I would like to thank all the people with whom I have been fortunate to interact during my fieldwork in Cape Town; especially Ismail Bey, Taliep Abrahams, Shawn Petersen, Adam Samodeen, Tape Jacobs, Ameer, Christopher Ferndale, Shahida Thole, Michael Abrahams, Eddie Matthews, Ronald Fisher, Abdurahman "Maan" Morris, Marian Leeman, Ismail Leeman, Ismail Morris and Kaatje. Please be assured of my gratitude.

I also would like to express my appreciation to the singers of the *Klopse* and the Malay Choirs, to the coaches and the musicians who trusted me and allowed me to record rehearsals while competitions were taking place: members and leaders of the Spesbona, the Fabulous Woodstock Starlites, the Kenfacts, the Woodstock Royals, the Tulips, the Starlites, the Continental Male Choir, the Zinnias, the Villagers, the Parkdales, the Young Men and the Morning Glories.

My stay and research in the Cape Flats would not have been possible without the support of Muneeb, Anwar and Firoza Gambeno: thank you for your warm welcome and innumerable teas and talks. I am also extremely grateful to the Wilsnagh family who made my stay in Mitchells Plain safe and fascinating: thanks to you, thank you for all the nights you spent telling me of the *Kaapse Klopse Karnival* in the Bo-Kaap.

Finally, I want to dedicate a very special word of thanks to Melvyn Matthews who took from his personal time to drive me all over the Cape Flats to meet various choirs and who shared with me his memories and his experiences of the Carnival. He also helped me to get a much deeper understanding of those who are involved in the Carnival and attend it. Melvyn, I could not have conducted this research without your support and your friendship.

* * *

DENIS-CONSTANT MARTIN

Research undertaken for this book would not have been possible without the support of the Stellenbosch Institute of Advanced Studies (STIAS), which very generously granted me three fellowships (2007, 2013 and 2015), during which I conducted investigations on *Kaapse Klopse* and Malay Choirs, and taped interviews with many participants in the New Year festivals. I am particularly grateful to Professor Bernard Lategan, STIAS' founding director, and Professor Hendrik Geyer, its director since 2008, as well as to Mrs Maria Mouton, personal assistant to the STIAS director, who organised my stays in Stellenbosch with the utmost kindness and efficiency. I also wish to thank the French Institute of South Africa (*Institut français d'Afrique du Sud*, IFAS) which, from the beginning, supported my research in Cape Town and granted a small subsidy for the publication of this volume, which is indeed highly appreciated.

Although I had for a long time been interested in South African music, and especially in South African jazz, I started doing academic research on Cape Town's New Year festivals and musics in the early 1990s. The programme dealing specifically with the New Year festivals, *Kaapse Klopse*, Malay Choirs and their repertoires was conceived at the request of Jean-Luc Domenach, then director of the centre to which I was affiliated: the Centre for International Studies (*Centre d'études et de recherches internationales*, CERI) of the National Foundation for Political Science (*Fondation nationale des sciences politiques*, FNSP). I realised it under the aegis of that CERI and then, after 2008, as a staff member of the Centre for the Study of Black Africa (*Centre d'étude d'Afrique noire*, CEAN) of the Bordeaux Institute of Political Studies (*Sciences Po Bordeaux*), which in 2011 was reorganised under the name Africas in the World (*Les Afriques dans le monde*, LAM). Without the support and encouragement I received from these centres and their successive directors (Jean-Luc Domenach, Jean-François Bayart, Christophe Jaffrelot and Christian Lequesne, at CERI; René Otayek and Céline Thiriot at CEAN and LAM), I would not have been able to develop a research programme that looked quite eccentric to many members of the academic establishment, in spite of the confidence and the intellectual stimulation I always received from my colleagues.

Simha Arom, Senior Research Fellow Emeritus at CNRS, has for several decades instructed me in ethnomusicology, advised on my research orientations and explained what I could not understand in the musics I studied. He has been a precious mentor whom I shall never be able to thank enough.

Investigations focusing on *moppies* were conducted within the framework of the research group GLOBAMUS (Musical Creation, Circulation and Identity Market in a Global Context),[1] led by Emmanuelle Olivier (National Centre for Scientific Research, CNRS) and funded by the French National Agency for Research (*Agence nationale de la recherche*). Research focusing on *nederlandsliedjies* was part of a programme initiated by Nathalie Fernando (Music Faculty, University of Montréal): Comparative Study of Aesthetic Evaluation Criteria and Taste Judgments (Comparative Musicology and Anthropology of Music Laboratory, Interdisciplinary Observatory of Musical Creation and Research, Canada).[2] Finally, research on Cape Town's New Year festivals contributed to the "virtual research laboratory" (Critical World),[3] organised by Bob White (Department of Anthropology, University of Montréal). Emmanuelle Olivier, Nathalie Fernando and Bob White sometimes supported my research financially, but more importantly, along with all the colleagues who participated in these groups, helped me to problematise my interests and devise appropriate methodologies to pursue my investigations into Cape Town's cultures.

In South Africa, many colleagues encouraged me, and provided information and suggestions that were invaluable: Sylvia Bruinders and Michael Nixon (South African College of Music) at the University of Cape Town; Stephanus Muller (Music Department and Documentation Centre for Music, DOMUS), Lizabé Lambrechts (DOMUS), Paula Fourie (then doctoral student in the Music Department), Simon Bekker and Kees van der Waal (Sociology and Social Anthropology Department), and Felicia Lesch, (Certificate Programme Co-ordinator and Outreach Co-ordinator, Department of Music) at Stellenbosch University. Cheryl Hendricks (Department of Politics and International Studies, University of Johannesburg) and Elaine Salo (Director, Institute for Women's and Gender Studies, University of Pretoria)[4] generously shared with me their intimate knowledge of Cape Town society and politics. Ongoing conversations with Christine Lucia (formerly with Stellenbosch University) on South African musics, with Zimitri Erasmus (Department of Sociology, University of the Witwatersrand) on coloured identity and creolisation, with Shamil Jeppie (Department of Historical Studies, University of Cape Town) on Cape Town's cultures and Islam in South Africa played a decisive role in my understanding of the relationships between festivals, musics and socio-political realities in Cape Town; I have not enough words to thank them for the inspiration they gave me. Finally, I want to dedicate a particular word of thanks to: Christopher Ferndale (Public Education and Outreach, Western Cape Provincial Parliament), a poet and one of the lynchpins of the Cape Cultural Collective who introduced me to the richness of Cape Town's cultural life; to Shamiel Domingo, who very generously shared time and documents with me and introduced me to the intricacies of *nederlandsliedjies* performances; to Firoza Gambeno and her husband, the late Kader Firferey, who gave me the opportunity to discover the ritual known as *gajjat*; and finally, to Rehana Vally (Faculty Teaching and Learning Committee, University of Pretoria) who, even before I could visit South Africa, educated me about the complexity, the vibrancy and the luxuriance of her country.

* * *

ARMELLE GAULIER AND DENIS-CONSTANT MARTIN

The two dedicatees, Messrs Anwar Gambeno and Melvyn Matthews understood, from the start, our respective projects and actively supported them to the extent that they eventually played a decisive role in our research on *Klopse* and Malay Choirs. They provided information, explanations and contacts in such a way that they became true partners in our investigations; it is impossible to tell how much we owe them.

We also want to thank Professor Shamil Jeppie who, in addition to his assistance in the course of our research, very graciously agreed to write a preface for this book.

We must indeed extend our appreciation to all the persons who accepted to spend time with us, who received us at their home, sometimes after a long working day, and accepted to talk to us and let us tape interviews, who allowed us to attend choir practices and to record them, who gave us material on *nederlandsliedjies* and comic songs; their names are listed at the end of this volume and they deserve our greatest gratitude. We have a special thought for those who have passed away since we met them; we hope we have been able to do justice to the experience they communicated to us. We keep particularly fond memories of Vincent Kolbe and Ismail Dante, for their kindness and their generosity; without their contribution, this book would not have been the same.

Muneeb Gambeno, a lawyer and a singer, guided us through the intricacies of the legal framework within which *Klopse* and Malay Choirs operate. Paul Sedres, an expert on Cape Town musics and cultures, not only translated *moppie* lyrics, but allowed us to understand better their innuendos and their specific comicality; he also very often identified the musical sources of *moppie* melodies. We deeply appreciate their friendship and their availability.

Finally, we want to extend our warmest appreciation to Tessa Botha who copy-edited our text with great meticulousness and made it easier to read and understand, as well as to François van Schalkwyk, a trustee of the not-for-profit, open access publisher African Minds. The collaboration between François van Schalkwyk and Denis-Constant Martin started when François was working at David Philip Publishers and edited and produced Denis-Constant Martin's *Coon Carnival: New Year in Cape Town, Past and Present*. Years later, he welcomed at African Minds Denis-Constant's subsequent projects on Cape Town musics with enthusiasm and trust. We feel very fortunate to work with a publisher with such an open mind, a great tolerance for English written by non-native speakers, and eager to make scholarly works dedicated to Cape Town and South Africa's cultures easily accessible through open access publishing. African Minds is the kind of home we hoped for when we began devising this project. Our hope has become a reality, thanks to François van Schalkwyk.

Notes

1. http://globalmus.net/?lang=en
2. http://mcam.oicrm.org/en/research-at-mcam/comparative-study-of-aesthetic-evaluation-criteria-and-taste-judgments/
3. http://criticalworld.net/
4. It is with great sadness that, at the time of proofreading, we learned of the untimely demise of Elaine Salo. She was a brilliant scholar and a wonderful person; she is and will be deeply missed (for a eulogy, see: Chris Barron "Elaine Rosa Salo: Feminist who spoke truth to power", *The Sunday Times*, 28 August 2016).

The Riverside Roses, Keep the Dream Malay Choir Board Finals, 2015

Foreword

Cape Town's public cultures can only be fully appreciated through recognition of its deep and diverse *soundscape*. We have to listen to what has made and makes a city. The ear is an integral part of the "research tools" one needs to get a sense of any city. We have to listen to the sounds that made and make the expansive "mother city". Various of its constituent parts sound different from each other, just as Cape Town might sound different to, say, Johannesburg. A Saturday morning in the markets of Khayelitsha or Gatesville looks and sounds very different to the Saturday markets closer to the mountain and greener, forested parts of the city.

Some, especially younger, people might prefer going about listening to their private, downloaded music through their headphones. However, many people listen to the range of radio stations operating in the city. Contemporary Western pop music has a large following through these radio stations, although "talk radio" has also come to have a great attraction. About the music, however, it's not only the latest or recent hits. There has been a long love affair with American R&B and "evergreens" from a range of popular repertoires. The daily aural experience of the city comprises the noise of cars and trucks, mixed with human chatter, sometimes barking dogs, and the popular radio stations or TV in the background. In some neighborhoods the Arabic call to prayer or *Adhan* might faintly project across the atmosphere at certain times of the day. Church bells are hardly audible these days, but they do still ring in some areas. This description is, of course, a simplification of a varied experience of sounds in the city.

And then there is the sound of the singing men and their choirs ("teams" they are called) in preparation for the longstanding annual Malay choral competitions. The lyrics from the various repertoires they perform are hardly ever written down. They are mostly in the memory and memorised, even if they are new compositions. There are texts of the hallowed "Dutch songs", but these do not circulate easily and widely. Researchers dream of finding lyrics from decades ago, not to mention a few generations ago — back to the early 19th century. However, there seems to be no publicly available "standard edition" of the canon of either the oldest traditional songs or the comic songs produced anew every year. This work by Denis-Constant Martin and Armelle Gaulier provides us with a very useful selection of these songs. More than that, the book is a critical sociological reflection of the place of these songs and their performers in the context that has given rise to them and sustains their relevance. It is a necessary work and is a very important scholarly intervention about a rather neglected aspect of the history and present production of music in the city. Some young people with fancy headphones might pull up their noses and condemn these music forms as relics from the past. But we can safely assume that when what most of them are now listening to has long been forgotten, the songs here studied will still have a deep resonance. Across many generations, the choral traditions have persisted and the choirs have never lacked for men to perform, or men and women to back their "teams".

This book is the collective product of two scholars, together with the assistance of many close collaborators from among the choirs who value the importance of this kind of research. However, it will not be out of place to mention, in the first instance, something about how a French scholar came to discover, and in a certain sense, also recover, as a research field, a musical form.

Denis-Constant made the music and performance cultures of Cape Town his focus in the early 1990s. Before then his research interests took him to various parts of Africa: from Algeria to Tanzania and Kenya; and from the Caribbean to the USA. He has written about aspects of the musical and expressive cultures, and the politics or connections among these areas, for each of these sites of research. Denis-Constant spent many years working in East Africa and when the opportunity arose to begin work on South Africa after the end of apartheid, he jumped at the opportunity. At that time, there were many possibilities, and an unlimited array of topics for researchers. He set about investigating the Western Cape's musical traditions that bring together a range of influences — created from local conditions, but also reflecting influences from across the Indian Ocean and the Atlantic. Although there had been some previous work on this, Denis-Constant brought his own intellectual formation to this area. His formal training was in the study of politics with a strong ethnographic bent, namely political anthropology, begun under the famous Georges Balandier. His later fieldwork and theorisation would develop around multi-ethnic, multi-cultural societies and their histories of performance and music-making, from reggae to rap, from jazz in the USA to jazz in Paris, from carnival in the Caribbean, eventually to carnival in Cape Town.

Those of us involved in the study of this part of South Africa — the Western Cape and the urban Cape in particular — have been fascinated by this French scholar. We have been, and perhaps still are, so Anglophone in our orientations in most things and also our approach to research. Denis-Constant brought a wealth, and world, of comparative learning and experience. His work has revitalised the historical–ethnographic study of popular culture and music in the Cape. And in the roughly two decades since his first encounters in the city and its peripheries he has produced a number of outstanding works – articles and books (and CDs) – that are essential reference works and reference points for theoretical insights and empirical details. They are eminently readable for scholars and the general reader alike.

In 1999, Denis-Constant's *Coon Carnival: New Year in Cape Town, Past and Present* brought together his fieldwork and insights for a general readership, but with his interpretive framework in place. Then appeared *Sounding the Cape: Music,*

Identity and Politics in South Africa in 2013. In between these years there appeared a slew of journal articles. These are major contributions to our understanding of the making of the soundscape, identities and texture of Cape Town, a part of South Africa that was first colonised by the Dutch, then the British; and that as a port-city has seen the comings and goings of men and women, and ideas and things, from across the globe. Denis-Constant, perhaps more than many other local scholars, has seen the possibilities for studying the region in a trans-regional setting. And, enthused by it, he recruited other Francophone researchers. This book is the product of Denis-Constant and Armelle Gaulier, his former PhD student who trained in ethno-musicology and carried out extensive fieldwork in Cape Town in the 2000s.

In this work, the two authors give us a selection of original texts and translations, as well as analyses of two genres emblematic of the choral repertoire, the *nederlandsliedjies* and the *moppies*. If these had not been invented in the 19th century, there would be no Malay choirs today. Expertise in these genres takes hundreds of hours of practice and much hardship. There are many performers who can perform and innovate (in the *moppies* or comic songs), but only a very few have attained mastery. There are standards and protocols to learn, observe and master. There is a classic body of *nederlandsliedjies* and an ever-changing body of *moppies*. These have not earned entry into any national music canon — they are never played on the radio, except for one or two really famous tunes on very local stations — and are very much limited to Cape Town. However, the authors argue that they are indeed works of art. The original words of the songs and their translations are presented, together with interpretive overview essays. Enjoy the songs and then listen to the choirs practising or performing at a competition.

SHAMIL JEPPIE
University of Cape Town

Drum Majors leading the Penny Pincher klops *at the Green Point Cycle Track, 1994*

Prologue

A word about words

Writing about South Africa always entails using words which have been, and still are, loaded with historically constructed meanings and located within complex and often ambiguous semantic fields. This is why we think it necessary to clarify the vocabulary that we use in this book.

"Race" and "racial" classifications

The authors of this book are French, which implies they are also Europeans. We are heirs to a history which saw the idea of "race" used at various periods to justify colonial oppression and the extermination of large numbers of our fellow human beings. Consequently, we, along with a majority of European and non-European social scientists, reject the meaning that has been given to "race" in the past, including the South African past, and feel uneasy when we have to use the word. Our attitude towards the use of "race" is based on French philosopher and political scientist Pierre-André Taguieff's considerations (Taguieff 2010).[1] The notion of "race" is scientifically – be it in biology or in the social sciences – null and void. However, the word and its derivations (racism, racialism,[2] racialisation[3]) are still used and "overused" (Taguieff 2010: 7). Given this "paradox" (Taguieff 2010: 7), it appears imperative to study how, by whom, when and why they were and are used.

The idea of "race" has for a long time been a structuring factor of South African society. Yet, definitions and uses of "race" have been characterised by variability, imprecision and arbitrariness. Anthony Christopher (2002, 2009) analysed in detail classifications imagined by South African authorities, especially on the occasion of censuses, starting with the Cape of Good Hope census of 1865, the first modern scientific census conducted in South Africa. His tables illustrate the many changes that affected the number and the names of categories in which people were put. As a matter of fact, as underlined by sociologist Deborah Posel, before 1948 each institution produced its own definitions and classifications, based on discretionary decisions made by bureaucrats or judges (Posel 2001: 89-92). On the whole: "The classification of population in South Africa in successive censuses was an integral part of the system of control exercised until 1994 by the dominant white group, which remained the one constant entity in the ever more rigidly enforced system" (Christopher 2002: 406). The advent of apartheid and the passing of the Population Registration Act, 1950, ossified "racial" categories, but could not give them a solid basis. It emphasised the constructed nature of the classification system by insisting on the notion of social "acceptation". For instance, it stated that: "A white person means a person who in appearance obviously is, or who is generally accepted as a white person, but does not include a person who, although in appearance obviously a white person, is generally accepted as a coloured person" (quoted in Christopher 2002: 405). However, observed Deborah Posel: "If the substance of the Population Registration Act did not fundamentally change the content of racial categories operative pre-1948, it radically transformed their form [...] For the first time, a racial classification would be uniform and immobile, established once and for all, to apply across the range of experiences subject to racialized legislation" (Posel 2001: 103). There were nevertheless a few modifications within the coloured category regarding the place of malays,[4] griquas[5] and Indians, included as subdivisions of the coloured group, or treated as separate entities (Christopher 2002).

After 1994, the post-apartheid governments decided that it was impossible to do away with previous classifications of the South African population. They continued using the four basic categories (whites, Africans/blacks, coloureds, Asians/Indians) but a fifth category ("Unspecified and Other") was added in 1996 to meet the demand of the Griqua National Council. Statistics South Africa (Stats SA), the official body in charge of enumerating the population, explained: "*Population group* describes the racial classification of a particular group of South African citizens. The previous government used this type of classification to divide the South African population into distinct groupings on which to base apartheid policies. It is now important for Stats SA to continue to use this classification wherever possible, since it clearly indicates the effects of discrimination of the past, and permits monitoring of policies to alleviate discrimination. In the past, population group was based on a legal definition, but it is now based on self-perception and self-classification."[6] This classification has not only been utilised for censuses, but provided a framework for assessing the impact of such legislation as in the Employment Equity Act of 1998 and the Broad-Based Black Economic Empowerment Act of 2003 (Christopher 2009: 107). It must also be noted that, for instance, the Broad-Based Black Economic Empowerment Act of 2003 made use of the umbrella category "black", which was theorised by the Black Consciousness Movement and encompasses all victims of apartheid: black Africans, coloureds and Indians/Asians[7] (Escusa 2015: 114). Such traces of the apartheid era clearly indicate that: "after apartheid, most South Africans' lived experiences continue to be shaped by racialized material and subjective realities" (Erasmus 2008: 172). This reality should not, however, conceal the fact that since 1994: "while race remains a key factor shaping inequality and vulnerability, it is now reproduced and spoken about differently" (Erasmus 2008: 173). Consequently, in certain instances, it still is necessary, for analytical purposes, to deal separately with people who have been or still are classified as belonging to the various historical population groups: Africans, coloureds and Indians/Asians. The term "Africans" is generally used to designate people who speak indigenous languages of the Bantu family. South African citizens speaking, or whose ancestors spoke, indigenous languages belonging to the Khoisan family, are often put, for historical reasons, under the category "coloured" and several groups of coloureds claim a Khoikhoi or San ancestry. Indians/Asians denote descendants of indentured workers brought from the Indian peninsula during the second half of the 19th century, traders and businessmen that came with or after them and other persons who came from India or Pakistan to South Africa in the 20th century (Ebr.-Vally 2001).

Coloureds

"Coloured" is probably the most contentious word in this terminology. It has been understood as a label arbitrarily imposed upon certain people by the authorities and used to create divisions among those who were oppressed and exploited under racial policies. In addition to this, it proved impossible to clearly define who could and who could not be classified coloured so large were the somatic, religious, linguistic and socio-economic differences between people put in a category that appeared basically as a residual category (not white/not African).[8] While it cannot be denied that the category "coloured" was effectively imposed and used to separate, it must also be acknowledged that the term was eventually appropriated by those whom it meant to circumscribe. In the 19th century, the South African population was usually divided into whites and coloureds, meaning Africans speaking Bantu and Khoisan languages, descendants of slaves and *mestizos* (Christopher 2002: 402). In 1865, the Cape of Good Hope census identified four groups of people living in the Cape Colony: Europeans, "hottentots", "kafirs" and others; in so doing, it divided the former coloured group in three and introduced a difference between "hottentots" (coloureds) and "kafirs" (Africans). This created an intermediate category which will persist as such until the end of the 20th century (Christopher 2002). According to anthropologist Rosemary Ridd: "'Coloured' arose as a miscellaneous category out of the difficulty British administrators found in trying to classify a substantial population that did not fit easily into a race group" (Ridd 1994: 51). Being classified coloured sparked off various reactions: "Among those classified as Coloured there have been different responses to being labelled. Some were content to call themselves Coloured, whether as a political statement (as Alex la Guma did within SACPO [South African Coloured People's Organisation][9]) or with resignation as a status group (a position Peter Abrahams[10] describes his family taking). The founders of the APO [African People's Organisation][11] presumably wanted to be thought of as African. Others called themselves 'non-White', 'South Africans' or 'just people' [...] The questioning of Colouredness represented a form of quiet resistance among people powerless to act more openly. It gave them a secret language and understanding which, ironically enough, contributed to a bonding and group consciousness while at the same time defying any attempt formally to lay this down in absolute terms" (Ridd 1994: 59).

These vacillations were in part due to the fact that former slaves began to toy with the idea of being coloured as distinct from "natives" as soon as the turn to the 20th century (Erasmus & Pieterse 1999: 169). Historian Vivian Bickford-Smith observed that: "In the course of the 1890s 'Coloured' or 'Cape Coloured' was increasingly adopted as a self-descriptive ethnic label by people who were not accepted as white and who did not think of themselves as Natives or Africans" (Bickford-Smith 1995: 201). Consequently, a community, cemented by feelings of belonging, began to coalesce and became progressively structured by internal social networks based in particular on religious and sports organisations (Bickford-Smith 1995). In the process, those who utilised coloured as a self-definition gradually changed its meaning; the negative definition of a residual category (neither Europeans nor Africans) was rejected to make room for the positive conception of a group characterised by resilience, solidarity and creativity.

Historian Mohamed Adhikari underlined that: "Even though the coloured status was to a large extent voluntarily adopted and the coloured identity largely elaborated by coloureds themselves, it nevertheless remained a second choice to their ultimate goal of assimilation into the superordinate society. Coloured identity was therefore not embraced in a spontaneous and positive expression of ethnic identity by its bearers, but was rather accepted with a mixture of tentative self-affirmation and helpless resignation to an unjust social order" (Adhikari 1993: 174). The ambiguity between positive self-assertion and acquiescence left open possibilities of negotiating with the authorities which have been highlighted by anthropologist Elaine Salo in her studies of Manenberg:[12] "the local residents utilised the coloureds' official place in the spatial, social and economic apartheid landscape and creatively inverted the official meanings of colouredness to reclaim a positive sense of identity, rooted within the moral sphere" (Salo 2005a: 174). These historical considerations are important because they provide a background that allows us to understand how the term "coloured" has been used since 1994, not only in legal texts, but by the very people so qualified.

As suggested by Zimitri Erasmus and Edgar Pieterse: "It is important to conceptualise coloured identities as relational identities shaped by complex networks of concrete social relations rather than seeing 'coloured' as a particular category of individuals and/or simply as an imposed name from a racist past. The value of this approach is its challenge to any notions of colouredness as homogeneous and/or an essentialist ethnic identity with fixed cultural boundaries as well as its acknowledgement of the particularity of identities" (Erasmus & Pieterse 1999: 183). This explains why so many people classified coloured have no qualms about calling themselves coloured and expressing their pride in belonging to this group. Francesca Inglese, an American student who conducted research on Cape Town carnival troupes in 2014, remarked: "During the course of my research, the majority of *Klopse* participants whom I interviewed proudly self-identified as coloured. Although many recognize the historically-constructed and lived fluidity of *all* racial categories, they conceptualize the term as an important means by which they navigate their relationships to history, place, and to one another, and recognize that it continues to be a lens through which others view them in their day-to-day lives" (Inglese 2014: 128). This totally concurs with what we experienced in the course of our own investigations in Cape Town: a large majority of our interlocutors, if not all of them, had no problem in calling themselves coloured and most often insisted on the fecundity and the originality of the group's culture. This is why we think it legitimate to use the word coloured in this book.

Malays and Malay Choirs

People called "malays" or "Cape malays" have been either treated as a sub-group within the category coloured or as an autonomous entity. The word was used by whites in the 1850s to designate Muslims; it was rapidly adopted by those who were referred to as such, mostly ex-slaves or descendants of Muslim political prisoners (Bickford-Smith 1995: 35). The term "malay" was based not on the origin of the people – very few of them actually came from the Malaysian peninsula and archipelago – but on the idioms they spoke, belonging to the Malay language family or creoles with a strong Malay component (Malayo-Portuguese creole). Malay became an appellation that allowed Muslims to be distinguished from other coloureds. It carried a rather positive connotation, malays being often considered as respectable and hardworking, especially because they did not drink. Many malays adhered to these representations and believed they were superior to other "non-whites", because of their religion, education and socio-economic successes (Haron 2001). However, the term malay and the idea of being malay have also been heavily contested (Vahed & Jeppie 2005). At the height of the anti-apartheid struggle, during the 1970s and 1980s, young activists chose to use the religious label and called themselves South African Muslims rather than Cape malays (Haron 2001: 2). But a few years later, after the collapse of apartheid, there was a "resurgence of Malay ethnicity" which manifested itself in the celebration of the tri-centenary of the introduction of Islam at the Cape (Haron 2001: 5; Ward 1995). Today, "the 'Cape Malay' identity continues to be a contested terrain; a terrain where there are a fair number of voices in support of and against it" (Haron 2001: 6). This situation derives in a large part from the fact that the label "malay" was used to divide people classified coloured and to create antagonisms between Muslims and Christians when, in most areas inhabited by coloureds, coexistence was friendly and inter-marriages were accepted. Historian Shamil Jeppie underlined the convergence of white intellectuals – fascinated by the exotic they saw in malays and intent on creating "racial" categories – and conservative Muslims wanting to control, religiously and socially, a specific community: "The idea of a definitive and original Malay background found its Muslim proponents among politically conservative Muslim elites in the twentieth-century. It inevitably found its white folklorists and ethnographers as well, most notably I.D. du Plessis, devoted to preserving aspects of the supposedly vanishing Malay culture, customs, language and so on. The separate national origin for the Muslims served excellently ruling class racialistic arguments and the development of segregationist policies – with their divide and rule rationale – which became the fully blown Apartheid from the late 1940s onwards" (Jeppie 1996b: 78). We shall examine in more detail how ID du Plessis contributed to consolidate the category "malay" and, especially, how he was involved in the creation of the Cape Malay Choir Board.[13] We are fully aware of the debates which developed around the label "malay". But, as with "coloured", we also acknowledge that the majority of our Muslim interlocutors expressed no reluctance at calling themselves malay, many finding pride in being linked to the history of Muslims in South Africa and relating strongly to what they considered their dignity and their contributions to building an original South African culture.[14]

In addition to that – although several alternative names exist, such as *Sangkore*, *Nagtroepe*, Male Choirs or *Mannekore*,[15] *Hollandse* Teams – a great majority of the choirs we shall deal with in the following chapters call themselves Malay Choirs and belong to one of the two main organisations: the Cape Malay Choir Board or the Keep the Dream Malay Choir Forum. There have been discussions within these organisations to decide whether they should change their name and stop using Malay Choir, or not. Anwar Gambeno, coach of the Young Tulips Sangkoor and president of Keep the Dream Malay Choir Board recalled: "In the beginning, they used to name the choirs *sangkore* [...] Then the new thing came along: malay. So everybody changed their name: Malay Choir. Then some other guy came along with another clever idea and said 'no, no, no don't say Malay Choir', he translated the thing directly into English and instead of saying *Sangkoor*, he gave the name Singing Choir, but obviously a choir sings [...] But you hardly hear the name *Sangkoor* anymore; you'll hear most of them say Malay Choir. But that's actually *Sangkoor*".[16] As a matter of fact, there were heated discussions in the 1990s about the use of the term "malay"; some argued that it should be dropped because of its "ethnic" connotations and also because not all members of the "Malay Choirs" were Muslims, that is "malays"; others considered that the word no longer differentiated people on the basis of their origin or religion, but had become a marker of particular cultural practices and consequently was inoffensive. Eventually, the proposition to substitute "male" for "malay" was rejected[17] and "Malay Choir" was retained. A similar discussion took place about the *kofia*,[18] the fez, which is an indispensable part of the singers' uniform. The choirs' representatives also decided that it should continue to be worn in competitions since it probably followed a Turkish and not an Indonesian or Malaysian fashion, and was not the emblem of an ethnic identity, but the component of a "cultural" dress. Consequently, in spite of all the ambiguities and contradictions attached to this term, we shall retain malay, when discussing the Malay Choirs.

Coons, minstrels, *Kaapse Klopse*

People participating in the New Year Carnival usually refer to the organisation they join for the occasion, as well as to the character they embody during the festivities, as "Coon". They say "I am a Coon"; a troupe captain talks about "his Coon"; and the carnival itself was for a long time called the "Coon Carnival" when the Afrikaans *Nuwe Jaar* was not used. There have been, at various periods, objections to the use of the word "coon" because of the meaning it had in the United States. "Coon" reached South Africa with blackface minstrelsy in the second half of the 19th century and carried with it ambiguities that were not clearly perceived, be it in the United States or in South Africa. Probably the most prominent "coon" in blackface minstrelsy was "Zip Coon": the central character in a song composed by George Washington Dixon, who also played the role on stage. An urban dandy, Zip Coon was generally opposed to Jim Crow, the rural dancer. The lyrics suggested that he had ridiculous pretensions: he was a "larned skoller" because he could sing "Possum up a gum tree" and some thought he could become "De bery nex President". Zip Coon apparently embodied an aspiration to socio-economic elevation that made whites nervous. However, a closer look at the music supporting the lyrics and at the persona of their author shows that behind the surface lay more complex meanings. The song could be the vehicle for real ambitions shared by young black and white working class people. George Washington Dixon was an advocate of the working class; he was suspected of being anti-slavery, and accused of being a mulatto himself (Cockrell 1997). Notwithstanding these intricacies – which were probably lost on most patrons of blackface shows – "coon" became in the United States an insulting way of talking about African-Americans, more or less synonymous with "nigger".

When the word crossed the Atlantic, it was appropriated by revellers celebrating the New Year in Cape Town; they understood it as the symbol of a bright, modern form of entertainment and it lost its racist acceptation. In 1994, a former carnival organiser and troupe captain explained what he understood when hearing the word "coon": "What is the coon? [...] It must be something the coon [...] the coon is a bird in America a black bird with a big eyes [...] that's a coon."[19] Taliep Petersen, a celebrated composer of songs and musicals who coached many carnival troupes, even became agitated when asked about objections to using the word "coon": "Now, now people don't [...] the Americans come and they don't want us to use the word coon because it's derogatory for the people. Here coon is not derogatory in our sense. For us the minute you talk coon, he sees New Year Day, he sees satin [...] and the painted [...] white around the eyes, black around the rest."[20] Members, coaches and captains of carnival troupes interviewed by Denis-Constant Martin in 1994 used the word "coon" without any reluctance. In the early 2010s, Channel Oliphant, a student at the University of the Western Cape who investigated the New Year Carnival, similarly noted: "I have found that those who participate find no derogative connotation to the word 'coon', although some do acknowledge the African-American derogative connotation. Furthermore I have found that various participants use the words 'minstrels', 'coons' and '*klopse*' interchangeably" (Oliphant 2013: 3). In spite of the general use of the word "coon" in Cape Town without any derogatory or racist connotations, there has been insistent pressure from South Africa and the United States to abandon the word.[21] While most people involved in the New Year Carnival continue to use "coon" when discussing between themselves the festivities and the troupes which participate in it, the word has now been replaced in official parlance and in the name of carnival boards. "Minstrels" has been used for some time, but again objections referring to the blackface minstrelsy[22] lexicon led to its abandonment. The words now generally used by carnival troupes and organisers and by their counterparts in local government, as well as by scholars, are *Klops* and *Kaapse Klopse* (literally "clubs of the Cape"). They come from the English "club" and allude to the first aggregations that sang and danced in the streets on New Year's Eve, which were frequently formed by members of social and sports clubs; moreover, phonetically it also "plays upon, and evokes the sound of the *ghoema* beat"[23] (Oliphant 2013: 3). In this case, we shall follow the trend and use *Klops* and *Klopse*.

Conclusion

To conclude this prologue, we want to reiterate that we treat "racial" and group categories, including "coloured" and "malay", as socio-historical constructions that have no biological basis; we reject any idea of cultural essence that would imprison individuals in unique, fixed and immutable group "identities" or "race"; we consider that cultural practices interact and cross-fertilise whatever the barriers that are erected to isolate them, that they evolve thanks to these contacts and the creations they spur; therefore we contend that cultures are never fixed and closed and cannot give birth to pure and unalterable identities. Accordingly, in this book, after taking cognisance of arguments presented by several authors (in particular, Eldridge & Seekings 1996: 519; Erasmus & Pieterse 1999: 169; Gqola 2010: 16; Vahed & Jeppie 2005: 281–282), we have elected to adopt the following conventions.

With respect to "population groups", we shall use the terminology found in censuses conducted by Statistics South Africa:[24] black African, coloured, Indian or Asian, white and other.[25] It seems legitimate and relevant to use these categories since they are no longer arbitrarily imposed upon individuals: people who are enumerated are now asked to choose under which one they want to be classified.[26] We shall write African and Indian or Asian with a capital initial, since they denote a geographic origin; black, coloured, malay, griqua and white with a lower case initial to avoid essentialising groups without single geographical roots. In addition to these five basic categories, we shall, whenever needed, distinguish people speaking languages of the Khoisan family: Khoikhoi and San. "Black" (with a lower case b), following the Black Consciousness definition, will refer to all people oppressed under segregationist and apartheid regimes, treated as a single aggregation: black Africans, coloureds and Indians or Asians. Finally, we decided to write "race" between inverted comas to emphasise that we consider that it is a social construction that should be studied as such, but that it does not cover a biological reality, except when used to talk about the "human race".

Regarding musical and carnival groups, as stated above, we will call carnival troupes *Klopse* (singular *Klops*) and choirs Malay Choirs.

Since this book is being published in South Africa, we have adopted the South African English spelling. However, when quoting other works, we have obviously retained the original spelling. Unless otherwise indicated, texts in French have been translated by Denis-Constant Martin. In cases where the French text is particularly intricate, the original has been reproduced in endnotes.

Notes

1. See also: Taguieff 2001.
2. "A conception based on a hierarchical classification of human 'races' according to which 'races' determines culture, history and social evolution" (Taguieff 2010: 115-116).
3. A conception which considers that "differences existing between human groups are caused by biological factors as defined or supposed in racial doctrines" (Taguieff 2010: 115).
4. On the use of capital initials, see: p. xxv.
5. Contemporary griquas are the descendants of children born in the 17th and 18th centuries of unions between white settlers who ventured into the interior of the Cape Colony and indigenous people, mostly Khoikhoi, but also San and Tswana. They speak Afrikaans and have for a long time been classified in the coloured category. During the 20th century, various movements such as the Griqua National Conference of South Africa and the Griqua National Council emerged, claiming an independent identity. They are represented in the National Khoisan Consultative Conference launched in 2001.
6. Statistics South Africa (1998) *The People of South Africa: Population Census 1996, the Count and How it was Done* (Report No. 03-01-17(1996)). Pretoria: Statistics South Africa. Available at https://apps.statssa.gov.za/census01/Census96/HTML/Metadata/Docs/count/chapter_1.htm [accessed 21 December 2015].
7. The conception of blackness developed within the Black Consciousness Movement was largely inspired by the writings and actions of African-American activists in the United States and their slogan "Black Power". Bantu Stephen Biko clarified its meaning for South Africa in a paper produced for a SASO Leadership Training Course in December 1971: "We have defined blacks as those who are by law or tradition politically, economically and socially discriminated against as a group in the South African society and identifying themselves as a unit in the struggle towards the realization of their aspirations." Available at http://www.sahistory.org.za/archive/definition-black-consciousness-bantu-stephen-biko-december-1971-south-africa [accessed 25 May 2015].
8. During the Parliamentary debate on the proposed Population Registration Act in 1950, WH Stewart, MP for the opposition United Party, stated that the Act was an "attempt to solve the unsolvable problem, the absolutely unsolvable problem as to what is actually a pure white person, what is a pure Coloured person (if you can get a pure Coloured person) and what is the subtle mixture between the two, and which is which and which is the other" (quoted in Ebr.-Vally 2001: 46–47).
9. The South African Coloured People's Organisation (SACPO) was launched in 1953; it fought against the attempt to remove coloured voters from the common voters' roll.
10. Alex la Guma and Peter Abrahams are two of the most famous coloured writers. Peter Abrahams (1919–2017) was one of the first South African writers to be internationally recognised. Abrahams left South Africa for England in 1939 and eventually settled in Jamaica in 1956; a novelist and journalist, the struggle against racism runs like a red thread through his works. Alex la Guma (1925–1985) was both a novelist and an activist who dedicated his life to fighting racism and apartheid. La Guma, a celebrated writer, was a member of the South African Communist Party, participated in drawing up the 1955 Freedom Charter and was one of the anti-apartheid militants accused at the 1956 Treason Trial.
11. The African People's Organisation (APO) was, from its foundation in 1902 until the early 1940s, the main coloured political force. Led by Dr Abdullah Abdurahman, it gathered together an intellectual and economic elite of educated and rather well-off coloureds and endeavoured to mobilise coloured voters to: "promote unity between the coloured races [...]

12. Manenberg is a coloured township located about 18 km from the centre of Cape Town. Established by apartheid authorities in 1966, it accommodates mostly low-income coloured people and is rife with gang-related violence; it has been made famous by Abdullah Ibrahim/ Dollar Brand's composition "Mannenberg", recorded in 1974.
13. See p. 6.
14. In a survey of visitors of the "300 years: The making of Cape Muslim culture" exhibition held at the Cape Town Castle in 1994, Kerry Ward came to similar conclusions (Ward 1995).
15. As in the *Tafelberg Mannekoor Raad*, which is no longer active.
16. Anwar Gambeno, interview with Denis-Constant Martin, Mitchells Plain, 13 April 2015.
17. The Keep the Dream Malay Choir Board was initially named the Cape Male Choir Board, but following a Western Cape High Court interdict judging that this name was "confusing similar" to that of the Cape Malay Choir Board, it had to change it.
18. Also spelt *kufija* or *koefia*, from the Arabic *kūfiyyah* (كوفية), from the city of Kufa) and Kiswahili *kofia*; it usually designates a small cap, frequently embroidered, worn by Muslim men. In this instance it is used to speak of the red felt cap, the fez, worn by Malay Choir members.
19. Achmat Hadji Levy, interview with Denis-Constant Martin, Lentegeur, 28 January 1994.
20. Taliep Petersen, interview with Denis-Constant Martin, Athlone, 15 January 1994.
21. Those who advocate the rejection of words such as "coons" or "minstrels" seem to adhere to a cosmetic conception of political correctness, which leads them to condemn ways of speaking that are common in countries or social milieus other than their own. They behave as if they want to impose upon speakers the only acceptations with which they are familiar. They seem to ignore the well-known fact that when words travel, in space or time, their meaning is often altered or changed. The word "dame" provides an illustration of how words are given various, sometimes opposing, meanings at different times and in different places. Originally, in French, *dame* referred to an adult woman and connoted elegance, distinction and high social status. In American movies of the 1940s and 1950s, "dame" was most often used colloquially to refer to women of ill repute, considered to be of easy virtue. In Otto Preminger's Laura (1944), for instance, Waldo Lydecker (Clifton Webb) takes exception to Laura Hunt (Gene Tierney) being taken for a "dame". In French, she would indeed appear as a *dame* and not as a *poule* ("dame"). The meaning of "dame", whether in French or in English, has over at least two centuries alternated between respectful-honourable, and derogatory-offensive.
22. The origin of "minstrel" goes back to the Middle Ages. Minstrels were musicians, poets, storytellers who entertained feudal lords. Although treated as servants, they were legitimate artists in their own right. It was only much later, in the 19th century, that the word became used to talk about comedians in blackface and entered into the names of troupes, such as the Virginia Minstrels.
23. See pp. 98–99.
24. Statistics South Africa is an official body "responsible for the collection, production and dissemination of official and other statistics, including the conducting of a census of the population, and for co-ordination among producers of statistics". *About the Statistics Act*: online. Available at http://www.statssa.gov.za/?page_id=830 [accessed 23 December 2015].
25. See for instance: *Census in Brief*: online. Available at http://www.statssa.gov.za/census/ census_2011/census_products/Census_2011_Census_in_brief.pdf [accessed 23 December 2015].
26. See: Question P 05, *Household Questionnaire* (Questionnaire A): 2: online. Available at http:// www.statssa.gov.za/?page_id=3852 [accessed 23 December 2015].

The Donegals Sangkoor during the Bo Kaap parade, New Year's Eve, 1993–1994

Introduction

The present volume represents the outcome of many years of investigation into Cape Town's New Year festival, and in particular into the musical repertoires performed by the two most important organisations that enliven them: the *Kaapse Klopse* and the Malay Choirs.

Origins and methods

Denis-Constant Martin has been conducting research on Cape Town's New Year festivals since the early 1990s and has studied, among other aspects of these festivals, the particular forms of choral singing that feature in the *Klopse* carnival and the Malay Choirs competitions. Armelle Gaulier, following fieldwork she carried out in 2006 and 2008, dedicated two Masters dissertations to original repertoires sung by *Klopse* and Malay Choirs: the *moppies* or comic songs and the *nederlandsliedjies*.[1] Their works were mostly written and published in French, which made them quite inaccessible to an English-speaking readership and especially for South Africans interested in these singing practices or involved in them. Generally speaking, little has been published in English on *Klopse* singing, Malay Choirs and their repertoires. Desmond Desai highlighted, as early as 1983, the social importance of what he then called "Cape Malay music" and included serious musical analysis in his ethnographical and sociological studies of *ratiep*[2] and *nederlandsliedjies* (Desai 1983, 1986, 1993, 2004, 2005).[3] However, the results of the greatest part of his research were presented in unpublished dissertations or in publications which were not easily available. The late Gerald L Stone, a linguist and psychologist, wrote what was probably the first academic study of the *Klopse* carnival (Stone 1971), a paper which was, as far as we know, never published. His work on the Afrikaans spoken by members of the coloured working class (Stone 1991, 1995) also shed an interesting light on the New Year festivals. In addition to Desmond Desai's and Gerald L Stone's pioneering works, a few papers and dissertations have subsequently been written, adding new dimensions to the knowledge of *nederlandsliedjies* and *moppies* (Nel 2012; Van der Wal 2009) or analysing the history and recent evolutions of the *Klopse* carnival (Baxter 1996; Inglese 2014; Oliphant 2013; Rahman 2001; Wentzel 2011). All in all, the number of publications in English on these aspects of Cape Town's culture remains extremely limited. We thought therefore that we could contribute to the understanding of the social and musical specificities of these songs and singing practices by making our own research available in English and adding it to the extant literature. The present volume is based on texts which have been written in French, either as academic dissertations or as articles published in Francophone journals. The core chapters dealing with *nederlandsliedjies* and *moppies* are not translations of the original texts, but result from an amalgamation of writings by Armelle Gaulier and Denis-Constant Martin; they may therefore be considered as original English texts. The two chapters in Part I ("Memory and Processes of Musical Appropriation") are adaptations of articles originally published in French by Denis-Constant Martin.[4]

Armelle Gaulier and Denis-Constant Martin worked according to the same methods: close observation of musical practices during rehearsals, singing competitions and concerts; interviews with musicians (singers, coaches and composers), experts and organisers; and collections of musical material, namely audio and video recordings produced by carnival and Malay Choirs competition organisers or original recordings made during rehearsals (Armelle Gaulier). Based on this composite material we conducted sociological (Armelle Gaulier and Denis-Constant Martin) and musicological (Armelle Gaulier) analyses in order to produce sociological interpretations based, on the one hand, on solid musical analyses and, on the other, on information and opinions conveyed by musicians and experts. Armelle Gaulier made two field trips to Cape Town. From July to October 2006, while working on *moppies*, she was accommodated by a family in Mitchells Plain, from where she visited *klopskamers*, observed rehearsals and went to interview captains, coaches and singers. She came back to Cape Town in 2008 and, from January to March, she resided first in the Bo-Kaap and then in Mitchells Plain; she conducted the same type of investigation as in 2006, but this time she focused on *nederlandsliedjies*. Denis-Constant Martin, who had for a long time been interested in South African music, began researching Cape Town's New Year festivals in 1992. Between 1992 and 2015, he visited Cape Town and Stellenbosch[5] frequently; he had the opportunity to observe the 1994 *Klopse* Carnival, as well as Malay Choirs competitions in 1994, 2013 and 2015. In the course of his sojourns in Cape Town and Stellenbosch, he spent time at the National Library of South Africa in Cape Town, perusing newspaper and academic articles containing information on *Klopse* and Malay Choirs; he also taped interviews with captains, coaches and singers and gathered a collection of CDs, VHS cassettes and DVDs of the carnival and of the Malay Choirs competitions. Interviews taped by Armelle Gaulier and Denis-Constant Martin were in most cases either semi-directive or non-directive; they were complemented by other interviews aimed at obtaining information on particular aspects of the topics under study, which were more of the question-and-answer type. All interviews were conducted in English. Although English was the mother tongue of none of the interlocutors, fluency in that language on both sides was sufficient enough to allow serious dialogues and afterwards to analyse the discourse of musicians, coaches and experts. Interviews were transcribed as literally as possible; in the quotations included in this book we have tried to render as faithfully as possible the manner in which the interviewees spoke.

Nederlands and *moppies*: From the "Cauldron of Coloured Experience"[6]

Individuals involved in the *Klopse* carnival and the Malay Choirs belong almost exclusively to the coloured group.[7] According to the latest census available, coloureds represent 42.4% of Cape Town's population and constitute the largest group, before black Africans (38.6%).[8] Although there have been variations in their share of Cape Town's population,[9] they have always occupied an important place in Cape Town's economic, social and cultural life. Contemporary coloureds are the descendants of people of extremely diverse origins,[10] among whom were a great number of slaves. Between 1658 and 1808, 63 000 slaves were brought to the Cape from the African continent (26.4%), India and Sri-Lanka (25.9%), Madagascar (25.1%) and Indonesia (22.7%) (Shell 1994: 41). For almost the entire period of slavery, slaves outnumbered burgher residents at the Cape (Mountain 2004: 21). Intensive intermixture took place, between slaves of various origins, and between slaves, Europeans and Khoikhoi. This resulted in an important demographic growth and in the emergence of a group of locally born slaves who constituted more than half the slave population after the 1760s (Shell 1994: 47). Processes of cultural exchange took place within groups of slaves, as well as between slaves and European masters. Historian Mohamed Adhikari noted that: "Interaction between master and slave clearly entailed a degree of cultural exchange between the two especially since they often lived and worked in close physical proximity to each other" (Adhikari 1992: 100–101). These interactions did not lead to the slaves' adoption of their masters' culture, but triggered the creation of original cultural practices. Songs were invented in the process from the combination of elements of Dutch folk songs[11] with elements of musics from the slaves' regions or origin. When slavery was abolished, a substantial number of emancipated slaves or free blacks already existed, who were competent musicians and music teachers; they were among the most dynamic actors of Cape Town's musical life during the second half of the 19th century (Martin 1999: chap. 3).

Appropriation of blackface minstrelsy
English and, later, American influences entered in the mix and brought new material to enrich Cape Town innovations. Troupes from the United States, sometimes also from Great Britain, staged a new conception of entertainment, the blackface minstrel show, which was almost immediately appropriated by coloured musicians and revellers celebrating the New Year. Their songs, skits, costumes, ways of speaking and instruments (especially the banjo) symbolised a modernity that could be construed as *mestiza*, "non-white", although it was embodied, at least in its first South African performances, by white comedians and musicians made up in blackface. After an initial phase which saw South Africans, and in particular coloureds, reproduce the ritual and style of the minstrel show,

appropriation again produced original practices. From the stage, the codes of minstrelsy reached the streets of Cape Town where they were fully integrated in the celebrations of the New Year, and especially in the spontaneous carnival that was taking shape at the end of the 19th century. New elements were introduced in the 1890s by African-American minstrels, Orpheus McAdoo's Virginia Jubilee Singers; some of their members remained in Cape Town and performed with local outfits when the group, faced with financial troubles, disbanded (Erlmann 1991; Martin 1999: chap. 5).

Islamic inputs
Other influences that played a decisive role in fashioning *Klopse* and Malay Choirs' repertoires and styles of singing came from the Muslim world. The first Muslims arrived at the Cape in 1658 as slaves or free servants of the Dutch (Baderoon 2014: 8). A group of political exiles from Macassar, including an important dignitary, Sheykh Yusuf — the leader of the local Khalwatiyyah Sufi order and an opponent to the Dutch conquest — contributed to sowing the seeds of Islam in South Africa (Dangor 2014). Before 1804, Muslims enjoyed limited religious freedom in Cape Town; they could practice their religion privately, but were strictly forbidden to proselytise: "Islam was tolerated — never encouraged, yet rarely seriously repressed" (Mason 2002: 9). A Muslim school was nevertheless founded in 1793 in Cape Town by Imam Qadi Abdul Salaam, known as "Tuan Guru" (Jappie 2011: 375-376). The first South African mosque was probably opened sometime between 1795 and 1804 and by the end of 1824 there were two large mosques in Cape Town and five smaller ones. The number of Muslims developed steadily: from less than 1 000 in 1800, Cape Town's Muslim population grew to around 6 400 in 1842, about 8 000 in 1854 and in 1867 nearly half of the City's population was Muslim (Jeppie 1996a: 151); most of this growth was due to conversions (Mason 2002: 13). Islam gave slaves — and in general all human beings who were marginalised by slavery and the colonial system — a sense of personhood and self-dignity. Pumla Dineo Gqola, in a perceptive study of the role of slave women, explained that: "It is only Islam that allowed the slaves to be fully spiritual beings inside an institutional religion. For slaves, Islam offered entry into recognition of their humanity with all the ensuing associations" (Gqola 2007: 36). Islam provided both a sense of community and the inscription in the worldwide family of believers; it planted deep local roots which were inseparable from global networks. Islam in Cape Town was permeated with Sufism.[12] Even if Sufism "did not constitute the dominant religious tendency among Muslims and their leaders" (Jeppie 1996a: 157), "Sufi Islam, with its esoteric teachings and psychological and physical cures was particularly appealing to the Muslims at the Cape, as it offered power and a haven for them to deal with the hostile social environment they faced" (Jappie 2011: 377). Consequently, Sufi brotherhoods attracted believers; Sufi rituals were widely practised (Mason 1999, 2002) and opened up an intense

field of musical activities. At the beginning of the 21st century, Muslims accounted for 9.7% of Cape Town's total population, and represented 17.4% of Cape Town's coloureds.[13] Muslims have always been in a minority, but their cultural influence has been much more important than their share in the local population. Cape Town Muslims have never been isolated from followers of other religions: "The communal nature of township living has allowed for close friendships to be forged across religious lines. Muslims in townships do not lead a drastically different life from their non-Muslim neighbours" (Motala 2013: 188). Marriages between Muslims and non-Muslims are not infrequent. This situation allowed for traits particular to Muslim musical practices to percolate into Cape Town coloured musics; furthermore, Muslims developed, just as other people, a taste for international and American pop songs. Orthodox Muslim authorities have from time to time attempted to warn against music and dance, especially in the context of the New Year festivals. In 1893, they condemned "the going about the streets singing and the jollification. It is all against our belief and religion" (quoted in Bickford-Smith 1996: 27). More recently, the Muslim Judicial Council again decried the *Klopse*: "the coons dancing through our streets are under no circumstances fitting expression of thanksgiving to Allah for emancipation in this day and age". And its Fatwa Committee decreed that "It is not permissible for a Muslim to belong to them neither to participate in it neither to pay a fee to see the carnival nor to watch it."[14] However, Achmat Davids, who was a respected voice on both religious and cultural matters, clearly expressed his views in a contribution on "Music and Islam" presented at a symposium on ethnomusicology in 1984: "I conclude therefore that neither music nor musical instruments are forbidden in Islam" (Davids 1985: 38).[15] Most coloured Muslims inhabiting Cape Town certainly support this opinion and this is why large numbers of Muslims participate in the *Klopse* carnival and why Malay Choirs comprise a majority of Muslims.

The development of *Kaapse Klopse* and Malay Choirs

In the 18th and 19th centuries, processes of mixing and blending musical features originating in very many diverse cultures set in motion creative dynamics, which produced original ways of conceiving and making music. The emergence of creole forms became especially manifest during the New Year celebrations. Groups of singers, often inhabiting the same building or the same block, took this opportunity to perform and parade in the streets; they donned costumes in styles and colours which made them distinguishable from other similar groups and hung streamers in their colours across the streets they walked. These singing groups were very often linked to clubs which organised social and sports activities; therefore they also became known as *Klopse* (clubs).

The formalisation of Klopse competitions

Historian Vivian Bickford-Smith dated the creation of the first choirs from the 1870s, and noted that a Star of Independence Malay Club was then already in existence (Bickford-Smith 1995: 37). For his part, the president of the Cape Malay Choir Board, Shafick April contended that Malay Choirs have been in existence since 1887.[16] He probably considered that the first clubs who marched and sang in the streets during the New Year festivities in the 1880s[17] were the originators of Malay Choirs, although they did not carry that name. In neighbourhoods such as District Six, Harfield Village and the Bo-Kaap, informal competitions between these singing clubs began to take place. In 1907, the contests were institutionalised and took place at the Green Point Cycle Track. The "Coloured Carnival"[18] was discontinued after a few years, but was revived in 1920 under the auspices of Dr Abdurahman's African Political Organisation (APO). In the following years, various entertainment entrepreneurs organised rival competitions at various venues (Martin 1999: chap. 6). At first it appears that there was no clear distinction between the organisations that are today called *Klopse* and Malay Choirs. Abduraghman Morris, the current president of The Young Men Sporting Club, one of the most successful Malay Choirs at the beginning of the 21st century, thinks that the very first Malay Choir was the forerunner of the choir over which he now presides: this was *Die Jonge Mense Kultuur Club* (The Young People's Culture Club). Several members of the Silver Tree Rugby Club participated in this choir, which was founded in 1938 and was based in an area known as the Dry Docks in District Six. Its name was later changed to the Young Men Sporting Club.[19]

The creation of the Cape Malay Choir Board

The following year, in 1939, an organisation was launched to gather various choirs active in the Cape Peninsula and formalise their competitions: the Cape Malay Choir Board (CMCB). It was founded at the initiative of ID du Plessis, a white academic and poet interested in "malay culture", who was to become an official of the apartheid regime, and Benny Osler, a famous white rugby fly-half. Members of the Dante family, Edross Isaacs and Achmat Hadji Levy played an important role in its early developments. The idea probably came from ID du Plessis and other Afrikaner self-appointed "experts" of coloured culture. They were disappointed by the fact that very little Afrikaans was heard during the *Klopse* carnival, and that *Klopse* sang mostly songs inspired by American jazz and varieties. In their idea, Afrikaans was an evidence of the links that tied coloureds to whites and to the "West",[20] albeit in a subordinate position:

> The fact that the Coloured coons sang imported songs was lamented both by Dr I.D. du Plessis of "Die Moleier en die Afrikaans Volkslied" fame, and Professor Kirby, who wrote "The Musical Instruments of the Native Races of South Africa." At one of the coon concerts last week Dr du Plessis and Professor Kirby suggest-

ed that the coons should combine, and get back to the melodies of
the country and its people. The Cape Argus, strangely enough, in
a sub-leader applauds the suggestion, and expresses its regret that
the indigenous song and music as preserved by the Malay Choirs
should be overwhelmed by foreign importations.[21]

ID du Plessis was fascinated by what he considered a "malay culture". On the one hand, he entertained an exotic vision of the malays as custodians of a special culture; on the other, relying on stereotypes about slaves of Asian origin — especially about the "Buginese" — fashioned during the times of slavery, he considered them as an "elite" among coloureds (Bangstad 2006: 39–40). He attempted to construct an imaginary model of the "original" malay and, in that perspective, endeavoured to find the roots of a "pure" malay civilisation in Cape Town (Jeppie 2001: 84–86). His vision of "the malay" was not just an idiosyncratic figment of his imagination; it was inscribed within a particular political and cultural context and eventually served a political agenda. ID du Plessis

> emerged at the moment of mobilization of Afrikaans-speakers
> and he was both mobilized and acted in a mobilizing capacity.
> Du Plessis answered the "calling" of nationalism in the early years
> as a journalist, poet and teacher. At the same time, he generated a
> cultural niche for Afrikaner poets and writers, yet he was attached
> to expressions of liberalism. Du Plessis' social and intellectual role
> was deployed through the categories of Romanticism and Social
> Darwinism stressing the "individual" and his release from social
> constraints, the obsession with the exotic (and sometimes erotic)
> and the "protection" of "weaker peoples" and their gradual evolu-
> tion. (Jeppie 1987: 21)

Eventually: "The purpose for which 'malay otherness' operated was to maintain a *divide et impera* policy in a local setting. The specific setting was white racial domination" (Jeppie 1987: 51). It is therefore no surprise that ID du Plessis ended up as Commissioner and later Secretary and Adviser for Coloured Affairs from 1953 to 1963. He did not, however, impose the creation of the CMCB upon reluctant choirs. His conception of malays as an elite, whose exclusive culture and places of dwelling (the Bo-Kaap) were to be preserved, resonated with self-conceptions which were rampant among educated and well-off coloured Muslims in Cape Town. The "reinvention of the malay" by ID du Plessis strengthened a sense of respectability and distinction that was adhered to by, for instance, the Cape Imams (Baderoon 2014: 15; Jeppie 1996a: 157) and is still shared by several Malay Choirs' leaders, who insist on not being confused with Coons. In any case, the creation of the CMCB caused a new distribution of repertoires between *Klopse* and Malay Choirs. *Klopse* would sing adaptations of imported songs, coming largely from the United States;

Malay Choirs would exclusively use Afrikaans and interpret the most traditional repertoires, *moppies* and *nederlandsliedjies* (until the late 1950s sung as combine chorus[22]), as well as original creations prepared for the solo[23] and combine chorus competitions. In 1949, Afrikaans *moppies* were introduced in Coon competitions, again probably following ID du Plessis' recommendations[24] and in about 1957 *nederlandsliedjies* became a full-fledged "item" in the Malay Choirs competitions, as suggested by ID du Plessis and Dutch musicologist Willem van Warmelo (Desai 2004; Van der Wal 2009: 59). Since 1950, *Klopse* have been singing arrangements of imported songs as well as Afrikaans *moppies* and Malay Choirs' competitions have featured four main "items": the two most important creole repertoires, Afrikaans *moppies* or comic songs and *nederlandsliedjies*, as well as solo and combine chorus, consisting mostly of original tunes, some of them modelled after foreign types.

The New Year Carnival

The format of the New Year festivals as they unfold today was fashioned in the 1950s and 1960s. The celebration opens with a parade of the Malay Choirs, known on this occasion as *Nagtroepe* (troupes of the night), which takes place in the Bo-Kaap and lasts from midnight till the wee hours of the morning. Choirs, including several that do not participate in the official competitions, march the streets in tracksuits, stopping in front of friendly houses where they sing and are treated to soft drinks, snacks and sweets. On the following morning, *Klopse* members gather at the *Klopskamer* (rehearsal place and headquarters of the troupe) and ready themselves for the competitions which will start in the afternoon; they dress in the particular "uniform" the captain has chosen for the year and make their faces up in bright and glittering colours.[25] Several carnivals take place at different venues: Vygieskraal stadium in Belgravia for the Kaapse Klopse Karnaval Association; the Athlone stadium for the Cape Town Minstrel Association (Oliphant 2013). The proceedings are more or less the same. There are about twenty categories of competitions (marches, songs, dances, orchestras, costumes, decorated boards, skits); they start on 1 January and continue for two or three weekends until the end of January. Competitions are judged by a panel of experts who, in total, award something like sixty trophies or more. Chanell Oliphant noted that: "The singing categories are judged based on pronunciation, the quality of the voices, and with regards to the choirs includes the harmonizing quality of the different voices. This in turn led to the reason behind hiring professional choirs and singers, which is reflected in the choice of bands as well" (Oliphant 2013: 81). Apart from competitions organised at stadia before paying audiences, the main event of the New Year festivals is the *Tweede Nuwe Jaar* (2 January) parade. All *Klopse* congregate on Keizergracht, the former entry into District Six, and march along a traditional itinerary which takes them through the town centre via Darling Street, Adderley Street and Wale Street.[26]

The customary proceedings of the festivals have been upset several times in the past. Apartheid caused important disruptions: the destruction of District Six and the forced removal of its inhabitants to distant townships (Jeppie & Soudien 1990) created severe difficulties for *Klopse* and Malay Choirs. Members no longer lived in the same areas; they had to drive, when they could afford it, or board taxis to go to the *Klopskamers*; buses had to be organised to bring them to the points where the parades started, which of course increased the costs of participating. In addition to that, various restrictions were imposed on the itineraries, on the right to march in town and on the stadia in which *Klopse* could perform. In 1968, Green Point having been declared a "white area" according to the Group Areas Act, 1950, carnival troupes were forbidden to use the stadium and to walk in its direction. In 1976, a total ban on parades was decreed by virtue of the 1956 Riotous Assemblies Act. It was not before 1989 that *Klopse* were again allowed to parade in the centre of Cape Town and perform both at the new Green Point Stadium and at the old Cycle Track.

The City of Cape Town's apprehension about carnivals

Automobile traffic had always been an excuse for the City administration to throw a spanner in the works of the carnival. This did not stop with the collapse of apartheid. Relationships between carnival organisers and the City Council have remained difficult. Negotiations have to be organised almost every year to try and find compromises allowing for the smooth proceeding of the parades. However new obstacles arise regularly. For instance, the preparation for and proceedings of the 2010 FIFA World Cup created unforeseen problems. Access to the new Green Point Stadium was refused to *Klopse* and even other stadia where Carnival competitions usually took place, such as the Athlone Stadium, were forbidden because the City was worried about the grass on the pitch being damaged by revellers' *takkies* (tennis shoes) (Wentzel 2011: 10). The gentrification of the Bo-Kaap meant the arrival of new inhabitants who resented "noisy" parades.[27] In 2015, the manager of the Taj Hotel,[28] located at the corner of Wale Street and St Georges Mall, expressed reluctance about choirs singing in front of his establishment.[29] Also in 2015, the *Tweede Nuwe Jaar* parade had to be postponed until 17 January because of a succession of Muslim festivals and a party organised for the African National Congress.[30]

The City would like to have one, and one only, interlocutor, which proves very difficult, given the rivalry that has always existed between carnival organisers. Regularly, a fusion of carnival organisations is announced, but it usually does not last long. In 2007, for instance, a memorandum of agreement was entered into between the two main carnival organisers, the Cape Town Minstrel Carnival Association and the Kaapse Klopse Karnaval Association.

This made provision for the appointment of a Road March Committee, in which both organisations would be represented. The committee should have been the sole partner of the City of Cape Town and should have become responsible for organising all aspects of the *Tweede Nuwe Jaar* Road March. However, eventually the two organisations clashed and went their own ways, although both still participated separately in the *Tweede Nuwe Jaar* march.

Hoping to bypass the carnival boards and avoid tedious discussions with them, the civic authorities also tried in 2012 to entrust the organisation of the festival to an event management company, a move which was obviously rejected by carnival organisers (Inglese 2014). However, in spite of all the hiccups in the relationships between carnival organisers and the City Council, the latter now heavily funds the event.[31] It provides fencing, security, traffic control, organises the presence of the South African Police Service and of medical personnel. In 2013, the council contributed ZAR 3.5 million to the carnival budget, to which must be added ZAR 350 000 for competitions and grants in support of *Klopse* from the National Department of Arts and Culture, corporate sponsors and the provincial government.[32] Whichever political party rules Cape Town,[33] civil authorities remain suspicious of a carnival in which working-class coloureds participate; carnivals are sometimes considered as a bit too unruly, and street parades are a cause for concern. However, while trying to secure better control of the event, the party in power supports the event because it attracts a large number of voters and is also a potential tourist attraction. Francesca Inglese, a graduate student in the ethnomusicology programme of the Brown College Music Department, accurately synthesised the attitude of the City authorities towards the New Year Carnival: "Together, these actions have created a general sense that city officials and culture brokers are using the Minstrel Carnival to present an image of Cape Town as diverse and inclusive, solely for touristic purposes, while marginalizing the needs and goals of the actual resident-participants themselves" (Inglese 2014: 140). Tazneem Wentzel, then a student at the Department of Sociology and Social Anthropology of the University of Stellenbosch, noted that "the Minstrel Carnival will remain the recurring logistical nightmare that annually walks both politically and poetically to haunt the city with a particular Minstrel form of discipline and disorder" (Wentzel 2011: 3).[34]

Carnival boards and *Klopse*

In the post-apartheid period, after a few years during which the *Klopse* Carnival seemed a bit subdued, it gained new momentum in the 2000s and 2010s. In 2014, over 60 troupes, comprising in total about 40 000 revellers, paraded through Cape Town (Inglese 2014: 128). There are today two main carnival organisations. The Kaapse Klopse Karnival Association (KKKA), whose chief executive officer is Melvyn Matthews, launched in October 2004. The KKKA is a non-profit organisation (NPO)³⁵ (former section 21 company) and is governed by 10 elected directors, who are selected from captains of "long-standing troupes". It consists of 30 troupes, comprising 300 to 3 000 members. The KKKA carnival is organised in two sections, the second one being reserved for larger troupes. Musical competitions are adjudicated by musically trained judges; marches and best-dress contests are assessed by experts drawn from the military. The KKKA entertains close ties with the Western Cape Street Bands, an association which trains young musicians who can later play for the *Klopse*.³⁶ The other major carnival organisation is the Cape Town Minstrel Carnival Association (CTMCA), headed by Richard "Pot" Stemmet and Kevin Momberg. CTMCA competitions are also divided in categories according to the troupes' size. *Klopse* in the "super league" comprise between 800 and 1 500 participants; the "premier league" troupes have 300 to 600, while "first-division" troupes comprise only between 100 and 300 members. Rivalry between these two organisations is intense, the more so since the management of public funds allocated for running the New Year Carnival has become a crucial issue.³⁷ The situation is made even more intricate because of links between certain *Klopse* and drug dealers,³⁸ and also because of political attempts to use the carnival to influence voters.³⁹

All *Klopse* are structured in a more or less similar fashion. They consist of an executive board, coaches and captains. For instance, the executive board of the Fabulous Las Vegas, based in Lentegeur, includes several persons in charge of different aspects of the club's life: a director, a president, a vice-president, a vice-chairman, a treasurer, a public relations officer, a coordinator, several trustees, a captain and a secretary. The Fabulous Las Vegas has specialised divisions: a Brass Band, adult and juvenile Choirs,⁴⁰ Drum Majors and the rank and file (Oliphant 2013). Another *Klops*, the All Stars from Mitchells Plain, is run by an executive committee (chairman, vice-chairman, two secretaries, two trustees, treasurer, and managers), who make the decisions about uniforms, various activities and the repertoire. The executive committee is assisted by a working committee, run by women, and captains selected by the team members. Its leader, Anwar Gambeno, decides on the songs to be performed during the carnival and coaches the singers. The *Klopse* organise their own sponsorships; the All Stars have been, for instance, supported by Nokia for several years.⁴¹ Most *Klopse* attract members who come from all over greater Cape Town. The Fabulous Woodstock Starlites, established in 1973, one of the founding teams of the KKKA, and a regular winner of the Section Two competitions, counted about 650 participants who came from areas such as Valhalla Park, Mitchells Plain, Bonteheuwel, and even Strand.⁴² Francesca Inglese, who worked with this *Klops*, drew a map showing the places where members dwell in relation to the location of the *klopskamer* (Inglese 2014: 130).

The map shows how removed from each other members are and indicates that some of them have to travel more than 35 km between the neighbourhood where they live and the *klopskamer*.

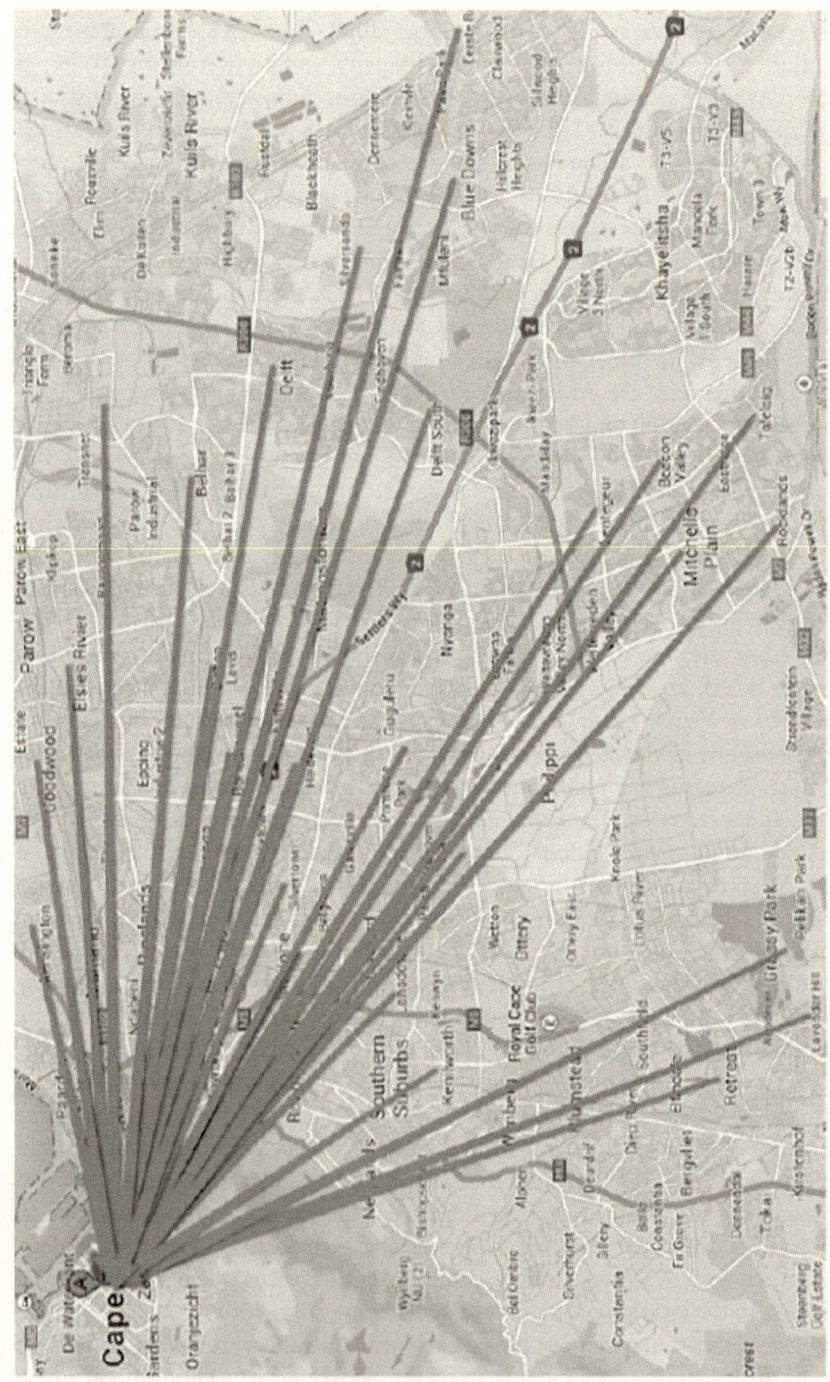
A map of Cape Town showing where members live in relation to the location of the klopskamer *(Francesca Inglese)*

Malay Choirs

Several *Klopse* are closely related to Malay Choirs; these links show that opposition between them does not always exist. The Pennsylvanian Crooning Minstrels are linked to the Shoprite Jonge Studente; the Heideveld Entertainers to the Young Men Sporting Club; and the All Stars to the Tulips; to give but a few examples. Malay Choirs hold their competitions after the *Klopse* carnival, usually between February and April.[43] The dates may be moved in case they conflict with Muslim festivals; no competitions can take place during the month of Ramadan. Choirs perform four or five song repertoires: *Nederlandsliedjies*, Afrikaans *Moppies* or Comic Songs, Combine Chorus, Senior Solo and Junior Solo, which is optional. Singing competitions are held in a hall which used to be the Good Hope Centre, although in 2016 they took place in the Cape Town City Hall.[44]

Malay Choir boards

The first board, the Cape Malay Choir Board (CMCB), was launched in 1939 and organised its first competitions in 1940 at the Cape Town City Hall with six participating choirs (Nel 2012: 37; Van der Wal 2009: 51). A new board, the *Suid-Afrikaanse Koorraad* (SAK, Council of South African Choirs) was formed in 1952 by dissident choirs that split from the CMCB because they refused to participate in events celebrating the tercentenary of the arrival of Jan van Riebeeck at the Cape. They said they could not accept the segregated organisation of the festivities and rejected the apology of apartheid which underlay them. Two further splits later affected the CMCB. First, in 1982, a few choirs launched the *Tafelberg Mannekoor Raad* (TMR, Council of Table Mountain Male Choirs). Secondly, in 2010, a successful businessman, the late Al-Hajj Mogamat Naziem Benjamin founded the Keep the Dream Malay Choir Forum (KTDMCF) with the support of his father, Al-Hajj MZ Benjamin (better known as "Hadji Bucks"[45]), leader of the Starlites Malay Choir. A large number of choirs decided to leave the CMCB and join the KTDMCF over disagreements about the financial management of the organisation and the centralisation of power in the hands of its chairperson. It is also said that several small choirs, who could not financially compete with the largest ones, considered themselves to be at a disadvantage and no longer stood a chance of reaching the highest levels of competitions; this caused discouragement among the singers and motivated them to join the new board. In 2013, the KTDMCF claimed 45 choirs (Keep the Dream Male Choir Board 2013) and 22 choirs participated in the preliminary sections of the CMCB competition. In 2015, the SAK was still alive, although its activities were very low key and it had only nine affiliated choirs. The TMR no longer exists.

Boards are non-profit organisations in terms of the Companies Act. Choirs are affiliated to a board; they participate in its competitions and can also apply for funds or sponsorships under the aegis of the board; they must include with their application a certificate from the board showing its NPO number.[46] Decisions in the CMCB are formally made at general meetings held every two or three weeks, to which each affiliated choir sends two or three representatives. The general meeting discusses all the rules and regulations, as well as the competition dates. Before competitions, the Cape Malay Choir Board issues each choir with a certain number of tickets, usually 200 or 300, which they have to sell; this is called the "Board share". The choirs may keep 50–60% of the profits, which are used, in addition to their own resources, to meet their organisational expenses. The KTDMCB is a subsidiary of the Keep the Dream Malay Choir Forum, a non-profit organisation. The KTDMCB is run by a 15-person executive; the most important decisions are made by a general council, in which all affiliated choirs are represented and an annual general meeting (AGM) assesses the activities of the board.

Malay Choirs

Most Malay Choirs have adopted a democratic type of organisation, which does not preclude the fact that some individuals (president, captain, coach) may play a prominent role when decisions are made. The Young Men Sporting Club, which is affiliated to the CMCB, for instance, is governed by its AGM, which gathers about 100 members; it elects officials and discusses the uniforms. The day-to-day affairs of the club (including the choice of uniforms) are run by an executive committee comprising a president, a vice-president, a secretary, two trustees, two managers and three additional members; they meet once a month. The president, who is also the coach of the choir, decides on the repertoire; he writes the combine and the comic song. The singer of the solo (Niel Rademan, a professional popular Afrikaans singer, who is hired for the competition) decides on what he is going to sing, in agreement with the president. In addition to monies the club can get from the board, it organises functions and karaokes at which collections are made. The Young Men also sing for the Heideveld Entertainers *Klops* and get paid for their services.[47] In the Shoprite Jonge Studente, also a member of the CMCB, the chairperson procures and appoints specialised music directors for each item in the competition. Since they aspire to become "more professional", they hire "professional people and academically qualified people [...] that can really give [the choir] the standard of the competition, makes us one of the best choirs, whether we do the singing, whether we do the marching".[48] They pride in having Kurt Haupt, the University of Cape Town choir conductor as coach for the combine chorus and the *nederlandsliedjies*, and Arlene Jephta[49] as voice-training supervisor. Comic songs are coached by an experienced musician, Ismail Jackson, who composes them and sings the solo part, although the choral accompaniment is also arranged by Kurt Haupt. In order to train the marching squad that competes in the Grand March Past and the Exhibition March Past categories performed during the Grand Finale, the Shoprite Jonge Studente have even gone to the extent of bringing out a retired admiral from Holland, Kos Peeters.[50] The Young Tulips Sangkoor, affiliated with the KTDMCB, is managed by a twelve-person executive committee that meets every two weeks. They have only one coach for the five "items", who chooses the songs and writes the comic and the combine.[51]

In spite of being called *Malay* Choirs, all choir members are not Muslims. It is estimated that about one-third of the singers belong to other faiths, mostly Christian.[52] However no singer is allowed to indulge in liquor or drugs.[53] Choirs must have new uniforms (suit, shirt, tie, shoes and socks, sports jacket and trousers for the New Year Eve's parade) made every year and risk losing points if they show in competition with a costume they have already worn. It was customary for choir members to pay for their uniforms. Nowadays, however, given the dire conditions in which many singers find themselves, members can no longer afford to spend more than ZAR 1 000 to buy the choir's outfits and receive them free of charge. This weighs heavily on a choir's finances: members of the Young Men Sporting Club are supposed to pay for their uniforms, but the young and the poor get them for free. In the Young Tulips Sangkoor, uniforms are given for free; and 90% of the Shoprite Jonge Studente singers cannot pay for their uniforms. All singers and musicians must wear a fez.[54] The champion of champions, at the end of competitions, wins the "Silver Fez".

The competitions

At CMCB competitions, choirs may comprise from 18 to about 100 singers; they are accompanied by instrumental ensembles composed exclusively of string instruments (including a piano), except for a *ghoema* drum used when *moppies* are sung. The best choirs now hire professional musicians or students from the music departments of the Cape Town and Stellenbosch universities. If women are not allowed to sing in the choirs during competitions,[55] they can play instruments, but must then wear a head scarf. The demand for musicians has become so high that the amount they ask for has increased tremendously, making it difficult for small (and less well-endowed) choirs to hire them. Abduraghman Morris, President of the Young Men Sporting Club, explained:

> For the Malay Choir, we have the pianist during rehearsals […] Up until a week or two before the competition day, I employ a guy who is in contact with the string quartet, I give him the music and he writes out the parts for each instrument of the string quartet and

then in the last week we all come together: the string quartet, because when we do our combine it usually consists of the string quartet with the piano, and then we rehearse like that. In competition we have the string quartet and a piano, plus guitar mandolin, banjo and double bass. For the combine, we only use the string quartet and the piano. For the other items, the nederlands and the comic, we use the full ensemble, plus the *ghoema* for the comic.[56]

The bursting in of backtracks

In the 1990s, sequencers began to be available in South Africa. Coupled with MIDI keyboards and computers, they gave access to immense sound banks and could reproduce the sounds of all instruments and even create original electronic sounds. Their arrival in the Malay Choirs and *Klopse* worlds disrupted the relationship between musicians and singers. It made it possible to rehearse a song to the background of a pre-recorded backtrack, which has been specially conceived, will never vary (and will never be late or stand the choir up), and is paid for once and for all, whereas musicians have to be remunerated every time they are needed. Many coaches complain about the cost of musicians. The size of the orchestras that accompany the singers in competition has significantly increased over the past thirty years. The orchestras now comprise up to forty instrumentalists and the cost of hiring such an ensemble amounts to several tens of thousands of Rands.

In competition, *Klopse* have for several decades resorted to backtracks. The CMCB still forbids the use of pre-recorded music and demands that choirs be accompanied by an instrumental ensemble, whose performance is marked on the evaluation reports. But choirs affiliated to the KTDMCB have decided to sing with backtracks, even *nederlandsliedjies*. Many choirs could not afford to pay the high prices musicians were demanding and they realised that it was cheaper to have backtracks made — which they could use both during the rehearsals and the competitions — than to hire a live orchestra. The decision to use backtracks allowed small choirs, with a limited financial capacity, to continue participating in competitions, thereby keeping their singers and maintaining their morale. However, the debate is still going on within the Keep the Dream Malay Choir Board and a few choirs' representatives would like to go back to having a band on stage during the competitions.[57] Anwar Gambeno, President of the KTDMCB, recounted how it happened:

> We debated this thing for a full year. What are we gonna do? There were for and against. At the end of the day, a majority voted in favour of the backtrack. There was an argument: let's do the ned-

erlands and the comic live, and we have the combine and the solo with the backtrack. That was shot down; we didn't want to make a mockery of the thing. So, we go backtrack. The backtrack has got its advantages and the backtrack has got its disadvantages. But the only argument that the guys are putting up against the backtrack is it is not tradition. Now according to the dictionary, tradition changes day by day. What is tradition today is not tradition tomorrow. But tradition at what cost? That is the problem here. So now you have a band, a stage band is another R 50 000. You can't afford that. So, what happens now, the choirs are closing. So, either you're sitting with making the Malay Choirs extinct because you don't want to change with the time and go for tracks, which I know I would prefer personally a live band, the banjo, the *ghoema* [...] I would prefer that personally, that's why when we do concerts with the group [The Young Tulips Sangkoor], we have that with the group so that we still have that type of thing alive. But in competition, I would prefer that myself, but they cannot afford it. But if you make your tracks properly, you still get the sound of the banjo, and you still get the sound of the mandolin, if you do it properly.[58]

Shawn Petersen, who coached the Kenfacs, agreed that backtracks help solve the problem of musicians who behave as mercenaries. He added that, as far as *Klopse* are concerned, since they perform outdoors, the sound of backtracks is often better — more balanced and clearer — than the sound of poorly amplified musicians. Moreover, it gives the coaches greater freedom in the choice of the instruments they want to associate with the voices.[59] However, Ismail Bey, a backtrack composer, affirmed that there must always be a banjo — "that identifies the *moppie*" says he — even a synthetic one, even if the timbre coming out of the backtrack is not as nice as that produced by a "real" instrument. But one must be cautious not to get carried away by the potentialities of synthesisers and add instrument upon instrument, to the point when the characteristics of a *moppie* are no longer audible.[60] To Shawn Petersen, the main problem with backtracks is that they cannot adjust in real time to what is happening on stage: modification of intonation or change of tempo. Even during practices, backtracks do not make allowances for trial and error, to improve the melody or the arrangement; they induce an imperative of formal perfection that must be attained before the backing CD is burnt. The composer must have in mind all the details of his tune, of the orchestral arrangement and of the combination between the two before he orders the backtrack from a specialist. Waseef Piekaan, a *moppie* composer, coach and singer, explained the difficulties faced by artists who do not write music:

> But if you, as the *moppie* writer, the person who makes or writes the *moppie*, if you can't make that tune go together before you

come to this guy that is only gonna make the music, that is only gonna press sounds, if you can't do that, then you are still not gonna have [...] it's not gonna work. So that comes from you first, and he just puts it together [...] You have to sing the tune to him a cappella and he has to hear it from your mouth and you have to sing it so right also, because [...] some of the tunes that I use are original tunes [...] so he doesn't know this tune, so you have to sing it so perfect to him, because if you're gonna sing it wrong and the backtrack is wrong, now you're gonna come to the choir and now the judges is going to hear, now musically it is not right, so you have to sing it note for note from your mouth for this guy so that he has to be able to program it right.[61]

Moreover, added Tape Jacobs, captain of the Beystart *Klops*, the consequences for the future of the music must not be underestimated: "Like a guy, if he doesn't see a man playing with the guitar, he won't be interested in learning [...] because he doesn't see the instrument. [Before] if you did see the guy was playing a certain instrument, you got the passion, man. But today you don't see the man, you just hear backtracks. Where is your passion now?"[62] The late Ismail Dante, musician, composer and former coach, also lamented that they "take the culture away" and do not encourage young people to learn music.[63]

Choirs in competition

Malay Choirs' core members practise regularly all year round. A few months before the competitions begin, they are joined by other singers who beef up the group and give more depth to the singing; rehearsals then become more frequent, longer and more intense. When contests used to take place at the Good Hope Centre one could see people congregate outside, under the trees surrounding it. Singers, with their family, greeted each other, discussed and tried to guess which choirs could win. Then singers and listeners entered the hall, where the heat was sometimes suffocating, in spite of huge fans located on each side of the stage. Inside, the atmosphere was at the same time tense and good natured. However, even at the City Hall, competitions remain a very enjoyable entertainment and the audience takes great pleasure in listening to the choirs, in admiring the talent of a *nederlands* singer who can produce beautiful *karienkels*,[64] in watching the antics of the comic soloist and relishing in the vocal timbre of the solo singer. But most listeners are also supporters: they entertain friendly or family links with one particular choir and expect it to win several prizes, if not the Silver Fez. They usually sit together on the same stand, they loudly applaud their favourite choir and often dispute the decisions of the judges when their champions are not given good marks. In the corridors and at the underground level, stalls are set up where typical malay dishes (curries, biryanis, samosas) and soft drinks can be bought.

Competitions may last for several hours, till after midnight and are interrupted for Muslim prayers. A stage is prepared for the singers, with a space reserved in front for the musicians, and an upright piano to one side. At the same level as the audience, an enclosure is set apart for the adjudicators. They must remain isolated and are forbidden to communicate with the singers, the listeners, and even the sound engineers; they can only talk to the board's officials. A Master of Ceremonies, alternating between English and Afrikaans, announces the choir that is going to perform, and gives the titles of the songs they will sing.

Each choir is allowed to remain on stage for no longer than 26 minutes "from the first strum or beat".[65] The competitions are organised like a championship. First, after a random draw, choirs are grouped in sections; according to their ranking in the sections, choirs are then allowed to participate in one of the three competitions: Premier Cup (CMCB) or Naziem Benjamin Cultural Cup (KTDMCB), those with a smaller number of points; the President's Cup (CMCB) or the Silver Plate Competition (KTDMCB), the intermediates; or the Top 8 (CMCB) or the Nedbank Super 12 (KTDMCB), the best. All will finally participate in a Grand Finale which takes place at a stadium and consists in competitions for: Drum Major, Best Dress, Float,[66] Grand March Past and Exhibition March Past. The end of the competition season is marked by the Champ of Champs, in which five choirs from the CMCB Top 8, two choirs from the President's Cup, and two choirs from the Premier Cup compete for the last time of the year.

Competitions are judged by a panel of "adjudicators" selected by the Board among people who have formal musical training (music teachers or music students at a university) or are considered as "experts" of *moppies* and *nederlandsliedjies*.[67]

Freedom and conventions

The rank and file of the *Klopse* and Malay Choirs are amateurs; they even have to, or are supposed to, pay for their uniforms, and audiences at stadia or halls where choir competitions take place must buy entry tickets. However, the festivals make it possible for a small number of people to earn a living or at least to draw part of their income from their involvement with *Klopse* and choirs: professional artists (singers, coaches, musicians); carnival organisers; tailors; importers of material and accessories, such as hats and umbrellas. The dominant discourse among participants nevertheless emphasises a love for music, a passion for the Cape culture and the determination to keep it alive.

"For the love of the sport"

Adam Samodien, a famous composer and coach, strongly asserts that he creates songs "for the love of the sport".[68] "Sport" is a word which is frequently used when discussing the New Year festivals. It underlines both the joy of playing carnival or singing in a choir and the omnipresent competitive spirit. "To me, it's just fun" concurred Ismail Dante,[69] whose family has been involved in the festivals since the end of the 19th century. To him, money is not what matters:

> That's why these guys they can't understand, they come to me, they ask me "How much do you charge?" I just laugh at it, I say "now look, I won't give you a price, but what I can do, I can coach, I play four instruments, put me in that category and you think of yourself what you can give me. Whatever you give me, I will say thank you, I appreciate it. Because at least, you came to me and asked me." Because, I say I don't want to know what the other guys are getting, that's not my business, but this is actually my pleasure, I enjoy myself with this thing.[70]

Other musicians, soloists or coaches are obviously less disinterested, but they nonetheless always insist on their passion for the "sport" and the culture.[71] Paraders, singers, coaches, organisers, leaders and audiences form a small world, which could be likened to what sociologist Howard S Becker called an "art world" (Becker 1982), crisscrossed by networks of social relations underlain by tensions between respectability (*ordentlikheid*) and lawlessness, regulations and organised disorder (Salo 2004, 2005a, 2005b). The festivals are the "big days" in the year; the time when revellers can feel free, whatever the tribulations and the humiliations they have to endure the rest of the year.

Many people feel a compulsion to participate in the festivals, even just as spectators in the streets or at a stadium. But participants experience something stronger: a mixture of extreme pleasure and freedom; the sensation that they become different, because they then live on another plane, in another universe. Two words express that: *deurmekaar* and *tariek*. *Deurmekaar* rhymes with *Nuwe Jaar*, just as in the West Indies, "bacchanal" echoes "Carnival". In Cape Town's songs, *Nuwe Jaar* is traditionally answered by *deurmekaar*. As an adjective it usually means confused or disorganised; it connotes disorder, chaos and even danger. Applied to the New Year, however, it acquires the much more positive meanings of fun and excitement, of pleasure and liberation from the constraints of ordinary life. *Tariek* explains even more precisely what the festivals are about. The word comes from the Arabic and is related to *tariqa* (brotherhood). In the language of Islam, more specifically of Sufi Islam, *tariqa* means the way, that is the journey leading to God, and the spiritual techniques which allow one to accomplish this journey. One of these techniques is the chanting of *dhikr* (literally the "memory of God") in order to glorify God and to reach spiritual perfection, a collective experience which often leads to a state of trance. As a matter of fact, *tariek* is used to describe the state of trance reached by participants during *ratiep*. According to the late Gerald L Stone, *tariek* means excitement, being carried away, being in a trance-like state (Stone 1971, 1991, 1995). *Tariek* is closely related to *deurmekaar* and consequently also connotes being mixed up, a state of social chaos, anomy. This word definitely has two sides; it means confusion and fun; it can be both positive and negative.[72] This interpretation is confirmed by members of Malay Choirs well versed in Muslim theology. They explain *tariek* in terms of the union of the positive and the negative, the difference and the complementarity of the physical and the spiritual, and the capacity of the latter to activate the former.[73] To the revellers themselves, pleasures and impressions of freedom experienced during the New Year festivals are similar to the state of trance reached by dancers who perform the *ratiep*. Melvyn Matthews, who has been participating in the carnival in various capacities since he was a very young child, reflected on this particular sensation:

> There must be some madness in this thing [...] DIE TARIEK [...] The tariek, this thing you put yourself in, in another frame of mind. You're now at another level [...] You're going to another level, you're getting to something else [...] I'll walk and I'll start to run and I'm getting to this fever now, that tariek [...] it's at the other level [...] You're now overflowing, you're now overflowing and not everyone can feel it because why, it goes deeper than what a lot of people can perceive.[74]

The place of women

In her masters dissertation on the "changing faces of the *Klopse*", Chanell Oliphant observed that "writings on the *klopse* seem to have gendered the performance to one of the masculine. This is embodied and stylized in the gears and the designs, which are what one would associate with male attire. The only visible sign of femininity and a stylization in design of clothes, and feminine behaviour were the *moffie*"[75] (Oliphant 2013: 86). As a matter of fact, a spectator watching the performances of *Klopse* and Malay Choirs can gain the impression that the New Year festivals are undoubtedly a man's world. Yet, women have always played an important role in the celebrations and their preparation, and their place is steadily increasing.

As we have seen, during the competitions women cannot sing in a Malay Choir; they can only play instruments (usually strings, including double bass and piano), provided they cover their head. However, girls and women join the male singers for practices and concerts outside official contests. They also sit in large numbers in the audience. Before competitions were formally organised by the Cape Malay Choir Board, some women were known as *nederlandsliedjies* soloists and could be heard at birthday parties or weddings. Mariam Leeman, a school teacher and amateur singer in her sixties at the time of the interview, recalled that in her youth she heard women singing in the choir, backing a male soloist, at weddings.[76] Ismail Morris, then coach of the Morning Glories, confirmed that women sang at weddings:

> You may find some women who are able to sing because their brother or husband used to be in a choir but there is no places where women could take part of the Ned. At wedding people don't sing anymore. Before it used to be fantastic, the brides' maids they had to sing, there were certain women that went to weddings that could sing lovely, but that has all died out now people don't sing, they hire a choir to come and sing or they play music.[77]

In private situations, women whose family is involved in the Malay Choirs, who have an uncle or a brother who sing solo can learn the *nederlands* repertoire and the art of *karienkel*, but they do not perform in public.

Women are present in the *Klopse*. Usually, they are not very conspicuous since they wear the same gear as the men. Their numbers have definitely increased since the early 1990s and women now also participate in the organisation and functioning of the troupes. In 1988, two women organised a carnival, and one troupe, the Famous New Blue Girls, was captained by a woman (Oliphant 2013: 87). More recently, the Heideveld Entertainers were "owned" by a woman[78] and the Hangberg Troupe was also captained by a woman (Oliphant 2013: 88). Women sit on the Las Vegas' Executive Board (Oliphant 2013: 88) and they form the core of the All Stars' Working Committee.[79] In the course of her field work with the Las Vegas in 2012, Chanell Oliphant "came across women participating in different roles, as 'soldiers', ordinary members, as supporters and as cooks in the stalls. Women came with their children, walked with their children and pushed their younger children who wore miniature gears in strollers" (Oliphant 2013: 88). Chanell Oliphant also noted that women in the *Klopse* were beginning to wear clothes or accessories that could distinguish them from the men: wigs, pearls, earrings; some even put on dresses instead of the customary pair of pants. She concluded "Thus here one sees a growing performativity of the female gender taking place by women" (Oliphant 2013: 88). In the same year, a troupe participating in the *Kaapse Klopse Karnaval* featured a woman singer; before there had only been a few occasions when women sang the "special item". KKKA's chief executive officer, Melvyn Matthews, explained that this illustrated the "stance of non-sexism" adopted in the carnival he organises (Oliphant 2013: 87).

In addition to their visible presence, women also play important supportive roles in the *Klopse* and the Malay Choirs. They prepare food and drinks served at rehearsals; many tailors who cut and sew the uniforms worn in competition are women; and they cater for singers and spectators at the competition venues. These roles are traditionally assigned to women in many male-dominated societies, including Cape Town coloured communities. The attractiveness of a woman because of her physical features and domestic abilities, in particular cooking, was described — tongue-in-cheek — in an old *moppie*, quoted by Shamil Jeppie in one of the first serious articles devoted to the Coon Carnival: *"Die Nonnie van Waalstraat"* (The Lady from Wale Street), which caricatures a woman assigned to the role of cook, who is at the same time perceived to be attractive. The song concludes "Let others say what they want/My heart is so glad/Where in the whole world/Will you get such a girlfriend?/I can't contain myself anymore/Must be at her side all day/O, she is a lovely thing/When she moves her little backside" (Jeppie 1990). While recognising that the place of women in the New Year festivals is mostly subordinate (although it is currently changing), one should not, however, underestimate its social and symbolic importance. Anthropologist Elaine Salo highlighted the fact that women actually occupied a pivotal position in coloured underprivileged townships where they acted both as guardians of moral values and respectability, and as protectors of young men, even when they infringed the law (Salo 2004, 2005a, 2005b). More generally, Pumla Dineo Gqola underlined the fact that food can be a vehicle for memory and that: "The preparation, selection and sharing of food becomes a space for sustenance of cultural memories in diaspora. When food is this vehicle, or one of them, the burden often falls on women" (Gqola 2010: 171). Among coloureds, whose history has largely been moulded by the experience of slavery, the feeling of belonging to a diaspora is rather weak, but the transmission of culinary traditions is definitely a means to establish roots in an ancient past, and a way of putting forward a creativity that contributed to giving Cape Town cuisine its originality. In this perspective, cooking runs parallel to making music and singing and may be seen as a practice that empowers women in situations of disempowerment. Gabeba Baderoon, a professor of women's studies and African studies, explained: "Even though implicated in patriarchal power structures, the ability to cook and to teach cooking is the locus of enormous power" (Baderoon 2002: 8). She added that cooking is "a concrete and immediate kind of artistry" and that food has the "power to shape place, time and social interaction" (Baderoon 2002: 4). She concluded that, within the framework of a male-dominated society, "food gave women power" (Baderoon 2002: 9) and "allowed young ones to display their creativity and capacity of innovation" (Baderoon 2002: 11). These remarks imply that even though men may be in the forefront, the "culture and traditions" they perform in competition could not be transmitted and perpetuated without the active participation of women, a participation that is apparently increasing, making access to new roles easier. This evolution may eventually make them more visible and bring them to the foreground.

The meanings of musical competitions

In every society, whatever the era, it seems that there have been musical competitions. Experimenting with music is a source of pleasure: pleasure of making music, and making it well, pleasure of listening, and of listening to nice-sounding music. Consequently, musicians strive not only to play well, but to play better, for their own satisfaction, and also for the enjoyment of their fellow musicians and of their audiences. They endeavour to play better than before, better than other musicians; they hope to be recognised in their time, if not to leave their mark in history (Helmlinger 2011). In order to be acknowledged and assessed, their efforts "to do better" demand that they be evaluated and compared with those of other musicians (Molino 2007: 1180; Nattiez 2009: 59). Such comparisons may be informal and based on vague impressions; they may also be institutionalised in the form of contests, in which judges apply precise criteria.[80] Judgements passed at the conclusion of a competition are based on particular conceptions of the good and the beautiful, which vary according to time and place and therefore "have only a strictly contextual and pragmatic value" (Lortat-Jacob 1998: 193): they are incessantly debated and adapted. Musical competitions can therefore be approached as situations in which aesthetic values are affirmed, as circumstances when criteria defining "beauty" — the greatest beauty — are put in play, at the same time applied and contested. To put it in a nutshell: competitions are moments when conventions encapsulating aesthetics, ethics and social norms appear in full light (Molino 2009: 374–375), the more so since human beings' propensity to discuss music and to theorise it (Nattiez 2009: 52) seems to be stimulated by the spirit of competition (Erlmann 1996: 35; Rohlehr 1985).

Beauty, tradition and identity

Discussions arising from the need to evaluate, to compare and to justify judgements passed on the qualities and defects of a piece of music or of its interpretation, are linked to questions pertaining to established forms and techniques which have furnished, for some time, the ideals of quality and beauty. Such discussions lead to an appreciation of changes and innovations, to the recognition, or not, of their capacity to open new fields of creativeness and invent beauties unheard of. Confronted with innovation, many actors of the music world resort to arguments based on a certain idea of "tradition". Discourses in terms of tradition usually link aesthetic conceptions to visions of society and in particular to social representations of the groups to which musicians and *aficionados* belong. What is at stake in these cases is the identity of a group confronted with new notions of modernity. Defined by Georges

Balandier as "movement plus uncertainty" (Balandier 1988: 161), the advent of a "new modernity" combines transformations in social and political structures, mutations in value systems and changes in behaviour. It awakens a sense of unpredictability, underpinned by a confrontation between, on the one hand, danger and degradation, and on the other hand, progress and improvement.

In the musical domain, competitions circumscribe space-times of introduction and trial of innovation: they are occasions which allow musicians to propose innovations, which can then be accepted or condemned, but which in every instance arouse discussions. Competitions provide occasions for assessing the intrinsic properties of what is new against the background of a debate on the validity of current canons, which implies questioning their relevance in a changing world. This shows that there is no rupture between tradition and innovation: reference to tradition, be it in discourse or act, clears the way for transformations (Schlanger 1995; Waterman 1990: 8). As suggested by folklore historian Charles W Joyner "innovation without tradition is no more satisfactory an explanation of folklore performance than tradition without innovation" (Joyner 1975: 261), a statement from which David B Coplan inferred that tradition offers "established structures of creativity" (Coplan 2001: 113). It has been empirically observed, for instance in North-Amerindian *powwows* (Scales 2007: 24) and Hawaiian *hula* dances (Stillman 1996: 372–374). Competitions are an excellent occasion to stretch tradition towards modernity, since they invite musicians to try and distinguish themselves from their rivals. In order to do so, they can "sing better, louder and longer than the others" (Lortat-Jacob 1998: 67); they can also introduce original traits in their performances to attract the listeners' or the judges' attention, hoping that novelty will seduce them (Avorgbedor 2001). Ethnomusicologist, George Worlasi Kwasi Dor, explained that, among the Ewe, innovation was not only accepted but expected:

> Indeed, despite stereotypes about the antiquity and traditionalism of African culture, the Ewe generally measure the creative potency of a social dance group by the rate at which it introduces newly-composed songs to its repertoire. Just as the Ewe assess affluence in part by how often one changes one's clothes, the "richness" of a group similarly resides in its performance of new songs, dance movements, and drum motifs. (Dor 2004: 30)

Aesthetic changes and social change

When an innovation is successfully introduced in competition, it tends to be adopted and to become a new aesthetic norm. Awarding a prize to a musician or a piece that displays originality has at least two consequences: it legitimates the changes that have been presented; it encourages participants to adopt in subsequent competitions what has been endorsed by the judges, because they expect that it will help them to be successful (Helmlinger 2008, 2011; Henry 1989: 91–92). This happens even in fields in which it is generally considered that nothing can be changed, such as Qur'anic cantillation (al Fārūqī 1987). Aesthetic evolutions are tightly linked to other mutations, related not only to identity but also to ethics (Averill 2003: 91–98). This is one of the reasons why debates on the definition of musical beauty are so passionate and often lead to contesting the judges' decisions (Weintraub 2001: 97–98). Musical competitions are not only about musical quality, but also about values shared within a social ensemble; musicians, organisers and listeners together strengthen or renew social values. During competitions a "spiritual *communitas*" (Gunderson 2000: 16) is formed and participants abiding by its accepted rules assert that they belong to it (Scales 2007: 24). This does not imply that communities staged during competitions are homogeneous and unified. Competitions are arenas in which ideas and forces clash, in which various forms of power are at stake. State authorities can try and use them to impose their ideology, as was the case in Suharto's Indonesia (Weintraub 2001: 87–88). Victims of domination and oppression can attempt to take advantage of competitive rituals and festivities to create an autonomous universe governed by rules and hierarchies markedly different from those of the dominant order. Veit Erlmann showed, for instance, how *isicathamiya*[81] choirs gained a relative independence through the particular organisation of their contests (Erlmann 1996: 134). These few examples confirm Jean Molino's contention that: "Aesthetic experience and aesthetic judgement result from two kinds of mixing: they combine the formal properties of the musical object with the affective and concerned reactions of the subject; they graft 'external' factors, that set in motion the intricacy of human relationships within a community, onto 'internal' factors" (Molino 2007: 1189). This is one of the reasons why musical competitions — institutionalised situations in which judgements are passed and motivated, taking into account aesthetic, moral and social values — may be considered as objects of research likely to: "reveal 'emic' oppositions underlying what participants in a culture recognise as 'good' or 'beautiful' musical experiences" (Molino 2007: 1173). In this perspective, musical experiences acquire the dimensions of total social phenomena and the debates and controversies surrounding them become "a privileged place where common references, perceptual schema, axiological frames are made explicit"; they offer "reliable indicators about value systems that are vying with each other in a given society" (Heinich 1998: 41).

* * *

It is from these premises that we have approached Cape Town's *nederlandsliedjies* and comic songs. We consider them as musical objects, whose intrinsic characteristics displayed in situations of competition may shed some light on mutations which are underway in coloured communities, affecting notions of history (including memory and understandings of tradition), culture and identity, and consequently the position of coloured communities within and their attitudes towards South African society at large. The first part will continue to present the theoretical grounds on which our analyses are based, focusing on questions of memory and meanings of musical appropriations. The next two parts will deal with the most original repertoires sung by *Klopse* and Malay Choirs: *nederlandsliedjies* and comic songs; they will propose sociological interpretations grounded in musicological analysis. In the conclusion we shall come back to some of the most important issues raised by the study of these two repertoires: the role of memory in creating senses of identity and community, the affirmation of resilience through music and the relevance of theories of creolisation for an understanding of dynamics at work in contemporary South African society.

Notes

1. Armelle Gaulier (2007) *Appropriations musicales et constructions identitaires, les chants moppies du Cap, Afrique du Sud*. Mémoire de Mastère 1, Département de musique, UFR Arts, philosophie, esthétique, Université Paris 8 – Saint-Denis; and (2009) *Emprunt musical et créolisation chez les populations coloured du Cap (Afrique du Sud): le cas des chants nederlandsliedjies*. Mémoire de Mastère 2, Département de musique, UFR Arts, philosophie, esthétique, Saint-Denis, Université Paris 8 – Saint-Denis.
2. The *ratiep*, also known as *khalifa*, is defined by Achmat Davids as "a sword game that is characterised by the hitting of a sharp sword across the arms or body or by driving sharp skewers through the thick flesh of the face without causing any blood to flow. The exercise is accompanied by drum-beating and an almost hypnotic chanting in Arabic" (Davids 1994a: 63). The *ratiep* is meant to demonstrate the strength of the spirit compared to that of the body. Although it is not considered orthodox by many religious authorities, it is encountered under different names in several Muslim societies from Morocco to India. Its existence in Cape Town has been noted since the beginning of the 19th century and it is probable that it was practised before then.
3. Among his sources, Desmond Desai cites: GM Theal (1964) *History of South Africa before 1795*. Stellenbosch: Stellenbosch University Press; H Lichtenstein (1928) *Travels in South Africa, Volume 1*. Cape Town: Van Riebeeck Society; Lady Duff Gordon (1925) *Letters from the Cape*. Cape Town: Maskew Miller; Isak D du Plessis (1972) *The Cape Malays*. Cape Town: Maskew Miller; J Campbell (1974) *Travels in South Africa*. Cape Town: Struik; JS Mason (1970) *The Malays of Cape Town*. Pretoria: State Library.
4. (2009) Traces d'avenir, mémoires musicales et réconciliation en Afrique du Sud. *Cahiers d'ethnomusicologie* 22: 141–168; (2013) Attention, une musique peut en cacher une autre, l'appropriation α et ω de la création. *Volume!* 10(2): 47–67. Used with the kind permission of the editors.
5. Thanks to fellowships granted by the Stellenbosch Institute of Advanced Studies (2007, 2013, 2015), to which Denis-Constant Martin wishes to express his gratitude.
6. This phrase was frequently used by the late Capetonian, ex-librarian and historian Vincent Kolbe to underline that, although all people classified coloured under apartheid were affected by racist laws, the way they lived through segregation and discrimination was not uniform: their experiences were diverse, although they were stirred in the same cauldron.
7. There have recently been notable efforts to open up the New Year festivals and include as non-competing participants ensembles drawn from other musical traditions. In the 2013 CMCB competitions, preliminary sections 3, 4 and 5 were introduced by "Guest Choirs": the Simon Estes Alumni Choir from Wynberg (Section 3), the Cape Town Welsh Choir (Section 4) and the Kensington Girls' Choir (Section 5), a fairly representative sample of Cape Town's population and of the various styles of choral singing that are practised in the "Mother City". According to Chanell Oliphant, who participated in and observed the 2012 *Klopse* carnival, *Klopse* are becoming increasingly inclusive. For instance, an outfit from Gugulethu, the Vulindlela Cultural Group, took part in the exhibition of the Woodstock Starlites: they played the drums and danced. It seems that black African artists are now regularly hired by troupes (Oliphant 2013: 91–92).
8. City of Cape Town (December 2012) *2011 Census*. Available at https://www.capetown.gov.za/en/stats/Documents/2011%20Census/2011_Census_Cape_Town_Profile.pdf [accessed 4 January 2016].
9. For a long time they were outnumbered by whites, whose proportion has drastically

10. Patric Tariq Mellet, for instance, after thoroughly investigating his ancestry, concluded: "My genealogical roots, as they emerged were a wonderful mix of peoples. There were 17 slave personalities including West African slaves, Indonesian slaves from Macassar and Indian slaves from the coast of Malabar, and locally born Cape Creole slaves. There were two Khoe personalities of Goringhaiqua heritage and another of probable Hessequa lineage. Then there were also a range of Europeans of French, Dutch, German, Swiss, Norwegian, English and Scots heritage" (Mellet 2010: 29).

11. Possibly first learned by female domestic slaves (Robert Shell, interview with Armelle Gaulier, Cape Town, 19 February 2008).

12. Sufism is a mystical trend within Islam. "The word '*Sufi*' can be translated by 'mystic'. At first it was used to denote the habit of wearing clothes made of wool (*suf* in Arabic), a symbol of poverty at the time […] In the 11th century the word *tariqa* (a path, a way) appeared, to denote all the recommended rites to be practiced by the *Sufis* during the *halaqat* [literally circle or meeting]. In musical terms, the meetings took the form of *sama'* or listening to songs of praise to the Prophet, together with the recitation of verses from the Koran, both designed to heighten the adept's concentration and spiritual awareness. Between the 9th and 14th centuries other religious exercises and practices were instigated, amongst them the *dhikr*, which has a double meaning, one limited, the other much broader. Its original meaning in Arabic was remembrance, the act of remembering. By extension it came to be applied to the oral account of the thing remembered, its repetition and the technique used for the repetition. Its usage in Sufism refers to the repetition of one of the names of God or the oral profession of the Islamic faith by the initiates, against a background of sacred poems recited by a hymnodist. This is a technique to be practiced in a group, accompanied by breathing exercises which increase the supply of oxygen to the brain, producing a state of trance or dizziness, or even total blackout" (Moussali 1999: 3). Sufism insists on the purification of the heart and the intensification of spiritual life in order to strengthen the connection with God. It is organised in orders or brotherhoods. During *dhikr*, music (vocal and instrumental) plays an important role. This implies that for Sufi Muslims music is not *haraam* (forbidden).

13. City of Cape Town (2012) *Census 2001 – Characteristics of Population: Distribution of Religious Affiliation by Population Group*. Available at http://web.capetown.gov.za/eDocuments/Religion%20(City-2001%20Census)_1772003165422_.htm [accessed 5 January 2015].

14. Murray Williams (2013, 4 January) MJC issues fatwa on minstrels. *Iol*. Available at http://www.iol.co.za/news/south-africa/western-cape/mjc-issues-fatwa-on-minstrels-1.1447535#.U3D6Za1dWup [accessed 10 July 2015].

15. Achmat Davids examined what the Qur'an and the jurisprudence of the Hadith say about music, and referred to Imam Gazzali (Hujjatu-l-Islam Imam Abu Hamid al-Ghazali, 1056–1111), a Persian philosopher and theologian, who wrote, in his *Alchemy of Happiness*: "The heart of man has been so constituted by the Almighty that, like a flint, it contains a hidden fire which is evoked by music and harmony, and renders man beside himself with ecstasy. These harmonies are echoes of that higher world of beauty which we call the world of spirits; they remind man of his relationship to that world, and produce in him an emotion so deep and strange that he himself is powerless to explain it. The effect of music and dancing

16. Nicole McCain (2015, 21 April) Choirs celebrated. *People's Post Woodstock-Maitland*.
17. *Cape Times*, Monday, January 4, 1886. "The frivolous coloured inhabitants of Cape Town, who take a holiday on the slightest pretext, indulged their peculiar notions in regard thereto by going about in large bodies dressed most fantastically, carrying 'guys', and headed by blowers of wind and players of stringed instruments, who evoked from their horrible monsters the most discordant and blatant noises that ever deafened human ears. At night time these people added further inflictions upon the suffering citizens of Cape Town in the shape of vocalisation, singing selections from their weird music with variations taken from 'Rule Britannia' and the 'Old Hundredth'. They also carried Chinese lanterns and banners as they proceeded through the streets playing their discords, beating the drum, singing and shouting, and the strange glinting of the combined light from the street lamps and the Chinese lanterns fell upon their dark faces, they seemed like so many uncanny spirits broken loose from — say the adamantine chains of the Nether World. But it was their mode of enjoyment and strange as it is that such noises should be regarded as pleasant, it showed at least the desire on their part to celebrate the birth of a new year".
18. *Cape Times*, 1 January 1907.
19. Abduraghman Morris, interview with Denis-Constant Martin, Colorado Park, 21 April 2015.
20. ID du Plessis explained that his work at the head of the Department of Coloured Affairs "although done on a basis of separation […] did not push the coloured man away but clasped him, as a Westerner, even more strongly, to the West" (Coloured people belong to the West, *Cape Times*, 26 August 1960).
21. Coons and Afrikaans Culture, "Ridiculous Suggestion", *Cape Standard*, Tuesday, 10 January 1939: 2.
22. The combine chorus is a choral piece sung with instrumental accompaniment but without soloist; the words are original and the music is based on a combination of snippets of melody borrowed from old or recent popular songs.
23. The solo is usually a popular song, a jazz standard or a "classical" aria; it is interpreted by a soloist backed by an instrumental ensemble, without any intervention from the choir.
24. "There are regrettably at New Year too many songs from Tin Pan Alley and too few from Schotsche Kloof [meaning here the Malay Quarter]. The individual troupes, particularly the juveniles among them, love the slow crooning songs which Bing Crosby can put over so well but which the Cape Town Gentlemen Jazz Singers or the Young Dahomey Crooning Minstrels, try as they wish, simply turn into something like a melting chocolate mould at a kids' party. Fortunately, in recent years, largely through the influence of Dr I.D. du Plessis, both the Malay Choirs and the troupes of Coons have been paying more attention to the songs of the Cape. Thus, they are giving the New Year Carnivals a more truly Cape flavour than they had before". Aschman, George (1948, 29 December) Cape's unique New Year Carnival of music. *Argus*. "A feature of the coon song competitions at the Green Point Track yesterday were the Afrikaans 'moppies' or 'liedjies'. The troupes were congratulated by Dr I.D. du Plessis, one of the judges, on bringing this innovation into their carnivals." (1949, 4 January) Thousands see Coon Carnivals. 'Moppies' a new feature. *Argus*.
25. It was during the period spanning the late 1980s to the early 1990s that the style of make-up changed and colours tended to replace black and white. This means that from the late 19th century to the 1980s, the dominant style of make-up was black and white.

26. Troupes are now bussed from their *klopskamer* to Keizergracht and from the junction of Wale Street and Bree Street, or of Wale Street with Rose Street or Chiappini Street back to their *klopskamer*. The parade draws more than 60 000 spectators into the central business district (CBD).
27. "Due to complaints in 2008, the city banned troupes from marching in the Bo-Kaap, apart from a few resident troupes that were allowed to march back home after the Carnival. In 2011, Carnival organizations banded together and took the city to court. The city drafted an official agreement stipulating that it would permit troupes to march in the Bo-Kaap only with the promise that they would immediately board buses and depart the city center after the parade" (Inglese 2014: 139).
28. Where, according to their website, a single room at this hotel costs between ZAR 3 205 and ZAR 8 750.
29. He wrote to the mayoral committee member for tourism requesting that the choirs "should just march past and into Adderley St without music […] This really is critical as I have a 100% full Hotel with very high-rate paying visitors, whom will SERIOUSLY complain if they cannot sleep due to this event." Quoted in: Wim Pretorius (2015, 31 December) Taj Hotel apologises for asking that Cape Malay Choirs not play music outside hotel. *News24*. Available at http://www.news24.com/SouthAfrica/News/taj-hotel-apologises-for-asking-that-cape-malay-choirs-not-play-music-outside-hotel-20151231 [accessed 4 January 2016]. The manager later apologised and promised to inform his guests about Cape Town culture and the New Year festivals.
30. Melvyn Matthews, interview with Denis-Constant Martin, Kensington, 22 April 2015.
31. According to Melvyn Matthews, chief executive officer of the Kaapse Klopse Karnaval Association: "It was not until 2012 that the city's Democratic Alliance (DA) government officially recognized the Carnival as an annual event and set aside a budget for it. Until then, Carnival associations were expected to apply for permission to parade and financial support from the city and provincial governments each year revealing the contingency and marginality of the practice." (Interview with Francesca Inglese, quoted in Inglese 2014: 138).
32. Kardas-Nelson, Mara (2013, 4 January) Kaapse Klopse still march to their own beat. *Mail & Guardian* online. Available at http://mg.co.za/article/2013-01-04-00-kaapse-klopse-still-march-to-their-own-beat [accessed 10 July 2015].
33. Since 1996, the successive mayors of Cape Town have come from the ranks of: the National Party, then New National Party, the African National Congress and, since March 2006, the Democratic Alliance.
34. This is probably the reason why in 2010 another "carnival" was inaugurated: "a Rio-inspired parade in March invented by a media company as a way to create social cohesion and showcase South Africa's diversity for tourists" (Inglese 2014: 140). This Cape Town Carnival is but a show, devoid of social substratum, lacking people's participation, meant to display a particular conception of South Africa's diverse cultures for the satisfaction of tourists (Wentzel 2011).
35. "An NPO is defined, in terms of section 1 of the NPO Act, as a trust, company or other association of persons established for a public purpose and of which its income and property are not distributable to its members or office bearers except as reasonable compensation for services rendered. Nongovernmental organisations (NGOs) and community based organisations (CBOs) are collectively known as non-profit organisations (NPOs). In some instance, NPOs are also referred to as Civil Society Organisations (CSO)." Available at http://www.dsd.gov.za/npo/ [accessed 29 June 2015]. These organisations can access funding from the National Lotteries Trust, NDA [National Development Agency] and other agencies and apply for tax exemption status from SARS [South African Revenue Service]. Available at

https://www.westerncape.gov.za/general-publication/all-you-need-know-about-registration-non-profit-organisations?toc_page=2 [accessed 29 June 2015].

36. "The Kaapse Klopse Carnival Association has started a project they hope will give young people an appreciation for music, art and life skills, while encouraging greater interest in the minstrels. The project, The Western Cape Street Bands Association, hopes to establish resource centres in various neighbourhoods where young people will be taught these skills. Venues have already been identified in Woodstock, Factreton and Athlone. Director of the Kaapse Klopse Karnival Association, Melvyn Matthews, came up with the idea after realising that the Minstrel Carnival was no longer considered a fun event. 'Our carnival has been around for a long time and it has been many things to many people. It has survived slavery, politics and poverty. This is our way of giving back, and the project is the first step to developing the carnival and helping to empower the city' said Matthews. The project has the support of various people, including Ed Backhouse's band and The Dixie Swingers, who host workshops every Saturday to teach people to read sheet music and play instruments. 'Opportunities to play with and enjoy other music groups are non-existent as the Coon players are effectively (musically) dyslexic. They are unable to read normal music' said Backhouse. Matthews and colleague Vic Wilkinson have committed themselves to teaching the minstrels, both young and old. Classes started in July and are held at the Ex-Serviceman's Club in Petunia Street, Parktown, Athlone. 'We are telling the stories of local Cape communities, and Coon classics are being harmonised to create richer sounds to accompany the enthusiastic colourful dancers and singers' said Backhouse. These classes are only the start, but are already an opportunity for the association to get young people off the streets. 'If we can take every kid off the street, put an instrument in his hands and teach him to play - then we have achieved our goal'" said Matthews (Mathy, Cindy (2005, 12 September) Cape minstrels to get music lessons. *IOL*.) Available at http://www.iol.co.za/news/south-africa/cape-minstrels-to-get-music-lessons-1.253241?ot=inmsa.ArticlePrintPageLayout.ot [accessed 26 June 2015]. The project, initiated by The Western Cape Street Bands Association, also aims at offsetting the effects of the professionalisation of musicians playing in bands backing *Klopse* and Malay Choirs. Melvyn Matthews deplored the fact that young people no longer have the opportunity of learning to play instruments during choir practices (Melvyn Matthews, interview with Armelle Gaulier, Mitchells Plain, 11 October 2006).

37. "Alderman JP Smith, City of Cape Town Mayoral Committee Member for Safety and Security, has handed in an official complaint to the Public Protector, calling for the investigation of more than R50m that has allegedly gone missing from the Cape Town Minstrel Carnival Association over the past 3 years. The complaint, lodged on Monday, 16 February, was made against the Cape Town Minstrel Carnival Association (CTMCA), specifically naming the association's chairperson Richard Stemmet and its chief executive, Kevin Momberg. The City believes that the CTMCA received money from various sources, including the City of Cape Town under false pretences, and large amounts of funds 'were misspent severely'. Smith says that donations of R57m, over the past three years, from the National Lottery have 'gone under the radar and remain unaccounted for'. The City of Cape Town also gave the Cape Minstrel Carnival Association an amount of R6m, under the impression that the Minstrel Association was under immense financial pressure and that they had no additional funds, other than those provided by the City of Cape Town. When questioned about the usage of the money, Kevin Momberg told *Carte Blanche* [an investigative TV programme broadcast on the private network M-Net] that the funds were used – and are going to be used – for an official Minstrels Museum, among other things. According to the investigative television report, the Cape Minstrels and their representatives, for example Shahieda Dolly Thole from the Cape Minstrel District Board, know nothing of

any museum". (2015, 16 February) Public Protector asked to probe Kaapse Klopse funds. *NEWS 24.com*. Available at http://traveller24.news24.com/News/Public-Protector-asked-to-probe-Kaapse-Klopse-funds-20150216 [accessed 6 January 2016].

38. See for instance: Shanaaz Eggington (2015, 15 January) "Drug high-flyer" key player in Cape Town minstrel mess. *Times Live*. Available at http://www.timeslive.co.za/local/2015/01/15/drug-high-flyer-key-player-in-cape-town-minstrel-mess [accessed 5 June 2015].

39. See for instance: (2013, 30 December) Fransman set to be minstrels' patron. *IOL News*. Available at http://www.iol.co.za/capetimes/fransman-set-to-be-minstrels-patron-1.1627319 [accessed 5 June 2015]; Anel Lewis (2014, 18 November) R6m is "not enough" – Cape minstrels. *IOL News*. Available at http://www.iol.co.za/news/south-africa/western-cape/r6m-is-not-enough-cape-minstrels-1.1781919 [accessed 5 June 2015] and Marianne Thamm (2015, 3 February) Western Cape ANC: Concern about Fransman's leadership grows. *Daily Maverick*. Available at http://www.dailymaverick.co.za/article/2015-02-03-western-cape-anc-concern-about-fransmans-leadership-grows/ [accessed 5 June 2015].

40. The adult choir used to be drawn from the Lavender Hill (Malay) Choir; in the early 2010s, the Las Vegas asked another Malay Choir, the Young Ideas, to help them improve their singing.

41. Anwar Gambeno, interview with Denis-Constant Martin, Mitchells Plain, 13 April 2015.

42. Armstrong, Aubrena (2014, 7 February) Passion keeps Woodstock Klopse going. *Woodstocklife*. Available at http://woodstocklife.weebly.com/download-woodstocklife.html [accessed 6 January 2016].

43. A third type of organisation, the Christmas Choirs or Christmas Bands, also hold their competitions after the *Klopse* carnival; since this volume is dedicated to choirs and choral singing, we shall not deal with them here. These Christian bands have been thoroughly studied by Sylvia Bruinders (2006/2007, 2012).

44. In July 2015, the Good Hope Centre was turned into a cinema studio; it will no longer be available for community events or concerts; consequently, the CMCB and the KTDMCB decided to use the Cape Town City Hall for their 2016 competitions. See: Lewis, Anel (2015, 10 February) Good Hope Centre to become film studio. *IOL*. Available at http://www.iol.co.za/news/south-africa/western-cape/good-hope-centre-to-become-film-studio-1.1815637#.VeBmUpdKYXg [accessed 28 August 2015].

45. He appears in a documentary film dedicated to Malay Choirs: *The Silver Fez* (Ross & Malan 2010). See also: (2015, 3 May) Bitter feuding among the Cape Malay Choirs has thrown a cherished tradition off key. *Sunday Times*. Available at http://www.pressreader.com/south-africa/sunday-times/20150503/283347585745961/TextView [accessed 8 January 2016].

46. Since *Klopse* and Malay Choirs are considered as organisations involved in socio-economic development, sponsors are able to get socio-economic development score card points for their Black Economic Empowerment (BEE) certificates, which improves their BEE rating. In addition to that, sums allocated to socio-economic development organisations are tax deductible.

47. Abduraghman Morris, interview with Denis-Constant Martin, Colorado Park, 21 April 2015.

48. Ahmed Ismail, interview with Denis-Constant Martin, Mitchells Plain, 22 April 2015.

49. An opera singer who performed, among other roles, Annina (Violetta's maid) in the 2011 production of Verdi's *La Traviata*, at Artscape, Cape Town.

50. *Shoprite Jonge Studente*, brochure published by the Shoprite Jonge Studente, 2015; Ahmed Ismail, interview with Denis-Constant Martin, Mitchells Plain, 22 April 2015.

51. Anwar Gambeno, interview with Denis-Constant Martin, Mitchells Plain, 13 April 2015; "Young Tulips S.K. Constitution", mimeographed document kindly provided by Anwar Gambeno.

52. Singers trained in Pentecostal or Sanctified churches are sought after because of their vocal qualities. For instance, more than half the members of the Calypso Malay Choir are said to

come from an Apostolic Church; André Rix, 25 February 2013, *Malay Choirs Open Group*, Facebook. Available at http://www.facebook.com/pages/Malay-Choirs/100634199977978#!/groups/98713196428/?fref=ts [accessed 17 May 2013].
53. See for instance: Nokia All Stars, Minstrels Rules and Regulations; and CMCB rules: "ANY MEMBER/S UNDER THE INFLUENCE OF LIQUOR OR DRUGS WILL NOT BE ALLOWED TO PARTICIPATE WITH HIS/THEIR CHOIR IS AUTOMATICALLY UNDER SUSPENSION", rule No. 8; "LIQUOR, DRUGS AND FIREARMS IS PROHIBITED AT ALL COMPETITIONS OF THE BOARD", Rule No. 9 (*"Cape Malay Choir Board competition rules and regulations"*, included in the Cape Malay Choir Board programme for the Top 8 and Grand Finale, 2011, p. 6).
54. "All affiliated choir members including MUSICIANS shall wear a FEZ as a headgear in all competitions. A choir contravening this rule will be disqualified of an item." (Rule No. 3, *"Cape Malay Choir Board competition rules and regulations"*, included in the Cape Malay Choir Board programme for the Top 8 and Grand Finale, 2011, p. 6). ID du Plessis contended that the fez was brought to the Cape by exiles from Indonesia. However, according to historian Robert CH Shell, Abubakr Effendi, a Kurdish Islamic scholar sent to Cape Town in the 1860s by the Ottoman Empire at the request of Queen Victoria, "was responsible for the Ottoman fez replacing the turban, *toering* and the head handkerchief as the distinctive Cape Muslim garb" (Shell 2006: 109).
55. A few choirs include girls and women when they practise or perform outside competitions.
56. Abduraghman Morris, interview with Denis-Constant Martin, Colorado Park, 21 April 2015.
57. Anwar Gambeno, interview with Denis-Constant Martin, Mitchells Plain, 13 April 2015.
58. Anwar Gambeno, interview with Denis-Constant Martin, Mitchells Plain, 13 April 2015.
59. Shawn Pettersen, interview with Armelle Gaulier, Cape Town, 3 October 2006.
60. Ismail Bey, interview with Armelle Gaulier, Mitchells Plain, 19 September 2006.
61. Waseef Piekaan, interview with Denis-Constant Martin, Mitchells Plain, 25 October 2011.
62. Tape Jacobs, interview with Armelle Gaulier, Mitchells Plain, 9 August 2006.
63. Ismail Dante, interview with Armelle Gaulier, Mitchells Plain, 7 September 2006.
64. Melismatic ornaments; see "Karienkels", chapter 3, pp. 92–95.
65. Rule No. 26, *"Cape Malay Choir Board competition rules and regulations"*, included in the Cape Malay Choir Board programme for the Top 8 and Grand Finale, 2011, p. 6.
66. Originally, large floats were carried on lorries or trailers; their size was later reduced so that they could be presented on tables and became known as "mini-floats".
67. See "The Juries", chapter 4, pp. 107–111.
68. Adam Samodien in Adam Samodien and Rashaad Malick, interview with Denis-Constant Martin, Woodstock, 12 October 2011.
69. Ismail Dante passed away in 2012, aged more than 70.
70. Ismail Dante, in Ismail and Gamja Dante, interview with Denis-Constant Martin, Hanover Park, 20 October 2011.
71. See for instance: Waseef Piekaan in: "No Copyright on *Moppies*, Yet?", chapter 5, pp. 168–171.
72. Gerald L Stone, personal communication to Denis-Constant Martin.
73. Adam Samodien, Magdie Luckie, Omar Petersen and Anwar Losper, interview with Denis-Constant Martin, Woodstock, 19 January 1994.
74. Melvyn Matthews, in Melvyn Matthews and Sakie "van Die Star", interview with Denis-Constant Martin, Woodstock, 17 January 1994.
75. In South African popular parlance, *moffie* designates a man who dresses and acts like a woman. It does not necessarily mean a homosexual, although it frequently does, but rather a male who acts out female characters, i.e. drag queens, cross-dressers etc. It originally carried derogatory connotations, which is still very often the case today. *Moffies* are put in the

limelight by *Klopse* during carnival parades and are a recurrent topic in *moppie* lyrics. See "*Moffies*", chapter 6, pp. 188–191.
76. Mariam Leeman, interview with Armelle Gaulier, Bridgetown, 12 February 2008.
77. Ismail Morris, interview with Armelle Gaulier, Athlone, 26 February 2008.
78. Kardas-Nelson, Mara (2013, 4 January) Kaapse Klopse still march to their own beat. *Mail & Guardian* online. Available at http://mg.co.za/article/2013-01-04-00-kaapse-klopse-still-march-to-their-own-beat [accessed 10 July 2015].
79. Anwar Gambeno, interview with Denis-Constant Martin, Mitchells Plain, 13 April 2015.
80. Examples of such contests abound. Among the Anlo Ewe (Ghana), listeners choose the winner (Avorgbedor 2001; Dor 2004). Similarly, at the end of Brazilian *desafios* or of Chilean *controversias*, the audience designates the most creative *repentista* or *payador*. But in Trinidad, it is a jury applying a strict scoring scale that ranks the best steel bands in the Panorama (Helmlinger 2011) and in Tanzania judges who must fill adjudication forms award the prizes at the end of *Kwaya* (choirs) championships (Barz 2000: 385). In the field of Western "classical" music there are indeed innumerable competitions: the Queen Elisabeth International Music Competition in Brussels, the China International Piano Competition in Xiamen; the Melbourne International Chamber Music Competition in Australia, to name but a few. And pop music hit-parades not only record, but sometimes contribute to making, successful songs (Parker 1991). Awards obtained in these competitions may be just symbolic and grant only prestige (Stillman 1996: 365); in most cases they mean large amounts of money and/or the promotion of winning artists (Weintraub 2001: 91).
81. An *a capella* genre of choral singing created by Zulu migrant workers in industrial centres and mining compounds; isicathamiya choirs regularly enter in competitions. See: Erlmann 1996.

Jereme Trumpeter & Johaar "Hadji" Kenny, moppie *soloists*,
Cape Traditional Singers, 2016

Part One

*Memory and Processes of
Musical Appropriation*

Anwar Gambeno playing the ghoema *with Johaar "Hadji" Kenny and the Cape Traditional Singers, 2013*

CHAPTER 1

Music behind the music: Appropriation as the engine of creation[1]

"Appropriation" has become a keyword in writings about music. It encompasses various forms of copying, borrowing or recycling, which lead to the production of a piece of music based on pre-existing elements. In the field of what is conventionally called "contemporary" music, composers use it profusely. It is one of the main composition techniques in recent genres of popular music (rap, techno, "world music") and is also widespread in African urban or Indian popular music. It is indeed the major technique used to compose *moppies* and combine choruses sung by Cape Town's Malay Choirs and *Klopse*. Appropriation is a universal method of musical composition[2] and its very universality invites us to try and understand how it is used, what it means in various contexts and how it is related to creation.

The universality of appropriation

A theory of appropriation was formulated in the late 20th century to draw lessons from the emergence of a movement in plastic and visual arts. Artists considered as participating in "Appropriation Art" used many different techniques, ranging from identical reproduction to reformulated forms of ready-mades and collages, a continuum punctuated by several intermediary procedures. "Appropriation Art" designated an ensemble of works and artists presented in a number of influential New York galleries during a decade spanning the late 1970s to the late 1980s. It was considered as: "the very 'language' in which the postmodernist debate was conducted" (Evans 2009: 14). Appropriation, however, was nothing new. The emergence of a diverse artistic movement gathered under this label contributed to draw attention to the term and the techniques it covered; this must not conceal the fact that appropriation has always been used, everywhere, by human beings involved in creative processes. To note the universality of appropriation necessarily leads to asking why it is so widespread and what social significance it may have in various social contexts. To look for answers to these questions, one may start from anthropologist Jean-Loup Amselle's theory of an "initial *métissage*"³, that is a *métissage* that had no beginnings, which, consequently, could never bring together pure and unmixed elements. Ethno-history actually brings to light infinite connections (*branchements*): cultures have always been invented and identities configured by mixing elements coming from societies considered, at one particular time, "different" (Amselle 1990, 2001).

Looking closely at how mixing and blending take place, it is obvious that appropriation is never unilateral: it is a multidimensional relationship that involves several agents (at least one who appropriates and another whose "goods" are appropriated) and impacts upon on their ways of being, as well as on their powers of innovation (Ziff & Rao 1997: 1–4). Appropriation is one of the modes of cultural transfer that is set in motion as soon as people or groups of different origins meet, whatever the situation of inequality and violence (slavery, colonisation) in which the meeting occurs (Gruzinski 1996, 1999; Turgeon 1996, 2003). It intervenes within the general mechanism of acculturation as defined by Roger Bastide: an ensemble of "processes that take place when two cultures are put in contact and interact: act and react one on the other" (Bastide 2006 [1998]). These processes cause changes in every culture that comes into contact with other cultures, and trigger creative dynamics. Serge Gruzinski, for instance, analysed how Aztecs in New Spain (Mexico) started, as soon as they were subjugated by Spaniards, to move from exactly replicating European models to inventing new aesthetic forms, and how, in turn, in the fine arts, their innovations influenced the European styles called "Mannerism" and "Grotesque" (Gruzinski 1996, 1999). In the first stages of colonisation, acculturation and appropriation implied immediate meetings of people: rubbing shoulders was a prerequisite for exchanges. Today, new techniques of communication no longer make that necessary. First, the discovery of printing and engraving stimulated the circulation and commercialisation of plastic models throughout Europe. Albrecht Dürer was one of the first artists to understand the benefits he could derive from having his works, identified by a logo, reproduced in large quantities and sold. Then, recording machines were invented, which made it possible to fix and transfer sounds and images; later the internet intensified and accelerated the circulation of cultural products, making it possible to access immediately almost any type of artistic creation emanating from any place in the world. Appropriation is not only about artistic productions, but also about aesthetic models. The examples of the Aztecs and Albrecht Dürer confirm it acquired this characteristic early on.[4] Focusing on a more recent period, anthropologist Bennetta Jules-Rosette, demonstrated that African tourist art represents the outcome of an intricate system of communication/interaction, in which African sculptors endeavour to meet what they assume to be the expectations of tourist art buyers and in this way contribute to fashioning these buyers' representations of what African art is. An aesthetic of symbolic exchange appears in this *mise en abyme* (Jules-Rosette 1984:

19, 220) that sheds an interesting light on the way several musicians found their place in the world music market.

Musicologist, Jean-Jacques Nattiez, following up on propositions by philosopher and linguist, Jean Molino, suggested that music should be considered as an "impure mix". He converges with Jean-Loup Amselle's theory of initial *métissage* and disproves notions of musical "purity" or "authenticity" (Nattiez 2009: 55). Such a primordial impurity is the consequence of what anthropologist, Georges Balandier, identified as a dialectics of inside and outside dynamics (Balandier 1951, 1971). Inside dynamics result from the impact of moral, social, economic and political mutations on musical activities. Within this framework, aesthetic research creates an additional, but autonomous, momentum. Outside dynamics arise from three inter-related phenomena: external constraints (especially commercial constraints linked to the treatment of music as a commodity); social representations of music from "elsewhere" (which can be depreciated and despised or valued because of an exotic fascination for faraway lands or a romantic idealisation of certain societies); and finally, choices made by musicians for reasons pertaining to the first two phenomena, as well as because of aesthetic preferences. Musical appropriation can therefore be defined as the adoption — spurred by internal and external factors and independent inclinations (which cannot be divorced one from the other) — of musical traits, genres, styles or elements of genres and styles coming from musical works or musical universes other than those of the borrower.

This is a universal phenomenon. In mediaeval Europe, troubadours writing in *lenga d'òc* (*langue d'oc*, an ancient form of Occitan) practiced *trobar*. The term, used to speak of a particular creative process, combined the notions of finding and composing; it clearly signified that troubadours' creations were based on reusing what they "found" to produce personal "finds". This is the reason why one piece, music and lyrics, could be rendered with many variants, using a composition method proceeding by addition (Thomas 1998: 36-38). In these times "composition was an organic process concerned with the past and the present while contributing to the future" (Thomas 1998: 36). To quote other works was a way of paying a compliment to fellow musicians and poets, and also of referring to meanings associated with these works. From the combination of the text of the work quoted with the text of the "new" composition, emerged complex correspondences: significations replete with contrasting and sometimes contradictory sentiments (Thomas 1998: 36). Later, all composers adopted similar attitudes. Johann Sebastian Bach, wrote musicologist Antoine Hennion: "never ceased to draw from others to imagine his music" (Hennion 2010: 42). Bach considered that God is the only creator and that, consequently, he, Bach, "does not create anything ex nihilo: he comments, he re-uses tirelessly already existing music, his own or other musicians', in order to ornament God's words" (Hennion 2010: 44). After Bach, most composers abandoned the idea that creation was only God's prerogative; they nevertheless continued unabatedly to draw from past and present popular and art music. In order to evaluate the extent of musical appropriation and to understand its consequences, J Peter Burkholder endeavoured to constitute the use of pre-existing music as an autonomous research domain. His goal was to study techniques of borrowing, relationships between various modes of borrowing and meanings of borrowings. He proposed more than two decades ago the outline of a typology and a timeline of musical borrowings which are still extremely useful (Burkholder 1994). In the history of Western art music, despite efforts made by historians and musicologists to hide it behind the myth of the individual genius, appropriation is ubiquitous.[5] It is widespread in orally transmitted music (so-called "traditional" music). Contemporary artists in the field of popular music make the widest use of computers and recent communication technologies to increase their stock of material ready to be reworked: "Undaunted by traditional conceptions of literary and intellectual property, fans raid mass culture, claiming its material for their own use, reworking them as the basis for their own cultural creations and social interactions" (Jenkins 1992: 18). For these musicians, "every sound that has been caught is liable to be used" (Kosmicki 2010: 100).

Musical appropriation

Musical appropriation is so prevalent that it is no longer enough to signal it in passing. It is necessary, as advised by J Peter Burkholder, to zero in on the reasons and the consequences of this practice.

What is appropriated?

Appropriation may concern styles or genres. When Johann Sebastian Bach qualified his suites as "French" or "English", when he titled a harpsichord concerto *Concerto nach Italienischem Gusto* (Concerto after the Italian Taste), he underlined his will to reproduce prevalent characteristics of the French, English and Italian music of his time that his audience would probably recognise. Claude Debussy and Igor Stravinsky adopted the same evocative approach when they took inspiration from American music. The fascination Afro-Cuban *son* exercised on Senegalese and Congolese young urban musicians led them to adopt not only songs, but a whole style of performance typical of Cuba (Shain 2002, 2009; White 2008). Ghanaian and Nigerian musicians rather looked to Trinidad and took to playing calypso (Collins 1989, 1996). Apart from these types of broad appropriation, there are more limited forms of borrowing: Béla Bartók from Hungarian and Slovakian popular songs, Leoš Janáček from Moravian songs or

Richard Wagner, who introduced in the prelude to *Tristan and Iseult*'s third act a Venetian gondolier's song under the guise of an English horn solo (Nattiez 1997). Among Indian composers of Bollywood soundtracks or pop songs, using and mixing pre-existing tunes is extremely common (Guillebaud 2010). One of the most remarkable examples of appropriation brings us back to European 17th century: Georg Friedrich Händel was so fond of Giacomo Carissimi's oratorio *Jephte* that he included note for note its final chorus in his own *Samson*.

Why appropriate?

Musicians decide to appropriate material they did not create for aesthetic reasons, for example for a particular sonic quality that will enrich the piece they are working on. They also often select what they appropriate according to the symbolic value they, and/or their audience, grant to traits typical of specific genres or musical cultures. In South Africa, the *ghoema* beat is included in works belonging to many genres, from "art" music to rap, in order to signify Cape Town and its history of mixing. Particular types of vocality and ornamentation techniques refer to the East and the Arabic world. Certain rhythmic patterns embody Jamaica and the myths surrounding reggae. In genres which appeared recently, such as rap, techno or "world music", one can hear a multiplication of borrowings within the same piece. Combinatory mechanisms have become a predominant mode of composition, made easier by sampling and dedicated computer software (Arom & Martin 2011). Samples can be transformed. They can also be treated in a way that allows listeners to recognise the source: their insertion in a new piece produces a double effect, namely sonic and symbolic. However, a combination of pre-existing tunes pre-dates the irruption of samplers and computers. In Madagascar and Reunion Island, as well as in many other parts of the world, composers used to memorise songs, distinctive traits of styles, genres and motives and assemble them according to their own imagination (Mallet & Samson 2010).

These various examples highlight how important a role technical innovations play in processes of appropriation. It cannot operate in identical ways when musicians work in an environment where they have to come face-to-face to exchange,[6] and when they find themselves in a world criss-crossed by virtual networks of communication. Ethnomusicologist, Peter Manuel, demonstrated how cassettes transformed the Indian musical landscape (Manuel 1993). Steven Feld and Annemette Kierkegaard showed that many genres of modern music could not have been conceived without a phenomenon which R Murray Schaffer baptised "schizophonia", the separation of sounds from the situation in which they were originally produced (Feld & Kirkegaard 2010). In every case, it appears that appropriation is not just a morphological operation; it also implies symbolic manipulations.

Situations of appropriation

Musical appropriation has to be understood against a background of both particular situations, such as slavery and colonisation, as well as of the development of a commercial market for music and of the repercussions of technological changes (cassettes, internet) on the circulation of "goods" in this market. Consequently, social conditions and technological mediations have to be taken into account when investigating relationships between power and music. When Johann Sebastian Bach or Georg Friedrich Händel "borrowed" from their colleagues, they did not think of it as "appropriation", but rather as a way of circulating music among peers. When Jesuits taught music to their indigenous flock in South America, or Christian missionaries to their followers in South Africa, they conceived music as a means to consolidate conversions and to instil in "heathens" the principles of European (Christian) civilisation. Both created a power relationship that imposed their culture and their faith as superior. The same mechanisms were at work in slave colonies of the Americas and the West Indies, but were indeed applied in a much more brutal fashion. In such situations, acquiring knowledge of the fundamentals of various European forms of music led indigenous converts in South America and African slaves in the so-called "New World" to develop an ability to play on symbols of European superiority. In a dialectical and contradictory manner, the internalisation of European pre-eminence was coupled in their mind with an increasing awareness that they could use the symbols of this pre-eminence, music among others, in order to fight European superiority and claim their own humanness.

As a matter of fact, relations of appropriation are frequently unequal. Johann Sebastian Bach was younger than Dietrich Buxtehude, but rapidly became considered as his equal, if not as a disciple who had surpassed his master. Composers of Indian pop songs and techno DJs work on an equal footing, even if differences in reputation and popularity exist between them. However, the globalised economy of music that conquered the world in the 20th century created positions from where powerful actors could capture the creations of subordinated people. Here again the relationship is replete with ambivalence. Ethnomusicologist, Steven Feld, emphasised that:

> Musical appropriation sings a double line with one voice. It is a melody of admiration, even homage and respect; a fundamental source of connectedness, creativity, and innovation. This we locate in a discourse of "roots", of reproducing and expanding "the tradition". Yet this voice is harmonized by a counter-melody of power, even control and domination; a fundamental source of maintaining asymmetries in ownership and commodification of musical works. This we locate in a discourse of "rip-offs", of reproducing "the hegemonic". Appropriation means that the issue of "whose

music" is submerged, supplanted, and subverted by the assertion of "our music". (quoted in Seeger 1997: 62)

The effects of ambivalences led Bruce Ziff and Pratima Rao to distinguish between *assimilative practices:* "a process whereby cultural minorities are encouraged, if not obliged, to adapt or assimilate the cultural forms and practices of the dominant group" and a*ppropriative practices*: "a process whereby dominant groups may be criticized and challenged when they borrow the cultural forms associated with subordinate groups" (Ziff & Rao 1997: 5–7). Such a dichotomisation brings to the fore power relationships that underpin cultural transfers and highlights the existence of different strategies related to various power positions. Yet it may be understood as a rigid opposition between attitudes and practices that are actually always intertwined. This is why it is probably more fecund from a heuristic point of view to continue using the general term *appropriation* to embrace the combinations of these attitudes and practices in all their complexity, while keeping in mind that: "power and the relationships of power can be construed as central to the concept of cultural appropriation [...]" because it implies a "differential access to sources of power and the consequences for cultures and cultural forms that flow from this differential access to power" (Ziff & Rao 1997: 5).

The transformative power of appropriation

The first stage of appropriation is unchanged reproduction, for example Georg Friedrich Händel's inclusion of Giacomo Carissimi's final chorus of *Jephte* in *Samson*. The mere practice of inserting a piece from a work by Giacomo Carissimi in an oratorio written by Georg Friedrich Händel transformed it, because the context in which it was placed was different. Analysts of "Appropriation Art" were quite aware of this. David A Mellor, discussing Richard Prince's "rephotographies", observed that they were "invaded — parasitized — by uncanny fantasies of forfeited existence" which permeated them with an "unintended and unwanted dimension of fiction" (Mellor 2009: 100). Photographer Richard Prince himself explained:

> Rephotography is a technique for stealing (pirating) already existing images, simulating rather than copying them, "managing" rather than quoting them, re-producing their effect and look as naturally as they had been produced when they first appeared. A resemblance more than a reproduction, a rephotograph is essentially an appropriation of what's already real about an existing image and *an attempt to add on or additionalize this reality onto something more real*, a virtuoso real, a reality that has the chances of looking real, but a reality that doesn't have any chances of being real. (Prince 1977; own emphasis)

In this case, reproduction is a manipulation aimed at re-signifying what is reproduced. In pop music, "cover versions" are necessarily unfaithful to the original: they compete with the initial production and between themselves. Just as with "remakes" in cinema, they have to show specific traits in order to attract buying listeners; they try to be "better", to be more "up-to-date". When it is a genre or a style that is appropriated, the transformative process is more powerful: appropriation gives birth to new trends, even though they may keep the name of what has been appropriated. Jazz has provided many examples, be it in France, with the emergence of "French jazz" (Martin & Roueff 2002), or in South Africa, with "African jazz" (Ballantine 2012). Ska, reggae and rap have produced the same effects.

Appropriation is even deliberately used to produce something new. Indian popular music is, again, a case in point: composers move melodies around; sometimes they mix them, they place new texts on pre-existing tunes (Guillebaud 2010; Manuel 1993: chap. 7). Gipsy musicians from Kossovo, and many other places, "handle a tune as raw material, out of which they tend to create a new product, their personalized version. In the process of molding the product, Gypsy musicians consider all musical features changeable" (Pettan 1992: 128). Their attitude is similar to that of jazz musicians who always considered interpreting *standards* as a stepping-stone to improvisation, which could be in the form of variations on the theme or of original melodies built on the chord progression of the song "interpreted" (Williams 2010). Jazz improvisation is at the same time impromptu and fed by formulas widely circulating in the world of jazz, the memory of solos which have made a strong impact upon musicians and audiences, and imitations of individual characteristics which have been integrated in innovative styles. We shall see how, in Cape Town, *moppie* composers assemble elements of pre-existing melodies to organise a new tune on which they place original lyrics in Afrikaans.[7]

Significations and resignifications

Transformations caused by appropriation are not only morphological. To be sure, they contribute to giving a particular aesthetic quality to works in which borrowings are inserted or which are edified on such borrowings. But borrowings refer to other pieces, to other composers, and to the societies they come from: they exhibit a relation that is heavy with symbolic significations. Philosopher Paul Ricœur considered that to appropriate amounts to making what is appropriated one's own in order to affirm or to recover the "act of existing",[8] to proclaim a desire to be (Ricœur 1969b: 323–325). Existing and understanding Oneself depend on the Other, on the Other's understanding (Ricœur 1969a: 20–21). Relations existing between the Self and the Other develop from the Other's presence in the Self and the recognition of the Other as another Self: they generate agency because they give the subject a power of initiative, an ability to change what the subject has appropriated from Others which appears as the portent of a capacity to change the world (Ricœur 1990). To understand the motives and significations of musical appropriation, it is necessary to start from the relationships between appropriation, identity, alterity and transformative power.

Appropriation can be used to improve a piece of music by giving it a particular "flavour" or by remodelling a conventional form. When composers work on an equal footing, this may consist of drawing inspiration from and paying tribute to a "master" or a respected colleague. This is frequent in European "art" music, jazz, techno and rap. Musicologist, Sabine Trébinjac, recounted that already in second-century BC China: "Hans considered that music, especially military music, had a particular power; to analyse the theft of the enemy's music in order to defeat him as a way of appropriating his luck and his virtue is therefore well founded" (Trébinjac 1997: 239). When composers are linked by uneven relations, appropriation acquires other dimensions. The appropriation of musical characteristics of a dominating group's music by dominated musicians seems to manifest an acceptation of its intrinsic superiority, but it also affirms the subaltern's capacity to do as well as, if not better than, the "masters" in their own realm. In Cape Town, amateur coloured singers of the Eoan Group gave outstanding performances of Italian operas in Italian (Eoan History Project 2013) and Trinidadians "bad boys" turned steel drum players gave amazing renditions of European "classical" hits (Stuempfle 1995). In such cases, the use of the Other's music amounts to a form of the symbolic cannibalism advocated by Oswaldo de Andrade in Brazil: "anthropophagic thinking" is selective, it implies absorbing what represents the Other's strength in order to acquire it, but it is capable of distinguishing the positive elements of the Other's civilisation and of rejecting what cannot be used to the "cannibal's" benefit (De Andrade 1995, 2015). Decades later, Haitian poet René Depestre developed similar ideas under the name "maroonage": "The socio-cultural history of the dominated masses of the western hemisphere is globally a history of ideological maroonage which allowed them, not to re-interpret the sword-brandishing, cross-toting and whip-waving Europe through an alleged 'African mentality', but to exhibit a heroic creativity in order to elaborate painfully new modes of feeling, of thinking and of acting" (Depestre 1980: 99). Here, "maroon" does not simply mean to escape, to flee the plantation, but also to take from the Master's possession what can be used to reconstruct a new life, a new comprehension of oneself. In this perspective, it may not even be necessary to abscond: the invention of a new practice, be it religious or artistic, may contribute to recovering self-esteem, the conscience of being human, even while in shackles.

Members of dominating groups also draw from the music of the dominated. In so doing, they affirm their capacity to "improve" the material they borrow, to cleanse it of its rustic or plebeian dirt and give it a legitimate form, resounding with rich harmonies. This is, for instance, what Greek composers Manos Hatzidakis[9] and Mikis Theodorakis pretended to do with demotic music or *rebetiko*, in a way emulating French composer Joseph Canteloube who "adapted" popular songs from Auvergne (a mountainous region of south-central France). However, the ambition of "art" music composers to "enhance" popular music does not preclude the fact that they can also be motivated by the will to pay tribute to the popular culture of their country. Peasants or urban workers, in spite of the exploitation they suffer, have also been considered as guardians of traditions, of an authentic national heritage which could be re-used and re-formulated in a nationalist perspective. Beyond a strict musicological interest, this is what led musicians such as Béla Bartók, Zoltán Kodály and Leoš Janáček to conceive works inspired by songs and dances they had heard, noted and sometimes recorded in the rural areas of central Europe. This type of work, including recognisable elements taken from the music of subjugated groups has indeed a political dimension: it can sound like a nationalist claim, but can also be heard as a protest against the oppression certain groups are submitted to. In South Africa, especially in the 1980s, "contemporary" composers such as Kevin Volans, Stefans Grové and Michael Blake inserted traits characteristic of black African music in some of their works, when white members of the rock ensemble, Bright Blue, quoted Nkosi Sikelel' iAfrika in an *mbaqanga*[10]-sounding piece, which became one of their greatest successes: "Weeping".[11]

Musicians borrowing from the music of people considered "different" often express, at least symbolically, the will to break away from the group in which they live, its traditions or the way it is governed. Such breaks are moved by identification mechanisms, which turn the people from whom music is borrowed into an ideal or a counter-model, in contrast to the organisation of the society to which the borrowers belong. When young urban African musicians wanted to demonstrate that they too belonged to a world of modernity and that such a world was not the preserve of Euro-Americans, they injected in their music elements from metropolitan pop repertoires, as well as from original West Indian genres that radically differentiated them from their rural counterparts (Collins 1989, 1996; Shain 2002, 2009; White 2008). In the United States, young whites who decided to play jazz when it was just budding (e.g. Bix Beiderbecke) or reinterpreted black rhythm and blues (e.g. Elvis Presley), distanced themselves, at least for a time, from their native milieu and its cultural norms.

Appropriation and identity

What is at stake in these examples (and many others could have been given) is the configuration and expression of identities and processes in which music plays an important role (Martin 2013: chap. 1). Ethnomusicologist, Nathalie Fernando, observed: "The question of identity is central to inter-ethnic borrowing. Characteristics of the Other's music may appear as potential material for building one's own identity" (Fernando 2007: 59). Musical appropriation relies on identifications which are one of the essential mechanisms of identity construction. Music allows one to hear a play on sameness and difference; it tries simultaneously to erase the differences of Others with whom borrowers identify and to produce differences within groups from whom borrowers want to distance themselves, be it their membership group or not. This play is one of the forms taken by the agency that Paul Ricœur linked to appropriation. It not only causes morphological changes, it also transforms symbolic significations attached to music and triggers what Peter Manuel called a process of resignification: "On a strictly musical level, appropriation can involve the active alteration, however subtle, of acquired styles, as competent imitation gives way to creative syncretism and further evolution. More importantly, however, appropriation is a socio-musical process, involving the resignification of the borrowed idiom to serve as a symbol of a new social identity" (Manuel 1994: 274). When pieces or styles of music circulate between groups, sometimes in surprising round trips, it generates chains of metamorphosis, such as Christopher Waterman brought to light in his study of several versions of the song "Corrine Corrina" (Waterman 2000).

Together, formal modifications and resignification in music manifest a transformative power that can be symbolically extended to lived realities: for subaltern groups, they hold an emancipating potential. The effort to exist and the desire to be which Paul Ricœur discerned in appropriation nourish a will to fight in order to bring about changes in situations of inequality and oppression. From a different premise, Marxist philosophers linked the appropriation of the means of production to the liberation from alienation, in the perspective of a total reinstatement of a denied or mistreated humanness (Cotten 1982). This link was analysed in detail by Perla Serfaty-Garzon, an expert in environmental psychology: "This type of possession aims at making something one's own, that is to adapt it to oneself and in so doing to transform this something into a prop supporting the expression of oneself. Appropriation amounts to grasping an object and exercising a dynamics of action on the social and material world with the intention to build the subject" (Serfaty-Garzon 2003: 27).[12] Many illustrations of the liberating potential of musical appropriation can be found. One of the most powerful is the use made of African-American religious songs, in which European Protestant hymns were upset (or transformed) by the mixing of hymns with conceptions of polyphony and polyrhythms coming from various regions of the African continent. The invention of black gospel in the 19th century associated musical innovations with a reinterpretation of certain aspects of Christian dogma put forward by European settlers and their descendants. This led to a theology of salvation no longer based on obedience, but on emancipation. The liberating potential of black spirituals was fully realised when these songs served first as communication codes for activists involved in networks known as the Underground Railway, which organised slaves' escapes; then as models for militant songs sung during the Civil Rights Movement (Martin 1998).

Appropriation and property rights

Until the 19th century, appropriation was free. When the notion of copyright was applied to music, and generated a number of related rights, it stirred up debates and legal controversies. Ethnomusicologist, Anthony Seeger, summed up the main issues of these disputes:

> The copyright law in force today is based on a number of cultural presuppositions, four of which are central to issues faced by ethnomusicologists. First, the law is based on the concept of individual creativity — individuals copyright products of their own creation. Second, it is based on the idea that an individual should receive compensation for a limited period of time, after which the idea may be used by anyone without paying a royalty. After the expiration of a copyright, music enters "the public domain" and royalties may not be collected on it. Third, the law leaves somewhat unclear the status of arrangements of "traditional songs". Fourth, the musical item copyrighted is item-title based. (Seeger 1997: 60)

These presuppositions are relatively new. Copyright was first instituted as much to punish individuals guilty of "subversive" writings (Foucault 1994: 799) as to protect the literary rights of writers. According to historian, Roger Chartier, it engendered a new economy of writing which put an end to: "the practice of collaborative writing that was demanded by patrons, troupes or theatre entrepreneurs and the reuse of stories already told, shared commonplace ideas, accepted formulae or the continuation of works which always remained open" (Chartier 2011: 282–283).[13] In 1831, the addition of musical compositions to the American law on copyright had similar effects (Mangolte 2010). But it was based on the ideas that a musical composition was necessarily produced by an individual composer, that it was possible to isolate singular works to which the law could be applied, and it implied for a long time that only written pieces of music could be registered. It therefore ignored a large part of musical production, probably the largest: so-called "traditional" music, orally transmitted and not written,[14] as well as many genres of today's music in which composition and performance set in motion an art of combining that necessarily implies borrowing (Kosmicki 2010; Mallet & Samson 2010).

The many loopholes that persist in the legal approach to musical property are the source of controversies regarding the "theft" of dominated people's "culture", a practice the Writers' Union of Canada defined in 1992 as: "the taking — from a culture that is not one's own — of intellectual property, cultural expressions or artefacts, history and ways of knowledge" (quoted in Ziff & Rao 1997: 1). This formulation remains clumsily braced on an essentialist notion of culture. A musician from a "rich" country who borrows from or imitates music from a "poor" country is perceived as a "thief"; however, musicians from "poor" countries often acknowledge the fact that they may benefit from such a "theft" because "rich" and famous musicians contribute to giving the material they have borrowed a large exposure and help introduce musicians from "poor" countries to the globalised music market (Guillebaud 2010). However, the fact that some musicians derive important revenue from works integrating elements taken from other cultures cannot be denied. The most famous example is that of the New Age "world music" practised by French duet, Deep Forest. They used ethnomusicological recordings to produce compositions that generated important financial gains, which were neither repaid to nor shared with the ethnomusicologist who recorded the original material and the person who performed it (Feld 1996, 2000; Zemp 1996). Californian lawyer, Sherylle Mills, considered that: "Deep Forest remains an excellent example of the alarming vulnerability of non-Western music in today's commercial music world. As the fate of the sampled music in Deep Forest reveals, current Western copyright schemes are inadequate for the protection of non-Western music and, consequently, are in desperate need of updating" (Mills 1996: 60). This highlights the combined effects of the legal individualisation of the creator, of the commodification of music and, consequently, of the application to artistic productions of rules conceived for commodities. Music, more than ever, generates financial benefits that provoke a struggle for their distribution. It may also disseminate deformed representations of the societies from which musical traits have been appropriated and be seen, within these societies, as offensive to the spirituality of the music. In spite of attempts to adapt laws to the reality of musical practices in every type of society, many problems remain. Essentialist notions of identity and cultural heritage carry a fixist conception of culture. It seems difficult to accommodate in Western law, in which originate international rules governing artistic property rights, notions of cultures emphasising their mutability, their ignorance of borders, their intense relations and their intricate entangledness, such as proposed by Édouard Glissant's theory of Relation (Glissant 1990). Bruce Ziff and Pratima Rao observed:

> It is one thing to try to retain a faithful rendering of a practice, such as a traditional method of storytelling (if this is possible); it is another to try to preserve the practice forever *only* in its current form (1997: 14) [...] The difficulty here lies in the law allowing creative processes to continue while responding to unacceptable appropriative practices, whatever these may be. (1997: 18)

An adaptation of laws on musical property rights allowed in some cases the redress of dishonest appropriation of particular pieces whose composer was known. Solomon Linda's heirs finally recovered the rights to his most famous song, "Mbube", after a long legal battle that involved influent personalities who could give evidence that Solomon Linda composed the song; this was thanks to archival material and recordings that were admitted as substitutes for written scores (Malan 2000).

Nevertheless, the challenge Bruce Ziff and Pratima Rao put forward has not yet been answered. In an ideal world, a solution would probably be to consider musical productions as common goods and put them under creative commons licenses.[15] This would facilitate a return to the free circulation of musical works and to their unrestricted appropriation for creative purposes, a conception that would resonate with pre-19th-century practices and is today shared by most techno DJs.[16] However, given that the present world is structured around wide inequalities, mechanisms would have to be devised to protect the rights of the most disadvantaged. Neither existing laws, nor adjustments that have been recently made, in Brazil for instance, in order to protect the rights of "communities" over their cultural productions, seem to bring satisfying solutions. Many measures have been criticised because it has been observed that: "proprietary approaches only benefit powerful people who are able to obtain that restrictions be respected. The application of proprietary approaches creates a risk of embezzlement and public servants or private actors may monopolise the benefits accruing from agreements they entered into as representatives of the communities" (Aigrain 2010: 173).[17] Alternately, to treat collective heritage as common goods would make it possible to: "acknowledge the rights of communities to receive benefits, in financial or other forms, when users of the common goods employ them in economic activities or utilise them as a basis for innovation". These benefits would be placed in a "security fund initially financed by states, then by levies on benefits realised by the users" (Aigrain 2010: 173).[18] Implementing such a system may appear somewhat utopian; to make do with present legal regulations, actors involved in music production — musicians, producers, ethnomusicologists, archivists, etc. — have to improvise *ad hoc* bricolages which include informal solutions (an ethnomusicologist delivers money directly into the hands of musicians, whose recording has been used for the soundtrack for an advertisement) and legal suits (as in the case of "Mbube").[19]

Appropriation and creation

To be able to freely appropriate, that is, borrow and transform already existing works, or not, changes the conditions in which creation can blossom. From time immemorial, everywhere, musicians have drawn from other musicians' ideas in order to invent their "own" music. If, in the past, composers had been submitted to the conceptions of artistic property that prevail today, one can imagine the number of claims which would have been lodged against Johann Sebastian Bach, Igor Stravinsky, not to mention Charles Ives.[20] There is a general agreement on the fact that: "Practically speaking, there is no 'creation from nothing' (ex nihilo). There is always something 'before the beginning', just as there is always something 'after the end'. Put another way, everything is 'all middle'" (Pope 2005: xv). Consequently, large numbers of creative musicians: "rather than to elaborate new ideas or concepts, are deft at revealing original correspondences between already existing forms. Their creations often sound like arrangements, variations or bricolages" (Guillebaud et al. 2010: 8).[21] New technologies multiply possibilities to discover and to use correspondences, to conceive original arrangements organised by bricolage. Creation more and more resembles an "assembly line" associating many "workers" who are not necessarily mentioned on concert posters or recordings' liner notes and whose names do not appear on the registers of copyright (Côté 1998: 73–88).

"Refreshers" and *"establishers of discursiveness"*

To recognise that arrangement and combination of pre-existing elements from many different origins are the basis of creation questions the very notion of creation: if every work results from assembling and mixing, what is original? A first answer consists in considering creation as a dynamics, a movement; as is creativity. Rob Pope, a professor of English who teaches creative teaching and writing strategies proposed that: "creativity will be provisionally defined as the capacity to make, do or become something fresh and valuable, with respect to others as well as ourselves" (Pope 2005: xvi). He explained: "fresh because this means more than just "new" or "novel" and because 'refreshing' may involve making strange things familiar as well as familiar things strange" (Pope 2005: xvi). Beyond a few puzzling formulations[22], the emphasis Rob Pope puts on the link between to become and to "refresh" must be considered seriously: it posits that refreshing (which can be understood as rejuvenation and renovation) pre-existing pieces in works resulting from combination is a mode of becoming. Creativity is a momentum which extends the effort towards existing and the desire to be, dispositions Paul Ricœur attaches to appropriation. Creation is loaded with symbolic significations; it is one of the reasons why it appears as an undeniable characteristic of humanness: as the expression of a will to exist as a full-fledged human being (Cassirer 1979).

Such characteristics of humanness may be instilled in a work by "refreshing" a musical style or genre: A noticeable modification of musical parameters may destabilise the pre-existing balance between these parameters and establish a new one. Musical history is marked by moments of renewal: for example, in jazz, the advent of be-bop in the 1940s, then of "jazz-rock" in the 1960s; in Trinidadian music, the modernisation of calypso imposed by The Mighty Sparrow in the 1950s, then the invention of soca by Lord Shorty (Ras Shorty I) in the 1970s. Such changes in what are, at a particular time, conventional parameters are evidence of a dynamics of creativity; however, they do not radically transform aesthetic languages. Attempting to understand what can constitute a real break, a rupture, Michel Foucault suggested that it was necessary to identify writers — but his line of reasoning can also be applied to musicians — who could be considered as "establishers of discursiveness",[23] because they "not only made possible certain analogies, they have made possible certain differences" (Foucault 1994: 805). "They have produced something more: they have made possible the formation of other texts and they have provided rules for it" (Foucault 1994: 804).[24] Many composers introduced ruptures in the conventional language of their time and often theorised them: Johann Sebastian Bach and Jean-Philippe Rameau, Arnold Schoenberg, Terry Riley; Ornette Coleman and the explorers of "free jazz". In many instances, it is impossible to identify individual musicians who introduced elements leading to a break. Several of them, not always known or recognised, have laid the foundations of a "new discursiveness": African-American musicians in the late 19th and early 20th centuries who, in several regions of the United States, invented a totally new conception of improvisation; urban youth, who attempted to distance themselves from American rhythm and blues and re-introduced Jamaican elements in their music, creating a dynamics that led from ska to reggae; techno DJs, who took advantage of new technologies to appropriate and manipulate sounds and brought about new treatments of timbre and sonic texture; Dakarois musicians, tired of playing replicas of Afro-Cuban music who initiated *mbalax* by drawing from several Senegalese rural sources. However, it is more difficult to single out such ruptures in orally transmitted music, which have only been recently recorded. Ghanaian musicologist, Kwabena Nketia, nevertheless insisted on the importance of studying mutations in African music, arguing that: "A musical culture must [...] be regarded as something dynamic and capable of growth or change in relation to the social and the musical or their juncture and as something that develops its own characteristic modes of expression and behavior" (Nketia 2005: 87). Another musicologist from Ghana, Kwasi Ampene, empirically applied this principle to a study of Akan music and analysed how some musicians introduced innovations that could be considered as establishing new rules (Ampene 2005).

Appropriation is at the heart of these creative processes. "Establishing discursiveness" is indeed initiated by individuals or groups of musicians. However, to create dynamics of original creation demands that the innovations they propose be accepted, taken over and appropriated by other musicians and their audiences. Roland Barthes announced the "death of the author" and emphasised the role of the reader: "A text consists of multiple writings, issuing from several cultures and entering into dialogue with each other, into parody, into contestation; but there is one place where this multiplicity is collected, united, and this place is not the author, as we have hitherto said it was, but the reader: the reader is the very space in which are inscribed, without any being lost, all the citations a writing consists of; the unity of a text is not in its origin, it is in its destination [...]" (Barthes 1984: 69).²⁵ If "text" is replaced with "musical work", "author" with musician and "reader" with listener, this assumption appears perfectly relevant for music. Musical creativity and creation appear as dialectic processes in which participate, on the one hand, initiators of change, "establishers of discursiveness", and on the other "judges" belonging to the worlds of musicians, of listeners, of commentators, who draw the attention of audiences to the works of music makers. In this perspective, musical creation must be apprehended with a "systemic approach". Mihalyi Csikszentmihalyi, a psychologist who dedicated part of his research to understanding creativity, explained: "[W]hat we call creativity is a phenomenon that is constructed through an interaction between producers and audience. Creativity is not the product of single individuals, but of social systems making judgments about individuals' products" (quoted in Pope 2005: 313). Cape Town *nederlandsliedjies* provide a good illustration of the position of music in social systems in which competition organisers, judges and music lovers play a decisive role.²⁶

Appropriation and hegemony

Appropriation is present at both ends of any creative process: at its beginning it provides material to be reworked or to get inspiration from; at its end, it puts in circulation new material which others can rework or draw inspiration from. Any music can enter into infinite combinations in various forms: written, oral, computerised or mixed. Appropriation gives a measure of changes occurring in musical languages and may signal the advent of "new discursiveness". It carries symbolic significations that weave relationships between the Self and the Other, and between identity and alterity. Consequently, it contributes to identity configuration. Appropriation has a definite relational dimension: it affirms that the knowledge of Oneself necessitates the presence and the recognition of the Other in Oneself and in one's desire to be (Ricœur 1990). Appropriation creates a dynamics of relations that contains a strong potential for inventing and transforming the world. The realisation of this potential is, however, subordinated to power relationships governing the world. In the epoch of financial capitalism, appropriation can consequently be used as yet another mechanism for exploiting dominated people's resources and, contradictorily, as a means which the same dominated people may use to fight domination symbolically, while it never ceases to build bridges facilitating exchanges. The multiplicity of functions appropriation may have makes it a stake in power struggles, one example being the opposition between a rigid conception of property rights as upheld by advocates of capitalism and free trade versus the open notion of common goods promoting unhindered exchanges between music makers and between music lovers. In this perspective, music appears as another arena where power struggles take place: a field of hegemony, in the Gramscian understanding, in which strategies of domination, acquiescence to domination and opposition to domination are at the same time pitted against one another and entangled (Roseberry 1994; Sayer 1994). This is why the study of musical circulations and appropriations can reveal subtle mechanisms of identity configuration and unsuspected workings of the dialectics of domination and resistance. Cape Town New Year festivals, as a whole, illustrate the complexity of these phenomena. A closer look at two choral repertoires sung by *Klopse* and Malay Choirs will illustrate how adjustments of existing notions of identities take place in a period of rapid mutations, and proceed by fine tunings, seeking to achieve new balances in a mix of identity conceptions and identifications. Fine tunings cannot iron out ambivalences which have developed over more than three centuries; therefore attitudes towards domination and identity configurations are still underpinned by hesitations, contradictions and ambiguities, which music is better able to express than most other artistic languages.

Notes

1. This chapter is largely based on: Martin, Denis-Constant (2013) Attention, une musique peut en cacher une autre, l'appropriation α et ω de la création. *Volume!* 10(2): 47–67.
2. Discussing the implications of creative commons in the field of knowledge, Giovanni Ramello stressed that "composition" relies on the re-arrangement of pre-existing elements: "It is no coincidence that the generic term denoting creative activity is 'composition' (we speak in effect of literary composition, musical composition, etc.) whose Latin etymology specifically invokes the above-described process: 'cum ponere' means literally 'to put together', suggesting that creation is first and foremost a novel arrangement of existing elements" (Ramello 2004: 5).
3. The words *métissage* (French), *mestizage* (Spanish), *mestiçagem* (Portuguese) do not have any exact translation in English. They cover complex processes which develop from the encounter of human beings coming from different backgrounds, who exchange, even under conditions of domination and violence, cultural knowledge and imagine original creations from their exchanges. It used to have a negative connotation, which has been in part overcome in theories of creolisation (Glissant 1997 [1969]: 213–214; Glissant 2007: 89). Hybridisation, rooted in biology, often connoting infertility, is not adequate. A phrase associating blending and mixing may be used in some cases.
4. The circulation and inter-influence of Greek, Etruscan and Roman forms provide other evidence of this process.
5. American composer Charles Ives (1874–1954) is the example *par excellence* of the use of appropriated music in original creations (Burkholder 1994).
6. Johann Sebastian Bach walked 400 kilometres to hear Dietrich Buxtehude in Lübeck; slave and slavers lived together in a system of violent oppression; Jesuits in South America interacted closely with the indigenous people they wanted to Christianise.
7. See Part Three: *Moppies*: Humour and Survival.
8. *L'acte d'exister*.
9. The few names cited do not constitute an exhaustive list of all composers who worked in this direction; they just illustrate a trend in which many other musicians participated.
10. In IsiZulu, *mbaqanga* designates cornmeal porridge, a poor people's staple food. It is used in popular music as a label encompassing all sorts of styles derived from the *marabi* matrix (Martin 2013: 135–137), based on a simple chordal structure: I-IV-V, usually played on a fast tempo. These styles ranged from types of African Jazz to Zulu popular song, as illustrated by musicians such as the Soul Brothers and Simon "Mahlathini" Nkabinde (Erlmann 1996: 83–87).
11. *The Best of S.A. Pop (1960–1990), Vol 2*. Johannesburg: Gallo Records, 1994 (CDREDD 610).
12. "L'objectif de ce type de possession est précisément de rendre propre quelque chose, c'est-à-dire de l'adapter à soi et, ainsi, de transformer cette chose en un support de l'expression de soi. L'appropriation est ainsi à la fois une saisie de l'objet et une dynamique d'action sur le monde matériel et social dans une intention de construction du sujet."
13. "l'écriture en collaboration, exigée par les protecteurs, les troupes ou les entrepreneurs de théâtre; le réemploi d'histoires déjà racontées, de lieux communs partagés, de formules consacrées, ou encore les continuelles révisions ou nombreuses continuations d'œuvres toujours ouvertes".
14. A notion of musical property does exist in some oral cultures; however, it rarely matches conceptions of artistic property as canonised in Western law. Anthony Seeger asked: "In the case of the Suyá Indians of Brazil, how does one register a song composed by a jaguar, learned from a captive over 200 years ago, and controlled not by an individual but by a ceremonial moiety?" (Seeger 1996: 90).

15. For a discussion of the benefits and limits of creative commons, see: Ramello 2004.
16. Guillaume Kosmicki explained: "A techno composer deliberately abandons property rights on his musical productions which, by essence, are bound to be mixed, recomposed and to be used as improvisation material by other musicians in live performances [...] The notion of copyright is fundamentally challenged by the principles on which the practice of this music is based; it implies *de facto* that the creator agrees to be dispossessed" (Kosmicki 2010: 110).
17. "les approches propriétaires ne bénéficient qu'aux puissants qui ont les moyens de faire respecter les restrictions, et que leur usage risquait de donner lieu à des détournements lorsque des acteurs administratifs ou privés s'approprieraient les bénéfices d'accords d'exploitation qu'ils passeraient au nom des communautés".
18. Soit "reconnu un droit des communautés à obtenir des revenus ou d'autres formes de bénéfice lorsque les usagers de ces biens communs les utilisent dans des activités économiques ou comme points de départ pour d'autres innovations [...] Une solution serait de recourir à un fonds garant, initialement alimenté par les États, puis constitué par des prélèvements sur les bénéfices d'usage."
19. A more detailed discussion of ethical problems raised by the circulation of "traditional" music and a presentation of solutions adopted by ethnomusicologists can be found in: Arom & Martin (2015): Chapter 3: Questions d'éthique.
20. At the time of writing (5 November 2015), we learnt that, following a complaint filed by the estate of Sergei Prokoviev, composer Hélène Blazy was condemned by a French court for using the "Dance of the Knights" from the Russian composer's ballet *Romeo and Juliet* (opus 64) in her inaugural music for the Burj Khalifa tower, the highest building of the world, erected in Dubai.
21. "les musiciens créatifs, plutôt que de produire des idées ou des concepts nouveaux, savent faire apparaître des correspondances originales entre des formes déjà existantes. Leur création ressemble souvent à de l'agencement, de la variation ou encore du bricolage."
22. Rob Pope defines creativity as: "extra/ordinary, original and fitting, full-filling, in(ter)ventive, co-operative, un/conscious, fe<>male, re ... creation" (Pope 2005: 52).
23. "instaurateurs de discursivité".
24. Ils "n'ont pas rendu simplement possible un certain nombre d'analogies, ils ont rendu possible (et tout autant) un certain nombre de différences." "Ils ont produit quelque chose de plus: la possibilité et la règle de formation d'autres textes."
25. The English translation of this quotation is taken from an English version of this text translated by Richard Howard; it can be found at *UbuWeb*, where the quoted passage appears on p. 6. Available at http://www.tbook.constantvzw.org/wp-content/death_authorbarthes.pdf [accessed 4 November 2015].
26. See Part Two: *Nederlandsliedjies* and Notions of Blending.

CHAPTER 2

In the footsteps of the future: Musical memory and reconciliation in South Africa[1]

French sociologist, Maurice Halbwachs, was one of the first to emphasise that memory is a social phenomenon, whereby elements from the past are reconstructed in and for the present (Halbwachs 1992). Halbwachs insisted on the necessity of approaching memory through social frameworks (*cadres sociaux*), within which memory is constructed and operates. Halbwachs mentioned that music can play a significant part in this process and suggested that relationships between music and memory ought to be reconsidered. In this perspective, the questions to be asked are: How can music contribute to organising memory? How can memory be kept in music and resurface through music, beyond the oblivion that conceals past events which are not, or have not been, utterable? Philosopher Paul Ricœur followed up on Maurice Halbwachs' founding contentions that we need others in order to remember; that memory is consequently a social phenomenon and that although memory deals with the past, it does not restitute it intact.

A "present of the past"

Collective interactions fashion a "present of the past" (Lavabre 1994; Ricœur 2006). Memory is constructed, transmitted and transformed within social groups; it is affected by their evolution, their position in larger ensembles, their interests and their interactions with other groups. Memory renders the past of social groups in the present; moreover, memory infuses what remains of the past with sentiments. In the process, memory contributes to transforming social groups into affective communities and entrenches collective bearings and behavioural norms. To achieve such a mutation (or transformation), choices are made in order to select from the past that which is considered relevant and useful for the present, and which can make the present meaningful and stimulate action. This is why several memories of the same past may coexist at a given time, and may evolve in different directions and underpin opposed strategies. Memory, therefore, is not history: "Not because history and memory differ like 'true' and 'false' but because history is moved by an aspiration to know, whereas memory is motivated by a political will and a concern for identity [...]" (Lavabre 1995: 1). History and memory are nevertheless intertwined, since history provides and permanently renews material for memory. In order to try and clarify their relationships, Marie-Claire Lavabre distinguishes between a historical memory, in which the past is used and exploited, and a collective memory, based on shared representations of the past. This opposition must, however, be nuanced because in actual fact historical memory and collective memory overlap; yet it is analytically useful because the first will only be accepted and gain legitimacy if it corresponds, at least in part, to the second (Gensburger & Lavabre 2005).

Interactions between historical memory and collective memory lay the foundations for a "pragmatics of memory, by virtue of which remembering is doing something [...]" (Ricœur 2006: 100).[2] What memory does is to explore the world in order to produce a *present of initiative*:

> Remembering, we said, is doing something: It is declaring that one has seen, done, acquired this or that. And this act of memory is inscribed within a network of practical exploration of the world, of the corporeal and mental initiative which makes us acting subjects. It is then in a present much richer than that characterizing sensible intuition that memories come back, in a present of initiative. (Ricœur 2006: 7772–7777)

In this perspective, memory appears as a condition for the subject's agency. Part of its work consists in selecting and re-elaborating from the past, in "inventing traditions" (Hobsbawm & Ranger 2012), in assigning meaning to their resurgence. This is done through interactions within social groups, which can be initiated by social or political "entrepreneurs". Remembering is doing something, what we have summarily described, in order to do something else: to act and encourage action in and on present situations, to propose strategic memories able to gather and stimulate political and identitarian mobilisations, whose aim will be to stir recollections and heal wounds (Chaumont 1997; Gensburger & Lavabre 2005).

Music may be used for identity claims, which are very often based on historical memories (Martin 2013: chap. 1). Identity constructions can rely on memory, because, wrote Paul Ricœur, of its narrative function:

> On the deepest level, that of the symbolic mediation of action, it is through the narrative function that memory is incorporated into the formation of identity. Memory can be ideologized through the resources of the variations offered by the work of narrative configuration [...] The narrative, Hannah Arendt reminds us, recounts the "who of action". It is, more precisely, the selective function of

the narrative that opens to manipulation the opportunity and the means of a clever strategy, consisting from the outset in a strategy of forgetting as much as in a strategy of remembering. (Ricœur 2006: 1312–1316)

Identity configurations use memory to argue that the identity put forward is legitimate because it is rooted in a reformulated past, at the heart of which features a group whose essence has remained unchanged. In such cases, memory stresses alleged ancient differences between the "Us" and the "Others"; it aims at homogenising the "Us" in the present because these differences are supposed to have existed in the past, and not to have radically changed since then. Memory tries to mobilise people by including them in a memorial narrative which should encourage them to identify with the group that is narrated, and which should convince them that the group needs to be supported, consolidated, and made more powerful. This generates rivalry and conflict between groups, which entails a competition of memories.

Music is frequently utilised to buttress identity strategies involving memory: music is endowed with a singular capacity to move, which can easily be instrumentalised. Philosopher, Vladimir Jankélévitch, considered that songs can have a persuasive effect and "subjugate by suggesting" (Jankélévitch 1983: 8). Music can be brought forward to give evidence of the ancient existence of a group, of its persistent differences with other groups. Historian Hebe Mattos provided an illuminating example of this use of music; she showed how, in Brazil, the rediscovery of musical and choreographic practices named *jongo* was used to give new dimensions to the memory of slavery. This contributed to freeing the memory from shame and to transforming it into a founding experience which, in the present, in a new political conjuncture, affirmed a persistent difference on which demands, especially land claims, could be based (Mattos 2003[3]). Memory may be used to emphasise differences, oppositions and conflicts. It may also bear traces of contacts, of exchanges, of links that were tied between individuals and groups in a more or less distant past; memories of sharing and coexistence may then serve to contradict and oppose memories of division and hatred, without necessarily erasing all remembrance of confrontations and violence. Such a contest between memories of sharing and creating together and memories of divisions, contempt and hatred seems to take place in post-apartheid South Africa. What is the place of music in these memorial rivalries?

Musical traces

The most obvious link between music and memory is their relationship to time. Memory re-elaborates the past in order to serve certain objectives in the present.

Music is characterised by a dual temporal dimension. On the one hand, it recycles in the present forms that were invented and established in the past; even avant-garde ruptures operate by differing from pre-existing norms and structures. On the other hand, music substitutes a particular sense of time for the "objective" time as given by scientific calculations. Music is constructed on several temporal parameters: tempo, meter and rhythm. The capacity to manipulate these parameters gives a feeling of power, of mastery over time; musicians seem to be able to accelerate, to slow down and even to suspend the flow of time, and listeners share in that gift. The very idea of *rubato*, of "stolen time",[4] and adventures in non-measured playing provide some of the most striking examples of how a sensation of freedom from chronometric time can be experienced in music (Caïn & Caïn 1982). Moreover, listening to the flow of music involves both apprehension of its content in an immediate time and instantaneous transformation of this present into a past that memory preserves more or less faithfully. Auditory "images" of the past, which are loaded with affects, are drawn within these frameworks (Caïn & Caïn 1982; Ricœur 2006: 108). Psychoanalyst, Guy Rosolato, asserted that music generates enjoyment from reminiscences[5] (Rosolato 1982). Another psychoanalyst, Alain de Mijolla, added that this kind of delectation is underpinned by the two modes in which music is inscribed in the mind. The first one can be likened to a mnesic trace, a condensed souvenir which has been reorganised or discombobulated; the second is the result of chains of associations, which gives listening to certain musical pieces "a little taste of *madeleine*"[6] (De Mijolla 1982: 13). Auditory images and enjoyable reminiscences derived from listening permeate mnesic traces that give meaning to music, and more especially memorial meanings that imbue what has been retained from the past with affectivity. The notion of trace leads back to the reality of rival memories and to the role of music in the confrontation between these memories.

Paul Ricœur distinguishes between three main uses of the word "trace": written traces, sometimes kept in archives, which may seem to belong to history, but can be absorbed by memory — from this point of view, musical works[7] can undeniably be considered as traces —; impressions pervaded with emotions left by a particular event, experienced or not;[8] and a corporeal and cerebral imprint[9] (Ricœur 2006: 257). Material traces, as well as corporeal imprints, can leave affective impressions and both generate the networks of associations which Alain de Mijolla mentioned. Paul Ricœur also underlined the importance of forgetting, which should not be understood as the opposite of memory, for: "There is forgetting wherever there has been a trace" (Ricœur 2006: 4219). This implies that traces may remain outside the immediate consciousness and resurge when emotional circumstances bring them back to the conscious level, or when memory entrepreneurs rediscover them, the one being often related to the other. There exists a "reserve of forgetting"[10] which sometimes holds unexpected resources to memory and history (Ricœur 2006: 4220). Envisioned in the light of these philosophical propositions, it appears that music can leave material, emotional and corporeal traces; traces which remain audible and make sense at certain times, but can be buried as archaeological vestiges under the dirt of amnesia or denial and reappear when circumstances or social actors summon them. Music participates in the three mnemonic modes Paul Ricœur identifies with regard to Edward Casey (1987): *reminding*, that is memory-aids, points of reference, reminders, clues that guard against forgetting; *reminiscing*, which makes "the past live again by evoking it together with others, each helping the others to remember shared events or knowledge [...]" (Ricœur 2006: 622); and *recognising*, through which "we are referred back by the phenomenon of recognition[11] to the phenomenon of memory as present of the absent encountered previously. And the 'thing' recognized is doubly other: as absent (other than presence) and as earlier (other than the present)" (Ricœur 2006: 630).

The *"gift"* of creation

Paul Ricœur nicely wrote that recognition is a "minor miracle of happy memory" (Ricœur 2006: 6151). Elaborating on this formula, at the risk of simplifying its meaning, it may be proposed that the re-union of memories — because it has the power to re-launch dynamics of sharing — is likely to make the truth of "forgotten" traces re-appear. It cannot, on its own, bring about "reconciliation", but it may participate in a global effort to fight present injustices, imbalances and prejudices inherited from the past. A history of exchanges — which took place in spite of violence, exploitation and contempt — and creation from these exchanges, that is, a history of creolisation, drawn from the "reserve of forgetting", will constitute an alternative to a persistent conception of South Africa as a juxtaposition of different entities of the type which was articulated by former president Thabo Mbeki in his famous "I am an African" speech (Mbeki 1998: 31-36). Beyond the rhetoric of reconciliation, true *recognition* — in the dual sense of knowing the Other again and being born again with the Other — will only derive from *recognising* — discovering again and acknowledging the existence of — ancient dynamics of creolisation which continue to stir South African society.

Music, in South Africa, constitutes one of the richest "reserves" in which perceptible traces of these dynamics have been preserved (Martin 2013). Black musics have been inadvertently presented with the "gift" of creation from inter-"racial" exchanges. Applying to South Africa lessons from Ronald Radano's analysis of the history of music in the United States (Radano 2003) enables an understanding of how the refusal of political and cultural white leaders[12] to recognise the potential of blending and mixing led them on the one hand to sterilise South African "official" culture and on the other to discredit manifestations of creole creation — including *boeremusiek*, replete with traces of cross-"racial" exchanges (Van der Merwe 2015). The denial of white South

Africans' involvement (even passive and unwilling) in creolisation and their stubbornness in sticking to the belief that "legitimate" culture could only originate in Europe left black South Africans in charge of imagining original forms and expressive modes, based on every musical conception present in the country, without consideration of "race" or origin. Some currents of popular music — mostly black, but including *boeremusiek* and several genres of "white" pop music[13] — are available for *reminding*: for re-calling social interactions, in which musical processes were intimately involved. In this respect, jazz provided a platform for intensive cooperation and a launching pad for indigenous innovation. The same musics can be employed with regard to *reminiscing*: because they grew out of protracted blending, they can re-awaken within groups, which are supposed to be different, memories of partaking and creating in common. Finally, they may initiate *recognising* by bringing forth memories of a past of cross-fertilisation and mutual enrichment. The role music could play should not, however, be idealised and lead to forgetting of a new type. *Recognising* aims to bring about consciousness of realities forgotten and denied; it requires a deliberate pragmatics of memory to make everyone acknowledge and accept these realities. Recognising cannot erase other memories that persist, for instance, in musical categories derived from the division of South Africa into ethnic and "racial groups" imposed during the greatest part of the 20th century, for example white music, Zulu music, Tswana music, Sotho music, coloured music, etc. Trust in memory's re-union[14] (Ricœur 2006: 6388) should lead to an assumption that the confrontation of the two memories of which music bears traces — a memory of division and violence; a memory of interactions and creation in common — will end in the latter prevailing over the former. It does not mean that memories of division and violence will disappear: they should remain acute, as testimonies of a bygone but unforgettable era, a necessary condition for edifying the future that was imagined during the struggle and initiated in 1994, following the country's first democratic elections.

The *"treasure chest"* of creolisation

From the outset of colonisation onwards, the history of what was to become South Africa has been particularly tragic and complex. It is a history of conquest, subjugation, extermination, slavery, racial discrimination and apartheid; it has been marked by various enterprises aimed at dividing and separating people on the basis of "racial" hierarchies and notions of purity (*suiwerheid*), entailing prejudices against and contempt for "non-whites" (*nie-blankes*). The 20th century witnessed a systematisation of segregation which reached an apex with apartheid; it was accompanied by an increasingly brutal repression of all attempts at escaping or fighting this oppression "of a special type". Yet, in spite of separations and violence, contacts, exchanges and creations from exchanges never stopped. Separations were "futile" and intertwining was "fertile" (Martin 2013), from the first encounters between Khoikhoi and European travellers to the liberation struggle, in which activists of every origin joined forces. Racist authorities attempted to introduce divisions in music by promoting hierarchies, placing at the top forms inherited from European "high" culture and supporting organisations dedicated to such forms. The same ideas guided the reorganisation of the South African Broadcasting Corporation (SABC), following which Radio Bantu was created in 1962, incorporating services in several African languages: Radio Zulu, Radio Sesotho, Radio Lebowa, Radio Xhosa, etc. The juxtaposition of services for white listeners in English and Afrikaans and Radio Bantu rippled into the recording industry and most records were released under labels corresponding more or less precisely to the SABC categories. In addition to this self-imposed policy, recording companies also had to obey censorship not only of music and lyrics, but also of record covers (Drewett 2008; Hamm 1991). These measures and their severe implementation made inter-"racial" collaboration more difficult, but could never totally prevent it. The measures pushed a number of musicians into exile and hindered physical meetings, but never stopped the circulation of musical ideas within South Africa and between the outside world and South Africa. The result was the recurrent emergence of genres and styles which, although they may have been inscribed within the circumscriptions of official "population groups", showed evidence that they were born out of creative dynamics of blending: from the first appropriation of European songs by Khoikhoi musicians to 1980s modern jazz; via Christian hymns composed by black Africans at the end of the 19th century; and through *marabi*, African jazz, *mbaqanga*, *boeremusiek*, *Klopse* and Malay Choirs' repertoires, rock, rap, and works by "contemporary" composers, to mention just a few. All these genres and styles taken together illustrate the power of creolisation, its capacity to fuse elements of diverse origins to eventually produce unpredictable creations (Glissant 1997: 16). They also constituted a kind of treasure chest in which testimonies of cross-"racial" creations were preserved, able to instigate a re-union of memories beyond forgetting. I have analysed elsewhere in detail processes whereby musical creation took place within each of the groups delineated by racist powers, while it was always spurred by influences and appropriations from outside their artificial borders (Martin 2013). Since 1994, re-unions, appropriations and blending made possible by private initiatives or public support have been extremely intense; aesthetic research regained the freedom to look everywhere for inspiration and material to be borrowed, then transformed. The question that remains open is whether the innumerable productions that have blossomed in South Africa's musical landscape since the 1980s (for the movement started before 1994) erected pillars on which could be built a bridge leading from *reminding* and *reminiscing* to *recognising*.

In other words, can music play an active role in the transmutation of a formal reconciliation – registered in law and imprinted in people's minds by the Truth and Reconciliation Commission (Darbon 1996; Krog 1998) – into the "freedom in harmony" sung by the Stellenbosch Libertas Choir?[15] One phenomenon is obvious: many traces of a past of exchanges, cross-fertilisation and creation, surface in the present South African cultural ferment, traces that run contrary to attempts at prolonging past divisions that can be seen in the fields of politics, culture and cultural policies. However, musical and cultural memories cannot be isolated from the social environment in which they may be mobilised. They have to be linked to what Paul Ricœur defined in ethical terms as "the aim of the 'good life' with and for others in just institutions" (Ricœur 1990: 240). This objective needs to be politically translated to inspire social and economic policies aiming at redressing inequalities which are no longer inherited from the past, but also result from transformations South Africa has undergone since 1994. "The 'good life' with and for others" cannot happen when rural poverty, urban slums, massive unemployment, unequal education, and differential access to basic social services, including health, persist. However, reorientations of public policies will not be enough; they should be complemented by in-depth efforts to change representations of South African society and representations that members of the various groups, which were previously circumscribed, entertain about members of other groups.

The contradictions of the transition

These representations remain full of contradictions and ambiguities. The latest *Reconciliation Barometer*, published by the Institute for Justice and Reconciliation available at the time of writing, presented and discussed the results of surveys conducted between 2003 and 2013 (Wale 2014). It described in detail the contradictions and ambivalences which are today rampant in South African society.

The *"shadow side"* of reconciliation

The *Reconciliation Barometer* showed, for instance, an intriguing discrepancy between a decrease in identification with South Africa as a whole and a marked decrease in "interracial mistrust". Language remained the main domain of identification for South Africans for 23.2% of the respondents in the 2013 survey; race increased from 11.8 % in 2003 to 13.4% in 2013; and ethnicity dropped from 15.1% in 2003 to 11.1% in 2013. During the same period, identification with South Africa dropped from 11.2% to 7.1% and the desire for a united South Africa decreased from 72.9% in 2003 to 55% in 2013 (Wale 2014: 15). However, what may look like an identity fallback is accompanied by a significant diminution of the number of South Africans who find that people belonging to "other groups" are not trustworthy: they constituted 40.6 % of the respondents in 2003 and 28.1% in 2013 (Wale 2014: 16). This downward trend may be linked to an intensification of social interactions. The number of South Africans who responded that they often or always talk to a person of another race rose from 25.5% in 2003 to 33.1% in 2013 and the number who said they often or always socialised with people from another race rose from 10.4% in 2003 to 23.5% in 2013 (Wale 2014: 21).

However, although South Africans have more opportunities to meet and interact with compatriots belonging to another of the historically demarcated groups, this does not mean that they really wish such interactions were more frequent: "both the desire for interracial talk and learning about the customs of others have decreased over time. In terms of the former, there has been a 12.9% decrease from 32.3% in 2003 to 19.4% in 2013. Similarly, the desire for learning about other races customs has decreased by 14.1% from 53% in 2003 to 38.9% in 2013" (Wale 2014: 24). These figures must also be appreciated against the background of the social distribution of the answers: the poor remain largely excluded from social integration. In 2013: "While the middle and upper LSM [Living Standards Measure] groups[16] are becoming more integrated, the poorer LSM groups remain almost exclusively black. The overwhelming majority of the poor continue to be black" (Wale 2014: 22). Commenting on the above-mentioned results (and others which are less relevant to our research) Kim Wale, the project leader for the *Reconciliation Barometer*, concluded: "An interesting contradiction emerges in the results. On the one hand, race relations are improving in terms of trust and interracial contact and socialisation. On the other hand, in terms of primary identity association, racial identity is becoming stronger as the desire for a unified South African identity decreases and agreement on the meaning of apartheid diverges across race" (Wale 2014: 35). The last sentence hints at the relationship between current attitudes and representations and memory; it shows that the reconciliation dreamed of in the 1990s is still far from being realised, an observation that shed some light on its "shadow side":

> Bringing reconciliation down from its transcendent heights into the realms of everyday lived realities faced by South Africans also requires us to face the contradictions of the transition and their impact on the present. These contradictions may be imagined as reconciliation's shadow side. This shadow of reconciliation is seen, for example, in the inequality and poverty we continue to witness in South African society, or in the misunderstanding, fear and anxiety generated around racial issues. (Wale 2014: 9–10)

When memory is specifically taken into account: "SARB results demonstrate the significance of engaging in a broader conversation about the meaning and relevance of South Africa's history" (Wale 2014: 36). This implies that, in order to defuse fears and anxieties, and in addition to vital policies of social redress: "It is important to find a balance between what is diverse and what is common so as to allow space for conflict within unity" (Wale 2014: 36).

Music is clearly not the only instrument that could help reach such a balance. Once again, the power of music will be extremely limited if it does not come as a complement to policies fighting inequalities, especially in terms of access to employment, education, health and basic services. But music can certainly participate in the conversation about the history of South Africa. A history of the creolisation of music in South Africa can demonstrate how, out of a large diversity that racist authorities attempted to ossify, developed not only styles and genres invented thanks to inter-"racial" and inter-ethnic influences and interaction, but original creations which testified to the uniqueness of South Africa. Every genre of South African music — whatever the label that was put on it — is, to put it briefly, mixed (*métissé*) and bears traces of influences and appropriations from other genres. Yet, every genre is also characterised by innovations that resulted from dynamics internal to the group where it flourished. Consequently, every genre of South African music displays *at the same time* specificities linked to its social environment and commonalities with other South African genres; the totality of these diverse musics constitutes South African music.

The *"bright side"* of joint creation

In past years there have been many instances of musical encounters which may contribute to alleviating current fears and anxieties about members of "other" groups' "customs". Jazz, as always, has been in the forefront of broad collaborations. After the demise of Moses Taiwa Molelekwa and Zim Ngqawana, other musicians, such as Shane Cooper, Carlo Mombelli, Kesivan Naidoo, Selaelo Selota, Kyle Shepherd, Dan Shout, Marcus Wyatt and Sisonke Xonti, to name but a few, kept the colour-blind creative traditions of South African jazz alive. Following up on new mixes inaugurated by Mango Groove, Freshly Ground proposed attractive pop fusions. MCs (i.e. rappers) of various backgrounds are associated in rap. Kwaito[17] fans can be increasingly counted among coloured and white South Africans; recently a white writer and singer, camouflaged behind the sobriquet Craigieji Makhosi, launched "Quite a White Ou" (Quite a White Guy), a humoristic kwaito song aiming at making "people aware of the enormous gap between the European and African cultures within South Africa".[18] The South African College of Music's Opera School at the University of Cape Town trained in a few years talented young singers who perform in South Africa and abroad; symphony orchestras and chamber music ensembles, such as the Odeion Quartet,[19] based at the University of the Free State, now comprise noticeable numbers of black African, coloured and Indian instrumentalists.

A *moppie*[20] presented during the 2008 *Klopse* Carnival told a fable which showed that representations of others were beginning to change. In November 2007, *Kaapse Klopse* are busy practicing the various items they will enter in the 2008 carnival competitions. In Netreg Road, not very far from the railway line which edges the township of Bonteheuwel,[21] the Netreg Superstars are rehearsing a *moppie*. Gathered in a shelter erected in front of a small house, isolated from the street by pieces of plywood and plastic sheets, covered with a tarpaulin, 20 to 30 singers (mostly men, some quite young) read on a carton board hanging from the wall the words they have to memorise. They are supported by a backtrack, on which the accompaniment of the song has been recorded. The coach organises the voices according to their range, indicates nuances that must be respected, and emphasises where the song must gain momentum. The singers have no musical training whatsoever; they do not read music, but they have good voices and display an acute musicality. They are lucky to work with an outstanding coach, Terry Hector. He used to play and sing in Taliep Petersen and David Kramer's musicals, and featured in particular in *District Six, The Musical*.[22] He is not only a remarkable comedian and singer, but also a clever composer of *moppies*. For the 2008 *Klopse* carnival, he prepared an original song titled "*Vusie van Guguletu*".[23] The hero of the story is a black African named Vusie, who came from Soweto to live in Gugulethu, a black African township, about three kilometres from Netreg. One day, he passes by the *Klopskamer* of a carnival troupe and hears them rehearsing a *moppie*. He is quite fascinated, comes in and asks if he can join them. The singers are a bit surprised, but accept and when Vusie starts singing, they discover that he has a fine operatic voice. He sings "like Pavarotti", and they find him *duidelik*, which usually means clear, understandable, crystalline, but can be understood here as very nice and refined. Vusie is integrated into the choir; he learns how to sing *moppies*, but in the process also influences his fellow singers to the extent that, eventually, their style changes: They sound "opera" and have, together with Vusie, invented an "opera *moppie*".

"*Vusie van Guguletu*" is obviously a parable, but as such it reveals ongoing mutations in representations which the different "population groups" categorised by apartheid entertain about each other. It suggests that music can help overcome prejudices and divisions, can contribute to leaving behind forgetting — forgetting of commonalities, of shared histories — and become an instrument of *reminiscing* that may lead to *recognising*. For a long time, in order to prevent a union of all victims of racism and apartheid against successive governments, the strategy of divide and rule implemented by the authorities instilled in the minds of coloureds a fear of black Africans, of "*kaffirs*".[24] Coloureds were made to believe that, although inferior to whites, they were superior to black Africans. Zimitri Erasmus recalled for instance: "For me, growing up coloured meant knowing that I was *not only* not white, but *less than white*; *not only* not black, but *better than black* (as we referred to African people)" (Erasmus 2001: 13; italics in the original). Similarly, black Africans were taught to despise coloureds, who were presented as people without history and culture, and as drunkards lacking education, sometimes called *amalawu*.[25] Bradley van Sitters, an activist fighting "mental enslavement" who claims to be "a proud Khoikhoi (man par excellence)" explained: "Growing up on the Cape Flats of South Africa, I was mistakenly stereotyped a 'amalawu', a Xhosa term roughly depicting people with no culture and no language of their own, the bastard children of Jan van Riebeeck [...]".[26]

"*Vusie van Gugulethu*" is just a fable which can be considered as a portent of changes to come, but cannot be treated as evidence that a complete transformation of representations has already taken place. Other examples nevertheless confirm that music is a terrain on which encounters may open a way to *recognising*. In Cape Town, choirs led by Phumelele Tsewu (Fezeka High School Choir, then iGugu Le Kapa [Pride[27] of Cape Town]) illustrate how various musical repertoires can be made to converge. They do not only sing arrangements of rural orally transmitted songs from Transkei and works by black South African composers, they also interpret *moppies* and Afrikaans songs. Singers, most of whom were born in underprivileged neighbourhoods, are filled with pride when they are acclaimed in concert halls after performing, in their own way, the diversity of South African choir music. Recently, they have collaborated with another choral group presenting *Klopse* and Malay Choirs' repertoires, the Cape Traditional Singers led by Anwar Gambeno. iGugu Le Kapa and the Cape Traditional Singers appeared in concerts where they first sung on their own, then joined voices to perform pieces drawn from their respective repertoires. The finale in which the two choirs intermingled appeared undoubtedly as a moment of great rejoicing, a time of *recognising*. However, it must be noted that these concerts did not take place in South Africa, but in France and the Netherlands.[28]

What does take place in Cape Town is the development of the Rosa Choir[29]. The choir was initiated by members of the Cape Cultural Collective, a group of poets, musicians and artists (most of them former anti-apartheid activists) dedicated to developing artistic creativity across the borders of the former "population groups".[30] They discovered that a translation of the emblematic *nederlandsliedjie* "Rosa"[31] existed in isiXhosa (Desai 2004) and realised that songs loved by black Africans, coloureds and whites could be translated and jointly sung by a group representative of the Western Cape's demographics. The collective decided to form a choir able to transcend "historical divides" and soon got support from the Institute for Justice and Reconciliation. They intended to combine "different cultural traditions in a project that is entertaining, transformative, inspirational and educational". They also emphasised that: "The project is about much more than just singing. It is about friendship, respect, tolerance, understanding and affirming the value of each person."[32]

Journalist Warren Fortune wrote that, according to Mansoor Jaffer, one of the co-founders of the Cape Cultural Collective, "the choir was creating a form of cultural integration that had the potential to destroy persistent apartheid ideologies". Mansoor Jaffer explained: "We want to break down the barriers of the past, the mental and physical restrictions that apartheid exposed to us."[33] The choir is diverse in terms of the origins and musical backgrounds of its members, who sing in the three most spoken languages of the Western Cape: Afrikaans, isiXhosa and English. The Rosa Choir regularly performs and a Junior Rosa Choir has recently been formed.

Towards a "radical reconciliation"

The Rosa Choir Project illustrates the observation made by anthropologist, Catherine Besteman:

> In Cape Town, it seems that nothing has changed and everything has changed [...] Since the end of apartheid, the terms on which people are mixing and the urban arena where people come together have changed in fundamental ways. The cultural and personal spaces of intimacy that people in Cape Town create when forging new groups and relationships are, in fact, really new [...] contemporary Cape Town allows for race to be deconstructed, reconstructed, and imagined in novel ways. Experimental identities allow creative Capetonians to redefine themselves and to transcend race. (Besteman 2008: 13–14)

Phumelele Tsewu, Anwar Gambeno, members of the Rosa Choir Project and the Cape Cultural Collective indisputably belong to the group of "transformers" Catherine Besteman identified in Cape Town: people who have chosen "to embark on transformative agendas that demand lifestyle changes, ideological investment, and the creation of new social worlds" (Besteman 2008: 192). They have chosen to work with music because music helps to bridge the gap between *reminiscing* and *recognising*. Since it is conceived in the examples presented above as a collective activity, music provides occasions for re-unions of memories, in which souvenirs of experiences, which were common, but lived differently, are confronted and blended. Participating in a choir implies rubbing shoulders with other people, mixing one's voice with other voices, and also spending time with them: to chat and exchange fragments of one's life with fellow members, who may not live far away, but in different styles and conditions. The common aim and the corporeal reality of standing close to each other in a choir contribute to transcending differences. In these conditions, the Other is truly *recognised*; all the implications of being *Oneself as Another* (Ricœur 1990) — the realisation that the Other is part of Oneself and that the Other includes part of Oneself; the acceptation that there is no Self without Others, whoever they are — are eventually acknowledged. Remembering in music and through music is indeed "doing something" (Ricœur 2006: 100); it launches a "present of initiative" which materialised in the joint performances of the Cape Traditional Singers and iGugu Le Kapa, the Cape Cultural Collective and the Rosa Choir Project.

* * *

These initiatives are still limited; they involve only small numbers of people. But they — along with jazz — show how music can help overcome divisions and preconceptions; how it can project hopes of a future underpinned by "the aim of the 'good life' with and for others", based not on oblivion, but on keeping alive the memory of past antagonisms in order to be sure not to reproduce them. Yet, as mentioned earlier, music can only contribute to such a process. A history of South African music as creole music, as a field for exchanges and common creation must be divulged, demonstrated and taught. It must be integrated in the concept of heritage[34] because, as emphasised by Nick Shepherd, heritage is "a site of active cultural construction" (Shepherd 2008: 125), a "sphere of practice in public life which presents a rich set of opportunities for confirming and contesting settled identities, and versions of the self and the nation" (Shepherd 2008: 126). Finally, music should be made part of a resolute programme of "radical reconciliation" such as proposed by Kim Wale:

> The concept of radical reconciliation [...] focuses on the relationship between economic inclusion and reconciliation. First, for radical reconciliation to proceed, issues of economic justice need to be central to the process of reconciliation. Second, the concept requires us to think more carefully about the relationship between different vectors of exclusion, such as class and race, in South African society. Third, radical reconciliation critiques the divisive nature of political party discourse which is counterproductive to the aims of building citizen's confidence and trust in governance institutions. Finally, radical reconciliation recognises that in order to address questions of economic injustice, we also need to build intersubjective awareness and social relationships across intersecting race and class boundaries. (Wale 2013: 7)

No doubt, making music together and singing together offer the possibility of building "intersubjective awareness and social relationships". This is demonstrated by the experience of the *Kaapse Klopse* and the Malay Choirs; their activities and their repertoires reformulate memories that play a crucial role in reconstructing the meanings of coloured identity and reassessing the relationship of the sense of belonging they imply with South African society as a whole.

Notes

1. This chapter is based in part on: Martin, Denis-Constant (2009) Traces d'avenir. Mémoires musicales et réconciliation en Afrique du Sud. *Cahiers d'ethnomusicologie* 22: 141–168.
2. References to Paul Ricœur's *Memory, History, Forgetting* are given according to Kindle's "location" numbering; all quotations from this book are taken from Kathleen Blamey & David Pellauer's translation (Ricœur 2006).
3. See: Hebe Mattos & Martha Abreu (dirs) (2005) *Memórias do Vativeiro*. Gragoatá (Brazil): Laboratório de História Oral e Imagem/Universidade Federal Fluminense. [Documentary film in Portuguese, also available with English or Spanish subtitles]; Hebe Mattos & Martha Abreu (dirs) (2007) *Jongos, Calengos, e Folias: Música Negra, Memória e Poesia*. Gragoatá (Brazil): Laboratório de História Oral e Imagem/Universidade Federal Fluminense. [Documentary film in Portuguese, but also available with English subtitles].
4. There have been many definitions and uses of the term *rubato*. According to *The Oxford Companion to Music* (1984) Oxford: Oxford University Press. p. 894: "*Tempo rubato* has been attached (and still is by some) to elasticity in tempo and rhythm in general, i.e. to the sum of all possible kinds of deviation from a strict clock-work regularity of beat from the beginning to end of a performance."
5. Guy Rosolato uses the French verb *jouir* which combines sexual and non-sexual pleasure; it can also be heard as *je-ouir* (I-hear) and is phonetically close to *jouer* (to play); these associations are encapsulated in the enjoyment (*jouissance*) that can be derived from music.
6. Alain de Mijolla refers here to Marcel Proust's "*petite madeleine*", the small cake that awakens souvenirs and sends one back to the time of childhood.
7. Of whatever type: written in staff or other notation (tonic sol-fa, for instance), orally transmitted, or preserved by various recording media, including computer memories.
8. Here, the notion of "traumatic event" introduced by historian, Michel Vovelle, seems particularly relevant (Vovelle 1992: 332-333).
9. Which can probably be linked to Roger Bastide's notion of motor memory (Bastide 1972).
10. Kathleen Blamey & David Pellauer translate *oubli de réserve* by "reserve of forgetting"; it could also be rendered by "forgetting in reserve" or "forgetting in waiting".
11. "Recognition" is an equivalent of the French *reconnaissance*. However, in Paul Ricœur's perspective, it may be useful to mention that, if *re-connaissance* is obviously built on *connaissance* (knowledge) and literally means "knowing again", it can also be heard as *re-con-naissance*: to be born again with (others).
12. Although not all white cultural actors, including, inter alia, David De Lange, Chris McGregor and Alex Van Heerden.
13. One can think of the 1989 *Voëlvry* tour, of rock groups such as Bright Blue, and of the lesser-known punk movement that was particularly abrasive; see: *Punk in Africa, Three Chords, Three Countries, One Revolution…*, a documentary film directed by Deon Mas and Keith Jones (2013), and produced by Jeffrey Brown. Auckland Park: Meerkat Media and Peligroso Productions (MVD 6189 D).
14. Kathleen Blamey & David Pellauer translate *retrouvailles de la mémoire* by "memory's finds", which literally means *trouvailles de la mémoire* and get over the prefix *re-*, again; "re-union" or "getting back together" would probably be more accurate translations of *retrouvailles*.
15. Stellenbosch Libertas Choir (2006) *Freedom in Harmony* (CD). See: http://libertas.co.za/ [accessed 18 November 2015].
16. "The LSM is a composite measure of the standards of living of the household that the respondent belongs to. It includes a range of items such as dwelling type,

telecommunications, domestic workers employed at household, water items, and sanitation services on site, ownership of consumer items and residence in rural or metropolitan area. The responses to these items are combined to create a single score for respondents, with category 1 representing the lowest LSM scores and category 10 representing the highest LSM scores" (Wale 2014: 21–22).

17. Kwaito became extremely popular among black African urban youth in the 1990s. It incorporated elements from house, garage and South African "bubblegum" pop music in an eclectic and electronic mix, based on a heavy beat. It is sometimes seen as the post-apartheid black popular music *par excellence* and now has many coloured and white fans.
18. Available at http://mayhemandmuse.com/quite-a-white-ou-white-guy-sings-kwaito/ [accessed 20 November 2015].
19. Available at http://humanities.ufs.ac.za/content.aspx?DCode=588; https://www.youtube.com/watch?v=QGPu6QHU814 [accessed 20 November 2015].
20. See Part Three: *Moppies*: Humour and Survival.
21. A very poor neighbourhood inhabited by coloured people, located east of the Cape Town centre.
22. *District Six*, © Stage Productions 2007 (DVD BLIK 16/DV).
23. The lyrics are reproduced below in Part Three: Appendix: *Moppie* lyrics.
24. From the Arabic Kāfir (كافر), infidel, unbeliever; used by whites in South Africa in a strongly derogatory way, first to designate Xhosa-speaking people, then all black Africans. It is nowadays an extremely offensive insult and people who utter it can be charged for *crimen iniuria* (see: http://constitutionallyspeaking.co.za/2012/07/16/ [accessed 20 November 2015]).
25. *AmaLawu* (singular *iLawu*) is an isiXhosa word originally used to designate Bushmen; it was then used to refer to coloureds in a derogatory way, which connoted lack of manners and education.
26. Van Sitters, Bradley (2012, 25 February). Coloured is not an identity: Learning to speak my ancestor's tongue again. Posted on the Archival Platform. Available at http://www.archivalplatform.org/blog/entry/coloured_is/blog [accessed 20 November 2015].
27. *iGugu* means pride in isiXhosa, but it is also a reminder that Phumelele Tsewu taught at the Fezeka High School in Gugulethu and that most members of iGugu Le Kapa started singing in the Fezeka High School Choir he created.
28. See: http://www.festival-automne.com/en/edition-2013/cape-traditional-singers-fezeka-youth-choir-traditions-vocales-cap; http://www.hollandfestival.nl/nl/programma/2015/cape-traditional-singers-igugu-le-kapa/; https://www.youtube.com/watch?v=aasdmE8AvKQ [accessed 20 November 2015].
29. I wish to thank Christopher Ferndale, a founding member of the Cape Cultural Collective, for introducing me to the Rosa Choir.
30. See: http://groundup.org.za/article/creating-cape-cultural-collective_949 [accessed 23 November 2015].
31. See: Chapter Three: The *nederlandsliedjies*' "uniqueness".
32. Rosa Choir Project, presentation brochure. See: https://www.youtube.com/watch?v=2dgJd9qA9cg; https://www.facebook.com/rosachoirproject/; https://vimeo.com/58749007 [accessed 23 November 2015].
33. Fortune, Warren (2014, 5 May) Cape choir united in song. *IOL*. Available at http://www.iol.co.za/news/south-africa/western-cape/cape-choir-united-in-song-1.1683705#.VlLh3b_3QXg [accessed 23 November 2015].
34. See: National Heritage Resources Act 1999 (Act No. 25 of 1999). Available at http://www.wipo.int/wipolex/en/details.jsp?id=5766 [accessed 7 December 2015].

Part Two

Nederlandsliedjies *and Notions of Blending*

Mustapha Adams, Nederlands *soloist with the Cape Traditional Singers, 2013*

CHAPTER 3

The nederlandsliedjies' *"uniqueness"*

Every Malay Choir competition generates among the audience a tremendous enthusiasm. However, the emotional attachment to *nederlandsliedjies*[1] is particularly strong. This repertoire is considered the most important because it embodies "tradition". It is the most sophisticated body of songs interpreted by Malay Choirs and allows singers to display both their technical mastery and their artistry. *Nederlands* are the exclusive preserve of Malay Choirs; winning a prize in this category is a source of delight for singers and listeners who support them. When we started investigating Malay Choirs, singers and coaches frequently told us that, if we wanted to understand what the choirs were about, we had to start with the *nederlands* because they have been transmitted from generation to generation by the "forebears". When members of the choirs discuss them, they show an undeniable pride and, at the same time, cannot conceal a sense of nostalgia. They usually associate these songs with a type of life that existed before the forced removals and was marked by festivities and social functions, especially weddings.

As a matter of fact, *nederlandsliedjies* are testimonies of the past, shrouded in the mist of time. Their origins probably lie in early interactions that took place between slaves and masters in the 17th and 18th centuries. Dutch songs — thence the name *nederlandsliedjies*: literally little Dutch songs — were appropriated by the slaves and transformed; they provided the basis for original creations that have been performed, not without changes but without interruption, until today. *Nederlandsliedjies* became favourites, sung during Muslim weddings (*bruids liedere*: bride's songs). Members of families and guests spontaneously burst into songs which had not been arranged or rehearsed beforehand, and did not necessarily feature a soloist. The original stock of songs dating back to the time of slavery seems to have been renewed several times at the end of the 19th century and at the beginning of the 20th century, by a Dutch sailor named Frans de Jongh, who brought new songs from Holland and gave them to a Cape Town singer, Rasdien Cornelius, who memorised them and contributed to their diffusion (Green 1951: 196; Nel 2012: 8, 25, 48; Van der Wal 2009: 62–63); then at the end of the 20th century by Dutch musicologist Willem van Warmelo (Van der Wal 2009: 59-63), who was involved with the Cape Malay Choir Board (CMCB). Whatever the date and the circumstances of their introduction in South

Africa, the music of these songs was orally transmitted and consequently underwent important transformations. At some point, which is difficult to ascertain, coaches and singers started to write down their lyrics, but here again previous oral transmission and a limited mastery of Dutch or High Dutch caused alterations or distortions in the words, to the extent that the lyrics of some songs became incomprehensible to singers and listeners alike.

Lyrics, language and music

Members of the Malay Choirs are quite loquacious about the origins of *nederlandsliedjies*. They see their roots in songs brought by Dutch settlers during the 17th century, which the slaves learned. The language in which the lyrics were written — which they call "proper Dutch" — is considered evidence of this borrowing. But, in most cases, when singers or coaches were requested to translate the words, they found it very difficult and could only provide the general meaning of the songs. However, they tended to consider the opacity of the words as further proof of the role that people, later labelled "coloured", played in the edification of South Africa, and as a denial of the stereotype forged by racist thinkers that they are a people without history. Today the transmission and learning of *nederlandsliedjies* relies on a mix of written and oral means. Coaches keep the words in notebooks they have received from their forebears or in personal files. The major Malay Choir boards often print selected lyrics in programmes or special booklets. During practices, the words of the song being rehearsed are written on carton board hanging from the walls of the *klopskamer* and memorised by the singers. In 1935 ID du Plessis published a doctoral thesis dedicated to the songs of "the Cape Malays"; it included the texts of several songs (Du Plessis 1935), which he might have somewhat tampered with. In 1942, MA Gassiep published a collection of *nederlandsliedjies* titled *Nederlandse volksliedjies soos deur Maleiers gesing* (Dutch songs sung by the Malays) (Gassiep 1942). The foreword to this book underlined, as noted by Professor Frank Hendricks, "That the Dutch is not pure Dutch as they sang it in these years, the oral tradition transformed the songs."[2] Furthermore, added Professor Vium van Zyl, those singing the *nederlandsliedjies* sometimes "do not know what they are singing and the Dutch is seldom correct Dutch [...] Sometimes they've got words that do not exist even in Dutch or in Afrikaans."[3] Academics, even though they are experts in Dutch and Afrikaans, find it difficult to decipher the lyrics of *nederlandsliedjies*. Coaches and singers are puzzled when they have to translate *nederlands* lyrics; this confirms that their texts have been altered to a point when they no longer correspond either to the norms of the Dutch language, or to those of standard Afrikaans and Cape Flats Afrikaans. This is why it has been difficult to give a "correct" translation of the *nederlands* mentioned in the present book. A telling example of the variations that can be found in different versions of the same song is *"U gydagte"*, which was sung by the Starlites Malay Choir[4] in the 2008 competition. Its lyrics can be found printed in AM Gassiep's collection, and also in a booklet published by the Cape Malay Board in 2011,[5] when it was again sung in competition by the Continentals:

Starlites' text[6] **(regular type = soloist's part** **underlined words = choir's part)**	U gydagte, <u>stel maar einde</u> Sy't gydink tog, <u>aan aan u minde</u> Maar sy't gydink tog, <u>aan die afen stoned</u> Op diederin tyd toen, <u>hy haar gaan verbonde</u> Gynoeg lat hy haar, <u>gaan vergeefen</u> En voor, <u>u allien maar allien</u> (x3)
AM Gassiep's text	U gydagte steld maar in Sy't gedink aan haar elend Sy't gedink aan dit awend stond Op die de tyd toe sy haar gaan verbonde Gynoeg laat sy haar toen begiefen En voor U alleen maar alleen
CMCB's text **(regular type = soloist's part** **underlined words = choir's part)**	U gydagte <u>steld maar einde</u> Sy't gedink tot aan <u>haar u minde</u> Want sy't gedink <u>tot aan u awend stonde</u> Op diederen tyd toen <u>hy aan haar verbonde</u> Genoeg laat hy haar <u>gaan vergiefen</u> En voor u <u>alleen maar alleen</u>

"Rosa" is today the most well-known, the most popular of the *nederlandsliedjies*. This love song is considered the "cherry on the cake" of the repertoire, and is systematically sung by the leaders of the choirs participating in one or other rounds of Malay Choirs competitions. At the end of the day, when the jury is deliberating, they gather on stage, burst into the song and succeed one another in taking the lead. Some think "Rosa" was the first *nederlands* song to have been composed. According to Mariam Leeman, a school teacher who is also an amateur singer: "The 'Rosa' *nederland*, it's all about this guy, he met this girl, she was 16 years of age and he went to ask her hand in marriage and then the parents accepted and he was very happy [...] That was the first *ned* ever that was sang and up till now we call it our anthem."[7] Actually, it seems that "Rosa" appeared during the late 1950s or early 1960s and rapidly became a favourite among singers and their audiences. This is why it is sometimes considered as the anthem of the Malay Choirs and was used as a kind of counter-national anthem, at a time when oppressed people did not want to sing "*Die Stem*", the apartheid state's anthem. According to Abubakar Davids, coach of the Continentals Malay Choir: "This song is called 'Rosa', it's one of our main songs that we always sing at weddings. And even in apartheid years, where we didn't want to sing our anthem, the national anthem of our country, because we were against what they were doing to us, so we sang 'Rosa' whenever there was a gathering of people, and then we used to sing that song as an alternative to our national anthem, yes."[8] However not every Malay Choir expert agrees with the notion of "Rosa" as an anthem. Ismail Morris, adjudicator for the *nederlandsliedjies* in the *Suid-Afrikaanse Koorraad* (SAK) competitions, strongly reacted to this assertion:

> Noooo! That is talking nonsense […] There is no such thing as an anthem, it is just because "Rosa" is the *ned* that everybody knows. Everybody knows "Rosa" because it's such a common *liedjie* you know. It's famous and everybody anywhere you get together at weddings, anywhere people will sing it. But to say it's an anthem they sort of made it into an anthem when the choirs have their last concert, they would all stand together and sing "Rosa". Why this one? I don't know, because in that time when I was a lead singer [probably in the late 1950s and early 1960s] "Rosa" wasn't even sung, we sang other songs, but today it seems the only song they know is "Rosa"![9]

Adam Samodien, former coach of the Woodstock Royals Malay Choir, former president of the SAK, concurred with Ismail Morris and argued that "Rosa": "Is not an anthem! All the songs are anthems." This is a proclamation that can also be understood as meaning that every *nederlandsliedjie* could be considered as an alternative to the official national anthem.

> "Sometimes you hear people talking", continued Adam Samodien, "but you say to yourself that nowhere in the *nederlandslied* is this particular paragraph prescribed. One evening me and my wife was sitting at the function and they call this guy on stage to explain about this *nederlandslied*, "Rosa". But the way he explained it, it didn't make sense to me, because those words were never mentioned in the *nederlandslied* "Rosa". You see, the lyrics saying "*dit was drie jaar daarna*", three month after, they find out that she was in love with this guy: "*toe kom haar ouers na my vra*", her parents came to him and asked him if he loves her with all his heart and soul. But there was never mention that the two of you must get married now, they never mentioned the word marriage. That is the statement this particular guy made, to my opinion, wasn't the correct answer as far as "Rosa" goes.[10]

Yet, the lyrics transcribed by both the CMCB and Desmond Desai (2004) mention the expression *trou akkoord* or *trou a'koord*, which means marriage agreement:

"Rosa", CMCB's version[11]	"Rosa", Desmond Desai's "Dutch-Afrikaans or Cape Malay" version (Desai 2004)
Laas toe ek een meisie bemin Hare naam Rosa Dear Sy was maar noemlik sestien jaren oud Sy was een meisie van haar woord *CHORUS:* Sy seg say sal nooit verlaat Sy seg and sy vollig myn waar ek gaan Rosa, Rosa diet, was hare naam En sy vollig myn waar ek gaan Dit was een aand voorlat Ontmoet ek vir Rosa op een straat Spraak ek met Rosa een woord Dit was die woord van trou a'koord *REPEAT CHORUS:* Dit was drie jare daarna Toe kwaam haar oujers na myn vra As ek vir rosa sal bemin Al met myn hart en siel vrinde *REPEAT CHORUS:* Rosa dear Rosa dear vollig my met jong smart	Laas toen ek een meisie bemin Haar naam was Rosa Dear Sy was maar noemlik sestien jare oud Sy was een meisie van haar woord *CHORUS:* Sy seg sy sal my nooit verlaat Sy volg (vollig) my waar ek gaan Rosa, Rosa dit was haar naam En sy volg (vollig) my waar ek gaan Dit was op een aand voorlaat Ontmoet ek Rosa op een straat Spraak ek met Rosa een woord Dit was die woord van trou [a'koord] Dit was drie jaar daarna Toe kom haar ouers na my vra As ek vir Rosa sal bemin Al met myn hart en siel, vriende

"Rosa" provides another illustration of the mode of existence of *nederlandsliedjies*: as is often the case with folk songs around the world, there is no "authentic" or "reference" version of a song; it exists only as a series of variants. Similarly, the meaning of its lyrics and the social signification that can be ascribed to them, are elusive and change from one listener to the other, from one expert to the next. The popularity of "Rosa" could also be explained by the emphasis it puts on faithfulness and commitment, even when lovers are compelled to move, and are possibly separated, a situation that seems to hint at the forced removals of coloured citizens in the 1960s and 1970s. Yet, no single song can be considered as carrying an indisputable signification; it is the repertoire as a whole which is endowed with a sense of historicity and a strong feeling of belonging to Cape

Town and South Africa, because it is rooted in slavery and has been the result of a series of creative acts. This becomes more obvious when music is taken into account. Professor Frank Hendricks remarked: "I picked up when they sing this thing [...] The lyrics are less important than the musical cohesion and the emotion and everything else they try to convey. So the lyrics is not the essential thing."[12] Indeed, the music is certainly the "essential thing" and should be studied more closely.

Desmond Desai's Afrikaans translation (Desai 2004)	Desmond Desai's English translation (Desai 2004)
Laas toe ek 'n meisie bemin het Haar naam was Rosa Dear Sy was maar skaars sestien jare oud Sy was 'n meisie van haar woord KOOR: Sy sê sy sal my nooit verlaat Sy volg my waar ek gaan Rosa, Rosa die het een hart En sy volg my waar ek gaan Dit was vroeg een aand Ontmoet ek Rosa in 'n straat Spreek ek met Rosa 'n woord, Dit was die woord van trou akkoord Dit was drie jaar daarna Toe kom haar ouers na my vra As ek vir Rosa sal bemin Met al my hart en siel, vriende	Last there was a girl I loved Her name was Rosa Dear She was but barely sixteen years old She was a girl of her word CHORUS: She says she'll never leave me She'll follow me whe'er I go Rosa, Rosa that was her name And she'll follow me whe'er I go It was early one morning When I met Rosa in a street I spoke to Rosa one word It was a word of marriage It was three years thereafter When her parents came to ask If I would love Rosa With all my heart and soul, friends

As a matter of fact, views expressed by singers and experts underline the fact that the words are not what is essential; they appear as a prop, which serves to support musical creation, that bears testimony to the resilience and inventiveness of people who were enslaved and then segregated and painted as inferiors by racist stereotypes. Against that backdrop, argues Adam Samodien, it is important to highlight the roots of these songs:

> Our forefathers, they sang only *nederlands* because they come
> from Batavia and all those and from the Nederlands itself and so
> they were slaves and they were singing, that's why we inherited the
> *nederlandslied* and we don't compose *nederlandsliedere* and they
> have passed it on from generation to generation, and we intend to

pass it on. Showing our roots yeah, showing the roots, where we come from."[13] However, since it is today forbidden to compose new *nederlands*, musical creativeness has to be fully invested in the way tunes are arranged.

Nederlands: Evidence of creativity rooted in history

Nederlandsliedjies are a responsorial type of song accommodating a particular relation between the choir (the *pak*[14]) and the soloist (lead singer or *voorsinger*: the singer who is in front). A song begins with four to eight bars of instrumental introduction (*die kop*: the head), at the end of which the *voorsinger* strikes up the song and is then joined by the *pak*, with whom he continues to sing before he solos again. The soloist must not only "beautify the song" with his ornaments; he must also guide the *pak*, and cue them so that they can come in at the right moment. *Nederlands*' structures vary considerably: they know no unique model. Most are only made of verses (e.g. "Rosa"); others also include choruses (this is the case of one of the oldest songs, "*Koningzoon*"). The soloist and the *pak* alternate and often dovetail, but the length of the solo parts and of the choral parts may vary during the same performance, and from one performance to the other. They all share the same harmonic foundations based on the tonic-dominant (I-V) progression which may be developed in tonic-subdominant-dominant (I-IV-V-IV-V-I), the bedrock of European tonal harmony, propagated in South Africa by Christian hymns. Tempos are generally slow or moderate (from 63 to 76 quarter-note beats per minute); this is given by the guitars, the bass (which may be a double-bass or a cello played pizzicato) and, first of all, by the banjo which, since *ghoema* drums are not used to accompany *nederlands*, plays the ubiquitous "*ghoema* beat" rhythmic formula.[15] The mandolin embroiders melodic counterpoints. It has become customary to add string instruments (often a string quartet, sometimes a larger ensemble) and a piano to the traditional orchestra backing Malay Choirs. They remain discreet and the written scores they play weave a harmonic carpet to enhance passages in the song or to punctuate it. The role they play is minimal, some even think insignificant. One may therefore wonder if their function is not more visual — symbolic: it exhibits the presence of European "art" music — than truly musical. During the performance of a *nederlands*, the singers in the *pak* "turn and swing" (*draai en swaai*); they move lightly following the tempo; they turn and swing their body. This helps the singers to keep the tempo and involves the whole body in the interpretation. A few experts also suggest a historical reason for these movements. Part of the repertoire comes from sea shanties sung by sailors and slaves who landed at the Cape. The singers' *draai en swaai* could be a reminiscence of moves made by people on a boat to keep their balance. In this instance again, *nederlands* are signified with reference to slavery and the history of the Cape.

Nederlandsliedjies are usually classified in two main categories: *minnaat*[16] *liedere*, love songs, the greatest number, and *seevart*[17] *liedere*, songs of sea voyages. The memory of slavery again underlies this latest category. Shamiel Domingo, one of the foremost experts on *nederlands* explained their origin: "*Seevart lied* means mostly the *liedere* that was sung by the sailors while they were on the ships. So they would row and the slaves would row the boat and then they would sing." However, both *minnaat* and *seevart* songs are interpreted in the same way, continued Shamiel Domingo, but: "Your love song is more in a slow rhythm as your *seevart*, which is more upbeat, more with rhythm, more to the way they rowed the boats."[18] Anwar Gambeno, coach of the Young Tulips Sangkoor and president of the Keep the Dream Malay Choir Board (KTDMCB) added a third category: *jaage*[19] *liedere*, hunter's songs in which a strong relationship to nature is expressed.[20]

Nederlandsliedjies were sung as soon as choir competitions were organised by the Cape Malay Choir Board, but sources differ as to the date when a specific category dedicated to this repertoire was introduced. Shafiek April, president of the CMCB and Shamiel Domingo contend that such a category existed when the first competition was held;[21] others, such as Gamja Dante, a musician and composer, consider that it was only created in the late 1950s, following a suggestion from Willem van Warmelo (Nel 2012: 54–55; Van der Wal 2009: 59). This difference of opinion resides, says Shamiel Domingo, in changes in the style of interpretation:

> SD: I can understand where the people who say "end of the 1950s" […] where they come from. What happened was the nederlands was sung in a combined form, it was a combined but with a lead singer and that they sung right from the start, from the word go. But nederlands, the way we are singing it today, with the rhythm and all that, where you have the lead singer and the choir responding, that was only introduced in the late 1950s.
> DCM: Did the name of the competition change?
> SD: No, no, no.
> DCM: There was from the start a competition called *nederlandsliedjes*?
> SD: As far as my research goes, yes.[22]

The clarification brought by Shamiel Domingo shows that the *nederlandsliedjies'* style of interpretation changed without affecting the specificity of the repertoire; as a matter of fact styles of interpretation continue to evolve and are today the object of heated debates, as we shall see below.

The repertoire

It is impossible to know precisely how many songs are officially accepted as *nederlandsliedjies* and can be used in competition. The figure most frequently quoted is about 300, but they have never been compiled in a systematic collection. A few *aficionados* claim to have gathered a great many songs and to have looked for their Dutch origins. The CMCB occasionally prints the words of *nederlands* presented in competition, but there is no published volume offering a comprehensive compilation of lyrics and transcriptions of the melodies. When video machines were common and accessible, CMCB competitions were integrally recorded and made available in the forms of VHS cassettes; now DVDs and CDs are sold directly by the Board, at competition venues or at the homes of some of its leaders.[23] They are not commercially distributed and cannot be bought in shops or online. The accumulation of these CDs and DVDs could lead to a better appreciation of the number and diversity of songs composing the *nederlands* repertoire. The various Malay Choir Boards strictly forbid the composition of new *nederlands*. This rule is never explained; it seems to be self-evident to all actors of the Malay Choirs' world. It may possibly be interpreted as a will to preserve the uniqueness of the repertoire, to canonise it as "tradition" because of its symbolic value. It has also been suggested that the judges adjudicating *nederlands* competitions would be disconcerted if confronted by songs they are not familiar with, as they would not be able to assess the quality of the rendition of a *nederlands* whose words and tune they do not know.

In the past, there have been a few attempts to introduce songs which were not part of the accepted stock into competitions; they have always been disqualified.[24] Ismail Leeman, who coached the Parkdales in 2008, once tried to propose an original *nederlands*: "In 1991 I made my own song, I had an opposition with one of the Young Mens [...] I was very good friend with him, but he objected. So I said if you have your objections, fine I will respect it. The objection is that I'm breaking off the tradition because you must preserve the tradition there."[25] Adam Samodien recalled that in the past he tried to compose a new *nederlands* on the suggestion of a Dr Manhaven, from Holland, who had been invited to adjudicate SAK competitions and asked a few coaches to try and compose new *nederlands*. Adam Samodien took up the challenge. He based his creation on a Dutch popular song, *"Arm Den Haag, de Weduwe van Indië"* (Poor The Hague, The Widow of the Indies)[26], a ditty that is replete with nostalgia of *kroncong*[27] and gamelan, of spices and exotic foods, suggesting a longing for the colonial Dutch East Indies. Adam Samodien was warmly congratulated for his achievement and remained quite proud of it. However, he did not remember the title he gave to his "new" *nederlands* and explained he composed it as he would have assembled a *moppie*: "I sat down and I was thinking: 'now how am I going to do this?' I took a line out of the one *nederlands* and I took a line out of another *nederlands* and you know a complete line, and then I reconstruct this way and that way until I got satisfaction. This is only a natural thing."[28] This *modus operandi*, which is used for composing *moppies* and combined choruses, is a logical technique to be used by someone who is recognised as one of the best *moppie* creators of the late 20th century. It also highlights that *nederlands* cannot be abstracted from a conception of tradition that supposes an uninterrupted chain of songs from the times of slavery until today and gives legitimacy to contemporary innovations. In spite of the prevailing conservative conception of *nederlands*, a few experts are not opposed to the idea of composing new songs. Shamiel Domingo, for instance, considered that a new category could be created to allow the presentation of such innovations: "There is no right and wrong in *nederlands* tune. I am of the opinion, that yes, maybe, they can still sing the traditional *nederlands*, but then they must have another category, the innovation [...] where they write their own *nederlands*, and they would sing it, present it in the traditional style, I would be happy with that."[29] Similarly, Ismail Leeman, coach of the Parkdales, explained that the *nederlands* tradition could be made to evolve: new lyrics could deal with contemporary issues and address problems coloured communities are today confronted with. That would also imply changes in melodic constructions, for changes in the syllables would cause divergences with the tunes. But composing new tunes would be problematic with regard to the "tradition": "If you sing like this in minor with a change of key it would be nice, but the so called tradition tells you not to do that. But I want to do it."[30] His determination was nevertheless shaken when he considered the uniqueness of the *nederlands*, a uniqueness that Ismail Morris, adjudicator for the *nederlandsliedjies* in SAK competitions, insisted on preserving: "You know the atmosphere what comes out of the choir that is something that is unique very, very unique because nowhere in the world you would find singing like *nederlands* singing, nowhere in Africa."[31]

Today the interdiction to compose new *nederlands* remains in force. To ascertain that a song belongs to the legitimate repertoire and can be accepted in competitions, a particular procedure must be followed. As far as choirs which are members of the CMCB are concerned, before a competition starts, they must inform the Board of their choice in order for the Board to endorse it. The Board bases its decision on the opinion of experts, usually elderly men, who have memorised songs they learned from their forefathers and sometimes keep the words in their notebooks. When lyrics appear too impenetrable, the Board sometimes suggests "corrections" so that the lyrics can be better understood. To keep the repertoire alive and prevent choirs from interpreting the same "hits" too frequently, a song that won first prize in a *nederlands* competition cannot be selected again by any choir during the following three years.[32]

Types of harmony

Tunes accepted as legitimate have been orally transmitted; at some point, after having been handed down from generation to generation by word of mouth, their words were written down and occasionally "revised". In spite of an insistence on conserving a closed corpus of songs, the "integrity" of *nederlandsliedjies* is not what matters most; coaches, singers, experts and enthusiasts are first of all interested in the style of interpretation.

Originally, it seems that *nederlands* were informally sung by groups of people, from which emerged, or not, a solo voice.[33] Before apartheid and forced removals, every coloured neighbourhood had its own variants of the lyrics[34] and developed its own styles of rendering the *liedjies*.[35] In the 1950s, the tempo became more rapid, and the sensation of acceleration was even increased by the introduction of the galop, which gave the rhythm more density and allowed the choir to sing with increased energy.[36] At weddings or social functions, and possibly even during the first competitions, the choirs' harmonies were not pre-arranged and were spontaneously organised, without any consideration for conventional (European) vocal registers or smoothness in vocal tones, the most important aspect of the interpretation being to sing with vigour and passion.[37] Later on, choral parts became organised in a way that makes the "second tenors" carry the melody, which is supported by the basses; baritones were added in the bass section and "first tenors" now embellish the tune in a higher register.[38] Nowadays, the *pak* sings in three- or four-part harmony, which brings it closer to European choirs, an evolution which was started with the combined choruses. Many coaches, singers and listeners hear it as the result of the influence of Welsh choirs, from Wales but also from South Africa.[39]

Names given to the different vocal parts within the *pak* vary from one coach to the other; this absence of standard terminology brings to the fore a will, on the part of the choirs and their coaches, to assert a musical individuality and, in spite of the fascination they may feel with classical European or Welsh choirs, to demarcate themselves from these "models". The wealthiest choirs now tend to hire academically trained conductors to coach their teams; however, many coaches cannot read or write music and prefer to coin their own vocabulary. Abduraghman Morris, the Young Men's coach, for instance, explained the logics behind the manner in which he classifies the voices in his choir:

> What you would say is your first tenor, I would say it's our second tenor. The highest for us is the second tenor, and the lower one, who sings the melody of the song, they are my first tenors. But I don't class them as tenors I say my first voices and my second voices. Cause if you sing a song "do, re, mi, fa, sol" [singing], that is the melody, that would be my first voice. Then I would say "do,

re, mi, fa, sol" [singing high], that is the second voice, that voice seconds this one. That is what I called the second voice, but it is not necessarily a second tenor.[40]

When talking about the second voice, Abduraghman Morris uses the Afrikaans word *skondeer*;[41] this confirms that his second voice has to accompany, to "second" in a higher register, the first voice which carries the melody. To give a summary illustration of the differences between Adam Samodien's and Abduraghman Morris' terminology, the table below shows their correspondence with European academic terminology:

Adam Samodien	Abduraghman Morris	European academic vocabulary
Second voice	Second voice	First tenors
First voice	First voice	Second tenors
Second lower voice	Baritone	Baritone
Baritone (= bass)	Bass	Bass

The terminologies used by Adam Samodien and Abduraghman Morris are basically functional: they organise the voices according to the role they play in the rendition of a tune.

Muslim influences

Occupying the front-centre of the stage, the *voorsinger* indeed plays a decisive role in the interpretation of a *nederlandslied*. The part of the *voorsinger* has become so prestigious that choirs able to afford it hire the talents of specialists, who are highly sought after. The *voorsinger* usually belongs to the first or second tenors; he must be endowed with a wide tessitura and be comfortable both in the high and low registers. He must necessarily be adept at phrasing with suppleness and fluidity — in order to embellish the melody with *karienkels* — and display subtle nuances in his vocal emission.[42] A nasal timbre is, according to some experts, a plus, but there is no general agreement on this. Being trained in the cantillation of the Qur'ān (*qira'at*, قراءات) or in performing the call to prayer (*adhan*, sometimes spelt *athaan*, أَذَان) is generally considered as nurturing the ability to ornament beautifully (Desai 2004: 5; Keep the Dream

Male Choir Board 2013: 11). Actually, several *voorsingers* have been or still are muezzins. Frequent references made by singers or coaches to *qira'at* and *adhan* illustrate the ties that bind Malay Choirs, and especially *nederlandsliedjies*, to Islam, and more particularly to Sufism. *Nederlands* and the wedding songs they are derived from appear to have emerged from an ensemble of religious rituals and to still bear some traces of them. According to Desmond Desai, *nederlandsliedjies* have been influenced by *djiekers* (from *dhikr*: ذكر) sung on the occasion of the Mawlid, celebrating the birthday of Prophet Muhammad (Desai 1983: 110–123).

One particular repertoire, the *salawaat* (*ṣalawāt*, praises to Prophet Muhammad sung in Arabic), follows a responsorial structure, with a choir and a soloist who executes ornaments similar to *karienkels*. According to Ibrahim Hendricks, the Parkdales' *nederlands* soloist, *salawaat* and *nederlands* differ because the one is religious and sung in Arabic, and the other secular and sung in Dutch or Afrikaans, yet they share some resemblance: "You know if you listen to it, it sounds the same. That's why the *nederlands* were basically the tradition that came out of this [of the *djieker*] you know, in the time of our forefathers."[43] However, there is no pre-arranged harmony in *salawaat*, which are in this respect close to what is sung during *gajjats*: depending on his voice range, each singer positions himself as he wishes vis-à-vis the others, some carrying the melody, others "seconding" them; from time to time one voice rises from the mass and develops *karienkel*-like ornaments. P*udjies* interpreted during *ratieps* or *khalifas* may have also contributed to the creation of *nederlandsliedjies* (Desai 1983: 110–123). What should be emphasised is that the musics of Islam have without any doubt contributed to the development of a secular repertoire of entertainment songs, many of them being love songs. They have instilled among Cape Town's inhabitants hearing habits, tastes and aesthetic norms, the influence of which goes beyond the communities of believers. For, as Lois al Fārūqī remarked, *à propos* of a competition of Qur'ān reciters in Kuala Lumpur: "The Qur'ānic chanting is the model for other forms of musical art in an Islamic culture so that it carries at the same time a great religious and a great aesthetic value" (al Fārūqī 1987: 221). It is exactly this type of value that can be heard in the art of the *voorsinger* and his talent in developing *karienkels*. It explains at least in part why a secular repertoire has retained characteristics from musics used in Muslim rituals, but has also acquired new features; this repertoire is now sung by choirs that do not comprise only Muslims.

The relationship between *nederlandsliedjies* and Islam is regularly emphasised by coaches, singers and experts. This is not so much because they want to characterise Malay Choirs as part of an Islamic culture; on the contrary, the same individuals also gladly signal the presence of non-Muslims in the choirs. What is at stake here is, again, the historical signification of the repertoire: it is completely intertwined with the memory of slavery, and with the part played by a group of Muslims in the emancipation of slaves before the official abolition in 1834.

These people were literate, and taught not only religion, but reading and writing. They constituted an intellectual elite who enjoyed a relative autonomy from the colonial powers and their prestige did not vanish in the 20th or 21st centuries.[44] To associate the creation of the *nederlands* repertoire with this history amounts to giving these songs a historical depth (which in a few discourses may even lead back to Indonesia) and to transferring some prestige from 19th century Muslim dignitaries to contemporary actors of the Malay Choirs' world.

"*East*" and "*West*" in *nederlandsliedjies*

In addition to the symbolic weight history confers on *nederlands*, in spite of the dearth of precise data regarding their appearance and evolution, their technical characteristics also contribute to the prominence they enjoy in the Malay Choirs' world. They epitomise an originality that could only develop in the particular "situation"[45] of the Cape. The songs intimate a particular understanding of slavery and underline the slaves' capacity to appropriate and transform elements of the masters' culture, and eventually to transcend the conditions they were forced to live in by creating new artistic forms and practices. Later the slaves' descendants, and eventually all those who were thrown into the "coloured" category, continued to develop and enrich these creations and, in doing so, symbolically refuted the stereotypes presenting coloured people as people without history and culture. That is why a coach like Abubakar Davids could proclaim: "For me there's something sacred in this culture."[46]

The originality of the *nederlands* is particularly manifested in two of their features that a brochure published on the occasion of the 65th birthday of the CMCB brought forward: "Nowhere else in the world do people sing songs the way we do, especially our 'nederlandslied' the soloist singing in quarter tones and the choir joining in on the European tonal scale — without the assistance of a conductor" (Cape Malay Choir Board 2004). In actual fact, the *voorsinger* does not sing in "quarter tones" when he embellishes the tune with *karienkels*.[47] The ornaments he adds to the original melody proceed by half- or whole tones.[48] However, the important point here is not so much the technical accuracy of the claim, but its symbolical meaning: it emphasises the performance (accomplishment and rendition) of musicians who have no academic training, who come mostly from the working class or the lower-middle class, and manage to master complex techniques that are supposed to be the preserve of artists specialising in Western "art" music and avant-garde contemporary music. The melodic contours drawn by ornaments thought to use "quarter tones" evoke an "Orient", from where originated a majority of the slaves, which contrasts with the "West" and its musics based on tonal scales. This complementary opposition is heard in the interplay between the *pak* and the *voorsinger*.

Desmond Desai, who was the first to undertake a serious study of *nederlandsliedjies*, suggested that:

> Cape Malay music, in particular the *Nederlandslied*, is an unique result of the (musical) culture of the people of the Cape. The *Nederlandslied* in its very form and style show the indebtedness to the "East" in terms of the *karienkels*, and also to the "West" in terms of the language and the harmonies. Thus, the *Nederlandslied* is an unique blend of "East" and "West". (Desai 1983: 164)

As we shall see below, this analysis may be clarified and specified. But it does underscore the musical tension that exists in *nederlands*.

The *pak* always strictly remains within the limits of the basic harmonic framework (tonic-dominant or tonic-subdominant-dominant). But the soloist frees himself from it by stringing together inflexions and passing notes that give his ornaments an "Eastern" fragrance, although the techniques of ornamentation he uses cannot be equated with anything known in Indonesian, Indian or Arab musics. The *nederlands*' beauty arises precisely from the contrast between the solid harmony and the steady pulsation of the *pak* and the freedom the soloist enjoys with regard to the chord structure and the meter of the tune. What is sometimes understood as a "meeting between the eastern and the western world"[49] attests to a special type of creativeness able to associate elements which are usually considered distinct and incompatible, to invent new elements from this association and eventually to display in a particular repertoire both the association of the original elements and the new ones which such an association nurtured. Against the backdrop of the ideologies that were dominant in 20th-century South Africa, this signifies a rejection of the idea that purity (*suiwerheid*) is the source of social cohesion and a condition for cultural worth. In this perspective, *nederlandsliedjies* embody a people born of mixtures and blending, and demonstrate that beauty can spring from "impurity" (*onsuiwerheid*).

Nederlands' specific features

Judges and audiences pay great attention to the quality of choral singing, to the elegance of the polyphonies and to the homogeneity of the *tutti*. But the *voorsinger* and his *karienkels* attract even more interest; the quality of his performance is a prerequisite for the success of an interpretation. Solo singers are free to choose the type of *karienkel* they want to use and the place in the melody where they will insert them. The melismas they develop when "*karienkeling*" have no relationship with the words: their aim is to embellish the melody. However, their precise positioning is decided during rehearsals by agreement between the coach and the *voorsinger* and cannot change afterwards during competitions, lest it would unsettle the choir and make it extremely difficult for the other singers to know when they have to come in. In addition to that, the number and the type of *karienkels* must be carefully selected to suit the melody.[50]

Karienkels: The art of ornamenting

Several hypotheses have been formulated regarding the origins of *karienkels*. Willem van Warmelo thought one source could be found in the *gamakam* of Indian classical music[51] (Desai 1983: 65). Other scholars, such as Wim van Zanten,[52] considered it highly probable that Indonesian *kroncong* left marks on the singing style of the *voorsinge*r. *Kroncong* is used to name: a plucked lute, the orchestra which features it, and a type of song. The word appeared at the time of the Portuguese presence in Indonesia, but was not used to designate a genre of music before the 20th century. *Kroncong* represents the first musical layer of Malayo-Portuguese creolisation:

> It is generally accepted that certain of the components of what is now called *kroncong* were introduced into Indonesia by sailors on the Portuguese ships that came to the islands in the 16th century in search of spices. While some of these sailors may have been white Europeans, most were "black Portuguese" — i.e., freemen and slaves from stations of the Portuguese trading empire in Africa, India, and the Malay Peninsula, who had assimilated elements of Portuguese language and culture and had become Catholic. (Yampolsky 2010: 16)

It is likely that creolised songs played on the *kroncong* lute or accompanied by *orkes kroncong*, in which there were already traces of African inputs, were brought to the Cape by Indonesian political prisoners, slaves or even Dutch colonists coming from Batavia; however, it seems impossible to ascertain a precise filiation between Cape Town songs and *kroncong*. Whatever they sounded like in the past, contemporary Indonesian *kroncong* songs feature a solo voice, with no choir accompaniment, and differ markedly from *nederlandsliedjies*. The question of *nederlands*' and *karienkels*' origins is still shrouded in doubt. However, what appears obvious is that they are creole innovations that appeared in the Cape "situation".

The art of *karienkeling* is considered a gift. It cannot be learned and accordingly is not formally taught. Singers are supposed to have it in their voice;[53] they develop it by listening to celebrated *voorsingers* and in discussions with their coach. Abduraghman Morris explained: "A good *karienkel* is actually the bending of the voice, going out of the note and back into the note. Now, some people say, and I also believe that, it is something that you're born with. You either can do it or you can't do it. I can't teach you to have a *karienkel*."[54] Since *nederlands* are interpreted only by coloured singers, it implies that only coloured people can inherit this gift.

There are various types of *karienkels*. Desmond Desai (1983) was the first to describe them precisely. More recently Stigue Nel tried to classify them using the terminology of European "art" music: turn (gruppetto), lower or upper mordent, trill and appoggiatura (Nel 2012: 78–89). The vocabulary used in the Malay Choirs is constructed on the generic Afrikaans term *draai* (turn). It distinguishes the following:

- *dipdraai* (*dip*: to go down): the singer first goes down, then back up; "I go down, I dip, then I *karienkel* from the dip up" explained Shamiel Domingo;
- *roldraai* (*rol*: to roll): a kind of trill; for Shamiel Domingo: "It's almost like I'm rolling it [sings]; you just roll the karienkels";
- *snydraai* (*sny*: to cut): elision of the end of a verse and ornamentation on the last syllable of the text actually sung until the end of the melodic segment corresponding to the full verse; this is a very challenging technique that can only be used by outstanding singers. Shamiel Domingo demonstrated it with the exemple of "Rosa": "*Sny* in Afrikaans means cut, to cut something. Like for example, this was excellently executed by the people from the Bo Kaap. You know there is a Mosque […] The oldest Mosque in Cape Town is the one in Dorp Street. Now, the Imam, the priest of that mosque […] him and his sons, they were masters of the *snydraai*. For example, you know, they sing "Rosa" […] "*Sy was een meisie van haar word/En sy sê sy sal my nooit verlaat*". Now everyone will sing [sings the complete last line]. Now if you are to *sny* that, then you take out the end: '*En sy sê*', you just sing *sê* instead of all those words [sings *sê* with *karienkels*]. You just sing the one word, all the other words, you just *karienkel* it out. Just the one word *sê*, you cut all the other words. You cut it out. But it can only be done by a very good singer."[55]

Karienkels occur frequently in the solo part; they diverge by a tone or a semitone from the original melody. In a version of "Rosa" interpreted by the Zinnias,[56] the soloist sings:[57]

Karienkels, example 1

Ibrahim Hendricks, the Parkdales' *voorsinger* gave another example of *karienkels* in his rendition of "*Wat Breg My Dat Liefde*"[58]:

Karienkels, example 2

"Good" *karienkels* sound as if they are improvised, which is not the case. They are jointly prepared by the soloist and the coach during rehearsals. Once they have made their decision, the type, duration and position of the *karienkels* will not be changed, to avoid confusing the *pak*. The moment when *karienkels* are executed is important. They rarely occur at the end of a line, except to emphasise the last sentence of the lyrics. The soloist always *karienkels* before the *pak* comes in. Ideally, insists Adam Samodien, a *nederlands* interpretation should be fluid and seamless: the soloist "brings in his *karienkels* to make it like it flows and there is no gap in between [...] You will always hear voices until you come to the next line."[59] In "*Treade Jongsman*", the Tulips' *voorsinger* begins (the words on which the soloist *karienkels* are written in grey, the passages where the *pak* sings are in boldface): "*Treade jongsman en kom luister*"; then the *pak* "seconds" the soloist who continues to sing and ornament: "*na myn klag*". The first verse of the song is organised as follows:

> Treade jongsman en kom luister **na myn klag**
> Treade jongsman (en) kom **luister na myn klag**
> Myn geniese dit was aldoor hoar **vriese**
> (Een) ander life meisie sy stond in **myn gydagt**

As can be seen in this example, the soloist may *karienkel* while the *pak* is singing. Ikeraam Leeman, who used to be the Woodstock Starlites' *voorsinger* explained: "My role for the lead singer is that I open the song and afterwards then the group supports me [...] The *karienkel* is that, it's not easy, [...] Every time you sing, it must be there and that belongs to the *nederlandslied* [...] The choir [...] they sing straight, I am always above them and when there is a gap in the song, I must fill that gap."[60] It is generally thought that only the *voorsinger* may *karienkel*. If singing during a *gajjat* can be considered as a forerunner of *nederlands* singing, it is to be noted that melismatic ornaments are introduced by one or the other of the choir members, not necessarily by the leaders. In most Malay Choirs it is the soloist who must carry the *karienkels*. But there have been a few examples of *karienkels* coming from the choir. Shamiel Domingo remembered one very special case: Issa Mohammed, who used to coach the Marines in the 1980s, chose to place an excellent *karienkel* singer in the *pak*, because when he stood in front of the choir his voice was much too loud; he therefore selected a more mediocre singer as soloist. The good singer would *karienkel* from the back, covering the voice of the mediocre one and coming out on top of the choir. The audience could not hear the difference and the Marines won many a competition.[61]

Aangee: The door to polyphony

In addition to ornamenting the melody, one of the most important roles of the *voorsinger* is to indicate to the *pak* singers when they have to come in; in Afrikaans this is called the *aangee*, a word built on the verb *gee aan*, to pass. It means that the *voorsinger* "passes" the melody to the *pak*, a delicate move because he must imperatively end his *karienkel* on the precise pitch and time where the other singers must enter. He has to avoid any gap between the solo part and the choral part; this implies that he must carefully control his breathing (he should not inhale before the *aangee*). He has to select rigorously the type of *karienkel* he uses to make the *pak* feel comfortable, and should neither *overkarienkel* nor *underkarienkel*; it is generally assumed that a descending ornament makes it easier for the *pak*, whereas an ascending *karienkel* makes their entering more difficult.[62] When the *pak* singers join the soloist, they *skondeer* (from *sekondeer*, to second);[63] they support him in a way that allows him to be "on top": to be clearly heard. Unity and solidarity within the choir are foremost. A good polyphonic organisation of the choirs is, in this respect, essential. It is demonstrated in the arrangement of "*Treade Jongsman*" made by Anwar Gambeno:

"Treade Jongsman"

This example shows that there is no gap between the vocal parts. The first and second voices are homorhythmic, almost in unison (except for bar five). The voices are usually organised in a harmonic relationship to the third, the fourth or the fifth, which generates a polyphony of chords best suited to supporting the soloist, especially when he *karienkels*. The bass voice has a more melodic part; its role is very important. Adam Samodien considers it as "the foundation of the song, of the voices [...] if the foundation is not there then there is a hollowness, the building can't stand without the foundations."[64] Abduraghman Morris detailed the moves of the basses: "What would happen is: if the voice goes up, the bass will go down, they'll go like that. And then when this one comes down, the bass will go up."[65] A description Abubakar Davids complemented: "The basses [...] will also do a sort of a *karienkel* in there, but the other voices will all be straight [...] Not throughout the whole song, only certain areas where they will do it, like at the end of a line, before we start the next line and they will fill that, they will just come around with the bass and then we're in to the next line again."[66] The melodic line sung by the basses is tightly related to the solo part and brought out by the other voices, which are always confined within a limited ambitus and never cross each other. The coach tries to obtain the best complementarity between the voices and a strong vocal homogeneity in order to achieve a delicate balance between the subtle ornaments the soloist unrolls, the counterpoint created by the basses and the base established by the other voices. Singing a *nederlandsliedjie* involves every member of the choir.

The orchestral accompaniment

The traditional ensemble backing Malay Choirs comprises the following instruments: banjo, guitar, *ghoema* drum (which may not be used with *nederldansliedjies* in competition), cello or double-bass and mandolin. The banjo is a reminder of the influence American blackface minstrels had on Cape Town musics at the end of the 19th century. It is the most important instrument for the *nederlands*; singers and musicians alike agree that they cannot be sung without its backing. The type of instrument used with Malay Choirs is a four-string banjo, the first string being tuned like the fourth; it produces a minor third when played with the second; the second and the third produce a major third; the third and the fourth strings, a fifth. For instance, the banjo played by Abubakar Davids, coach of the Continentals, is tuned as follows: D-B-G-D. The function of the banjo is both harmonic and rhythmic; it gives the tempo and supports the *pak*'s harmonies. It also sometimes plays short melodies behind the singers. The harmonic and rhythmic role of the banjo is particularly obvious during the introduction (*die kop*) as can be seen in the transcription of the parts played by the banjo, the mandolin and the bass in the introduction of "*Gaaf Maria*" as sung by the Continentals Male Choir:[67]

"Gaaf Maria": Introduction

The mandolin has an exclusively melodic role and intervenes between passages sung by the *pak*. The bass provides the harmonic basis usually following a tonic-dominant progression, which is confirmed by the transcription of the beginning of the bass part in *"Treade Jongsman"*, as interpreted by the Tulips:[68]

"Treade Jongsman", Bass

Guitars play chords that strengthen the harmonic foundation laid by the bass and follow either a particular rhythmic pattern: ♩ ♫ ♩ ♩, or double the patterns played by the banjo (see below).

It is prohibited to use the *ghoema* drum in CMCB *nederlands* competitions. However, it can be heard during practices and seems to be tolerated by the SAK.[69] When a *ghoema* is present, the drummer beats the following patterns:

* ♩ ♫ ♩ ♩

* ♩ ♫ ♫♫

* ♪ ♩♫♫ ♪ ♩♫♫

Even when the *ghoema* is absent, the *ghoema* beat resonates behind the singers. The banjo takes over the role of the drum and plays the following formulas:[70]

* ♩ ♩ ♩.♩ ♩.♩ (*"Treade Jongsman"* by the Tulips)

* ♩ ♩ ♩.♩ ♩ (*"Ugydagte"* by the Starlites)

* ♩ ♩ ♩.♩ ♩ (*"En ek hep daar hop"* by the Woodstock Royals)

In every instance, we find the figure ♩.♩ ♩ or a version of the same developed by splitting[71]: ♩.♩ ♩.♩; they are all equivalent to the *ghoema* beat. The tempo of *nederlands* is slower than that of *moppies*, but the same rhythmic pattern underlies both repertoires. This shows how ubiquitous the *ghoema* beat is in the music of the Malay Choirs and helps understand why it has become a sonic symbol of Cape Town, used in jazz, pop music, "art" music, musicals, and rap. It is probably because it reproduces the *ghoema* beat that the banjo is deemed indispensable to singing *nederlandsliedjies*. It is, in the words of Abubakar Davids, who himself plays the instrument: "The backbone of a *ned*, you don't sing a *ned* without a banjo. It must always be there, it plays the leading part in the *ned* [...] The banjo is the priority, you must have a banjo for the *ned*, that's tradition."[72] Being related to rhythms animating the Zulu *indlamu* dance, *marabi*, *mbaqanga* and African Jazz, having also absorbed influences from rhythms brought from India, Indonesia and Madagascar, the *ghoema* beat, and the banjo which renders it in the *nederlands*, embody the creolising creativity that unfolded at the Cape and in the rest of South Africa, and underline the coloured people's contribution to the invention of original musics (Martin 2013: 351–354).

The galop

Nederlandsliedjies' performances feature a strong rhythmic complementarity between instruments and voices. It can be perceived in the relationship that links the banjo to the solo voice. Let us compare the rhythmic pattern played by the banjo with the melody the *voorsinger* sings and embellishes, as in the two following examples:

"Rosa",[73] banjo and solo voice

"*Wat Breg My Dat Liefde*",[74] banjo and solo voice

If we now superpose the two banjo parts:

"*Rosa*" and "*Wat Breg My Dat Liefde*", banjo parts

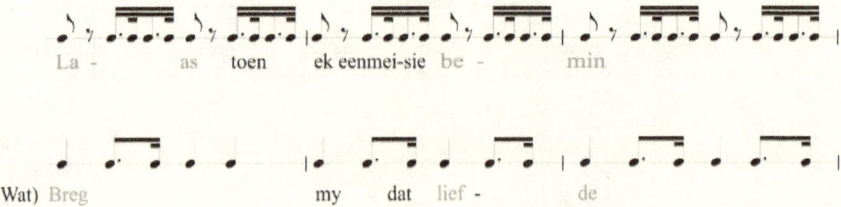

It appears that the first one ("Rosa") redoubles the second one ("*Wat Breg My Dat Liefde*"). This technique is called the "galop".[75] Ismail Dante recalled that in the 1940s, when the competitions started, *nederlands* were sung on a slow tempo, which was not always comfortable for the singers and caused them to sing out of tune. Today the tempo has speeded up, and a few years ago the galop was introduced:

> They started like what they called the galop style [...] The singer he sings the same way [...] We [the instrumentalists] as we play, we just pick up the tempo to give the *nederlands* a more lively effect. It's only the lead singer, he sings normally. But we boost the music, we're on the same timing with the choir and the musician, but we're looking for the choir to be happy [...] Some guys say it's too fast, but we explain to them: "it's not the tempo, you must sing ordinary, we'll do the tempo, but you just sing exactly as you should sing." It gives them more *umpf* [energy, vitality] because like that they want to sing.[76]

In other words, the musicians densify the rhythm by splitting, but they keep playing on the same tempo and the same pulse as the choir. Brothers Ismail and Gamja Dante, who played, respectively, cello and banjo or guitar with several Malay Choirs, are considered as the initiators of the galop. Not only did they densify the rhythm, but they used to improvise little dialogues, complementing the interplay between the soloist and the *pak*. The galop results from a choice made by the musicians and the coach, but is not introduced in every *nederlands'* interpretation. It illustrates how the *nederlands* "tradition" has been, time and again, transformed, and that these transformations have been endorsed by most members of the Malay Choirs' world. Ismail and Gamja Dante did not hide their pleasure at the success of their innovation:

Gamja: Actually, after we did that then everybody follows.
Ismail: It was in the late [19]50's. It sounds a bit boring for us with the slow tempo.
Gamja: The people around us seemed bored.
Ismail: Everybody started enjoying themselves. We just double up [the tempo], for them [the singers] the ned is good now because there is powerness in it, now there is more power and there is like you say happiness in it.
AG: What about the competition, do you double up the tempo as well in it?
Ismail: Yes we do it and we're successful at it, you know.[77]

The Dante brothers consider that the introduction of the galop does not in the least distort the tradition. Yet, it is undeniable that contemporary styles of interpretation differ from those that prevailed thirty or forty years ago. *Nederlandsliedjies*, or for that matter Malay Choirs, were rarely recorded in the

1950s and the 1960s, not to mention before. However, an LP was published in the early 1970s that gives a fair idea of the manner in which the Malay Choir repertoires were interpreted more than forty year ago. On this recording, "Rosa" is sung on a steady tempo, without a galop interlude; the soloist *karienkels* less than he would do today and his *karienkels* always proceed by half-tones or whole-tones; and when it is possible to isolate the banjo, it plays the *ghoema* beat.[78] This LP provides some historical depth and contains material which helps assess both the permanence of "tradition" and the extent of changes that happened after it was recorded.

* * *

When people involved in the world of the Malay Choirs discuss the beauty of *nederlandsliedjies*, they do not pay much attention to the melody, as it has been recorded in memories and orally transmitted, and even less attention to the words, both aspects of which are supposed to represent the Western or European component of the repertoire. Listeners may be sensitive to the sentiments they convey, but that is secondary. What comes first is the manner in which a song is rendered: the sophistication and the cohesion of the *pak*'s polyphony, the ingenuity the arranger shows in renewing old songs, the elegance, subtlety and smoothness displayed in the *voorsinger*'s *karienkels* and the ability of the latter to pass on the melody to the *pak*. Coach, arranger (when he's not the same person), singers and instrumentalists must together contribute to giving the performance *voema* (vigour, energy, momentum) and exhibit *snit*, that is a genuine musical artistry.[79] We have approached the *nederlandsliedjies* from a technical point of view and attempted to present a precise description of the repertoire. We now need to try and understand better the aesthetic conceptions that underpin the appreciation of this artistry and relate them to broader notions of "tradition" and coloured "identity" within contemporary South Africa.

Notes

1. The abbreviations *Nederland(s)* and *ned(s)* are also frequently used, especially in spoken language, as substitutes for *nederlandsiedjies*.
2. Professor Frank Hendricks, Department of Afrikaans and Nederlands, University of the Western Cape, interview with Armelle Gaulier, University of the Western Cape, 20 February 2008.
3. Professor Wium van Zyl, Department of Afrikaans and Nederlands, University of the Western Cape, interview with Armelle Gaulier, University of the Western Cape, 8 February 2008.
4. The complete Malay Choirs' names usually include the words "Malay Choir", "Male Choir", "Sporting Club", "Sangkoor", and are sometimes preceded by an adjective such as "Young" and/or by the name of a sponsor; in common speech, however, the appellation that distinguishes them from other choirs is only mentioned: "the Continentals", "the Starlites", "the Young Men", "the Jonge Studente", "the Tulips".
5. Cape Malay Choir Board, Nederlands Liedjies Songs Choral Competition, 5, 6, 11, 12, 13 February 2011, Good Hope Centre, Cape Town.
6. On the basis of the sole text used by the Starlites, Professor Wium van Zyl suggested the following interpretation: "It seems to me that what they're singing means that 'your idea or your thought brings an end to it'. So at the next line is *Sy't gydink togI*, *tog* means although the situation is now different, she still thinks on *u minde*, she still thinks about your love. But she still thought *avond stoned* which is twilight, romantic evening, that's what I detect. *Op diederin tyd toen, hy haar gaan verbonde*, that was the time when he [...] asked her to marry him or in an informal way there was a bond between them, they were married. But again *Op diederin* that is not 'proper' Dutch [...] Yes, it could have been but she still thinks about the evening when he proposes to her, *verbonde* is a little bit stronger than proposing: He talked about marriage [...] *Gynoeg lat hy haar, gaan vergeefen*, enough that he forgives her, something like that, again it's not a 'proper' sentence. *En voor, u allien maar allien* and for you alone, you alone. It is enough that he can give her forgiveness, so I think what it says is [...] he thinks she still loves him, he thinks there is love enough that he can forgive her that she left him. He thinks that she's still thinking about him. So if this is what I understand, this is kind of a complicated situation. But that is what I can understand from this, and I'm sure somebody else can say I'm speaking nonsense." Professor Wium van Zyl, interview with Armelle Gaulier, University of the Western Cape, 8 February 2008.
7. Mariam Leeman, interview with Armelle Gaulier, Bridgetown, 12 February 2008.
8. Abubakar Davids, interview with Armelle Gaulier, Athlone, 22 January 2008.
9. Ismail Morris, interview with Armelle Gaulier, Athlone, 26 February 2008.
10. Adam Samodien, interview with Armelle Gaulier, Woodstock, 24 January 2008.
11. Cape Malay Choir Board, Nederlands Liedjies Songs Choral Competition, 5, 6, 11, 12, 13 February 2011, Good Hope Centre, Cape Town.
12. Professor Frank Hendricks, interview with Armelle Gaulier, University of the Western Cape, 20 February 2008.
13. Adam Samodien, interview with Armelle Gaulier, Woodstock, 29 January 2008.
14. This may be an allusion to the "pack" (forward players) in rugby teams, a reminiscence of the time when choirs were linked to sports teams. In order to avoid confusion between the full choir (soloist included) and the backing choir, we shall use the word *pak* when talking about the latter (the choir without the soloist).
15. See: pp.98–99.
16. From *minnaar*: lover, beau, gallant.

17. From *see*: sea and *vaart*: cruise.
18. Shamiel Domingo, interview with Denis-Constant Martin, Wynberg, 22 May 2013.
19. From *jaag*: hunt.
20. Anwar Gambeno, interview with Denis-Constant Martin, Mitchells Plain, 15 May 2013.
21. Shafiek April, interview with Denis-Constant Martin, Hanover Park, 20 May 2013; Shamiel Domingo, interview with Denis-Constant Martin, Wynberg, 22 May 2013.
22. Shamiel Domingo, interview with Denis-Constant Martin, Wynberg, 22 May 2013.
23. The CMCB strictly forbids any private shooting of photos or recording of videos during their competitions, whereas the SAK and the KTDMCB tolerate them. The KTDMCB also burns DVDs of its competitions.
24. Sallie Achmat, then chief adjudicator, KTDMCB, interview with Denis-Constant Martin, Landsdowne, 20 May 2013.
25. Ismail Leeman, interview with Armelle Gaulier, Kensington, 5 March 2008.
26. Lyrics by Willem Wilmink, music by Harry Bannink. This song was made famous in the Netherlands by Wieteke van Dort nicknamed "Tant Lien", a Dutch singer and actress, born in Surabaya (Dutch East Indies) then under Japanese occupation. *"Arm Den Haag"* was originally published on her first solo LP: *Een Fraai Stuk Burengerucht* (Netherlands: Philips, 1975, No. 6410 088).
27. *Kroncong*, also spelt *keroncong* or *krontjong*, is the name of an Indonesian plucked lute and of a musical genre in which this instrument was originally used; see: Becker 1975, Heins 1976, Kornhauser 1978 and Yampolsky 2010, and: p. 92.
28. Adam Samodien, interview with Armelle Gaulier, Woodstock, 29 January 2008.
29. Shamiel Domingo, interview with Denis-Constant Martin, Wynberg, 15 October 2011.
30. Ismail Leeman, interview with Armelle Gaulier, Kensington, 5 March 2008.
31. Ismail Morris, interview with Armelle Gaulier, Athlone, 26 February 2008.
32. These rules pertain to the CMCB competitions; they do not seem to be different in the SAK and the KTDMCB competitions.
33. Rushdien Dramat, interview with Denis-Constant Martin, Athlone, 17 October 2011.
34. Anwar Gambeno, interview with Armelle Gaulier, Mitchells Plain, 19 January 2008.
35. Ahmed Ismail, interview with Denis-Constant Martin, Landsdowne, 13 October 2011.
36. The galop designates a technique that results in making the rhythm denser by splitting; that is, by dividing up the total duration of a given sound into shorter values; see, "The galop": pp. 99–102.
37. It is still possible to hear such a type of responsorial singing in which the choir shifts from heterophony to spontaneous polyphony and a soloist occasionally emerges from the collective during Muslim religious rituals known as *gajjat*. A *gajjat* (also called a *werk*: a work, a duty) is a Sufi ceremony that takes place at the home of a believer, during which a group of specialised singers chant and sing praises to Prophet Muhammad. *Gajjats* are held on Thursdays and are considered a spiritual preparation for Friday prayers. Their function is social, as well as purely religious: in District Six, on the occasion of *gajjats*, the better-offs shared food with the poor. The *gajjat* may be compared with the Malaysian *Ratib al-Haddad*, but is musically different, since at the Cape, choirs sing in harmony. Denis-Constant Martin wishes to thank Anwar Gambeno, the late Kader Firferey and his wife, Firoza Gambeno, as well as Cheikh Fayzal Gool and members of The Caravans of Light who allowed him to attend and record two sessions of *gajjat* (at Mr and Mrs Firferey's home, Rondebosch East, 27 October 2011 and 3 April 2015). We also wish to express our gratitude to Professor Shamil Jeppie (Department of Historical Studies, University of Cape Town) who generously shared with us information about the *gajjat*.
38. Adnaan and Abduraghman Morris, interview with Denis-Constant Martin, Athlone, 21 May 2013.

39. In 1978, Welsh singers living in South Africa founded the Welsh Male Voice Choir of South Africa: Cor Meibion Cymru's The Sons of Wales' Choir. Available at http://www.cmcda.co.za/ [accessed 19 August 2013]. In 1982, Welsh Capetonians, in turn, launched a Cape Welsh Choir. Available at http://www.capewelshchoir.co.za/ [accessed 19 August 2013].
40. Abduraghman Morris, interview with Armelle Gaulier, Micthells Plain, 9 January 2008.
41. In standard Afrikaans: *sekondeer*: to second.
42. Rushdien Dramat, interview with Denis-Constant Martin, Athlone, 17 October 2011.
43. Ibrahim Hendricks, interview with Armelle Gaulier, Parkwood, 18 February 2008.
44. Research conducted by Achmat Davids and Shamil Jeppie contributed to a better knowledge of this group (Davids 1980, 1994a & b, 2011; Jeppie 1996a).
45. In the acceptation suggested by Georges Balandier when he defined the "colonial situation": The totality of relationships existing between the settlers' society and the coloniseds' society. Their interpenetration, generating both exchanges and antagonisms, laid the foundations for new systems of thought and action, including inventions in the religious and artistic domains (Balandier 1951).
46. In Ross & Malan (2010): 37'39".
47. And there are many choirs, elsewhere in the world, who sing without a conductor.
48. See pp. 92–95.
49. Mr Salie, interview with Armelle Gaulier, Athlone, 14 January 2008.
50. Shamiel Domingo, interview with Denis-Constant Martin, Wynberg, 22 May 2013.
51. *Gamaka*, also known as *gamak* or *gamakam*, is an ornamentation technique used in classical Indian music. It is not just decorative, but gives ragas their particular colour. *Gamaka* is a type of inflexion proceeding by oscillations between adjacent and distant notes.
52. Wim van Zanten, interview with Armelle Gaulier, Paris, 17 June 2008. Armelle Gaulier wishes to thank Wim van Zanten for his availability, his willingness to listen to her recordings of *nederlands* and comment them.
53. Rushdien Dramat, interview with Denis-Constant Martin, Athlone, 17 October 2011.
54. Abduraghman Morris, interview with Armelle Gaulier, Mitchells Plain, 9 January 2008.
55. We are especially grateful to Shamiel Domingo who very kindly provided precise explanations about the interpretation of *nederlandsliedjies* during an interview with Denis-Constant Martin, Wynberg, 22 May 2013.
56. Private recording by Armelle Gaulier, Mitchells Plain, February 2008
57. The transcriptions provided below are, to a certain extent rhythmically approximate; they do not aim at an absolute accuracy, but at exemplifying the development of ornaments.
58. Private recording by Armelle Gaulier, Parkwood, 18 February 2008.
59. Adam Samodien, interview with Armelle Gaulier, Woodstock, 24 January 2008.
60. Ikeraam Leeman, interview with Armelle Gaulier, Woodstock, 28 January 2008.
61. Shamiel Domingo, interview with Denis-Constant Martin, Wynberg, 15 October 2011.
62. Sallie Achmat, Shamiel Domingo and Felicia Lesch, interviews with Denis-Constant Martin, 2013.
63. The word *jawap* is also sometimes used; it means "answer" in Malay languages and is generally utilised in the context of religious repertoires; Sallie Achmat, Shamiel Domingo and Anwar Gambeno, interviews with Denis-Constant Martin, 2013.
64. Adam Samodien, interview with Armelle Gaulier, Woodstock, 24 January 2008.
65. Abduraghman Morris, interview with Armelle Gaulier, Mitchells Plain, 17 January 2008.
66. Abubakar Davids, interview with Armelle Gaulier, Athlone, 22 January 2008.
67. Private recording by Armelle Gaulier, Athlone, 21 January 2008.
68. Private recording by Armelle Gaulier, Mitchells Plain, 8 January 2008.
69. In 2008, one of the choirs participating in the SAK competitions included a *ghoema* drum in

the orchestra backing the singers. The judges did not disqualify them, not knowing whether it was forbidden, as in the CMCB competitions, or allowed. This tends to confirm that there is nothing musically illogical in the use of a *ghoema* in the performance of *nederlands*. Nevertheless, the deciding authorities in the CMCB continue to ban *ghoemas* in *nederlands* competitions because, they say, the sound is too loud and covers the voice of the singers. This may have been a valid argument in the 1940s or early 1950s, when sound systems were not very powerful, but seems no longer credible today. As a matter of fact, the drum does not drown out the voices of singers when they perform comic songs. This interdict may just have to do with a certain conception of the "tradition" the *nederlands* are supposed to represent.

70. Recorded by Armelle Gaulier during private practices: "*Treade Jongsman*", Mitchells Plain, 8 January 2008; "*U gydagte*", Athlone, 14 January 2008; "*En ek hep daar op diese dag*", Woodstock, 24 January 2008.
71. *Splitting*, musically speaking, is a method that consists in dividing up the total duration of a given sound into shorter values.
72. Abubakar Davids, interview with Armelle Gaulier, Athlone, 22 January 2008.
73. Private recording by Armelle Gaulier, Mitchells Plain, February 2008.
74. Private recording by Armelle Gaulier, Parkwood, 18 February 2008.
75. The "galop" was an up-tempo dance characterised by a 2/4-time signature. It was extremely popular in England and Germany during the 19th century (mostly between 1825 and 1875) and was often played at the end of a quadrille.
76. Ismail Dante, in Gamja and Ismail Dante, interview with Armelle Gaulier, Mitchells Plain, 17 January 2008.
77. Gamja and Ismail Dante, interview with Armelle Gaulier, Mitchells Plain, 17 January 2008.
78. Du Plessis, ID (1973) *The Music of the Malay Quarter, Cape Town, Sung By the Central Malay Choir*. Musical Research. Johannesburg: Gallo (DLPA 165/6).
79. *Snit* means to cut; to edge; to fashion; to fit. This word brings additional value to the music since it seems to have been borrowed from the religious lexicon. It is, for instance, applied to the recitation of the Qur'ān; it is also used with reference to the singing of *Qasidahs* (a Muslim repertoire of entertainment songs; see: Martin 2013: 118–120); Shamiel Domingo, interview with Denis-Constant Martin, Wynberg, 2013.

CHAPTER 4

The meanings of blending

In the previous chapter we attempted to provide a detailed description of *nederlandsliedjies*, introducing as much as possible the vocabulary used by performers and listeners. In the following chapter, we focus on the quality of *nederlands* performance in competitions, as it is understood by specialised judges, but also by singers, coaches and audiences. To that effect, we shall summarily analyse adjudication reports filled by judges sitting in the juries who evaluated the eight best choirs participating in the "Top Eight" (the highest league) *nederlands* competitions of the Cape Malay Choir Board in 2011 and 2013. This analysis will be complemented by information collected in the course of interviews with experts, judges, singers and coaches, and opinions expressed on a dedicated Facebook forum.

The juries

Until 2015, Malay Choirs competitions took place at the Good Hope Centre, a concrete structure erected in 1976 at the place where the morning market was held before the destruction of District Six. Its main hall could accommodate up to 7 000 spectators, but had poor acoustics. The organisation of space is not radically different in the City Hall, where competitions took place in 2016. Not very far from the stage, in the front-centre, several judges (also called adjudicators) sit in a box which is supposed to isolate them from the audience, the officials of the board and the singers: their attention must be focused on the choir who is performing, and no one must influence their decisions. They can only communicate with a designated member of the organising committee, and they may not talk to singers, coaches, sound system engineers or members of the audience. The judges should not under any circumstances disclose decisions made by the jury before they are officially proclaimed from the stage. Every judge marks the performances; the marks are then aggregated by the chief adjudicator and the averages are copied on an adjudication report, accompanied by commentaries. Each participating choir is ranked in the individual category they have participated in, and also ranked within the group they were part of, according to the overall average mark (the addition of marks attributed in the various categories) they have obtained. Adjudication forms are handed over to representatives of the organising committee. The judges then climb on stage to proclaim the results and the Master of Ceremonies warns: "The judges' decision will be final [...] There will be no insulting of the judges and no assaulting of them." The judges then leave the building, protected by about thirty bodyguards. This is a worthwhile measure, since, in the past, a few judges have been threatened or assaulted, so intense is the passion triggered by these competitions.

Composition of juries

In the past, CMCB judges, who are selected by the President of the Board, used to be chosen from white music specialists, who were considered "neutral". They were, it was assumed, less likely to be included in friendship networks existing in the Malay Choirs world, and more competent, because academically trained. However, this was also the reason why their expertise was regularly questioned, and their decisions criticised. Their competence in European "art" music was no guarantee that they could assess the quality of the Choirs' performances, especially in the repertoire deemed the most "traditional", the *nederlandsliedjies*, whose technicalities and aesthetics they were not familiar with. Today, this is no longer the case and most judges are coloured.[1] Yet, many among them are still music teachers, trained in European music, which remains a case for arguing that they do not possess the insight necessary to evaluate Malay Choirs and, in particular, the *nederlands*. To try and render this argument void, CMCB authorities now often appoint experts (former singers or coaches) from the Malay Choirs' world, as judges or advisers to the judges.

Until 2012, juries were changed at every step of the CMCB competitions but, starting in 2013, the same persons must now sit through the whole championship. The *nederlandsliedjies* category is adjudicated by a separate panel, headed by a chief adjudicator, and advised by an expert, who does not vote, but explains to the other judges the specificities of the repertoire and what they should take into account in their ranking of performances. The chief adjudicator and the adviser have to make sure that judges do not apply criteria to *nederlands*, based on the rules of "art" music. In addition to that, judges are invited to attend seminars, where they are told about the particularities of the repertoire.[2] On the spot advice and training sessions are far from unnecessary, since many adjudicators, in particular white music students, are not at all familiar with the intricacies of a *nederlands* interpretation. Some of them occasionally express the perplexity they feel when they have to evaluate and mark the rendition of a form of choral singing which is new to them, and is based on rules which are markedly different from those they have been taught. One of the students, who is an experienced choir conductor, confessed: "When I first heard a *nederlandslied*, I was very very excited because I did not know that it existed [...] I am, for example, not allowed to deduct marks for what my conductors have always called 'scooping', or approaching the note from below."³

Juries contested

Despite efforts to train the adjudicators and to give them advice regarding the most important aspects of a *nederlands* interpretation, and even though information about the criteria used to assess the choirs is circulated among captains, coaches and singers, many participants still consider that a certain fuzziness continues to enshroud the rules they are supposed to follow. Abduraghman Morris, for instance, thinks that *nederlandsliedjies* are more and more appraised according to musical criteria conceived for combine choruses and borrowed from European "classical" music. In his view, *nederlands* are different:

> Yeah it's something you sing from inside, you sing from your heart. If you do a combine chorus you are very restricted you don't sing too loud, you don't sing too soft, sometimes you must sing fast, sometimes you sing slow, you've got movement, you've got crescendo, you've got decrescendo, you've got all of those things, that is combine chorus. You are controlled, *Nederlands* is no control. *Nederlands* you sing from your heart and you sing loud, you actually express yourself and that unfortunately with some of the adjudicators is not taken in the way that they should [...] Now lot of people feels like that the *nederlands* shouldn't be judged on the same criteria of the combine chorus, right?⁴

Arguments about the judges' decisions and the comments they write on adjudication reports are recurrent. After the Tulips' interpretation of "*Treade Jongsman*", Anwar Gambeno commented on a judge's remark, underlining that, since there are many variants of the same song, a particular individual, even a judge, does not necessarily know them all, and should not blame a choir for singing a variant he ignores:

> He says that that *kop* belongs to another *ned* but this other *ned* is totally different to what he is talking about. But now it was maybe changed two generations before us, so our forefathers gave it down to us the way we know it now. But now he goes into the original roots and he finds that no, no, no that is not the

> way he was taught. Now different areas sung the *nederlandslieds* differently, so he was most probably taught by somebody in Salt River, who sang the *kop* that way. And other people was taught like "*Maan*" [coach of the *nederlandsliedjies* for the Tulips] was taught from somebody in Cape Town who sang the kop that way, in District Six. But now if I go to another guy in Claremont who is also a top man in *ned*, he will teach it to me in a different way. You see when things get spread by word of mouth, oral tradition, it will always differ.⁵

Changes due to oral transmission and the diversity of variants peculiar to different parts of Cape Town make judgements on their legitimacy and the quality of their execution delicate and induce coaches to be careful; they sometimes try to get "clearance" beforehand from the judges regarding the version they intend to sing in competition. Rules are less rigid in the SAK, and also it seems in the KTDMCB. After a choir has performed in a SAK competition, the judge issues a written report to explain the mark he has given them. In 2008, after the Woodstock Royals sang "*Ek Hep Daar Op Diese Dag*", Ismail Morris commented: "A very good opening. Good tempo for this song. Good band. Diction good. Excellent *karienkels*. Choir and lead singer connect beautifully. Good harmony, a very good ending."⁶ What transpires from this report, and from many others we have been able to look at, is the subjectivity of the judges' appreciation. The boards attempt to circumvent the problem by appointing several judges and providing them with an expert, which oftentimes makes it difficult to assemble a jury. The pressures which the adjudicators have to face are an additional factor. Ismail Morris, who for many years adjudicated the *nederlandsliedjies* in the SAK competitions, underlines the reluctance expressed by people who are asked to judge Malay Choirs competitions: "You see they can't find the right people because the people are a bit worried; because they get abuses from the audience, because they get threatening letters and threatening phone calls, it's out of hand you know."⁷

Some choirs also hunt down "forgotten" songs, which judges are not likely to know, in order to sound more original and have the originality of the song taken into account, more than the quality of its interpretations. The choice of a particular song is sometimes surrounded by secrecy, and family and friends are used to obtain "rare" *nederlands* from people knowledgeable about the repertoire. Ismail Leeman explains:

> Certain choirs don't know *liedjies* and certain choirs know a lot so when they would sing a *liedjie* they would now prefer to sing an uncommon *liedjie*, and to keep it secret until the day they're gonna do the competition. It would stay amongst either you or the choir and you will never distribute it amongst friends [...]

They are singing maybe thirty to fifty different *liedjies* each year and you need to wait three years before doing it again. But it's like a repetition of the same thing which is not really the problem, the tradition is there. But there were only three or maybe five choirs out of the lot who will come with a special blend and, unfortunately, they are not ready to help any other choir. So you'll come to the same opinion I would actually prefer to keep my *liedjie* and for fifty years I will take a new one because I need to win and be special. I am not contributing to the tradition, I'm useless in this tradition, I might be useful in my choir but I'm not doing great things into the community and that is the main point.[8]

It is the meaning of "tradition" that is, once more, at stake in this instance. The behaviour of choirs trying to exhume forgotten songs is motivated by the belief that by presenting "old" songs they will benefit from a favourable bias because they will appear as carriers of the "tradition". However, this conception is countered by those who argue that the priority is to allow the repertoire to evolve, and to improve the quality of the singing. Discussions about *nederlandsliedjies* have been dominated for several years now by a tension between "heritagisation" and revitalisation, which overflows the banks of music and generates symbolic meanings about coloured identity and South African society at large.

The criteria of a "good" interpretation

In the CMCB, rules governing the assessment of choirs are adopted during meetings in which the leaders of the board, experts and representatives of the choirs participate. As a result, they enjoy strong legitimacy, which does not prevent their being hotly discussed. They have not radically changed over the past thirty years, but have been slightly adjusted at times. The most important modifications were the introduction of a new criterion, "balancing" (relationship between the voices within the *pak*) in 2004 and the increase of the percentage attributed to the *voorsinger*, which went from 10% to 15% in 2013, then from 15% to 20% in 2015.

The 2007 seminar

During the 2007 seminar organised by the CMCB, adjudicators were first warned: "The privilege of adjudicating is a sacred trust and a great responsibility." Their role was defined as: "Lifting the standard by communicating clearly, honestly, tactfully, and professionally"; to this end, they were requested to "be committed to the development of the sport [...]" and "provide objectivity". In short, they must adopt a "Triple C approach":

- COMPLIMENT
- Provide CRITICISM
- Conclude with COURSE OF ACTION to inspire choirs to improve.

Adjudicators have to form their opinion only from "what is presented during those few minutes choir is on stage" and "cannot evaluate a choir based on previous renditions or reputation, whether good or bad".

Coaches were advised to take heed of the following advice regarding the main criteria:

- tempo: some *liedere* to be sung within a specific tempo range and must suit the lied; tempo must be maintained throughout;
- rhythm: don't change the rhythm;
- music: no disparity between musicians;
- harmony: can be enhanced by singing the correct key; other aspects of harmonising to consider, such as: intonation & blending to polish harmony part; you need to back off (eliminate) as much vibrato as possible; establish if you want to sing 2, 3 or 4 part harmony; ascertain who sings the melody of the lied (on occasion, baritone can also carry melody);
- the lead singer: don't sing a lied out of your range; breathing is important; sing in your own voice (so that you are not confused with the choir); the clear voice is more pleasant to listen to; you only have so many notes available to put your parts into to follow the beat, too many "*karienkels*" which the notes/tempo would allow.[9]

The 2015 guidelines

In order to give more legitimacy to the juries' decisions, the CMCB instituted in 2015 a "Nederlands Committee". This body is composed of six or seven experts coming from choirs affiliated to the Board and is in charge of drawing criteria for the adjudicators; usually two of its members sit with the judges and advise them on the quality of *nederlands* interpretations. The decision to create this new committee has been prompted by changes in the composition of the jury and the fact that some new judges were not extremely knowledgeable about *nederlandsliedjies*. For the same reason, new guidelines for coaches, singers and adjudicators were issued:

Nederlands criteria, CMCB, 2015[10]

1	Lead singer	20%	(a) Does the Lead Singer (LS) sing in tune (on the note)? (b) How is the LS's example of karienkel singing? (c) Does the LS's *aangee* connect with the choir? There should be no pause or breath before the choir starts to sing the *skondeer*, except in the case of a *wip-draai* or chorus line. (d) Can the LS handle the key and carry the melody throughout the lied? (e) Is the LS's breathing at the right place? (normal rules of phrasing) (f) Is the LS's voice placing of his melodic line in the right place? Does he decorate the melodic line, and not simply duplicate the first tenor? (g) Is the LS's balance with the choir correct? Not too overpowering? (h) Note: the introduction line of the LS is allowed by means of the *riffling*[11] of the music.
2	Choral Ensemble	50%	The following four categories form part of this section:
2.1	Harmony	15%	
2.2	Overall Intonation	15%	(a) Does the choir sing in tune? (b) Does the key of the song suit the choir?
2.3	Variation	10%	Is there a degree of variation evident in the song? Note: Echo or repeat singing is not allowed in the body of the lied, only at the end or "langdraai" of the song, and not too long.
2.4	Balancing	10%	(a) Do the choir voices harmonise well? (b) Is the choir balanced — not one individual or voice group overpowering the other?
3	Music	10%	(a) Are the instruments in tune, individually, and with each other? (b) Do the musicians change chords in sync with each other? (c) Is the transition of modulation between the ensemble and the choir correct? (d) Is the rhythm and tempo consistent throughout the lied, especially before or after a *wip-draai* or chorus line? (e) Does the pace or tempo of the music do justice to the beauty of the lied? (f) Does the quality of the instrumental accompaniment compliment the performance? (g) The piano is allowed in the accompaniment, in a secondary capacity, *not* in the introduction. (h) If no banjo is used, marks will be deducted from this category.

	Tone Quality (of the choir)	10%	(a) Is the overall tone quality of the choir robust, harmonious and full, not harsh or "shouted"? (b) Is there a balance between the LS and the choir? (the choir should not overpower the LS)
5.	General Presentation	10%	(a) Does the general presentation adhere to the accepted norm of the Nederlands lied as presented by the choir? (b) Was the lied successfully executed?

These guidelines clearly complement recommendations made at the 2007 seminar and do not markedly diverge from them; the only important change concerns the percentage allotted to the lead singer. Stresses remain on the good execution of *karienkels* and *aangee*, precise intonation and cohesion, voice balance and nice harmonies. It is interesting to note that the new guidelines demand of the choirs both "robust and full" tone quality and underline that it should not be "harsh or shouted": an association of qualities that sounds like a compromise attempting to satisfy both the supporters of tradition and those of modernisation.

Adjudication reports

At the end of each performance, judges have to compile adjudication reports. They give a mark for each of the criteria defined by the Board[12] and add commentaries which may, depending on the year, bear on the overall performance or on specific criteria. The total amounts to a score out of 100. A comparison of forms used in the 2007, 2013 and 2015[13] Cape Malay Choir Board *nederlands* competitions shows that there have been a few changes.

In 2007, 2011 and 2013, "Ryhthm/Tempo" constituted one criterion counting for 10%, whereas in 2015 this was amalgamated into a larger "Music" section, the percentage of which has remained 10%. "Lead Singer" came third in 2007 and 2011, after "Rhythm/Tempo" and "Music", and counted for 10% in 2007 and 2011. This was brought up to 15% in 2013, and 20% in 2015; and now occupies the first position on the sheet. In 2007 and 2011, "Variation" was worth 15%; this was decreased to 10% in 2013 and did not change in 2015. In contrast, "Harmony" increased from 10% in 2007, to 15% in 2011. "Overall Intonation" has lost its weighting, from 20% in 2007 down to 15% since 2011. "Balancing" counted for 15% in the 2011 reports, but diminished to 10% in 2013 and 2015. Finally, in 2007 the two separate categories, "General Presentation" and "Outstanding Performance", were respectively worth 10% and 15%; in 2011, they appeared fused and were together awarded 10%, then "Outstanding Performance" disappeared and "General Presentation" was given a weighting of 15% in 2013, and then 10% in 2015.

CMCB criteria and their weighting

2007	2011	2013	2015
1. Rhythm/Tempo = 10%	1. Rhythm/Tempo = 10%	1. Rhythm/Tempo = 10%	1. Lead Singer = 20%
2. Music = 10%	2. Music = 10%	2. Music = 10%	2. Harmony = 15%
3. Lead Singer = 10%	3. Lead Singer = 10%	3. Lead Singer = 15%	3. Overall Intonation = 15%
4. Harmony = 10%	4. Harmony = 15%	4. Harmony = 15%	4. Variation = 10%
5. Variation = 15%	5. Variation = 15%	5. Variation = 10%	5. Balancing = 10%
6. Overall Intonation = 20%	6. Overall Intonation = 15%	6. Balancing = 10%	6. Music = 10%
7. General Presentation = 10%	7. Balancing = 15%	7. Overall Intonation = 15%	7. Tone Quality of the Choir = 10%
8. Outstanding Performance = 15%	8. General Presentation / Outstanding Performance = 10%	8. General Presentation = 15%	8. General Presentation = 10%

The most salient modification highlighted by this comparison is the promotion of the lead singer, both in terms of the position he occupies on the form and of his role in securing a good mark for his choir. This clearly signals that his style of singing, in particular his execution of *karienkels* and *aangees*, forms an essential part of what is considered a good rendition of a *nederlands*. This is all the more important, given the fact that he embodies "tradition" and displays an art which cannot be learned and is considered an innate talent: the gift of *karienkeling*. His weight is, however, counterbalanced by the emphasis put on the polyphonic organisation of the *pak*: if "Harmony", "Variation", "Balancing" and "Tone Quality of the Choir" are considered together, they amount to 45% of the marks in 2015, whereas "Harmony" and "Variation" alternated between 25% and 30% between 2007 and 2013. One may presume that the introduction of the "Tone Quality of the Choir" criterion and the number of points the three categories taken together allow the choirs to gain, reflect and endorse the increasing sophistication of the polyphonic organisation of the voices. Furthermore, the small diminution of the percentage allocated to "Overall Intonation" and "General Presentation" testifies to a general improvement of the choirs in terms of intonation, dress and behaviour on stage.

Commentaries written down on the 2007 and 2011 adjudication reports[14] dealt with the choir's interpretation in general. From 2013 on, the forms gave the judges the possibility to formulate specific remarks regarding each of the criteria. In 2011, they dealt mostly with the cohesion ("consistency", "togetherness") and steadiness of the choir, the quality of the harmonies ("clarity of harmony", "good balance in variation and harmony") and the balance of voices within the *pak*. The choice of tempo and its good adaptation to the melody, the relationship between the soloist and the *pak* ("lead singer and choir must complement each other"), the entertainment quality of the performance ("good performance and very entertaining") were also sometimes highlighted. When they focused on the *voorsinger*, judges occasionally questioned the adaptation of the melody to his voice range; they praised fluid and relax phrasing and good voice timbres, noted when breathing was clumsy and deplored poor intonation and lack of microphone control. Comments accompanying the 82.75 % awarded to the Young Men, who won the *nederlands* Top 8 competition in 2011, gave a fair idea of what is expected of a good choir: "Lead singer was very relaxed, and has a very good tone. Breathing of the lead singer was very good. Choir is well balanced, and managed to keep their posture throughout the lied. Lead singer and choir worked together well from the start of the lied to the very end. A pleasure to the ear."

Comments on the choirs' performances were obviously inspired by recommendations made during the 2007 seminar. The 2013 adjudication reports are more detailed, since they provided space for specific comments on each of the criteria. They, again, insist on the steadiness of rhythm and tempo, which should not be hurried ("relaxed pace, *not rushed*"). Instrumentalists must show regularity and style in their accompaniment ("supportive ensemble", "strong support", "effective accompaniment", "*statige ondersteuning*" [elegant accompaniment]); the orchestral scores should not be too close-knit ("complex structure", "interesting harmonies"/"the texture of the orchestration is a bit too dense"). Sometimes the quality of the strings, especially of the banjo and the mandolin, is underlined ("interesting added sixths in banjo"). The soloist is first expected to deliver good *karienkels* ("karienkels finely articulated", "karienkels have a spiritual quality to them", "karienkels fold beautifully into one another", "*karienkels met groot gemak gesing*" [karienkels sung with great easiness], "melodically and rhythmically complex karienkels", "beware of over-karienkelling"); the judges also pay attention to the precision and smoothness of the soloist's *aangees* and to the characteristics of his voice ("lovely, clear and expressive voice", "spiritual", "exceptionally bright tone", "*baie goeie tegnik*" [very good technique], "moving performance"). The *voorsinger* must fulfil his responsibilities as lead singer without hesitation; a judge, for instance, advised the Calypsos' *voorsinger*: "*Sing met mer selfvertroue, jy klink bietjie versigtig*" [Sing with more self-confidence, you sound a bit cautious]. Harmonies must be solid ("*skondeer* mostly solid"), bring momentum to the interpretation ("*die koor het mooi momentum gekry*" [the choir has got a beautiful momentum]), yet sound natural ("choir is rehearsed to the point of becoming distracted and ploughing on regardless"). The interpretation can be made more interesting by nice variations ("complexities of harmonies and rhythmic changes very effective") and precisely executed *wipdraais* ("wipdraai *a capella* successful, strong", "wipdraai cleverly brought song back to original time", "lovely wipdraai in 6/8"). Judges dislike forced tones, rough sounds, vociferous singing: the choir must be careful not to overshadow the lead singer. Comments entered in the "General Presentation" section delineate a somewhat fuzzy interpretation model, which probably indicates hesitation on the part of some judges, if not differences of appreciation. They praise confidence; a robust, but not forced, sound; a correct and becoming ("*netjiese*") interpretation, well-rehearsed but not over-practised. Everything must aim at producing an elegant interpretation ("*staatige vertolking*"), a performance which is both pleasurable ("*genotvolle uitvoering*") and moving ("very moving performance", "very intensely, expressively performed"). A good illustration of the judges' vacillations is given by the final comment made on the Jonge Studente's *nederlands* in 2013: "This Nederlands is extremely refined — perhaps up to the point of losing some of the traditional musical DNA that one associates with the form. A most enjoyable performance. Well done!"[15]

However imprecise they may be, these commentaries bear heavily on the styles of interpretation which the choirs choose to adopt in competition. A coach must see to it that his singers conform as much as possible to the board's criteria and the judges' expectations. As one coach put it: "If you sing something that pulls the things from the judges and the people, then you've got a winner."[16] That does not preclude the fact that several coaches and aficionados complain that adjudicators tend to assess *nederlandsliedjies* as they would combine choruses and ask of the choirs a polyphonic refinement modelled on Western, and especially Welsh, choirs.

Reactions to changes in the choirs' harmonies

Most Malay Choirs now sing, as do European choirs, in three- or four-part harmony, an evolution which started with the interpretation of combine choruses, a repertoire sung by the whole choir, without a soloist, backed by the same instrumental ensemble as the *nederlands*. Abduraghman Morris explained how he composes a "combine", a method followed by most of the coaches we interviewed:

> I would listen to a song, for example, if you listen to one in the car then I would memorise [singing] that starts for a combine chorus. So I would take that song and I'll get a key on the guitar let's try G it doesn't work let's try A, let's try C, right? [singing] that's the melody, right? Second tenor that's what you sing and I say you guys are first tenors and you'll say [singing higher] you'll get yours, and then the bass will go [singing] and that's what you would do. Everybody will listen to the other guys singing and fit your voice in.[17]

A few years later, he specified:

> Especially now with the internet, I go on the sites of like the Welsh choirs or the international choirs and I listen to pieces that they sing and then I try and get hold of the music that they sing. I get hold of the music and I have somebody to play out all the different voices' notes and then I write a story judging on the mood of the song and I write all the words and then I put it up on a board and I actually physically teach it to the guys to the different various group voices.[18]

The composition process adopted by most combine chorus composers is similar to the one used for *moppies*.[19] Some choirs even adapt pieces written by Western "classical" composers and add Afrikaans lyrics. The "Hebrew slaves' Chorus" from Giuseppe Verdi's *Nabucco* has been used as a combine, and so has a four-part arrangement of "Nessum Dorma" from Giaccomo Puccini's *Turandot*. Choirs able to give a good rendition of such reworking of "art music's" famous arias or choruses have been rewarded. This has created a trend which Adburaghman Morris, along with a great number of his colleagues, follows. However, he resents the fact that a small number of very wealthy choirs can afford to hire academically trained coaches:

> In my case, I've got no formal musical training but for the last five years we have been winning combine chorus and *nederlands*, and we are competing with the people who have got the music degree and our choir is biting them you know? Because again it comes down to our type of competition, you know, you can't just take a song and sing it like that, it's got to have that flavour, that malay flavour and that you can only put in by somebody who is in my position. I am not praising myself but somebody

who comes from the roots, who knows what the people like, who knows what the adjudicators like [...] When they started doing those types of combine they get music sheets with all your different voices and then they said all right but if they've four voices in a combine, first tenor, second tenor, baritone, bass why are we using three voices in the *nederlands*? Surely we could use four voices in the *nederlands*. And then we found a better harmony point, now more choirs are starting to do it. But of the three choirs that I teach, it's only the Young Men who do the *nederlands* in four-part harmony. Tulips and the other choir that I teach, they haven't got [...] they are not technically at that level yet.[20]

As a matter of fact, a baritone voice is now frequently added as a fourth part in *nederlands* harmonies. Abduraghman Morris's ambivalence is very telling about the attitude of many coaches regarding the increasing sophistication of the polyphony and the role formally trained coaches and arrangers now play in some choirs. On the one hand, he seems quite critical of innovations brought into *nederlands* singing; yet, on the other, he follows suit. The apparent contradiction in his statements is solved by his insistence on rooting every innovation in the "community", on giving them a special flavour. This amounts to disqualifying (mostly) white musicians — because, in spite of their knowledge and skills, white musicians cannot master the idiosyncrasies of coloured and malay aesthetics — and enhancing aspects that appear to be part of coloured identity. Abduraghman Morris is keen on acquiring the virtuosity of Western choirs, but intends to use it to improve an art which is intrinsically part of coloured or malay culture and evinces at the same time a long-standing tradition, a specific creativity and a capacity to participate in modernising movements.

The "traditionalists" still object to the evolution of *nederlands*, because it seems to break with a "tradition" coming from spontaneously bursting into wedding songs, in full throat and throttle, without any concern for harmonic organisation. Yet, if one listens to recordings made over the past twenty or twenty-five years, the magnitude of the changes does not seem so great. There has been a gradual shift towards increasing the number of vocal parts in the polyphony and arranging their relationships more carefully. But choirs have abandoned singing in full throat and adopted a distribution of voices according to their range a long time ago. However, mutations that have recently taken place, promoted by choirs such as the Jonge Studente, are experienced as a disruption: the increasing number of choirs interpreting *nederlands* as combine choruses has caused "a bit of consternation in the community"[21] and discussions on "tradition" and "modernisation" have become more and more heated among coaches, singers and aficionados.

Conceptions of blending

Competitions strongly influence aesthetic conceptions in paradoxical ways. Judges who are perceived (including sometimes by themselves) as ignorant of the "culture" apply criteria defined and adopted by representatives of the "community". In spite of the criticisms their decisions spark, their aesthetic orientations are accepted and adopted by the coaches, because they are formally legitimate (they are supported by the authority of the CMCB) and because coaches assume that by following them they stand a greater chance of being rewarded in the next competition. These paradoxes confirm that the evaluation of *nederlands* (of the repertoire and of its performance styles) is grounded on a plural aesthetic, which accommodates different value systems. These value systems do not necessarily conflict with each other, but commingle and eventually lead to judgements which, whatever hesitations and ambivalences may underlie them, result in rankings. Adjudication of the performance of a repertoire, whose beauty is assumed to be the result of blending, is therefore approached from mixed points of view. According to Abduraghman Morris:

> The adjudication today is a mix. There is a lot of western influence in the musical background. In the early years, we have the older experienced lead singers from yesterday, who sang in their youth, they used to sit in adjudication of the item. So, what have happened is they have become less, and with the advent of the choral competition, the westernised adjudicators were sorted out to come and sit in adjudication of the choirs, and they automatically applied a lot of the western musical criteria to what we do. And I think the big swing or the big change away from the cultural maintenance aspect of the lied is the advent of the competitions, because every choir is looking for the edge, to be better than the next one.[22]

Musical blending is at the source of the repertoire's tradition and of its "sacred" character. It symbolically evokes social and cultural mixing, an issue that runs through the history of South Africa, especially with regard to the situation of people classified coloured. An echo of the link between musical blending and cultural mixing can be heard in recent discussions around *nederlandsliedjies*.

Aesthetics under debate

Groups of connoisseurs created a Facebook Forum (Malay Choirs Open Group) where they exchanged views about trends in *nederlands* performance. We have looked at comments posted during and after the 2013 competitions and tried to identify the main arguments introduced in the discussion.[23] At first glance, they look like a new version of the quarrel of the Ancients and the Moderns, pitting partisans of tradition against supporters of modernisation. "Traditionalists" consider that judgements passed during the CMCB competitions endanger the "community's culture". Adam Samodien, who was for many years chairperson of the SAK, explains their point of view: "We got a rough time trying to maintain this culture, because when it comes to competitions, the adjudicators, they don't know our culture [...] it's a heavy task for us, we must then either convert to the Welsh Choir type of singing, which means we have to move away from our culture, and our heritage is so very important to keep it in possession or…".[24] In other words, singers should follow in the footsteps of their forefathers and continue singing *nederlands* like *djiekers* or *gajjats*, keeping the spirit of spontaneous harmonies and natural voices.[25] One participant in the Facebook Forum wondered: "Why is it that in some teams, the pak skondeer like they singing a combine? What happened to that raw and powerful way the pak sang that was filled with so much emotion it would give you goosebumps."[26] Judges are made responsible for a lamented evolution: "That's the thing the judges don't neesd to knw the culture. They jusst need toi knw the choral part. Makes u think that maybe its not about our culture anymore [...] So that's the quesstion is our culture worth a first prize?"[27] The uniqueness of *nederlands*, the jewel of the "culture" is at risk[28] because current transformations amount to a process of Westernisation,[29] and if it goes on: "So soon we be singing a Welsh Nederlands."[30]

Other, less conservative, coaches share the opinion that judges are adulteration mongers. Ahmed Ismail, chairperson of a choir who is at the forefront of the movement to "improve" the *nederlandsliedjies*, emphasises that choirs participate in competitions in the hope of winning a prize, and that: "If you do not sing according to the criteria, you will not win a trophy."[31] He considers that judges know their business because they have academic qualifications. More important, he thinks that traditional ways of singing inherited from weddings were practised by people who were workers and sailors, who lacked musicality. Today, it is imperative to improve techniques and styles; this is the reason why he hired Kurt Haupt, the University of Cape Town choir conductor, to transform the collective singing of the choir:

> Kurt [Haupt] has, for the last four years, put so much innovation into our *nederlands*, innovation in the sense that we still keep to the structures, we still keep to the traditional sides of the *nederlands*, but when it comes to harmonies, that is where we differ from other choirs, and we have been very very successful for the last three years now from the adjudication point of view, because of the harmonies that we do.[32]

Shamiel Domingo, to a certain extent, concurs with Ahmed Ismail: "We've got to enhance our singing, there is not one choir today, especially in the *nederlands*, that sounds like a Welsh Choir or a church choir, or any choir, they're still traditional *nederlands*, the only difference is they pronounce the words better and nicer than these choirs who want to go according THEIR idea of traditional singing [...] Today the singing is more beautiful than 30 years ago."[33] An opinion that can also be read on the Facebook Malay Choirs Open Group: "I just think that we musnt think too deeply on this in terms of 'losing tradition' but more like enhancing a well preserved item."[34]

Many coaches adopt a similar middle-of-the-road position. They do want to win prizes, but believe that it is possible to improve the quality of singing without adulterating the tradition. A good example of this approach is given by the Young Men, who have been successful in recent competitions. Adnaan Morris, who used to coach them, considered that:

> It is a very much good to the ear, to hear it. It is a good thing I think, the bringing out of the harmonies, and the balancing and the movement of the lied, I think it is a good thing. But the only thing is we've just got to be careful, because we regard the *nederlands* as a traditional item, it's a traditional song, and we've got to keep the tradition and the heritage, try to keep it as pure as possible. Some choirs have taken a further step now by what is called intersinging of voices, syncopation and all this, that is something that is being frowned on by the sort of traditionalist."[35] The Young Men sing elaborate harmonies, but refrain from introducing *wipdraais* and *stopdraais* in songs which did not originally include them. They pay particular attention to maintaining the structure of the songs they interpret, so that their melodies can be clearly heard and their "mood" well preserved:
>
> The enhancement from our side will purely be on the choral aspect of it, with the different voices, the harmonising, the blending of the voices.[36]

Several participants in the Facebook Malay Choirs Open Group agree: "We must innovate and bring freshness but not at the expense of our tradition.ill say this again [...] we are who we are bcoz of our uniqueness.dnt let us become ordinary."[37] This uniqueness, of the *nederlands*, of the tradition, of the culture, of the coloureds, must be preserved and passed on to the next generations. It manifests a capacity to appropriate, blend and create from blending. It tells of a history that goes back several centuries and has been characterised by tribulations and suffering, which nurtured adaptation and innovation. Most choirs make a deliberate effort to recruit young, sometimes very young, singers. They are taught not only to sing, but also to know their history as encapsulated in the tradition inherited from the "ancestors". They are featured in the Junior Solo competition and, when they grow up to be talented young adults, can become *voorsingers*. This was the case of Ismail, then Mustapha Adams with the Tulips.

Aesthetics, social values and identity

In his introduction to the works of linguist and semiologist, Jean Molino, musicologist Jean-Jacques Nattiez suggested that: "The aesthetical judgement is a symbolic form about a symbolic form" (Nattiez 2009: 59).[38] This assertion takes a particular meaning when associated with Jean Molino's insistence on the anthropological foundations of the aesthetic experience (Molino 2009: 343). From this perspective, it is possible to approach debates on *nederlandsliedjies* as dealing not only with a musical repertoire and the ways it is interpreted, but also with the social context in which this repertoire is performed. The example of North-American pow-wows invites us to look at musical competitions as arenas of cultural struggles, where the status of communal values is at stake: Which ones should be retained from the past? Which ones should be brought forward in the present time to symbolically define the community? (Scales 2007: 23). Discussions about *nederlands*, a "unique and sacred tradition", emblematic of a "culture" would then appear as a symbolic means to deliberate on possible configurations and reconfigurations of coloured identity. The debate may sound like a particular instance of the recurring opposition between tradition and modernity, in which both parties nevertheless agree on the impossibility of altering the characteristics of the solo part; that is, of the one aspect of the *nederlands* which is construed as representing the Eastern origins of both the songs and the people who sing them. *Karienkels* are "untouchable"; therefore, the dispute focuses on the *pak*. The debate centres around stagnation as opposed to progress, or, in other words, tradition as opposed to adulteration. Welsh choirs are used as a standard against which is appreciated the extent of progress/adulteration. They occupy a particular place in South Africa's musical landscape and can be perceived from different perspectives. They belong to the West, both from the geographical and the musical points of view; their members are white and male; and their musicality is universally celebrated. Yet, they are neither English nor Dutch; they embody a form of cultural autonomy within the United Kingdom and perhaps recall the memory of a colonial conquest.[39] Welsh choirs have a very long history and are said to have participated in choral competitions (*eisteddfodau*) since the 12th century.[40] These characteristics can arouse contrasting reactions among coloured people. Welsh choirs can be seen in a positive light because they provide a model for excellence and come from a history of oppression and contempt, but can also be viewed in a negative light because they are white and Western, and a carrier of pernicious influences. However, this opposition should be seen, not as an unsolvable antagonism, but as the manifestation of a plurality of coexisting perceptions. French sociologist Nathalie Heinich contends that one of the attributes of Art is to reveal "the plurality of value systems which coexist not only in a single society, but also within the same individuals" (Heinich 1998: 42). The *nederlands* debate does not categorically oppose tradition and modernity. It deals symbolically with the legacy of the colonial situation, the particular oppression that was imposed on scheduled categories of people and the various possible ways to cope with these experiences in post-apartheid South Africa. It highlights the uncertain status of blending and mixing in contemporary South African society and questions the place and function of appropriation in creative processes, which contribute to identity configuring.

Identity and politics in the Western Cape

The permanence of the name "coloured" in the 20th century covered social transformations that changed a classificatory category imposed by fanatics of a racial hierarchisation into a group,[41] within which emerged multiple feelings of belonging (Erasmus 2001; Martin 2001). The entity that became a group remained nevertheless heterogeneous, criss-crossed by somatic, religious, socio-economic, geographical and political differences. Various conceptions of coloured identity took shape in the cauldron of coloured experiences. Some of them radically rejected the label coloured; others accepted it because it was tied to (very) limited privileges granted by the government. Many eventually adopted it, only to subvert the signification that the government ascribed to it. Repertoires sung by *Klopse* and Malay Choirs were used, consciously or not, for this purpose (Martin 1999) because their very existence contradicted the stereotypes of which coloured persons were the victim: people without history or culture, a mere "appendage" to the whites.[42] The "new" South Africa changed coloured people's situation in several respects: all segregation laws were abolished and policies of "positive discrimination" were implemented to promote "previously disadvantaged" people. This benefitted many individuals, who accessed high positions in the civil service or in private corporations, were able to launch their own businesses, and got wealthier; others made a career in politics and became MPs, national ministers and provincial prime ministers. Some of those whose families had been forcibly removed managed to come back and resettle in the neighbourhoods where they or their parents used to live; others bought or rented houses in areas formerly reserved for whites. They registered their children in good schools (often former Model C schools) and prestigious universities. However, for the majority, nothing much has changed: the poor continue to be condemned to living in townships rife with violence, to sending their children to mediocre schools and to enduring unemployment.

New realities lived by coloured people, and their perceptions — often summed up in the frequently heard phrase: "Yesterday we were not white enough, today we are not black enough" (Adhikari 2005) — had political implications. Coloured citizens are in a majority in the Western Cape; since 1994 their votes have decided who governs the City of Cape Town and the Western Cape Province. In 1994, many coloured voters were anxious and did not know what to expect; they did not feel the African National Congress (ANC) would take care of their problems and fell victim to crude National Party (NP) propaganda. They contributed to the NP's victory in the City and the Province. Yet, interviews conducted in 1994 made it clear that they had no real sympathy for the inventors and perpetrators of apartheid, but were instead moved by the idea that: "Better the devil we know than the one we don't."[43] In subsequent elections, coloured voters were reassured and gave the ANC a plurality, but they were eventually disappointed by policies they perceived as benefitting mostly black Africans. Consequently, they shifted their support to the Democratic Alliance (DA),[44] possibly encouraged by the merger of the Independent Democrats (ID)[45] with the DA.[46] The Western Cape Province was successively governed by National Party or New National Party (NNP)[47] premiers from 1994 to 2004, then by ANC premiers from 2004 to 2008, then by Helen Zille, the DA's leader.[48] The City of Cape Town was headed by an NP/NNP mayor from 1994 to 1996, then by ANC mayors from 1996 to 2000 and finally by NNP and DA mayors since 2006.[49] The steady decline in voters' support for the ANC during the first decade of the 2000s,[50] compounded by internal tensions within the ANC, often interpreted as an antagonism between an "Africanist" faction and a "coloured" one, resulted in the quite widespread perception among the ANC's national leaders that coloured citizens of the Western Cape are disloyal and aligned with whites.

Misunderstandings between the ANC leadership and many coloured citizens in the Western Cape started as soon as the party was unbanned and began reorganising its internal structures. The political conditions of the times led the ANC to prioritise the unity of formerly segregated people, a unity that was necessarily to be realised under the aegis of the ANC. As a consequence, every organisation that had been involved in the struggle against apartheid was supposed to join the ANC. In the Western Cape, a major consequence was that the United Democratic Front (UDF) was invited to dissolve itself. Launched on 20 August 1983, the UDF was an umbrella organisation accommodating all kinds of movements, bound by their common will to fight for a democratic and non-racial South Africa. It acted as a relay for the outlawed ANC. The UDF strove to "knit together local struggles in one stream", it created "a sense of awe" and succeeded in pushing back "the frontiers of what was politically possible" (Seekings 2000: 93, 22, 119). It was extremely popular, in particular among coloured youth.

The UDF was banned in 1988, but eventually decided to "unban" itself in 1989. After the ANC was legalised again in 1990, there were heated discussions, especially in the Western Cape, as to whether the UDF should be maintained or dissolved. It was eventually resolved to dismantle it in August 1991, much to the chagrin of many activists who thought that it could have continued to play an important role, beside and in support of the ANC (Seekings 2000). The UDF embraced differences and its activists came from all walks of life and every group; it was spearheaded by a coloured minister of the Dutch Reformed Church, Allan Boesak, and Anglican Archbishop Desmond Tutu. The UDF managed to create synergy between people from various linguistic, religious and cultural backgrounds. The return to — as a matter of fact for many of them the adhesion to — the ANC was not satisfactory; they felt they had to conform to a mould that was too rigid. Large numbers of former anti-apartheid activists distanced themselves from post-1994 politics; they invested their energies in their professional activities or in non-governmental organisations. Between 1999 and 2009, some activists stopped voting for ANC candidates, abstained or supported other parties: the ID, the Congress of the People (COPE) and even the DA.

Citizens who resented apartheid, but did not fight it head-on, often caught in the net of effective patronage networks put in place by the NP and its local councillors, could not, in these conditions, be seduced by the ANC and elected to support other parties. The 2009 watershed, when the DA gained a majority of votes in the Western Cape Province, was the result of the convergence of disenchantment felt by citizens who had previously supported the ANC and of dissatisfaction caused by ANC policies implemented when its representatives were in power.[51] The impression that the ANC did not care for diversity and did not, in particular, take into account the specificities of coloured experiences became widespread and was probably reinforced by the style of Jacob Zuma, who was elected national president in 2009. Abubakar Davids, coach of the Continentals, articulated it as follows:

> Then Mandela came along, but you know what? Not much has
> changed. These places, for people who live here, life is still heavy,
> heavy, heavy. You know, my people, the so-called coloureds of
> Cape Town, many of us feel like we are lost in a no-man's land
> between Europe and Africa. I'm not sure where we fit in. That's
> one reason why the choirs are so important. You must understand,
> the Malay Choirs is one place where you are always accepted, no
> matter who you are or what you've done.[52]

The "no-man's land" Abubakar Davids talks about is not only political or socio-economic, it is also cultural and has eventually to do with a certain conception of coloured identity. For historical reasons, the fashioning of black (i.e. African, coloured and Indian) identities was underpinned by an unstable balance between self-assertion, based on fleeting definitions of the home group's characteristics, especially in the field of culture; transforming appropriation of the culture of the dominant groups; and identification with overseas' societies and cultural practices. To human beings who were treated as inferior and confined in separate categories, themselves enclosed in a fortress of a country, music offered privileged channels of symbolic identification. It allowed them to keep in touch with the wider world and to interact with people classified in other categories (Martin 2013). Music stirred up and put in the spotlight creativity which testified to the invention of alternative modernities, construed as non-exclusively white, mixed and allowed the overcoming of alleged differences between human beings.

Jazz provides an excellent example of the intricate relationship between musical creation and the formulation (and reformulations) of black identity (Martin 2008). Even before jazz, as such, emerged in its South African form, blackface minstrel shows were a vehicle for identification with an idealised representation of the United States, and fertilised *Isicathamiya*, *Klopse* and Malay Choirs. The complex and changing links between self-assertion (propped up with permanently reinvented "traditions"), appropriation and borrowing from groups, which could be identified with, naturally engendered the coexistence of several value systems and fostered ambivalence when particular practices had to be assessed, whether in South African society at large or in specific forms of competition. Music's multiple expressiveness, set in motion by the combination of various parameters (such as melody, harmony, rhythm, etc.) makes it an exceptional field for the concurrence of different value systems. In Malay Choirs' repertoires, the association of a polyphony of chords with *karienkels* symbolically projects a type of unity composed of heterogeneous elements. Discourses on *nederlandsliedjies* emphasise contrasts between the (more and more) European sound of the *pak* and the supposed Eastern origins of *karienkels*; between the originality of the music and the opacity of the lyrics. These contrasts are (dis)played against the background of the *ghoema* beat, which epitomises the specificity of the music of *Klopse* and Malay Choirs, while it hints at ties with many African and non-African rhythms.

Readjusting the balance in the mix

Nederlands sound like a demonstration of the fertility and beauty of blending, which resonates with the history of coloured people. A commonality of differences nurtured by contacts, exchanges and blending appears in today's South Africa as a singular phenomenon, on which renewed notions of coloured identity could be founded. It contrasts markedly with discourses of homogeneity developed about whites and black Africans.[53] It also leads to reconsidering the notion of heritage, as it is promoted by, among others, the national Department of Arts and Culture.

Disputes about "tradition" are rife in the Malay Choirs world; yet, they have never stopped coaches and singers from introducing changes in their styles of singing and some argue that evolution is the best way to keep tradition alive. To come back to Nathalie Heinich's advice on how to conduct sociological studies of the arts, we agree that: "It is decisive to consider seriously the empirical reality of ambivalence as the coexistence of heterogeneous elements that split the subject but cannot be reduced to one dimension, one order of value only — the subject himself being most often unaware of his internal splitting" (Heinich 1998: 51–52).

Nederlandsliedjies amalgamate heterogeneous elements. Judges and enthusiasts appraise their qualities and beauty in judgements based on several value systems, in which they often express ambivalence. The criteria defined by CMCB authorities are in part inspired by principles drawn from European "art" music. Judges, however, are required not to evaluate *nederlands* according to the principles of European music. The percentage allocated to the *voorsinger*, who represents what is considered as an unalterable "tradition" rooted in the East, has been regularly increased during the course of the current decade. The main bone of contention between "conservatives" and "modernists" is the harmonisation of the *pak*. Yet, arguments advanced in discussions do not so much oppose the "Orient" and the "Occident", but are focused on two notions of tradition. One argument refers to practices transmitted by "the forefathers", which legitimate a form of collective self-assertion grounded in a long history. The other proposes not to reject or annihilate what has been inherited, but to enhance and improve it: to spur progress by continued appropriation, a creative strategy which has always been the engine of musical innovation and displays evidence of a capacity to invent a specific form of modernity.

The study of changes in *nederlands'* interpretation styles and controversies around them show that there is a general agreement on construing the repertoire as an expression of group affirmation: as an evidence of coloured people's history and cultural creativity. This understanding is particularly acute because many perceive the post-apartheid phase of South African history as an episode when, once again, coloured culture (and the group who has developed it) is threatened. The history of people who were labelled coloured in the 20th century began with slavery and continued through racism, segregation and forced removals. It is a history of survival and resilience, which has demonstrated their ability to cope, in many different ways, with domination and contempt, and to overcome oppression, either by fighting it openly or by apparently bowing to it and subverting it. In today's South Africa large numbers of coloured people feel marginalised, think that their problems, especially in terms of living conditions and education, are not properly dealt with, and that what they consider their culture is not recognised. These are reasons why new conceptions of coloured identity are brewing. In these conditions, behind considerations of the beauty of *nederlands* and the emotion the songs convey, behind arguments about the various styles of interpretation heard in competitions, a debate is taking place on the possibility of reconfiguring coloured identity in the 21st century. Malay Choirs' aficionados, coaches and singers, jointly work, through their very differences, towards readjusting the balance between the components entering in the mix that constitute the *nederlands* and underlie notions of their beauty. In so doing, they contribute in their own way, through discussions about an artistic practice that seems far removed from social and political concerns, to reconfiguring coloured identities.

* * *

Studying *nederlands*, first from a formal point of view, then from a sociological approach, shows how the multidisciplinary analysis of a musical genre considered, both from within and without, as emblematic of a social group (or subgroup) leads to a finer understanding of the subtleties, ambivalences and contradictions which underpin attitudes towards social and political change. Combining musical analysis with an investigation into discourses about stylistic changes appears particularly fecund in this respect. Focusing on music allows us to go deeper than the surface of polemics about electoral behaviour in the Western Cape and to undermine unequivocal notions of what would be one single coloured identity. It suggests that social representations of mixing and blending, in which human beings and their practices are encapsulated, are deeply permeated with hesitations, uncertainties and anxieties. The uneasiness that ensues relates to balances within mixes, as well as to the place and the acceptance of mixing in South Africa and affects coloured citizens — in some instances "splits" them, as Nathalie Heinich would write. It bears upon the very idea of "coloured identity" and confirms that, under that common-sense notion, the reality is made up of diverse conceptions of coloured identity, separated by many nuances, both related and differentiated by protracted experiences. Such an interpretation of the social meaning of a musical practice — embracing a musical genre, a repertoire and styles of interpretation — can only be considered as valid if the music is carefully described, with reference to the concepts and words of its practitioners, for they carry symbols likely to reveal mutations that stir up social groups.[54]

Notes

1. A few of them are still recruited from white students coming from the University of Cape Town and the University of Stellenbosch music departments.
2. Shamiel Domingo, former chief adjudicator for the *nederlands* with the CMCB, interviews with Denis-Constant Martin, Wynberg, 15 October 2011 and 22 May 2013, and Felicia Lesch, then chief adjudicator for the *nederlands*, interviews with Denis-Constant Martin, Stellenbosch, 7 October 2011 and 15 May 2013. We would like to express a particular gratitude to Mr Domingo who gave us a printed copy of the *PowerPoint* presentation he made during the *nederlandsliedjies* seminars he conducted in 2007 and 2009.
3. From the diary of a judge participating in the adjudication of the 2011 competitions; kindly communicated by the judge to Denis-Constant Martin.
4. Abduraghman Morris, interview with Armelle Gaulier, Mitchells Plain, 17 January 2008.
5. Anwar Gambeno, interview with Armelle Gaulier, Mitchells Plain, 19 January 2008.
6. Copied by Armelle Gaulier from Ismail Morris' report.
7. Ismail Morris, interview with Armelle Gaulier, Athlone, 26 February 2008.
8. Ismail Leeman, interview with Armelle Gaulier, Kensington, 5 March 2008.
9. Text abstracted from: CAPE MALAY CHOIR BOARD, *Nederlands Seminar*, 12 August 2007, PowerPoint printout kindly communicated to Denis-Constant Martin by Shamiel Domingo; although parts of the PowerPoint presentation have been omitted, the original version has been retained in the sentences quoted here.
10. Reproduced from a document kindly communicated to Denis-Constant Martin by Abduraghman Morris, Colorado Park, 21 April 2015.
11. Abduraghman Morris clarifies the meaning of riffling in this context: "In other words, you can […] before you start singing the music is riffled, and you can sort of [sings a short melodic line] and then the music starts, that is allowed." Abduraghman Morris, interview with Denis-Constant Martin, Colorado Park, 21 April 2015.
12. We shall focus in the following paragraphs on CMCB adjudication reports; the criteria used by the KTDMCB, are by and large, similar, the most notable exception being the inclusion of a category "stage personality" for the lead singer.
13. This comparison is based on documents Denis-Constant Martin has been able to consult: a few of the 2007 and 2015 reports, and all the adjudication reports filled in by judges during the Top 8 (finals) *nederlands* competitions in 2011 and 2013.
14. The quotations inserted between brackets have been extracted from the assessment reports we have been able to copy.
15. Jonge Studente's adjudication report, Top 8, *nederlands* category, 2013.
16. Mogamat Stoffels, coach of the Continentals, in Ross & Malan (2010): 7'35".
17. Abduraghman Morris, interview with Armelle Gaulier, Mitchells Plain, 17 January 2008.
18. Abduraghman Morris, interview with Denis-Constant Martin, Colorado Park, 21 April 2015.
19. See Part Three, *Moppies*: Humour and Survival
20. Abduraghman Morris, interview with Armelle Gaulier, Mitchells Plain, 17 January 2008.
21. Felicia Lesch, interview with Denis-Constant Martin, Stellenbosch, 7 October 2011.
22. Abduraghman Morris, in Adnaan Morris and Abduraghman Morris, interview with Denis-Constant Martin, Primrose Park, 21 May 2013.
23. Malay Choirs Open Group. Available at http://www.facebook.com/pages/Malay-Choirs/100634199977978#!/groups/98713196428/?fref=ts [accessed 17 May 2013]; the idiosyncratic spelling used in some posts has been retained in our quotations.

24. Adam Samodien, in Adam Samodien and Rashaad Malick, interview with Denis-Constant Martin, Woodstock, 12 October 2011.
25. Rushdien Dramat, Anwar Gambeno, Abdullah Maged, interviews with Denis-Constant Martin, 2011.
26. Faik Fredericks, Malay Choirs Open Group, 26 April 2013.
27. Moeniel Jacobs, Malay Choirs Open Group, 24 February 2013.
28. Muneer Burns, Malay Choirs Open Group, 18 February 2013.
29. Moeniel Jacobs, Malay Choirs Open Group, 11 February 2013; Anwar Gambeno, interview with Denis-Constant Martin, Mitchells Plain, 11 October 2011.
30. Moeniel Jacobs, Malay Choirs Open Group, 18 February 2013.
31. Ahmed Ismail, interview with Denis-Constant Martin, Landsdowne, 13 October 2011.
32. Ahmed Ismail, interview with Denis-Constant Martin, Mitchells Plain, 22 April 2015.
33. Shamiel Domingo, interview with Denis-Constant Martin, Wynberg, 15 October 2011.
34. Thaabied Dante, Malay Choirs Open Group, 18 February 2013.
35. Adnaan Morris, in Adnaan Morris and Abduraghman Morris, interview with Denis-Constant Martin, Primrose Park, 21 May 2013.
36. Ibid.
37. Muneer Burns, Malay Choirs Open Group, 19 February 2013; position approved by: Riedwaan Amlay (11 February 2013), Thaabied Dante (18 February 2013) and Moeniel Jacobs (26 February 2013).
38. See also: Nattiez 1990, Part II, "The semiology of discourse on music".
39. Most independent Welsh principalities were conquered by Edward the First between 1277 and 1283.
40. The appellation Eistedfodd (plural Eistedfoddau) has been adopted by black intellectuals, white social workers and South African liberal organisations that started choral competitions in 1931. The choirs' friendly rivalry was seen as encouraging both musical and social improvement (Erlmann 1996: 226). South African Eistedfoddau are still very popular today and welcome choirs belonging to every musical culture of the country (see: "The National Eisteddfod of South Africa". Available at http://www.eisteddfod.co.za/ [accessed 2 September 2015]).
41. Following historian Gérard Noiriel, "group" is taken here to mean a social entity which is the result of "the subjective identification of the group's members to the spokespersons and the symbols that give the group its unity" and "category" to designate a human aggregate constituted by "a bureaucratic effort of identity assignment which demands an 'objective' identification of individuals classified within abstract entities defined by law" (Noiriel 1997: 31, emphasis in the original; see also Brubaker et al. 2006).
42. The phrase was coined by Jan Christiaan Smuts, Prime Minister of the Union of South Africa from 1919 to 1924, and again from 1939 to 1948 (Lewis 1987: 210). JBM Hertzog, Prime Minister from 1924 to 1939 explained very bluntly that "the coloured" "owes his origin to us and knows no other civilisation than that of the European (although he is sometimes lacking in appreciation of it), and even speaks the language of the European as his mother tongue" (quoted in O'Toole 1973: 97). When apartheid was not far from collapsing, the wife of the then Minister for Internal Affairs and future State President, Marike de Klerk, still contended that: "They [the coloureds] are the left-overs. They are the people that were left after the nations were sorted out. They are the rest. The coloureds were always under the wings of the whites. They have never been on their own [...]" (*The Sunday Tribune*, 5 February 1983; quoted in Adhikari 2005: 13).
43. When talking about whites, and more specifically Afrikaners, working class coloureds usually use the words "*Die Boere*", which clearly refer to a history of domination.

44. The Democratic Alliance resulted from the fusion of several liberal and conservative parties. It entered into a short-lived alliance with what remained of the New National Party in 2000–2001, and later absorbed Patricia de Lille's Independent Democrats in 2010. Its orientations are globally liberal in socio-economic matters and it claims to govern with more efficiency than the ANC. DA leaders point to their running of Cape Town and the Western Cape as an illustration of their claim. The DA was still recently perceived as a "white" party; it underwent a swift transformation under Helen Zille's direction and young blacks have been rapidly promoted to leadership positions. On 10 May 2015, the DA's electoral conference elected for the first time a black African as leader of the party.
45. The Independent Democrats were launched in 2003 by a former Pan Africanist Congress coloured activist, Patricia de Lille, with a platform emphasising the fight against corruption. In 2010 a merger agreement was concluded between the Independent Democrats and the Democratic Alliance. Consequently, the ID did not field candidates in subsequent elections and ID members were included on DA ballots.
46. Which resulted in Patricia de Lille being elected Mayor of Cape Town.
47. The New National Party was founded in 1997, when the National Party left the government of national unity; the name change was an attempt to distance the "new" organisation from the party that ran the country during apartheid. It later entered into an alliance with the DA, and was eventually swallowed by the ANC.
48. https://en.wikipedia.org/wiki/Premier_of_the_Western_Cape [accessed 2 September 2015].
49. http://www.sahistory.org.za/topic/cape-town-mayors-and-other-city-officials [accessed 2 September 2015].
50. Western Cape provincial elections results:

	ANC	NP/NNP	DP/DA	ID	COPE
1994	33,60%	56,24%	4,18%		
1999	42,62%	34,38%	14,18%		
2004	46,11%	9,44%	26,9%	7,97%	
2009	31,55%		51,46%	4,68%	9.06%
2014	32.89%		59,38%		0.59%

DP: Democratic Party; NNP: New National Party
Source: Independent Electoral Commission of South Africa. Available at http://www.elections.org.za [accessed at different dates between 1999 and 2015].

51. This summary of Western Cape and Cape Town political history since 1994 is obviously very broad and does not do justice to its complexity; for more detailed descriptions and analysis, see: chapter 7 "'*Pourquoi devrait-on forcément avoir un leader coloured?*': l'ANC du Western Cape, ou une anomalie institutionnelle disputée" ("'*Why should we necessarily have a coloured leader?*': ANC in the Western Cape, a contested institutional anomaly") in Darracq 2010; also see Cornelissen & Horstmeier 2002; Eldridge & Seekings 1996; Hendriks 2005.
52. In Ross & Malan (2010): 21'56".
53. These discourses do not totally conceal the reality of differences and mixing, yet they put the emphasis on ideas of exclusive heritages knitting together "Europeans" on the one hand and black Africans on the other. In spite of their attempts at doing justice to all South Africans, whatever the group they were formerly classified in, Presidents Thabo Mbeki and Jacob Zuma seem to have adhered to a conception of South Africa as a juxtaposition of different peoples and cultures. The "I am an African" speech by Thabo Mbeki provides an illuminating example of this conception (Mbeki 1998: 31–32).
54. Georges Balandier introduced the idea of "social revealers" that can be studied to "detect the streams of change under the dead waters of continuity" (Balandier 1971: 86).

Part Three

Moppies: *Humour and Survival*

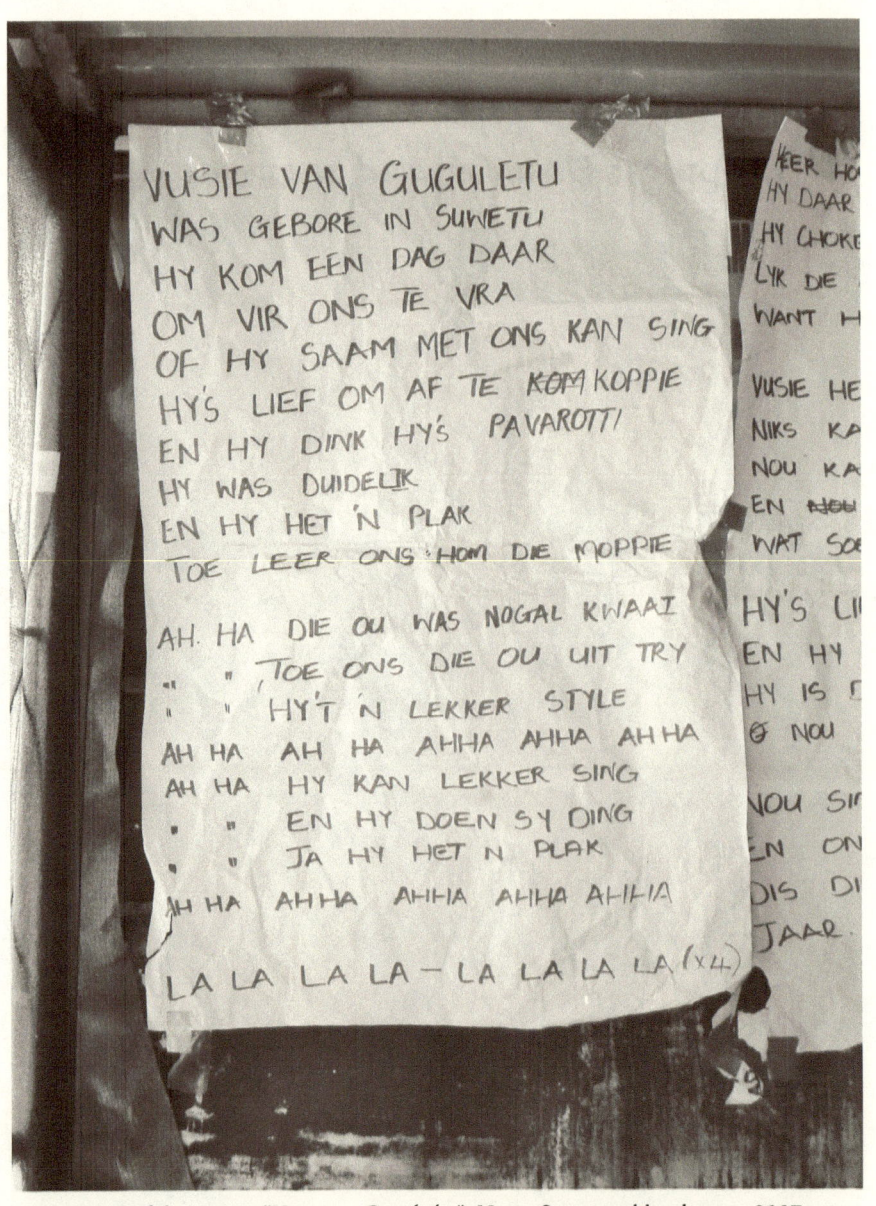

Lyrics of the moppie *"Vusie van Gugulethu", Netreg Superstars* klopskamer, *2007*

CHAPTER 5

Assembling comic songs

Besides *nederlandsliedjies*, comic songs are the most popular of Cape Town's repertoires. Often referred to as *moppies*, or just "comics", their name clearly signals that their lyrics and their performance must convey a form of funniness. In English, "comic" connotes humour, comedy, jocosity that instils among listeners pleasurable feelings of amusement. The Afrikaans term *moppie* signifies something that is pervaded with humour, frequently with a tinge of teasing and mocking. It is derived from the Dutch word *mop*, which designates funny stories and jokes. In South Africa it is mainly used with reference to Cape Town's comic songs. Comic songs or *moppies* are the only body of songs to be interpreted in competition both by *Klopse* and Malay Choirs. They occupy a central place in musical practices associated with the New Year and are particularly dear to the heart of people who were classified coloureds during the largest part of the 20th century. They are considered emblematic of Cape Town's musical idiosyncrasy because they are rhythmically built on a pattern that has come to symbolise the "Mother City" in many genres of music originating from there: the *ghoema* beat,[1] that "with its displaced beat serves as a poignant metaphor for a community that still bears the scars of apartheid dislocation" (Bruinders 2012: 2). The importance of *moppies* in music created by people who are in large part descended from slaves, who have been oppressed and despised, invites us to question the function of humour, and its usefulness, in situations of institutionalised domination and abasement.

Like *nederlandsliedjies*, *moppies* are interpreted by a soloist (*voorsinger*) and a choir (*pak*) in a responsorial relationship. Words most often deal with problems encountered in everyday life, but treat them with irony and facetiousness. They describe odd behaviours and take the mickey out of characters considered typical of certain groups of people. The tunes of *moppies* are composed in the form of potpourris stringing together snatches of melodies borrowed from popular songs heard on the radio, on TV, and nowadays on the internet. Afrikaans words are put to these assemblages. The composition process is exactly the same whether *moppies* are sung by *Klopse* or Malay Choirs; as a matter of fact, the same songs can be used in each of these groups' competitions. A difference may nevertheless exist in the way singers are accompanied. *Klopse* and Malay Choirs used to be backed by instrumental ensembles; however, for several decades *Klopse* have adopted backtracks instead of orchestras playing on stage. Among the Malay Choir boards, the Cape Malay Choir Board (CMCB) still demands that singers be accompanied by musicians appearing in the flesh, while choirs affiliated with the Keep the Dream Malay Choir Board (KTDMCB) now resort to backtracks.²

Meanings of the comic

The comic aims at making people laugh. It usually results from a humoristic description of certain situations, from the embodiment of certain individuals which create a contrast, a disparity or a contradistinction between a norm and the way it is applied, between different levels of the reality, or between various forms of knowledge (Gendrel & Moran n.d. a & b). Yet, as underlined by German philosopher Arthur Schopenhauer, the comic is "unremittingly guided by a demand for seriousness" (Gendrel & Moran n.d. a). French philosopher Vladimir Jankélévitch, talking about irony (associated with teasing and mocking) added:

> Humorous irony [...] hints at the impalpable seriousness of appearances: irony banters, but in the very way it mocks it is possible to read truth as in an open book. The humorist also plays, however his seriousness is extremely far away [...] In order to decipher humour, it is therefore necessary to apprehend it at three levels; one must understand: The farce that lies in the serious simulation; then the deep seriousness that permeates the mockery; finally the imponderable seriousness that is encapsulated in this seriousness. (Jankélévitch 1964: 173)³

Vladimir Jankélévitch points out the enigma of an apparent contradiction between laughter, amusement caused by comic and humour, and a lived reality of social and moral relegation aggravated by difficult, if not miserable, living conditions. He suggests that this conundrum could be solved by paying careful attention to the relationship between funniness and the seriousness of the truth. In this perspective, truth is not an abstract notion, but the product of experiences in the real world. Life is serious, especially for oppressed people, but can be transfigured by comic and humour, the figures and codes of which pervade social representations shared by members of a group who speak the same language and adhere to the same social codes (Jankélévitch 1964: 42; Sibony 2010; Williams 1991). According to psychoanalyst and philosopher Daniel Sibony: "Laughing amounts to saying 'I am not alone, I am manifold'" (Sibony 2010: 66–67).⁴ It implies that individuals are not isolated and cannot be reduced to assigned characteristics — as was the case in 20th-century South

Africa — but that they can decide to be multiple and diverse, in particular because they can choose their identifications. Music offers a wealth of possible identifications; forms of comic shared within a group combine a desire for diversity and the strengthening of social ties, for: "The collective revels in being together and keeping on" (Sibony 2010: 113).[5]

These initial considerations frame the way we approach Cape Town's Afrikaans comic songs: as a repertoire characteristic of a particular social group — people who were classified coloureds — which is today performed in specific social conditions, namely *Klopse* and Malay Choirs competitions; a repertoire in which songs are clearly defined as comical, funny, humorous, aiming at producing a collective laughter among audiences gathered on specific occasions. These conditions — competitive performances dedicated to particular audiences, in which being together and expecting laughter are intertwined — materialise Charles Baudelaire's idea that the comic lies primarily in who laughs: "The comic, the power of laughter is in who laughs, and not at all in what is laughed at."[6] Having quoted the poet, philosopher Francis Jeanson elaborated on his statement:

> Laughter must be understood as being at the same time intentional and spontaneous. It is intentionally operated; however beyond this intention, it is impossible to ascribe to laughter any *cause* or any *reason*, only occasions, pretexts, at most motivations [...] I do not laugh *because* of something which is *intrinsically comical*: I laugh according to a specific intention, and in so doing *I make appear funny to me* the event *à propos of which I laugh*. (Jeanson 1950: 87–88)[7]

The seriousness, even the drama of lived realities, contain elements that can be seen through the lenses of humour and staged in circumstances when laughter is necessary and expected because it reaffirms not only life, but an autonomous way of life in spite of multiple constraints imposed by domination. Laughter then opens a new vision of a reality that is both cherished (because of the group's sodality) and hated (because pervaded with scorn and discrimination).

The origins of *moppies*

In the Malay Choirs and *Klopse* worlds it is generally considered as an undisputed fact that *moppies*, written in the Cape dialect of Afrikaans, are derived from *ghoemaliedjies*, literally *ghoema* drum songs. They used to be performed during informal social functions, such as picnics on the beaches or street merrymaking. It has sometimes been argued that *ghoemaliedjies* had an Indonesian origin and were a southern African adaptation of *kroncongs* and *pantuns* (Winberg 1992). However, if it is possible, even probable, that slaves born in the Indonesian archipelago were familiar with these repertoires in the form they had in the 17th and 18th centuries, it is impossible to find in the *ghoemaliedjies*, which are still known today, or in *moppies*, prosodic or musical evidence of such an origin (Martin 2013: 112–113). The only feature common to *pantuns* and *moppies* is the humoristic treatment they apply to the topics they deal with, a characteristic that can be found in innumerable song repertoires around the world.

Ghoemaliedjies

Two different types of *ghoemaliedjies* may be distinguished. One evinces a Dutch influence on structure and rhythm, but words were adjusted by the slaves to their everyday lives. In the other, the rhythm, form and lyrics of Dutch songs have been more or less preserved; the words, however, have been reorganised and consist in the juxtaposition of various stories in order to produce a parodic effect. In this case, argues Christine Winberg: "We have in these songs not only a remarkable instance of a tradition that has persisted for three hundred years, but a working-class version of South African history" (Winberg 1992: 81). The lyrics of *ghoemaliedjies* were not fixed, and new lyrics were unceasingly imagined and adapted to changing circumstances, especially when they made fun of powerful individuals or authorities. *Ghoemaliedjies* and *moppies* are creole songs that emerged at the Cape from the blending of musical practices originating in all the regions from whence came the people who rubbed shoulders in the Cape "situation": Indonesia, India, Madagascar, Mozambique, West Africa and Europe. The Netherlands probably left a particular mark, since their *mopjes* (little jokes in songs) were also brought to southern Africa.

Performers and aficionados of *moppies* are convinced that they appeared during the times of slavery and assume that they were used to mock masters, a very plausible hypothesis for which there is, as far as we know, no unquestionable evidence. What cannot be disputed is that they were used for entertainment and celebrations.[8] The first trace of a creole song, probably pre-dating the creation of *ghoemaliedjies*, can be found in the record of a 1707 trial, at the end of which a certain Biron was condemned "for singing dubious ditties 'half in Malay, half in Dutch' in the streets of Cape Town" (Winberg 1992: 78).[9] One may surmise that if Biron's ditties were judged "dubious" that was because they were humorous and/or irreverent, a transgression compounded by the fact that they were uttered in a lingo which, described as half-Malay, half-Dutch, was probably a proto-form of Afrikaans.[10] Etchings and paintings from the 18th and 19th centuries, showing scenes of dancing and singing and featuring drums and other musical instruments, correspond to orally transmitted descriptions of *ghoemaliedjie* performances. In

1866, the *Cape Times* ran a story on New Year festivities which mentioned that: "At night time these people added further inflictions upon the suffering citizens of Cape Town in the shape of vocalisation, singing selections from their weird music with variations taken from 'Rule Britannia' and the 'Old Hundredth.'"[11] The variations on "Rule Britannia" were rather ironical. We have no information about the way they were sung and the beat they were put to, except that they sounded "weird" to the ears of a white reporter, which may mean that they differed from the usual way the song was interpreted and that they incorporated traits characteristic of *ghoemaliedjies*. Regarding the lyrics, we may surmise that they were identical or at least close to those collected by Christine Winberg:

> King Pluto said to England
> 'Look beyond the blue seas;
> I'll place the Transvaal in your hands'
> And the gold fields sing along:
> Come Britannia, the civilizing one,
> Make the nations into slaves…
> People not as crazy as you
> Must slowly learn your laws…
> Your tyranny will soon humble
> Those that call this land their own…
> O foggy Island, what a lot of
> Crazy rogues you have by the hand.[12]

Generally speaking, wrote historian Vivian Bickford-Smith, *ghoemaliedjies* "were often (sometimes sexually crude) parodies or burlesques of Dutch folk songs, and satirized figures respected by owners or employers. Some *ghoemaliedjies* contained veiled threats towards the latter. Others offered comments on events, sometimes in satirical form" (Bickford-Smith 1994: 302). The transition from *ghoemaliedjies* to *moppies* probably occurred sometime during the first half of the 20th century. Most musicians agree on the fact that the tempo of *moppies* is faster than that of *ghoemaliedjies*.[13] *Moppies* have retained an interlude played in a slower tempo than the rest of the songs, which may be a remnant of *ghoemaliedjies*. Musician and composer Ismail Dante explained:

> The ghoema came out first, the ghoemalidjies came out first from the picnics, from the old people where they used to sit around, when they start singing. They didn't have a cello, they only had a guitar and a banjo, and then they have the gammie, the ghoema you know. The ghoema gives them the rhythm of the whole thing. How could it be slow or fast, then from there as things go on, the years go on, people try to write their own comic songs, the moppie, from where they heard the ghoemaliedjie […] it is through the

> ghoemaliedjie that there is a comic song, that [...] that they had the moppie now, because the ghoemalidjie was the moppie before. Only as we grew up, we pick up the tempo.[14]

The link established between *moppies*, *ghoemaliedjies* and slavery gives *moppies* a historical depth, which definitely makes them a valuable heritage. Shawn Pettersen, coach of the Kenfacs *Klops* insisted:

> The moppie is, it is traditional, it is part of the slave songs which they did before, like I speak here about the older days, when the guys got to get on the Parade[15] [...] In other culture it will just be part of cultural songs, just one particular song that makes us remember about what happened in the past.[16]

Moppies, like *nederlandsliedjies*, provide evidence of a history, and of a contribution to history, that was denied by racist prejudices against coloured people. The permanence of an artistic medium based on humour and satire is a reminder of a protracted attitude of resistance to slavery and oppression, albeit largely symbolic and expressed through allusions in coded language. It also illustrates processes of creolisation and relationships between creolisation and challenging domination, while it confirms that resistance may take many different forms.

Informally performed when they were invented, *moppies* became a concert repertoire; at the beginning their lyrics were often, if not always, improvised; they are now specially composed. Today, *moppies* are one of the main items in the competitions of *Klopse* and Malay Choirs. As mentioned previously, Afrikaans *moppies* were introduced in the *Klopse* carnival of 1949, following pressure from ID du Plessis, who thought that Afrikaans was not given enough room. Yet, if *Klopse* had to submit, they made a point of not adopting songs composed by Afrikaners and made up their own songs, in their own way and in their own language. Melvyn Matthews, chief executive officer of the Kaapse Klopse Karnaval Association, recalled that ID du Plessis wanted them to sing about the *Boere Plaas*, the white farm and the countryside, a favourite topic of Afrikaner ditties.[17] Instead, *moppie* composers extended the tradition of *ghoemaliedjies* and produced songs in which they could tell about their experiences, even if indirectly. And they also kept singing English *moppies*.

Incomplete memories

Most of the artists who compose *moppies* do not know how to read or write music. Whether they invent a melody, arrange it for choir and soloist or teach it to singers, they do everything by ear. They used to memorise songs they heard on the radio or in musical films; nowadays, they record them on cell phones or computers. Abduraghman Morris, president and coach of The Young Men Sporting Club, explained:

> I've got a very good ear: I listen to something and I can recall it and repeat it and that is why when I get the combine chorus with different voices, I will go to a pianist and he will play the first tenors, melody, and I will record it; and he plays the second tenors melody and I will record it, and the baritones and the basses. And I will place the wording on that: I will listen to my music, and I will go over it and over it, put it in my head and then I will give it over to the club. How I go about it is the first tenors, I will make a CD of the tune and I will give each one a CD: "That is your [...] you listen to that tune." So that is how they get au fait with the thing.[18]

Composers approach *moppies* in exactly the same way; they have to produce a new one every year, sometimes they even compose several songs for different *Klopse* or Malay Choirs. Once presented in competition a *moppie* is rarely sung again; a few songs have been performed in subsequent competitions or in off-competition concerts, but they are exceptions. *Moppie* creators do not usually keep track of the titles or composers of the songs they assemble in their potpourris. Most of them do not even archive their own productions. Some keep notebooks where the lyrics they have penned are preserved; others just stock loose-leaf sheets of songs they presented in former years; many tend to consider that what belongs to the past must remain there. Recordings made by carnival organisers or Malay Choir Boards now make it possible to compile a systematic inventory of *moppies*, at least for a few decades; but, as far as we know, this has not yet been done. Songs produced before competitions were recorded can only be preserved in the memory of coaches, singers and listeners. This is why it has been extremely difficult to go back in time and analyse elements of social representations present in ancient *moppies*.

According to veterans Michael Abrahams, Eddie Matthews and Ronald Fisher, musical instruments used during the New Year parades of the 1950s were banjos, cellos, tambourines and bones;[19] on this background, said Michael Abrahams: "The men that walked behind, they made little *moppies* [...] they don't sing the whole song, just 8 bars [...] and those years they used to jog."[20] When marching in the streets, revellers used to run to the rhythm of the *moppie* they were singing. In those times, there were no *ghoema* in the parades; the beat was given by the cello: if a *ghoema* had been added, it would have overpowered the cello. Today there are no longer cellos in bands backing marching *Klopse*, but a great many *ghoema*s can be heard. They were introduced in the early sixties when brass instruments began to supersede string instruments, and rendered cellos inaudible. As a matter of fact, parades are today very different from what they were sixty years ago. *Klopse* members hardly sing; brass bands are in charge of the music. Marching drums have been introduced in orchestras, alongside *ghoema*s and tambourines, and are very popular with young musicians wishing to emulate American college bands.[21] Banjos have also tended to disappear, an evolution lamented by our panel of veterans. For Michael Abrahams "that isolates the members [...] it is not one group together". And Eddie Matthews added: "Now the *ghoema* will go, they've got a bass drum. It's going to fade away, the *ghoema* is going to fade away."[22] Individuals join a *Klops* because they want to be part of a bright and resounding troupe, to be seen in shiny outfits and accompanied by a forceful orchestra which will increase their pleasure and contribute to their reaching that particular state of mind they call *tariek*.

Many members of a *Klops* only march and parade; they do not participate in singing competitions. Ismail Bey, a backtrack composer, distinguished *die singers* from *die springers*:

> Which means, "the singers" and "the jumpers", the guys who sing and the guys who are the jumpers with the Coons [laughing] [...] So during the year you will have say 50 or 60 guys in your practice room, they are the singers, that is your foundation, then you get the people who just want to boast and brag, go with the parading, you don't see them! Look, in this game, Coon carnival game, you can never say how big your troupe is going to be. You get 50, 60 guys and that is all you see, but comes the end of the year, you see 900, 700, where those people come from? They want to go with that troupe, because that troupe has got a very nice big brass band and that is what about Coon carnival is all about, that is not about the singing anymore.[23]

Anwar Gambeno, captain of the All Stars *Klops*, concurred: in the carnival, most revellers are primarily interested in their troupe winning a prize; the love of singing comes second.

> That's a very serious question. Because that question: what makes the trophy so important is why? That is the reason why people join up with Coon troupe and with Malay Choir, because they want to win the trophy. Not everybody is with the Coon troupe or with the Malay Choir because they like the music or their love to the culture or the religion. You've got to reach a certain stage in this game, where trophies are not the main consideration anymore [...] Because when you start out in this game it is all about the trophies [...] Every song writer would like to have his song on top of the hit parade, because that's the same with the Coon Carnival,

at the end of the day you'd like to win the trophy. But it is important why? Firstly if your troupe doesn't win trophies, you won't have members. Secondly, if your troupe doesn't win trophies, you won't have any supporters because people only support the winner. Thirdly, if your troupe doesn't win trophies, no corporate sponsors will even give you the time of day.[24]

The prestige gained by a troupe or a choir in competition shines on every individual member: it brings stature and nurtures self-esteem. That was particularly the case before forced removals. Anwar Gambeno remembered: "Before apartheid, before the Group Area, when everybody lives in District Six, in Harfield, in Bo-Kaap, where there were five and six and seven, ten troupes in one community, the status was enormous. Now that is also changed."[25] Tape Jacobs, captain of the Beystart *Klops*, also regretted this evolution:

> What actually happens today in our music world, there is no improvement we are just implementing another culture into our music world [...] It is like that, it is a fact. I will tell anybody of that, we have lost a lot of our own music writers. We have lost a lot of them through the system, because the guys don't do it anymore for the love and for the passion of it. They are doing it for name and fame, you see. They want both.[26]

Finally, with the collapse of apartheid, South Africa reconnected with the rest of the world. New images, new sounds, new influences reached the Cape and attracted young musicians and young members of choirs and *Klopse*. Their references are now the Rio de Janeiro or New Orleans carnivals; not only jazz, soul and American pop songs, but rap and marching bands. Coaches and captains have to take their tastes into account if they want to entice them to join their teams. South Africa's new dispensation has also made it easier for tourists to visit the country; they come in great numbers to enjoy the Cape during the austral summer, which is also the time of the New Year festivals. *Klopse* captains and civic authorities dream of making the carnival a tourist attraction; in the meantime, the Coons have become emblematic of the development of an original culture in Cape Town. They are invited to perform at many public events, and get paid for their services. Troupes are now allowed to busk at the Victoria and Albert Waterfront.[27] Carnival associations are also subsidised by the City of Cape Town and the provincial government. There is now a widespread feeling that being involved in a *Klops* or a choir can bring money. Tastes, attitudes and expectations are definitely changing. However, even if the styles of interpretation evolve, the substance of the repertoire is not directly affected by these changes. The way *moppies* are composed, in particular, remains basically unaltered.

Com-posing *moppies*

At the beginning, it seems that *moppies* were collectively elaborated and organised by the coach and the singers, practice after practice. This is also the method that brothers Gamja and Ismail Dante or friends Adam Samodien and Rashaad Malick followed when they composed songs:[28] they worked together on the music and the lyrics, assessed if they fitted well together, and mutually tested their ideas. *Moppies* always rest on the *ghoema* beat; the melody is based on this pattern and is constructed by assembling snippets (musicians use the word "snatches") borrowed from diverse repertoires, but mostly from South African, American or British popular music, which are, when necessary, linked by short original passages. *Moppies* are literally *com-posed*: melodic snatches are *placed with* other melodic snatches.[29]

From heterogeneity to consistency

To be able to com-pose a *moppie*, musicians need a fantastic musical memory. They must know a considerable number of songs; they keep increasing their stock by listening to the radio, watching musical films and TV and listening to records. Until recently, they memorised everything and, for instance, did not hesitate to see the same movie several times to be sure they remembered correctly all the songs it featured. Today they rely more and more on the option of recording music from radio, TV or the internet on their cell phones, which they also use as an oral notepad to preserve ideas that come to their mind, wherever they are. However, underlined Anwar Gambeno, *moppie* melodies should not be just patchworks:

> You know we can't read music, so we can't write music [...] But we can hear music and we have very good ears. So what do we do? We listen to the popular songs, and we take, we actually pinch the tunes, but never ever take one complete song, we pinch a tune from Shirley Bassey and we pinch a tune from Elvis Presley and we pinch a tune from Michael Jackson and we bring that together and then we use it. But you'll always find that it makes sense.[30]

Assembling a melody proceeds by trial and error, with the help of a familiar partner (such as Rashaad Malick with Adam Samodien), of a co-composer (brothers Gamja and Ismail Dante provided a good example of such a relationship), or within the choir during rehearsals. A sequence of melodic fragments is tried; then the composer and his friends or associates check whether it "works" or not.[31] According to composers, Taliep Abrahams and Anwar Gambeno, the selection of particular melodic elements is based on three criteria: their own personal taste, the compatibility of the melodic line with a fast tempo and the will to appeal to the youth. *Moppies* also have a pedagogic ambition; these composers consider that they must convey a message, that they must especially highlight the dangers of gangsterism and drug abuse, which are prevalent in many coloured townships. For such messages to be heard, target audiences must be attracted by the music that carries them. This is why *moppies* often include borrowings from international pop music latest hits, which are sometimes mixed with older favourites. Taliep Abrahams explained:

> I can give a message over a *moppie*, also about this drug that the kids use, I wrote something about that also "The Tik",[32] to indulge in it. Because it makes you see things that you don't normally see, you see you're walking in the air, and there are lots of things that you think that you do but you won't normally do. So I say: "Stay away from that, it is just something bad for health and you will just put yourself into bigger and bigger trouble. So stay away from this. Children don't do that. Go to school, get education, read books." And in that way you get the message across to them, through the medium of the song.[33]

Since new *moppies* have to be entered in competitions every year, composers have to meet the challenge of using songs which are popular at the time when they write and finding particular ways to insert them in an original ensemble, so that various *moppies* performed during the same competition do not sound the same. *Moppie* melodies must be at the same time distinctive and evocative of the present.

When *moppies* are composed, some musicians begin with the music, others with the lyrics: there are no rules in this respect, but in any case they must eventually tie everything into a coherent whole. It is this "whole" that will be appreciated, both by the adjudicators and by the audiences; it is the melodic logic of the entire song that will inscribe a *moppie* in people's memories. The quest for coherence and logic implies selecting melodic fragments that "go well together". Waseef Piekaan, a young singer and comedian who was the coach and soloist of the Kenfac *Klopse* and composed "*Sokkie Bokkie,*"[34] a *moppie* awarded at the end of the 2012 carnival, explained: "Somehow I manage to get the one tune going into the next tune by using either a similar tune, a tune from a different song coming into that, but very similar to that tune, so it flows perfectly into that tune."[35] Anwar Gambeno, who belongs to an older generation, shared the same point of view:

> At the end of the day, you listen to it and you recognise that this is Michael Jackson, that is Beyoncé, and that is Ricky Nelson, you recognise the tunes, but when you listen to it as a whole, as a com-

plete thing, a complete SONG, you find that it is different. You understand? Because all those tunes have been brought together to make one whole thing.[36]

Waseef Piekaan clearly expressed his ambition: "What I am striving or actually want to work towards is getting a *moppie* structured exactly like a song, when it's one tune rolling but getting different feels within that tune."[37] In order to produce that effect, the chord structures of the various songs should be identical or compatible, so that their succession generates a feeling of continuity, which does not preclude the introduction of contrasts which change the mood of the *moppie*.

Coherence in alterations

The goal of coherence sometimes involves making slight modifications to borrowed fragments. Alterations in the original melodies aim at producing harmonic coherence and also at adjusting them to tempo changes that are now common in *moppies*. Somewhere during the performance of a *moppie*, the tempo is slowed down. It spices up the song and gives it a new momentum, but should never prevent the listeners from recognising the original tune. It is also during this interlude that the funniest words must be clearly articulated.[38] Such modifications are usually done by ear, from intuition. Gamja Dante explained how he proceeded:

> We use that [a tune], but we don't make the same, we don't do the same, we take, as I said, a note out there, put the other note in there, whatever it is, then we come up with our own in there. When I hear "Oh that is a nice song", now you can just think "OK, what can I try now?" I take the last note and I put it there, I take that note and I put it there and […] This is how I do.[39]

In every *moppie* one can hear an alternation of borrowed elements and original segments. When Anwar Gambeno has conceived the beginning of a song, he foresees what will come after, but he must find a way to bring the next melodic fragment in:

> I have a tune, but how do I get there? So I have got to compose my own little piece so that I can get there […] Yes I create my own tunes as well […] in my mind […] I can sing it but I can't write it […] you see […] and then I memorise it […] I sing it over and over and over until I know […] So as I am driving, I got my phone and I record [laughs].[40]

Composers also recycle fragments of older *moppies*. A few of them have become hits of sorts, like "*Mavis van Bishop Lavis*", by Boeta Omar Adams of the Fabulous Woodstock Starlites[41] or "*Die Toyi Toyi*" by Adam Samodien. Nowadays, when a coach decides to use a *moppie* composed by another coach-composer, he should ask the composer for permission to use it: it has become an implicit rule that he can't just take it; he must buy it, but this has not always been the case.

When a coach uses an already existing song, he may select only one part of it, change one of the borrowed fragments or substitute new words. "*Die Toyi Toyi*" provides such an example. This *moppie* was originally composed by Adam Samodien. It was adopted by Anwar Gambeno and the Young Tulips Sangkoor, as well as by several other choirs and *Klopse*. The Tulips' version, retitled "*Ons Hoor*" (We Hear, the *incipit* of the song), includes a new final verse which pays homage to Nelson Mandela. Similarly, Taliep Abrahams recalled that he was once approached by the coach of another *Klops*, who wanted to use his composition "*Queen van die Moffie*". After being granted permission, the coach found that the last part of the song was too "old-fashioned" and asked if he could change it; this was again accepted and he eventually substituted a fragment of "YMCA" by Village People with a fragment of "Go West" by the Pet Shop Boys.[42] Both "YMCA" and "Go West" are usually considered to be gay anthems, but the replacement of "YMCA" with "Go West" was clearly motivated by a will to bring the music up to date ("YMCA" was released in 1978 and "Go West" in 1993) in order to allude to the recent passing of a South African law legalising same-sex marriages.[43] Another reason for borrowing fragments of pre-existing songs is that, according to Ismail Bey,[44] it makes it easier for singers to memorise new words if they are already familiar with the melody.

The significance of borrowing

Abduraghman Morris acknowledged that most of the borrowed snatches of melody come from "famous numbers, or songs that the people can relate to and like". Then the composer writes "a story upon it and fit in different tunes and the most important part of it is it's got to be comical, you gotta be able to laugh, to laugh, because it's called the comic song".[45] *Moppie* composers draw from countless sources: "A Little Night Music" by Wolfgang Amadeus Mozart; "La Bamba", made famous by Ritchie Valens; songs interpreted by Al Jolson, Ricky Nelson, Frank Sinatra, Elvis Presley, Roy Orbison, Shirley Bassey, Michael Jackson, Céline Dion, the Beatles or Village People; tunes from blockbuster films such as *Grease* or *Dirty Dancing*; these are just a few examples. Melodic borrowings may have a symbolic dimension: arias (even if it is just "*Funiculì, Funiculà*"[46] sung with a seemingly operatic voice or the "Chorus of the Hebrew

Slaves" from Giuseppe Verdi's *Nabucco*) point towards European "art" music; "*Que viva España*" is a clear allusion to Spain; "*Mbube*", "Meadowlands" or just a bass line, or a chord progression evoke black Africans or African cultures, while melodies taken from Afrikaans songs (such as "*Kaptein (Span die Seile)*" by Kurt Darren) represent Afrikaners.

In every instance, there is a mix which associates *moppies* with a coordinate system locating Cape Town within a world of twinkling modernity, and links coloured people with this outer world, as well as with South Africa. The music of *moppies* contributes, in its own way, to fighting negative stereotypes that racist ideologies forged about coloured people; it proclaimed, until the end of apartheid, that efforts made by the government to keep them prisoners of their "racial group" and of their townships were in vain, because they could escape in imagination and in music.

American influences

The early influence of blackface minstrels on the music of Cape Town was mentioned in the introductory chapter. This marked the beginnings of an ongoing fascination with the United States of America, which has not abated today. It surfaces in many interviews and in *moppie* lyrics, sometimes included as a broader notion of "overseas". Shawn Petersen, coach of the Kenfac *Klops* told of his inspiration: "It comes from abroad, from overseas, but we make it a Cape Town thing, by just placing our flavour, our culture, it speaks about our culture."[47] This is illustrated by a line from the *moppie "Die Goema Dans"* by Abbassie Dramat: "*Dis grebring oor die see en gemeng met die ritme hier*" (it is brought from overseas and mixed with the rhythm here). In this *moppie* most melodic fragments are borrowed from American songs; "overseas" seems therefore to designate the United States. American influence can also be found in "*Fiesta Tyd*" (Fiesta Time); its last part is based on "*La Bamba*", a song which became famous thanks to Ritchie Valens' interpretation and to the film bearing the same title, dedicated to the story of his life.[48] "*Fiesta Tyd*" gives a humorous picture of the New Year Carnival. It describes a parade, which features revellers disguised as famous pop stars: Dolly Parton, the country and western singer; reggae luminary, Peter Tosh; Tony Danza, who played the housekeeper in the US sitcom *Who's the Boss?*; and Michael Jackson. All these stars were from the United States, with the exception of Peter Tosh, who hailed from Jamaica, which is also from across the Atlantic. "*Fiesta Tyd*" is but one illustration of the attraction exerted by American (in its broad sense) musics on South African black people in general and on coloured people in particular.

At the end of the 19th century, Orpheus McAdoo's Virginia Jubilee Singers were already being acclaimed and their performances contributed to fashioning an idealised vision of the United States as "a land of plenty, the Black Utopia as such" (Erlmann 1997: 9). These feelings were reinforced on several occasions. In 1901, the Right Rev. LJ Coppin, of the African Methodist Episcopal Church (AMEC) of the USA, told a Cape Town audience of the "remarquable progress made by the Coloured man in America, no similar history on record".[49] American Freemasons and, obviously in a different way, the AMEC, exercised a long-lasting influence on black populations. Marcus Garvey (1887–1940), founder of the Universal Negro Improvement Association and African Communities League, a forerunner of Pan-Africanism, who moved between Jamaica, the United States and Great Britain, had a following in Cape Town (Lewis 1987: 107). *The Cape Standard*, a newspaper with a large readership among coloured people, published on several occasions positive stories about the USA. The interest of Peter Abrahams, one of the greatest coloured novelists, was stirred after hearing Paul Robeson sing "Ol' Man River" (Couzens 1982: 328–329). In the 1970s and the 1980s, Western Cape young activists merged the ideals of Black Power with the ideas of Black Consciousness; there were vigils and marches to the tune of "Amazing Grace".[50] Although in a completely non-militant manner, the names of many *Klopse* (Martin 2000), and also of several gangs (one of the most notorious just call themselves "The Americans") carry the same enthralment for the United States. A myth was created and circulated through innumerable channels that made the USA a land of plenty, and first of all, a land of opportunity for "colored" people, who could see their talents blossom there and invent their own modernity. Such an idealised representation stood in sharp contrast to South African realities. Identification with the United States, or more broadly with the Americas, nourished aspirations for a better life, in which despised people could recover their pride. *Moppies* were one of the small tributaries that flowed into a large river of hope.

"Art" music

"Art" music of European origin provides another source for borrowing, although much less important than American musics. The inclusion of excerpts of "A Little Night Music" by Wolfgang Amadeus Mozart, of the "Chorus of the Hebrew slaves" from Giuseppe Verdi's *Nabucco* in a *moppie* or the introduction of an episode of operatic singing, as Terry Hector did in "*Vusie van Guguletu*",[51] refer to a musical genre that occupied, and still occupies, a particular place in the musical landscape, and musical imaginary, of South Africa. Such appropriations can be considered ambivalent. On the one hand, they pay reverence to what has been ideologically constructed as the "highest" form of music by people who governed South Africa until 1994, people who decided on cultural hierarchies which were at least in part interiorised by members of the social group to which the creators of *moppies* belong. On the other hand, appropriating pieces considered emblematic of European, "white", "superior" music signifies a capacity to absorb it, to master it to the point of reshaping it that amounts to symbolically proclaiming "we also participate in that culture, we are entitled to reformulate it according to our tastes and desires, and we have the ability to do it". *Moppies* entertain with "art" music a relationship that is not radically different from that of the *nederlandsliedjies*, although given the nature of the repertoire, the relationship manifests itself in the melodic composition, rather than in the choir's style of singing.

References to both American music and "art" music must be placed against the background of an obligation to address current problems with humour. Composers of *moppies* draw their inspiration from the media: radio, television, the internet, sometimes local or foreign CDs and they strive for the best adequacy between the lyrics' topic and the musical substratum of the song. They must answer three related concerns: they want to please the younger part of their audiences, to attract youth to *Klopse* and choirs, and to send them a message. Therefore, *moppie* composers tend to select current hits, either local or international, even if their musical style does not really correspond to their personal taste: they prioritise musical efficacy in order to make the message audible and listened to.

Pop musics from all over the world

We shall now focus on a few songs which have been quite successful and provide good examples of how composers select the melodies they want to use when they produce a *moppie*.

"*Sokkie Bokkie*" was performed with success by the Kenfac *Klops* during the 2012 carnival. It was composed by Waseef Piekaan, a young musician and comedian who coached the team and sang the solo part in the competition. As the song was being rehearsed at the time when Denis-Constant Martin interviewed him, he was able to indicate precisely the sources of the musical borrowings on which he had built the melody of his *moppie*.[52] After an original introduction which he himself conceived, he strung together fragments of: "Baby" by Canadian (then) teenager Justin Bieber,[53] a world hit between 2010 and 2012; an old Cape Town song, whose title Waseef Piekaan could not remember; "*Kaptein (Span die Seile)*" (Captain, Hoist the Sails), by Afrikaner songster Kurt Darren;[54] "*Baby Tjoklits*" (Baby Chocolates), a South African hit by another Afrikaner artist, Gerhard Steyn;[55] "Wavin' Flag", by Somali-Canadian K 'naan,[56] which was used as a promotional anthem by a famous soft drink brand during the 2010 Soccer World Cup that took place in South Africa; and finally, "Bottoms Up" by African-American singer and rapper Trey Songz.[57] Waseef Piekaan's musical choices confirm that *moppie* composers make a particular point of attracting youth by using songs they know and like; in this particular case, it seems clear that, by combining South African songs by Afrikaner composers and international best-sellers, he was sketching a new representation of South Africa, in which the local (coloureds and Afrikaners) are included in the global (international popular music).

Older musicians may dig out from a more distant past: American songs, jazz standards, soul music, old *moppies* or South African songs. Segments of melodies can be selected because they flow well into each other and altogether produce a gamut of dovetailing moods. They are also used to symbolise other people, other cultures and other lands. A few bars from "Meadowlands" by Strike Vilikazi, from "Mbube" by Solomon Linda, from "Homeless" by Paul Simon and Ladysmith Black Mambazo, evoke black Africans and their cultures. Such allusions may even be reduced to a bass line, a typical chord progression taken from *kwela*[58] or *mbaqanga*.[59] As we have seen above, opera, or what sounds like it, represents Europe and its "art" or legitimate "classical" music. Sometimes, the symbolism lies in the interplay between the borrowed melody and the original lyrics that go with it, and the new words written by the composer of the *moppie*. For instance, Ismail and Gamja Dante used in their patriotic song "*Ons Land Suid-Afrika*", a fragment of "A Golden Dream", a tune which was sung in the *American Adventure* show staged in the Epcot at Walt Disney World Resort in Orlando, Florida,[60] to reinforce their own lyrics:

"*Dit is ons land, ons land Suid-Afrika
Ons mooie land van mooiheid en plesier*"

[This is our country, our country South Africa
Our superb country of beauty and fun/pleasure]

Here two patriotisms merge and identification with the United States is again suggested. Anwar Gambeno played on the phonetic proximity between "shake" and "Shaik" to underline the catchphrase of the third verse of his *moppie "Die Son"*.[61] When the soloist sings "Shaik Zuma Shaik", to hint at the special relationship Jacob Zuma entertained with Schabir Shaik,[62] he parodies the music and the original words of "Whole Lotta Shakin' Goin' On", made popular by Jerry Lee Lewis:[63] "I said shake it, baby, shake it." Be it in "*Sokkie Bokkie*", in "*Ons Land Suid-Afrika*" or in "*Die Son*", the combination of original words, borrowed melodic fragments and lyrics initially associated with these fragments, form a symbolic system that implies references to situations and people, which resonate with the listeners' experiences.

"*Die Goema Dans*"[64] by Abbassie Dramat was performed by the Malay Choir, Die Angeliere and the *Klops* the Kenfacs in 2006, both using a backtrack realised by Ismail Bey. It can be broken up into an introduction, five parts and an "outro" (coda). The introduction is based on "A Little Night Music" by Wolfgang Amadeus Mozart; the first part, like the fifth and the "outro", have probably been penned by the composer; the second part is taken from "Can't Take My Eyes Off You", a song by Bob Crewe and Bob Gaudio, made popular by Frankie Valli in 1967;[65] the third, from "All My Loving", by John Lennon and Paul McCartney, interpreted by the Beatles; the fourth part was based on "YMCA", a song by Henri Belolo, Jacques Morali and Victor Willis, sung by Village People. This *moppie*, which celebrated "*ghoema* pop music" explained how music "brought from across the sea" is "mixed with the local rhythm"; the result was a Cape Town creation illustrating the motto "Local is *lekker*" (local is nice, pleasant). The selection of a collection of international successes — one of the best known pieces of European "classical" music, along with pop hits from the 1960s and 1970s — emphasises the ability to appropriate famous tunes from overseas and to transform them into something local, demonstrating coloured people's contribution to a variegated modernity by inventing something new: a "*ghoema* pop music".

Adam Samodien was unquestionably one of the cleverest *moppie* composers of the late 20th century. His song "*Die Toyi Toyi*"[66] can be taken as an example of his skills. Composed in 1993, it described the political atmosphere of the times:

>*Ons lees in die koerante*   We read in the newspaper
>*Die Kaap is aan die brand*   The Cape is on fire
>*Ons sien op die TV*   We see on TV
>*Hoe brand die squatter kamp*   The squatter camps are burning
>*Die riot-squad was daar*   The riot squad was there
>*Om hulle uitmekaar te jaa*   To disperse them all

Adam Samodien complemented the depiction of dramatic events with considerations of everyday life, this time defusing its harshness with humour:

>*Eers het ons nie geworrie nie,*   Before we did not worry
>*Toe was alles tax free*   Then everything was tax free
>*Maar toe kom die GST, maar nou is die VAT*   But then came the GST,[67] and now it's the VAT[68]
>*VAT op coffee, VAT op tea,*   VAT on coffee, VAT on tea,
>*Daar's VAT op vleis and reis*   There's VAT on meat and rice
>*Maar niks op n' stompie nie*   But nothing on spliffs

Then he came back to events taking place in this turbulent period:

>*Hulle het uit die werk gebly*   The people did not go to work
>*Vir die twee dae stay away*   For a two days stay-away
>*COSATU het gesê dat hulle vrydag vol sal pay*   COSATU said all workers would get full pay
>*Die een jol voor met 'n flag in die hand*   One leads with flag in hand
>*Die anders kom agter aan*   All the others follow after him

With these words, Adam Samodien manages to paint a moment in a time of sudden changes. He uses words that relate immediately to his listeners' perceptions and therefore address the anxieties they feel, because they cannot foresee what will eventually come out of marches, strikes and increased taxes. But he soothes his audience by introducing a joke suggesting that whatever the government wants to impose (new taxes, for instance), people will always manage to find a way of escaping it (by smoking *stompies*, meaning butts of *dagga*, cannabis). This song met with large success in the 1994 carnival and was later interpreted in concert by various choirs. One of these choirs was the Young Tulips Sangkoor, whose coach, Anwar Gambeno, somewhat modified the words of the last verse. It begins with onomatopoeias usually associated with toyi-toying: "Hi, Hi/Ya Hi".[69] Adam Samodien gave his understanding of *toyi-toyi*:

> This people that are doing the *toyi-toyi*, they've got problems and they want to rectify, so they go in masses to the government or wherever they want to, to unions and things like that, to get their things right, they want more pay [...] They want less hour to work and things like that. Now they march with big banners, it says "the one is marching in front with a big banner or with a flag." You see the emotion and the feeling of the people doing the *toyi-toyi* is serious [...] The *toyi-toyi* comes from the African people. The *toyi-toyi* originated from the Africans but when it comes to *toyi-toyi*, you people might call it a strike [...] But we use a method that Africans use."[70]

To underline the black African element in the *moppie*, Adam Samodien used a part of "Meadowlands" by Strike Vilikazi "to give it a more African flavour" said Rashaad Malik, a long-time friend of Adam Samodien's.[71] "*Die Toyi Toyi*" illustrates the integrative function of humour, and consequently of *moppies*. The *toyi-toyi* "comes from the African people", but when it appears necessary to protest "we use a method that Africans use". Everybody is united in *toyi-toying*, a mingling musically highlighted by the inclusion of "Meadowlands", a song that was written to protest ambiguously against forced removals[72] at the time when the inhabitants of Sophiatown[73] were expelled.

"*Wilhemina die Moffie*"[74] was composed by Abduraghman Morris and sung by the Young Men Sporting Club in the 2015 Top Eight competition of the CMCB, where it won first prize. Although the song was still very fresh in the memory of the composer, he could not recall precisely from where he borrowed the various elements he assembled to compose it.[75] Abduraghman Morris remembered that he took something from a song performed by Californian pop-rock band, Maroon 5, but could not give its title, and it seems to have been so transformed in the *moppie* that it is no longer recognisable. Then he recycled parts from another very popular moppie, "*Joe se Barber*".[76] He also included segments of "Macarena";[77] of "Blurred Lines", composed by American singers and songwriters Robin Thicke and Pharrell Williams;[78] and of an old Afrikaans folk song, "*O Die Donkie*", which provided the basis for the words of the gimmick.[79] The original words: "*O die donkie/O die donkie/Die donkie is 'n wonderlike ding*" (Oh the donkey/Oh the donkey/The donkey is a wonderful [a very funny] thing) became in the *moppie*: "*O die moffie/O die moffie/Die moffie is 'n wonderlike ding*" (Oh the *moffie*/The *moffie*/The *moffie* is an amazing thing).[80] Finally Abduraghman Morris used a part from "an old Beatles' song", the title of which he has forgotten, probably "From Me to You".[81] Here again, a favourite *moppie* and an old Afrikaans folk song were mixed with international hits to suggest a vision of South Africa, and Cape Town, in which indigenous cultures are inserted into a world of globalised modernity.

The *ghoema* beat

Borrowed melodic fragments are adapted to the length of lines and verses. They also have to correspond to the *ghoema* beat, the most important characteristic of the repertoire. This rhythmic pattern is played on the *ghoema* drum, hence its name, although, as we have seen, it can also be expressed behind *nederlandsliedjies* by a banjo, a cello or a double bass. The *ghoema* beat carries a strong symbolic value. It is the heartbeat of the New Year festivals and means a lot to revellers and musicians, such as Ismail Dante:

> For me, the meaning of the *ghoema* means a lot of things. It gives you rhythm, it gives you inspiration to […] you just want to be with the thing, you know, you just want to be with the thing, the sound is so nice that you, every time you just want to have the *ghoema* in your hands and to play with it, because you're with the guitar and you hit the rhythm."[82]

*Ghoema*s conduct *Klopse* when they march in the streets and parade at stadia; they make lookers-on and spectators irresistibly move their bodies to its rhythm. The *ghoema* beat induces *tariek*, this altered state of consciousness where one feels free from all constraints, where everything seems possible. What may sound at first like a trifling rhythmic pattern generates extremely powerful sensations. This is probably the reason why it has become a symbol of the New Year festivals; a time when life begins again and is celebrated, in spite of the tribulations that it carries along. By extension, the *ghoema* beat has come to mean Cape Town musical cultures: a sonic blazon which all musicians, whatever their style or the genre they perform, introduce in their creations to evoke the "Mother City". It was the defining feature of a style of jazz which emerged in Cape Town during the 1980s, baptised "Cape Jazz", which provided the soundtrack of many anti-apartheid protest marches and meetings organised by the United Democratic Front (UDF) (Martin 2013: 241–242; Roubertie 2012: 87). The *ghoema* beat continues to bring momentum to *langarm*, to which many working class coloureds dance every weekend.[83] It has furnished the central topic of a successful musical by Taliep Petersen and David Kramer titled *Ghoema*, which revisits the history of Cape Town and especially of the slavery period.[84]

Rhythmic patterns

The *ghoema* drum (also *goema* or *gammie*) is a single-headed struck drum, hit alternately with both hands. It is made by assembling staves, which are maintained with metallic circles and covered at one end with a springbok (*antidorcas marsupialis*) skin. The shape of the *ghoema* drum reproduces that of wine barrels, which were used in the past to make the drums.

The *ghoema* beat can take various forms, which may be played during the same interpretation: the basic pattern is always enriched by variations. Anwar Gambeno, for instance, played the following formulas on *"Die Son"* during a practice recorded by Armelle Gaulier in 2006:

Intro

a)

or

or

b)

c)

On *"Die Toyi Toyi"*, he played:

a)

b)

or

c)

or ♩♩♩ ...etc

or ♩♩♩ ...etc

Instrumental conclusion: ♩♩♩ ...etc

These two examples show that the basic pattern of the *ghoema* beat is: . Played on the *ghoema* drum, it can also be expressed by a banjo. In "*Die Son*", for instance, the banjoist played:

a) ♩♩♩ ...etc

f) ♩♩♩ ...etc

c) ♩♩♩ ...etc

Orchestras backing Malay Choirs always include a *ghoema* drum. *Klopse*, and also Malay Choirs affiliated with the KTDMCB, use backtracks in which the sounds of drum kits and banjos are synthetically reproduced. The pattern played by the drum machine during the introduction of "*Die Goema Dans*", recorded during a rehearsal of the Kenfac *Klops* was:

Introduction:

♩♩♩ ...etc

then:

♩♩♩ ...etc

On fast tempi, the synthetised drum kit[85] actually played the following combination:

The transcription shows the presence of the pattern: ♩♩, which is one of the possible variations on the basic pattern: ♩♩. Ismail Bey, who realised the backtrack played during this rehearsal, always uses this pattern: "[When] you get to the fast part there is just one beat to it. If you listen to that [the rhythm played by the computer] you get the *ghoema* [...] So the whole of the *moppie* is based on that, it is built on that, you get your drum pattern that is the beat, because this is how I identify the *moppie* today. The beat, that beat."[86] The "musical identity" of the *moppie* resides in the rhythmic pattern:  or , repeated twice in a 4/4 bar. It is the indigenous basis that allows all sorts of borrowing and sets in motion the mechanism of appropriation: the transformation of what is "snatched" from an infinite number of sources into a musical form that is unmistakably Capetonian. Both *Klopse* and Malay Choirs play this pattern: it is clearly heard in *moppies*, and also underlies *nederlandsliedjies* sung by Malay Choirs.

Melody, countermelody and harmony

Among the instruments backing Malay Choirs, guitars and banjo have a particular role: they establish the melodic-harmonic foundations of the songs on the *ghoema* beat. They may also propose variations or countermelodies during the introduction or the conclusion. Violins have essentially a melodic function; they play in unison with the choir or draw a countermelody. *Klopse* backtracks usually include trumpets, which play the same role as the violins with the Malay Choirs; they can also interpolate short answers at the end of a phrase sung by the *pak*. The bass drives the harmony and plays the root note and the fifth of the succeeding chords. When *"Die Toyi Toyi"* was being rehearsed by the Young Tulips Sangkoor, the bass played the following line during the conclusion:[87]

On *"Queen van die Moffie"*, by Taliep Abrahams, recorded in 2006 by Armelle Gaulier during a rehearsal of the Spesbona *Klops*, the bass played:

Characteristics of *moppies*

The *ghoema* beat is the one element that musically identifies a song as a *moppie*; the bass line gives harmonic coherence to a melody built from bits and pieces and steadies the tempo. The banjo cements the base on which the choir can firmly stand by fusing the rhythmic pattern, the harmonic progression and the tempo. *Ghoema* drum, bass and banjo must lead the singers across tempo changes that are part and parcel of the performance of a *moppie*.

Another characteristic of *moppies* is that they encompass an alternation between fast and slow tempos. These variations do not obey any general rule and a change of tempo may or may not correspond to a transition to another melodic fragment. Composers generally try to keep the melodies they borrow recognisable; a change of tempo may make it easier for listeners. In the songs analysed for this study, we found at least two tempo changes, sometimes more, ranging from a slow 80 quarter-note beats per minute to a fast 176. In "*Queen van die Moffie*", for instance, the beginning, the end and a middle part are sung to the "reference tempo", but there are two intermediate parts which rely on slower tempos:

a), b), c) ♩=160
d) [1] ♩=108
d) [2] ♩=160
e) ♩=112
f) instrumental conclusion: ♩=160

Anwar Gambeno insists on the importance of these changes. They give the performance a stronger momentum and make the song more attractive. They invite audiences to listen more attentively to the words, and facilitate a better understanding of their message.[88]

The structure of *moppies*

There are no fixed rules pertaining to the internal organisation of *moppies*; it varies greatly according to the composer's ingenuity. However, a careful analysis of a selected number of *moppies* showed that a common general structure can be brought to light. The following table is an attempt to describe this structure. It must be understood as an "ideal type", which is actualised in many different versions in competitions when composers, coaches and choirs want to distinguish themselves from other contenders. The same song may also be performed with different structures at different stages of the competition, or at successive competitions.

Formal structure	Harmonic progression	Tempo changes	Voices
Introduction: Instruments and voices	‖: I-IV-V-I-IV-V-I :‖ (repeated x times)	Slow or fast tempo	unison
Part A	⁄⁄.	Fast tempo	unison
Part B	⁄⁄.	Fast tempo	unison
Part C	⁄⁄.	Slow tempo and/or modulation	Harmonisation of vocal parts (to the third, the fourth, the fifth, etc.)
Part D (may include the *gimmick**)	‖: I-V-I-V :‖ (repeated x times)	Slow tempo	Call and answer: soloist/ *pak*
Part B	‖: I-V-I-V :‖ (repeated x times)	Fast tempo	unison
Conclusion or "*outro*": instruments and voices; instruments	‖: I-IV-V-I-IV-V-I :‖ (repeated x times)	Fast tempo	Harmonisation of vocal parts (to the third, the fourth, the fifth, etc.)

**gimmick* : see below, pp. 164–166

Moppies are sung by a soloist and the *pak* in a call-and-answer format. The solo parts are not fixed: their length may vary, as well as the moment when the soloist comes in. The instrumental "outro" is always played in Malay Choirs competitions, but may be omitted by *Klopse*, who are usually asked not to stay on stage too long. A good example is "*Die Goema Dans*": when rehearsed by the Malay Choir Die Angeliere, it ended on an instrumental conclusion, which the Kenfac *Klops* did not play.

Verses

In the chart given above, the various parts identified as A, B, C, etc. correspond to different melodic fragments. Each part may include one or several verses. The length of verses may vary within the same song and melodic phrases do not necessarily have the same bar structure. Lines must be rhymed, yet rhymes may be changed within a verse, and are not always placed at the end of lines. "*Joe Se Barber*" (Joe the Hairdresser), a *moppie* composed by Taliep Abrahams, was sung in 2007 by the Spesbona *Klops*;[89] the F part includes three verses (bold type and underlining in the text of the lyrics indicate consonances and alliterations; capitals at the end of a verse signal rhymes):

*Festive **sea**son bly **die** plek V**O**L*	During the Festive Season the place stays busy
***D**ie (queue) is so lank jy sal sw**ee**r d**aa**rs 'n J**O**L*	The line is so long you'd swear there's a party
*Twee speak**er**s by **die d**eur music klop d**aar d**EER*	Two speakers at the door bellow music violently
***D**ie b**er**gies dans d**aar** voor **d**EUR*	The tramps are dancing at the door
*As jy se **d**at jy nou pension krY*	If you say you get a pension
*Sal hy jou h**are** vir half prYs snY*	He will cut your hair half price
*Jou b**aa**rt sk**eu**r hy vern**I**ET*	Your beard he shaves for you
*M**aa**r (war) jy net moet w**I**ET*	But what you should know
Jou pension boekie moet hy sien	Your pension book he must see
*Boeta Joe se hy's kl**aa**r en ged**AA**N*	Bra Joe says he's completely exhausted
*Hy's moeg van heeldag op sy voete st**AA**N*	He's tired of being on his feet all day
*'n mens voel somtyds fl**O**U*	And sometimes one feels like fainting
***D**aarom moet Ta J**O**E sy voete in w**a**rm water h**O**U"*	That's why he has to soak his feet in warm water

As can be seen in the transcription, this part includes melodic variations. The melody has been "snatched" by Taliep Abrahams from a song of which he does not remember the title. He adapted it to fit the words of each verse, as obvious in bars 11 and 15. The corresponding lines are constructed according to a metre different from the first verse:

Fe-stive-seas-on-bly-die-plek-vol	= octosyllable
Die (queue)-is-so-lank-jy-sal-sweer-daar-s 'n-jol	= decasyllable
Twee-spea-kers-by-die-deur	= hexasyllable
mu-sic-klop-daar-deer	= pentasyllable
Die-ber-gies-dans-daar-voo-r-deur	= octosyllable

The organisation of rhymes is not fixed: it can follow an aabb pattern, as in the first and third verses, or an aabbc as in the second. Some lines do not even rhyme with others. There are obvious plays on consonances and alliterations, which are often intended to produce a comic effect[90]. In the present example, one can notice alliterations in **s / z , i , d** and consonances with the sounds: er, aar, oor. Verses can be strung together in various fashions. The singers may stop at the end of a verse and leave the orchestra or the backtrack to play by themselves during one bar, as was the case in "*Joe Se Barber*"; the soloist may also fill in the gap between two verses, as in "*Ons Hoor*";[91] finally, the soloist and the *pak* may sing together a bar *a capella* between two verses, as in "*Fiesta Tyd*".[92]

Choral parts

Singers are grouped together according to the range of their voice. When using Western terminology, coaches distinguish between tenors, second tenors, first bass and second bass. However, the arrangements of *moppies* do not always separate the voices, for they sing mostly in unison. When they sing in harmony, they usually sing chords by fourths, by thirds or by fifths. In the recording of "*Ons Hoor*", several intervals can be noticed (the lines at the top of the transcription represent the interplay between the voices and illustrate the technique of dovetailing (see below):

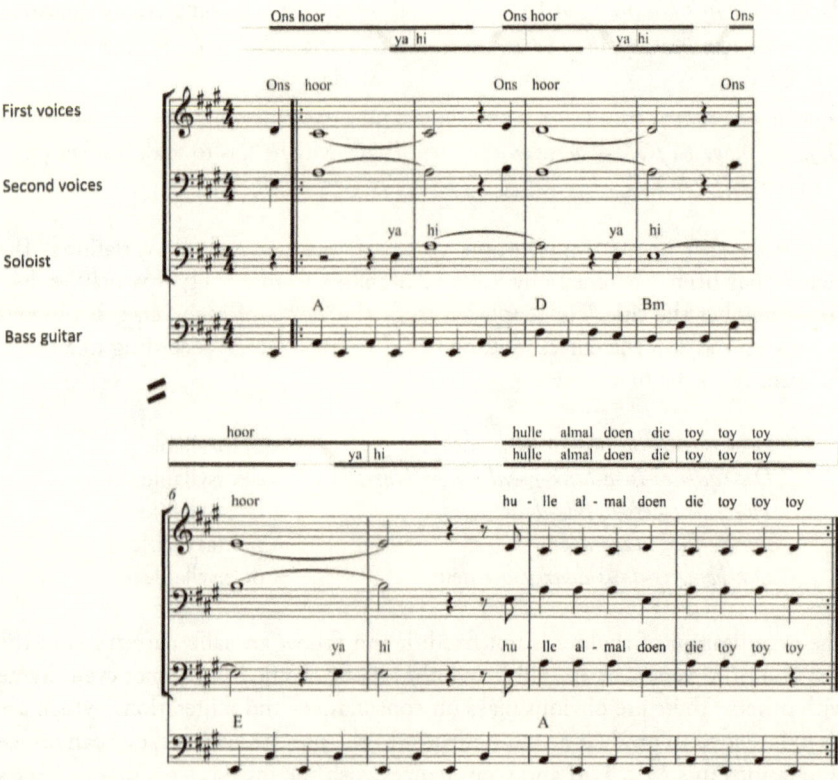

The transcription highlights the various intervals used in the polyphony: perfect fifth, major second, minor third or major seventh. It also shows that voices move mostly in homorhythm, even if there are short episodes of counterpoint. Each coach has his own method to teach his choir the various parts of a song. Shawn

Petersen, for instance, begins by teaching the main voice to all the singers in the choir, then he harmonises it. Anwar Gambeno hears the different parts in his head and teaches them to the singers he has organised according to their range. Adam Samodien works with his wife: he asks her to sing the melody, while he tries several harmonisations and records them on cassettes. Another technique frequently used in *moppies* is dovetailing: this consists of the swapping and overlapping of voices; the soloist and sections in the *pak* alternate without a gap. While a section in the *pak* or the soloist is finishing a musical phrase, another group of voices begins to sing and then continues when the first group has stopped. It can clearly be seen in the following transcription of a recording of "*Die Goema Dans*" by Abbassie Dramat made during the 2006 competitions of the CMCB:

Usually, one or two parts of a *moppie* feature dovetailing; this creates a momentary effect of complementarity and continuity which, alternating with passages in homorhythm, underlines the collective ethos that underpins the singing of comic songs. A coach who arranges a *moppie* is free to make use of various techniques, such as the ones described above, but he must adapt them to the voices and singing abilities of the choir or *Klops* members. The Fabulous Woodstock Starlites participated in both the Malay Choirs and the *Klopse* competitions; this is why, even when they appeared as a *Klops*, they comprised only male singers. When they rehearsed, singers were placed in a semi-circle and grouped according to their range: tenors, second tenors, first and second basses. Selected members of the choirs acted as section leaders and assisted the coach. The coach insisted on a good balance of timbres and adjusted the different parts in order to achieve the sound that fitted the song best. He sang to each section the part they had to interpret, while pointing to the words written on a board hanging from the wall of the *klopskamer*. If the singers "got lost", the coach played the backtrack and sang over it the part they had forgotten. The coach of the Spesbona *Klops* worked differently. The group was more important than the Woodstock Starlites and he used a microphone to address singers. At the beginning of the rehearsal all the singers sang in unison, with sometimes a second voice at an interval of a third. The singers were mixed; they included men and women, girls and boys, and their position did not seem to depend on their range. The Woodstock Starlites and the Spesbona are but two examples of the type or organisation adopted during practices; there are indeed many others. Arrangements will also depend on the composition of the choir and the singers' skills. It is obvious that they will differ if the choir is mixed or comprises exclusively males. Similarly, musicians adapt their parts to the choir they play with and transpose when necessary.

Gimmick and body movements

One of the important parts of a *moppie* is called the "gimmick"; many coaches assume that the singularity of the gimmick plays a decisive role in the assessment judges make of the performance of a *moppie*. The gimmick must introduce an element of surprise and make the audience laugh. "*Die Son*", composed by Anwar Gambeno in 2005, provides a very good example of gimmick. It is musically based on "Whole Lotta Shakin' Goin' On"; referring to Elvis Presley's version. Anwar Gambeno took the catch-phrase: "I said shake it, baby, shake it" and replaced it with "Shaik Zuma Shaik"; on stage, the whole body of the soloist emulated Elvis Presley's antics. He explained that he was inspired by the phonetic closeness of "Shaik" and "shake", which he found quite amusing and thought he could use it to make a particularly sensational gimmick:[93]

Ou Shaik is daai ou, hy sê hy's van die A.N.C	Shaik is a big shot, he says he's from the ANC
(Shaik Zuma Shaik Shaik Zuma)	(Shaik Zuma Shaik Shaik Zuma)
Die Son vra Mo vir wie het hy die brood gegee	*Die Son* asks Mo[94] whom he gave the dough to
(Shaik Zuma Shaik Shaik Zuma)	(Shaik Zuma Shaik Shaik Zuma)
Hy sê hyt 'n vriend, hy het geen antwood nie	He says he's got a friend but he's got no answer
Zuma sê Shaik het hom niks gegee	Zuma says Shaik gave him nothing
(Shaik Zuma Shaik Shaik Zuma)	(Shaik Zuma Shaik Shaik Zuma)
Hy is net skuldig as die hof hom nov straf jee	He is only guilty if the court finds so
(Shaik Zuma Shaik Shaik Zuma)	(Shaik Zuma Shaik Shaik Zuma)
Maar hy's nie meer in onse Parlement nie	But he is no longer in our Parliament
En ons sê, Shaik Zuma Shaik (x4)	And we say, Shaik Zuma Shaik

A few years later, as the Schabir Shaik affair was no longer in the news, Anwar Gambeno decided to change the gimmick and to poke fun at an old-time friend, Melvyn Matthews, chief executive officer of Kaapse Klopse Karnaval Association, who also sings with Anwar Gambeno's Cape Traditional Singers. The composer explained that, in the *moppie* spirit, laughing at a friend amounts to paying him tribute. The new words were:

Ou boeta[95] Mellie wat het jy gemaak?	Brother Mellie, what have you done?
Die Son het jou gevang is jy dan vaak	*Die Son* has caught you, were you asleep
Allie mense staan nou op (nou op)	All the people are now rising to their feet (to their feet)
Hulle was soe diep geskok (geskok)	They were so shocked (shocked)
Ou Mellie skree "hou nou op" (hou op)	Old Mellie shouts "stop it!" (stop it!)
My vrou gat my nou uitskop (uitskop)	My wife's gonna kick me out (kick me out)
Toe hy byrie huis ankom (ankom)	When he got home (got home)
Was sy vrou soe dom vestom (vestom)	His wife was so dumbfounded (dumbfounded)
Slaan hom met 'n biesemstock	She chased him with a broom
Ja ou Mellie bly ma dom	Yes, old Mellie stays thickheaded

Dom, dom, dom, Dom dom, dom	Stupid, stupid, stupid, stupid, stupid, stupid
Daar was 'n hele skelery	There was a big argument
(kyk hoe haloep Mellie,	(see how Mellie runs,
kyk hoe haloep Mellie)	see how Mellie runs)
Toe Mellie op die frontpage daar veskyn	When Mellie appeared on the front page
(kyk hoe haloep Mellie,	(see how Mellie runs,
kyk hoe haloep Mellie)	see how Mellie runs)
Hulle het hom in die Main Road nous sien ry	They saw him driving along Main Road[96]
Toe sê Die Son hy het met a moffie gevry	So *Die Son* said he had been making love to a moffie

Other examples of gimmicks are the inclusion of excerpts of "La Bamba" in "*Fiesta Tyd*" by Ismail Dante and the reference to *toyi-toyi* in "*Die Toyi Toyi/Ons Hoor*". In a gimmick, the song from which borrowings have been made should remain identifiable and the relationship between the melody, the original words and the new words constitute one of the mechanisms on which the comic of the *moppie* is based.

When performing a *moppie*, singers dance to attract the attention of the audience. Choirs now tend to develop sophisticated choreographies involving everyone, but the soloist still plays an important role. He has to bring forward the comic in the song, both by his singing (choice of timbre and range, stops and new departures that should not break the song's momentum) and his body language that still includes hand movements (made more visible by wearing white gloves) inherited from 19th-century blackface minstrels. The words are brought to life through his performance: The soloist has to be funny and to imagine antics embodying the text. In "*Die Vlooie*"[97] (The Fleas) by Adam Samodien, he wriggles and scratches endlessly where fleas are supposed to have bitten him. According to Ismail Dante, the soloist may move as he feels it, but he must mime the *moppie*. Mujait Booysen, who was a soloist with the Kenfacs, explained: "You have to carry over the comic, for the *ghoema* dance you have to show the dance [...] You can't really explain what is going to happen."[98] That is, the soloist may improvise his movements on stage, keeping in mind his role as mediator between the song and the audience. However, his moves are usually finalised during practices, the more so since they now have to match the *pak*'s choreography. In every case, both the singers in the *pak* and the soloist must always follow the tempo. In "*Die Son*", the soloist "is" at the beginning the boy who sells the tabloid in the streets and shouts the main titles:

Ons sien 'n laatie staan op die hoek stan en rook	We see a youngster standing smoking at the corner
Hy is die laatie wat die koerante verkoep	He is the youngster that sells the newspapers
Hy skree, Die Son, die skinder koerant!	He shouts *Die Son*, the gossip newspaper
Ja, jy kan jou mind opmaak	Yes you can make up your mind
Die Son sien nou alles raak	*Die Son* now sees everything
Dis laat die mense praat	It makes the people talk
Die Son, Die Son, die skinder koerant	*Die Son, Die Son*, the gossip newspaper

Comes the gimmick, he shakes his whole body and moves his legs in a parody of Elvis Presley's stage attitudes. In "*Die Toyi Toyi/Ons Hoor*", he dances the *toyi-toyi*, leads the protest march and pretends to smoke when he proclaims: "*Daar's VAT op vleis and reis/Maar niks op n' stompie nie*" (There's VAT on meat and rice/But nothing on spliffs).

Yet, from the point of view of the adjudicators, the role of the *voorsinger* is very important, not so much because of the way he "dances" the song, but rather because of the way he sings and establishes his relationship to the choir. Felicia Lesch,[99] who used to adjudicate the Cape Malay Choir Board competitions, explained:

> We don't judge the antics of the lead singer. You know what happened? There was a time when the lead singer focused entirely on the judging panel, only looked at us, never looked at the audience, never connected with the audience and the antics became suggestive and just too horrible, too lewd to look at, and there were small children in the audience and we found it was inappropriate. There were sexual overtones because of the lyrics and then, the rest of the choral singing disappeared behind the antics. Then we had a workshop and we [the judges] explained that we are really not interested that much in what the *voorsinger* does, we want the choir to be a unit, and what they do has to be supporting the *voorsinger*. The *voorsinger* must have a voice. If the *moppie* is solely a choir and the *voorsinger* always only sings with the choir and you don't hear him singing his solo, then that's not a good *moppie*. We need to know that the *voorsinger* can sing and that he can do the leading and that the choir can follow him, and the rhythmic changes, you know, they do it so naturally, what other choirs would struggle with, they fall in so naturally, from slow into fast, into the *ghoema* rhythm, it just flows from one to the other [...] we do judge the balance of

the choir because sometimes the choir gets excited and then the voices get louder and they shout and then we can't hear what they are saying. So we do expect them to still articulate [...] The choir and the soloist MUST be as one. They MUST stick to the theme of the *moppie*. If the *moppie* is not comic, it gets a low mark, even if it was really well sung.[100]

No copyright on *moppies*, yet?

With reference to *moppies*, the notions of author and composer are largely irrelevant; most artists involved in creating *moppies* remain anonymous, although some songs may continue to be associated with the group that performed them. Sometimes the name of the composer of a song, which has been extremely successful with audiences and has won several awards, is remembered (Omar Adams with "*Mavis van Bishop Lavis*"; Adam Samodien with "*Die Toyi Toyi/Ons Hoor*"; Anwar Gambeno with "*Die Son*"). Composers themselves used to consider that once a song had been sung, it was *passé*: they had to concentrate on writing new *moppies*. Adam Samodien confessed that he did not systematically keep the texts of his own compositions. Rashaad Malick explained: "When they've done them, the merit is gone [laughs]" and Adam Samodien added: "Because [...] the compositions was for the love of the sport, I never had the idea of compiling all those things."[101]

Composers of *moppies* get paid by choirs and *Klopse* in their capacity as coaches who prepare the performance. As a matter of fact, when they are hired to coach the *moppie* item, it implies in most cases that they will provide the song. When the coach is also the leader of the group, he obviously writes the *moppie* that will be entered into competition. However, a *moppie* composed by a coach may be used by other teams, *Klopse* or choirs, the same year or later. The teams who "cover" a successful *moppie* "buy it or they get permission to use it. They have to find out who's not using it, but they don't really bother."[102] *Moppie* composers are aware that they work with musical material that is, in most cases, copyrighted, and know that "snatching" bits of melody from commercially circulated songs could raise a few problems, although the practice of borrowing pre-dates by many decades the discovery that there are laws and regulations defining artistic property rights. Ismail Dante explained:

We borrow the tune from different songs, because if you're gonna use the whole thing, the whole musical thing, then people can put in trouble, because you're using their tune, their melody. Now, if you break away from that melody and put in another melody, from then on to another melody, they can't say it's their melody.[103]

As a matter of fact, it seems that no complaint has ever been lodged against *moppie* composers for their use of copyrighted melodies, probably because since *moppies* are not commercially circulated and have hardly been recorded; they are not visible on the international landscape of commercial music. Moreover, legal suits may eventually prove too costly since *moppies* do not generate any profit. In the other direction, there is at least one example of a Cape Town traditional song that has been "snatched" by commercial pop musicians. *"Daar Kom die Alibama"*, the anonymous anthem of the New Year festivals (Martin 1999: 83-84), which appeared at the end of the 19th century has been and still is played in Cape Town in many various ways by white and coloured bands and singers. It appeared on a Boney M album titled *Ten Thousand Lightyears*[104] under the name "The Alibama", and was credited to Sandy Davis, Frank Farian and Reyam.[105] The corresponding video clip seems to have been removed from YouTube,[106] although a version of the same song, including only the calendar part of *"Daar Kom Die Alibama"* (*"Januarie-Februarie-March"*), still appears on the CD *Kalimba de Luna*[107] under the title "The Calendar Song", attributed this time to Frank Farian[108] alone, and this version can be seen on YouTube.[109]

The intrusion of international show business in the world of the Cape Town New Year festivals — *"Daar Kom Die Alibama"* is but one example, others may wait to be discovered — has heightened the awareness of benefits that could accrue from composing and copyrighting songs and could change the attitude of *moppie* composers, and even transform the way they are conceived. Until now, a successful *moppie* brought its creator prestige and fame, which usually did not last long, but could lead to a reputation as a clever composer. A few songs could linger on while the name of their tunesmith was forgotten. What was produced for the New Year festivals belonged to them and did not cross any borders; the songs remained aloof from the universe of business and royalties. Today, in a world governed by competition and profit, which the "new" South Africa gladly entered after 1994, beauty for its own sake, pleasure brought by the "sport", prestige and reputation may not be enough to motivate the production of *moppies*. The youngest of the songsters we interviewed, Waseef Piekaan, who pursues a successful career as an actor and stand-up comedian, has other ambitions:

> At the end of the day this is a sport, but it's also a business. Like the *Kaapse Klopse* is a business [...] Now a guy like me who is coaching must still be paid, but I'm not at that level where I will say I'm doing this only to be paid, I will do it but like everybody else I have expenses, I must get from point A to point B, so I must get something out of it [...] But in truth, truth is that it does not matter about the money. Because in truth, if there was not any

money, I would coach comics, I would sing comics, because I love doing it, you know, I love to put a tune together [However] I want to write a moppie that is going to be an original song, an original moppie. None of the tunes is going to be used from any song: my own compositions all the way through. Once we achieved that on a moppie song, even on a nederlands song, if you write your own nederlands, or anything that's involved with the Kaapse Klopse, combine also, if you write an original piece of music, it becomes your piece of music, and that piece of music can then be registered and then it can be played on the radio.

Waseef Piekaan elaborated: when a choir sings a *moppie*, they sing twenty tunes with original words. According to the present system of copyright, such as applied by SAMRO (Southern African Music Rights Organisation), royalties should be paid to twenty different composers, which of course neither *Klopse* nor Malay Choirs can afford.

> That's how we do it, but that's not right. According to how the system works, how SAMRO works and all these music people work, it's not right. So if we can then write a moppie that is original, that is your tune, and it's viby, and it's lekker, and it's got this banjo, and you've got the outjies [chaps, fellows] singing in the background, then we are going to be successful, and we can copyright it, it can be played on the radio, covered by other bands [...] That is what I want to achieve in my lifetime still. Within the next two or three years, it's my ambition to change the face of moppie for all times, so that we can have moppies played on the radio, not just pop songs [...] We have to progress with time. So for example, I wrote a moppie, that happened last year, it was my moppie, five or six teams, on our very stadium, was singing the same moppie that we were singing, and then two on the other stadium was singing the moppie that I wrote, and then on another stadium there was another two singing that same moppie. Now we were competing against ourselves, I was competing against myself about eight times[110] [...] But now, if I had copyrights on that moppie, if I had registered that moppie and I went so far, I could have gone to that choirs and say "You cannot sing that moppie".[111]

Waseef Piekaan's projects do not seem to have materialised yet, but if he, or someone else, were to realise them, it would alter the whole notion of comic songs to a point where it will no longer be possible to speak of *moppies*, but where they will become the equivalent of Trinidad's calypsos. His dream may not be shared by many of his colleagues, and even less by the leaders of *Klopse* associations and

Malay Choir boards. However, he articulates a new desire for recognition and the material gains that could go with it. His ambitions manifest the impact on the world of the New Year festivals of conceptions and ways of doing coming from globalised entertainment, already transformed by widespread internet practices.

* * *

The manner in which *moppies* are created is not exceptional. They represent a case of transforming appropriation, something that has been practised by musicians in every era, in every genre — popular and "highbrow" — and in a multiplicity of forms. What is unique about Cape Town comic songs is the combination of borrowing ("snatching") melodic fragments from already existing songs, of assembling and reorganising them so that they fit a particular rhythm pattern (the *ghoema* beat), and associating them with original lyrics in colloquial Afrikaans. By using these combined techniques, *moppie* com-posers achieve coherence; they avoid discontinuity by adjusting their "snatches" so that the way they are stitched together allows listeners to perceive them as wholes, while some of their component parts remain recognisable. *Moppies* demand artistry and skill; these talents are geared towards producing a comic effect: the songs must be funny, they must make listeners laugh, whatever the topic they deal with. But there is seriousness behind the comic. The funniness of *moppies* alludes to realities that have to be acknowledged, and sometimes confronted, and the song's humour often carries more or less implicitly a serious message. This is what we would now like to turn to. After describing the creative processes through which *moppies* are produced, we will now focus on the content of the songs and on what they may convey.

Notes

1. See pp. 155–157.
2. In this chapter and the following, we discuss *moppies* on the basis of detailed studies of two overlapping corpuses of songs. Armelle Gaulier collected several songs during practices preceding the 2007 competitions and was given recordings of songs performed earlier. She decided to analyse *moppies* performed both by *Klopse* (members of the Kaapse Klopse Karnival Association, KKKA, or the Kaapse Klopse Association, KKA) and by Malay Choirs and selected those which were frequently mentioned in interviews she conducted with coaches. In these interviews, she asked composers to provide translations of the lyrics and had these translations checked by an expert in order to avoid misinterpretations. Denis-Constant Martin gathered the words, or parts of the words, of more than seventy *moppies*, collected from their authors during interviews conducted in 2011 or reproduced in Armelle Gaulier's MA dissertation (2007) and from Anne Marieke van der Wal (2009), who herself reprinted several old songs from ID du Plessis' collection (1935). Paul Sedres translated these lyrics into English and has also been of invaluable assistance in explaining some of the innuendos and allusions they contained and in identifying the original sources of the melodies. We wish to express our utmost gratitude to Paul Sedres, who has always been ready to help us in our investigations and oftentimes provided information and advice, without which we would not have been able to conduct our research.
3. "L'ironie humoresque […] fait allusion au sérieux impalpable de l'apparence: l'ironie plaisante, mais dans sa moquerie on lit la vérité à livre ouvert; et l'humoriste joue, lui aussi, seulement son sérieux est infiniment lointain […] L'interprétation de l'humour a donc trois niveaux à franchir: il faut comprendre la farce qui est dans la simulation sérieuse, puis le sérieux profond qui est dans cette moquerie, et enfin le sérieux impondérable qui est dans ce sérieux."
4. "Rire, c'est dire qu'on n'est pas seul, qu'on est multiple."
5. "Le collectif se réjouit d'être ensemble et de se maintenir."
6. "Le comique, la puissance du rire est dans le rieur et nullement dans l'objet du rire." Baudelaire, Charles (1884) De l'essence du rire. In *Curiosités esthétiques*, tome 2. Paris: Calmann-Lévy. p. 370. See: http://baudelaire.litteratura.com/ressources/pdf/oeu_27.pdf [accessed 23 November 2011]; quoted in: Jeanson 1950: 59.
7. "il faut concevoir le rire comme étant à la fois intentionnel et spontané. C'est dire qu'en dehors de l'intention qui le commande, on ne saurait pas plus lui trouver des *causes* que des *raisons*, mais seulement des occasions, des prétextes, et tout au plus des *motivations* […] je ne ris pas *à cause* d'un événement *en lui-même comique*: je ris selon une certaine intention, et, ce faisant, *je me fais apparaître comique* l'événement *à propos duquel* je ris" (italics in the original).
8. Adam Samodien and Rashaad Malick, interview with Denis-Constant Martin, Woodstock, 12 October 2011; Abubakar Davids, quoted in Van der Wal 2009: 87.
9. Christine Winberg quotes Du Plessis 1935: 41.
10. In the 18th and 19th centuries, the usual vehicular language at the Cape included many elements from Malay languages, some of which have been retained in contemporary Afrikaaps (Davids 2011).
11. *The Cape Times*, 4 January, 1886.
12. Winberg, Christine (1992) The 'Ghoemaliedjies' of the Cape Muslims: Remnants of a slave culture. Unpublished paper, University of Cape Town, quoted in Bickford-Smith 1994: 302.
13. Anwar Gambeno, interview with Denis-Constant Martin, Mitchells Plain, 11 October 2011.
14. Ismail Dante, interview with Armelle Gaulier, Mitchells Plain, 7 September 2006.

15. The main square in Cape Town.
16. Shawn Pettersen, interview with Armelle Gaulier, Cape Town, 3 October 2006.
17. Melvyn Matthews, in Gamja Dante and Melvyn Matthews, interview with Denis-Constant Martin, Victoria and Alfred Waterfront, 17 October 2011.
18. Abduraghman Morris, interview with Denis-Constant Martin, Colorado Park, 21 April 2015.
19. Two pieces of wood rhythmically banged together, a legacy from the blackface minstrels.
20. Michael Abrahams, in Michael Abrahams, Ronald Fisher and Eddie Matthews, interview with Armelle Gaulier, Mitchells Plain, 11 October 2006.
21. Many of them have been fascinated by *Drumline*, a movie showcasing American high school and college marching bands, directed by Charles Stone III, USA, 2002.
22. Eddie Matthews, in Michael Abrahams, Ronald Fisher and Eddie Matthews, interview with Armelle Gaulier, Mitchells Plain, 11 October 2006.
23. Ismail Bey, interview with Armelle Gaulier, Rocklands, Mitchells Plain, 23 September 2006.
24. Anwar Gambeno, interview with Armelle Gaulier, Mitchells Plain, 11 October 2006.
25. Anwar Gambeno, interview with Armelle Gaulier, Mitchells Plain, 11 October 2006.
26. Tape Jacobs, interview with Armelle Gaulier, Mitchells Plain, 9 August 2006.
27. The largest commercial mall in Cape Town, patronised by South Africans and foreigners.
28. Gamja Dante is today over 80 years old; Ismail Dante passed away in 2012, aged over 70; Adam Samodien was born in 1935, and Rashaad Malick is several decades younger.
29. To compose comes from Old French *composer* "put together, arrange, write" a work (12c.), from *com-* "with" + *poser* "to place"; from Late Latin *pausare* "to cease, lay down" and *cum* "with". Available at http://www.etymonline.com/index.php?term=compose [accessed 18 September 2015].
30. Anwar Gambeno, interview with Denis-Constant Martin, Mitchells Plain, 11 October 2011.
31. Adam Samodien, in Adam Samodien and Rashaad Malick, interview with Denis-Constant Martin, Woodstock, 12 October 2011; Ismail and Gamja Dante, interview with Denis-Constant Martin, Hanover Park, 20 October 2011.
32. Crystal methamphetamine, also known as crystal meth. Available at https://www.unodc.org/unodc/en/frontpage/tik-meth-in-cape-town.html [accessed 27 February 2015].
33. Taliep Abrahams, interview with Armelle Gaulier, Mitchells Plain, 18 September 2006.
34. *Sokkie* hints at *sakkie-sakkie*, a dance to the rhythm of *vastrap*, very popular among patrons of *langarm* functions (balls traditionally held by coloured people); various types of music, reorganised to fit the *vastrap* rhythm, can be used to dance the *sakkie-sakkie*. In the present case, *sokkie* signals an international modernity seamlessly inserted in chorographical and musical practices with deep local roots. *Bokkie* literally means small antelope; it is used here in the sense of "baby", "darling".
35. Waseef Piekaan, interview with Denis-Constant Martin, Mitchells Plain, 25 October 2011.
36. Anwar Gambeno, interview with Denis-Constant Martin, Mitchells Plain, 11 October 2011.
37. Waseef Piekaan, interview with Denis-Constant Martin, Mitchells Plain, 25 October 2011.
38. Ismail and Gamja Dante, interview with Denis-Constant Martin, Hanover Park, 20 October 2011.
39. Gamja Dante, in Gamja Dante and Melvyn Matthews, interview with Denis-Constant Martin, Victoria and Alfred Waterfront, 17 October 2011. Gamja Dante's description of his technique may seem a bit fuzzy. Like many of his colleagues, he finds it difficult to put into words what he does very easily and very cleverly because he has never benefitted from any formal music education. Yet, his talent and his skill have made him one of the most respected *moppie* composers. In order to analyse more precisely how *moppie* composers work, it would be necessary to select a corpus of *moppies*, identify all melodic borrowings, compare the way they are inserted in *moppies* with the original melodies, chord structures and rhythms of the songs from which they have been "snatched", and eventually to come out with a

"transformation model". This has not been possible in the present work, but it does suggest a fascinating direction for further research.

40. Anwar Gambeno, interviews with Denis-Constant Martin, Mitchells Plain, 4 December 2001 and 11 October 2011.
41. Felicia Lesch, interview with Denis-Constant Martin, Stellenbosch, 7 October 2011.
42. Taliep Abrahams, interview with Armelle Gaulier, Mitchells Plain, 21 September 2006.
43. Following the passing by Parliament in November 2006 of the Civil Union Act authorising the marriage of same-sex couples, the new version of the moppie says: "*Moffie kyk wat gaan aan wat gaan aan/Dis in die skinder koerant skinder koerant/Dis wettig nou in ons land/ 'n man kan trou met 'n nogge man man man man*" [*Moffie*, look what's happening, what's happening/ It's in the gossip paper, gossip paper/It's legal now in our country/A man can marry another man, man, man, man].
44. Ismail Bey, interview with Armelle Gaulier, Rocklands, Mitchells Plain, 23 September 2006.
45. Abduraghman Morris, interview with Denis-Constant Martin, Colorado Park, 21 April 2015.
46. A popular Neapolitan song (lyrics by Peppino Turco; music by Luigi Denze), composed in 1880 to celebrate the opening of the first cable car — *funicolare* — on Mount Vesuvio; recently made famous worldwide by Luciano Pavarotti and the Three Tenors.
47. Shawn Pettersen, interview with Armelle Gaulier, Cape Town, 3 October 2006.
48. Born Richard Steven Valenzuela, Ritchie Valens (1941–1959) was an American singer and guitar player who is considered as one of the pioneers of Rock and Roll; he also paved the way for Chicano Rock. His greatest hit was "La Bamba", based on a Mexican folk song, which he recorded in 1958. He died in a plane crash in 1959, aged only 17. The film *La Bamba*, directed by Luis Valdez, starring Lou Diamond Phillips as Ritchie Valens, was released in 1987.
49. *The South African Spectator*, 4 May 1901.
50. A hymn written by John Newton, captain of a slave ship, following a vow made during a tempest. In the 20th century, this song became a favourite in African-American churches and was sung by demonstrators during the civil rights movement in the 1950s and 1960s.
51. The lyrics are included in: Part Three Appendix: "*Moppie* Lyrics".
52. Waseef Piekaan, interview with Denis-Constant Martin, Mitchells Plain, 25 October 2011.
53. http://www.youtube.com/watch?v=KSnda5-o654 [accessed 18 February 2013].
54. http://www.youtube.com/watch?v=oLlIlJPTMkw [accessed 18 February 2013].
55. http://www.youtube.com/watch?v=M0YXQnNSfNE [accessed 18 February 2013].
56. http://www.youtube.com/watch?v=Igh5aldPLI4 [accessed 18 February 2013].
57. http://www.youtube.com/watch?v=ekAXPCphKXQ [accessed 18 February 2013].
58. *Kwela* was a musical genre featuring pennywhistles (tin flutes). It was invented in the 1950s by urban young black Africans who mixed various South African elements (Tswana music for reed pipes, Zulu music for flageolet), with imported American elements on a steady swing beat (Allen 1999).
59. *Mbaqanga* (*umbaqanga* in isiZulu means a thick cornmeal porridge) is a generic term that covers a wide array of black African popular music genres, based on a basic chord progression (usually I-IV-V-I on a four bars cycle) played in the 1960s and later.
60. The first verse of "A Golden Dream" is: "America, spread your golden wings/Sail on freedom's wind, across the sky/Great bird, with your golden dreams/flying high, flying high".
61. This *moppie* speaks of the popular daily Afrikaans tabloid newspaper, *Die Son* (*The Sun*), which was modelled after British tabloids and first published in 2005. Its provocative headlines, humorous language and sharp twists of phrases provide a mix of comic fodder, information and gossip. More than any other mainstream publication it dares to use the "Kombuis Afrikaans" (Lit. "Kitchen Afrikaans", a creolised, patois mixing Afrikaans and English) spoken by a large sector of the coloured population in Cape Town. It soon outsold

all other newspapers in South Africa, even emerging as a relevant node of influence in topical debates about cultural identity, especially among the coloured population (Paul Sedres, personal communication to Denis-Constant Martin). The lyrics are included in: Part Three Appendix: "*Moppie* Lyrics".

62. Schabir Shaik is a South African businessman who financially supported Jacob Zuma when he came back from exile. He was involved in dubious dealings with the French consortium Thompson-CSF and suspected to have arranged for bribes to be paid to Jacob Zuma. Schabir Shaik was condemned on 8 June 2005 to 15 years' imprisonment, but was released on medical parole on 3 March 2009. In his 2005 verdict, Judge Squires stated that there was "overwhelming" evidence of a corrupt relationship between Schabir Shaik and Jacob Zuma. Although the evidence was finally considered not conclusive enough to bring Jacob Zuma to court, he was dismissed from his position as deputy president of South Africa. A series of legal battles ensued at the end of which all charges against Jacob Zuma were eventually dropped. He was elected president of the ANC in December 2007, then president of the Republic in 2009; he was re-elected in 2014.
63. "Whole Lotta Shakin' Goin' On" was first recorded by African-American rhythm and blues singer, Big Maybelle, in 1955. The authorship of the song has been disputed: Big Maybelle's version is attributed to DC Williams, but it is generally credited to Dave "Curlee" Williams and James Faye "Roy" Hall. The most popular version was recorded by Jerry Lee Lewis in 1957. It was covered by Elvis Presley in 1971.
64. The lyrics are included in: Part Three Appendix: "*Moppie* Lyrics".
65. Frankie Valli (Francesco Stephen Castelluccio) was an American pop singer who was the leader of the vocal group, The Four Seasons. Available at https://www.youtube.com/watch?v=PzpWKAGvGdA [accessed 21 September 2015].
66. *Toyi-toyi* is a dance which originated in Zimbabwe and was adopted in apartheid South Africa by black African people marching and protesting in the streets. Demonstrators hammer the ground with their feet and move their torsos, while chanting slogans. It has been used in most political protest marches in South Africa since the 1970s. The lyrics are included in: Part Three Appendix: "*Moppie* Lyrics".
67. General Sales Tax.
68. Value Added Tax.
69. Probably derived from the Zulu interjection *hhayi*: no, stop, don't.
70. Adam Samodien, interview with Armelle Gaulier, Woodstock, 6 September 2006.
71. Rashaad Malick, in Adam Samodien and Rashaad Malick, interview with Denis-Constant Martin, Woodstock, 12 October 2011.
72. "Meadowlands" was written by Strike Vilikazi in 1956. It is a good example of double-entendre in song. The government understood that it supported their actions, while to black listeners it sounded like a protest hymn. The lyrics were sung in three languages: SeSotho, IsiZulu and Tsotsitaal (a street lingo combining English, Afrikaans, IsiZulu, SeSotho, and SeTswana) and could indeed suggest various interpretations: abidance by the authorities' orders or refusal to move. Available at http://www.ekayasolutions.com/FRS003/FRS003ClassLectures/Meadowlands.pdf [accessed 22 September 2015].
73. Sophiatown was a predominantly, but not exclusively, black African suburb of Johannesburg, one of the very rare areas in South Africa where black Africans had freehold rights. It became a cradle of cultural creativity, spurred in the musical field by the Anglican cleric, Trevor Huddleston, and his jazz band. It was subsequently declared a "white area" and in 1955 black Africans were removed to Meadowlands, Soweto; coloureds to Eldorado Park; and Indians to Lenasia. Sophiatown was razed to the ground, rebuilt as a white working class neighbourhood and renamed *Triomf* (Triumph) (Lodge 1981).

74. The lyrics are included in: Part Three Appendix: "*Moppie* Lyrics".
75. Abduraghman Morris, interview with Denis-Constant Martin, Colorado Park, 21 April 2015.
76. The lyrics are included in: Part Three Appendix: "*Moppie Lyrics*".
77. A song made popular by the Spanish singing duo, Los del Rio, which became an international hit in 1995–1996.
78. "Blurred Lines" was clearly inspired by Marvin Gaye's "Got to Give It Up", which led to a legal suit for copyright infringement opposing the Gaye family and Bridgeport Music, the publisher of "Blurred Lines".
79. An essential part of the *moppies*, where the original melody must be easily identifiable and humour is often based on a play of words, particularly sharp (see: pp. 164–166).
80. In Afrikaans folklore, the donkey and its cousin, the mule, are strongly associated with rural humour. This song celebrates the donkey as a "*trekdier*" (a "transport" animal or "beast of burden") and as a country people's companion when there were no modern means of transportation. The reference to the donkey in "*Die Moffie van Wilhemina*" can be understood as jestful, poking fun at a *moffie* who herself frequently uses humour as a means of putting up with the scorn and intolerance she is confronted with in her everyday life (Paul Sedres, personal communication to Denis-Constant Martin).
81. By Paul McCartney and John Lennon, 1963.
82. Ismail Dante, in Ismail and Gamja Dante, interview with Denis-Constant Martin, Hanover Park, 20 October 2011.
83. *Langarm* is a social gathering centred around dancing. Originally, it referred to a dance style in which partners stretched their arms horizontally; today dancers move as they wish. The saxophone, and the way it is played, are more important than the tunes themselves: popular hits and original compositions are played on a fast tempo and adapted to the rhythms of *vastrap* and the *ghoema* beat (Holtzman 2006; Martin 2013: 108–110).
84. *Ghoema, Original Cast Recording*. Cape Town: Blik Music, 2005 [CD Blik 12].
85. On backtracks, the drum kit is usually constituted of: a hi-hat, cymbals, a snare drum, a bass drum and sometimes a cow bell or a tom-tom.
86. Ismail Bey, interview with Armelle Gaulier, Rocklands, Mitchells Plain, 23 September 2006.
87. Transcription from a recording made by Armelle Gaulier in 2006; the part of the acoustic double bass was then played by an electric bass, which does not alter the line actually played.
88. Anwar Gambeno, interview with Armelle Gaulier, Mitchells Plain, 31 August 2006.
89. Recorded in 2006 by Armelle Gaulier during a practice of the Spesbona. The lyrics are included in: Part Three Appendix: "*Moppie* Lyrics".
90. See "Tik" by Adam Samodien: pp. 192–193.
91. An arrangement by Anwar Gambeno on "*Die Toyi Toyi*" by Adam Samodien, recorded by Denis-Constant Martin; included in the CD: *South Africa: The Cape Town Minstrels*. Paris: Buda Music, 2002 (CD No. 1986102).
92. A *moppie* by Ismail Dante; from a cassette recorded in undocumented circumstances; kindly communicated by the composer to Armelle Gaulier. The lyrics are included in: Part Three Appendix: "*Moppie* Lyrics".
93. Anwar Gambeno, interview with Armelle Gaulier, Mitchells Plain, 31 August 2006; Anwar Gambeno, interview with Denis-Constant Martin, Mitchells Plain, 11 October 2011.
94. Mo Shaik is a brother of Schabir Shaik. He is an important government official; he was previously head of the South African Secret Service and is now head of the international unit of the Development Bank of Southern Africa.
95. *Boeta* is an affectionate nickname derived from *boet* (brother); it is generally used when addressing older people, but not necessarily relatives; it can also be used, as in this instance, as a term of respect. It can be translated as brother, friend, old chap.

96. The Main Road (M4) is a major Cape Town thoroughfare going from the city centre to the Cape Peninsula.
97. Van der Wal 2009, "Appendix 2": 34.
98. Mujait Booysen, interview with Armelle Gaulier, Kensington, 11 October 2006.
99. Felicia Lesch is Certificate Programme Co-ordinator, Outreach Co-ordinator, Department of Music, University of Stellenbosch.
100. Felicia Lesch, interview with Denis-Constant Martin, Stellenbosch, 7 October 2011.
101. Adam Samodien and Rashaad Malick, interview with Denis-Constant Martin, Woodstock, 12 October 2011.
102. Felicia Lesch, interview with Denis-Constant Martin, Stellenbosch, 7 October 2011.
103. Ismail Dante, in Ismail and Gamja Dante, interview with Denis-Constant Martin, Hanover Park, 20 October 2011.
104. Berlin: Hansa Records, 1984, CD 206 555.
105. Available at http://en.wikipedia.org/wiki/Ten_Thousand_Lightyears [accessed 18 February 2013].
106. Available at http://www.youtube.com/watch?v=cQtmibS0weA, where Paul Sedres noticed it in March 2012. On 18 February 2013, when this video was requested at the above mentioned address, the answer was: "This video is not available." We wish to thank Paul Sedres for this information.
107. Paris: Carrère, 1984, CD 13582.
108. A German author, composer and producer. Available at http://de.wikipedia.org/wiki/Frank_Farian [accessed 18 February 2013].
109. Available at https://www.youtube.com/watch?v=jDtDP5ZrhYE [accessed 12 June 2015].
110. Taliep Abrahams related the same type of experience to Armelle Gaulier: Taliep Abrahams, interview with Armelle Gaulier, Mitchells Plain, 21 September 2006. "*Die Toyi Toyi*" was interpreted both in the Afrikaans *moppie* competition and in the Special Item competition by several *Klopse* during the 1994 carnival.
111. Waseef Piekaan, interview with Denis-Constant Martin, Mitchells Plain, 25 October 2011.

A moffie *leading a* klops *in the Tweede Nuwe Jaar march, Wale Street, 1994*

CHAPTER 6

Behind the comic

The music of comic songs is not written. The lyrics are. During practices they are inscribed on carton boards that hang from the walls of the *klopskamer*. Singers read them and memorise them as they learn the part they have to sing. *Moppie* lyrics are always original; composers have to produce new songs every year. During the same festive season, some compose several songs for various teams or different competitions. A *moppie* tells a story in a humorous way, even if the topic is not amusing; there have been "comic songs" which addressed serious and even dramatic issues: drug abuse; domestic violence; overcrowded dwellings in District Six. But it is the combination of a situation — a competition of *comic* songs, the listener's expectations, the manner in which the topic is handled and the choice and arrangement of words — that confers comicality on the song.

Themes in *moppie* lyrics

A thematic analysis of more than 70 *moppies* or parts of *moppies*, complemented by texts collected by Armelle Gaulier in 2006, shows that they tell mostly of characters and small everyday events particular to life in Cape Town's coloured townships: a conjunctivitis epidemic, in the course of which a cat turned pink (Abdullah Maged, "*Pang has Pinkeye*");[1] the Oxford pants craze of the 1940s, told by Kaparie January;[2] a wedding to remember (Ismail and Gamja Dante, "*Die Bruilof van die Jaar*", The Wedding of the Year);[3] a sensationalist gossip newspaper ("*Die Son*", mocked at least twice: by Abdullah Maged[4] and Anwar Gambeno[5]).

The New Year festivals

One of the most frequent topics of *moppies* is the New Year festivals, the very occasion for which they are produced and performed. These festivals are not depicted with irony or raillery, rather with an emphasis on happiness and being together, sometimes aroused by the excitement expressed in the word *deurmekaar*. As mentioned in the introduction, the word literally means confused, muddled,

179

disorganised but, in the context of the New Year festivals, it connotes a form of joy leading to freedom from all ordinary constraints, almost to an altered state of consciousness (*tariek*), in which anything is possible.[6]

"*Fiesta Tyd*" (Fiesta Time) by Ismail Dante provides a good illustration of the way the *Tweede Nuwe Jaar* parade and its preparations are pictured in song. The composer explained what he wanted to convey in this *moppie*:

> "Fiesta Tyd" is like when New Year comes in and everybody is happy. Now everybody is happy and they say it is a time for happiness […] Then the music, they are playing this music and now they come to enjoy this music. And everybody is doing the rumba as the band is playing, everybody enjoy themselves and now everybody is doing a different type of movement with their bodies, you see […] Now everybody is together and everybody sings together, now everybody is going to parade, to enjoy themselves in Cape Town. Everything is going very nice there and everybody is enjoying themselves […] If you feel like you want to do the action of Michael Jackson you're free to do it. Now you might attract the attention of the other people to watch you: "look that girl is doing Michael Jackson".[7]

The people are overtaken by a particular form of excitement even before the parade begins:

Fiesta, al die mense hou daar van	Fiesta, all the people love it
Fiesta, al die mense sing en dans	Fiesta, all the people sing and dance
Fiesta, dis die tyd van plesierigheid	Fiesta, it's the time for merriment

The emphasis is put on "*al die mense*", everyone: the parade involves the whole collective, fused in joy and fun. Then, Ismail Dante indicates that joy and fun are linked to a feeling of freedom: revellers are free to be who they want to be; no identity is ascribed to them by outside authorities; they can identify with anyone, and behave in a non-conventional manner. This is part of the essence of carnival everywhere, but in Cape Town, identification is mainly directed towards stars from across the Atlantic: Dolly Parton, the country and western singer; Peter Tosh, the reggae singer; and Michael Jackson. These characters are embodied with irony; they are caricatured. Dolly Parton's imposing bosom is described as the headlights of a Cadillac or Chevrolet:

Kyk wie kom nou hier aan	Look who's coming
Dis nou Dolly Parton met haar headlights aan	It's Dolly Parton with her headlights on

The seriousness that underlies such a depiction resides in the fact that stars are freely selected and represent fame and recognition, in spite of, or maybe because, they are worlds apart: it is difficult to imagine two persons as dissimilar as Dolly Parton and Peter Tosh. The possibility to be what one wants to be — white, black, anything in between or any mix, but a celebrity — even if only for the short duration of the *Klopse* carnival, was all the more important when the song was written, before the collapse of apartheid.

Die "*Ghoema Dans*", composed by Abbassie Dramat and arranged by Ismail Bey, brings to the fore the music of the festivals, and encapsulates it in the *ghoema* drum and the *ghoema* rhythm:

Ons sing 'n goema pop musiek	We sing a *ghoema* pop music
Dit laat my voete jeuk en dit gee my skoens tariek (Ja)	It leaves my feet itching and puts my shoes in a trance (yes)
Die klopskamer is waar jy my sal kry	The *klopskamer* is where you'll find me
Nou wys vir my die goema dans	Now show me the ghoema dance
Sit jou in 'n trans	Puts you in a trance

The music, and especially the *ghoema* rhythm, induces *deurmekaar*, the combination of disorder and intense pleasure. Shawn Pettersen, who coached the Kenfacs *Klops*, equated it with a spell:

> It puts you under the spell, this music, this ghoema dance is putting you under the spell, what are you going to do about? And you actually experience being in a crowded position and having to see people in a trance, people just going wild, people that you won't see go wild. Once I have been in, I was "extra wild", "extra wild". Yeah up till 2–3 o'clock in the morning [...] I just actually be in a different place, it just gives off the freedom and the expression of your culture.[8]

What is suggested here is that the "culture" has been so repressed, so dismissed as insignificant, that it needs a "spell" to make it appear in full light. Music reinforces the liberating power of the New Year festivals, at least for the time it lasts. Music reaches all listeners, including the lookers-on and when a band marches in the streets and plays a carnival tune, spectators usually react and start dancing; some of them follow the musicians, adopting a characteristic swaying step. Many genres of music can be played;[9] in most cases they are fine-tuned to fit the *ghoema* rhythm. The *ghoema* and its beat feature prominently in "*Die Goema Dans*":

Ons sing 'n goema pop musiek [...]	We sing a ghoema pop music [...]
Mense luister hierse goema ding [...]	People hear this, it's a ghoema thing [...]
Hoor die ritme wat soe lekker klink [...]	Hear the rhythms that sound so nice [...]
Die ritme vloei soe deur my aare [...]	The rhythms flow through my veins [...]
Dis 'n goema ding loat ons bring [...]	It's this ghoema thing we bring [...]
Dis gebring oor die see en gemeng met die ritme hier	It was brought from across the sea and mixed with the local rhythm
So was die goema gevier [...]	That's how the ghoema was celebrated [...]

Here the drum and the *ghoema* rhythm become the lynchpin of the festivals, and of an ensemble of practices construed as a culture. They sprang from "*hier*" (here), they are a local creation. But a creation that has not been achieved in isolation and continues to be fed by external elements. The "culture" therefore is moved by the capacity to borrow, to absorb and to transform to a point where what has been borrowed becomes local, and "*lekker*" (nice and pleasant). The *ghoema* drum and the *ghoema* rhythm are not only emblems of Cape Town, they are also the symbols of a creativeness able to refashion anything, thanks to unbroken contacts with the outside world, in spite of all the efforts the apartheid government made to lock coloured people up in confined townships.[10] This is what is condensed in the phrase "*goema ding*" (the *ghoema* thing): a complex dialectic of inside and outside dynamics that generates original products and practices; something quite close to the definition Édouard Glissant gave of creolisation: "an unpredictable energy of overcoming"[11] (Glissant 1997: 16). What *ghoema* symbolises is a creolising culture, something that should be considered with pride, which has a long history and will continue to develop. The words are quite explicit about this:

Dis 'n goema ding loat ons bring	It's a ghoema thing we bring
Dis 'n kaapse kultuur en dis hoe ons mense vuue [...]	It is a Cape culture and this is how our people get on fire [...]
Vertel die skinder bekke die goema gat hier bly [...]	Tell the gossipmongers the ghoema is here to stay [...]
Jy lyk verniet soe skaam	You don't have to be ashamed

These feelings are now integrated in multiple feelings of belonging that can be piled up, from the neighbourhood which people inhabit to South Africa as a whole. In "*Kabola*",[12] Abubakar Davids celebrates "*'n Kaapse Kultur*", a Cape Town culture which combines enjoying to be together and the unbreakable feelings of belonging that root coloured people to the "Mother City", South Africa's matrix. The character of Kabola in Abubakar Davids' *moppie* embodies these feelings:

Hoza Hoza ja (2x)
Kabola die oujaar is weer om
Dis Nuwe Jaar
Dan raak die mense deurmekaar
Hoza
Fiesta tyd is hier in die Kaap [...]
Kom jol saam die ding ruk hier en daar

Ons is almal saam [...]
Kabola Kabola dis Suid-Afrika!

Hoza Hoza, yes (x2)
Kabola, the old year has passed
It's New Year
Then the people all get deurmekaar
Hoza
Fiesta time begins in Cape Town [...]
Come and let's have fun together,
    the "thing" pulls here and there
    [i.e. everyone's having a great time]
We are all together [...]
Kabola Kabola, that's South Africa!

In 2008, Abubakar Davids set the New Year festival against the backdrop of the "new" South Africa. The initial call "*Hoza*", which most probably comes from the isiZulu *woza* (come) was heard in several recent *moppies* and symbolises black African people; the association of "*Hoza*" and "*Ons is almal saam*" (We are all together) suggests a new perception of ties linking coloureds and black Africans: they all can become *deurmekaar* – happy, joyful and free – together.

Everyday life and politics

Many *moppies* tell a story inspired by everyday life. In this case, the lyrics must obey some narrative logics, as does for instance "*Joe se Barber*",[13] a song composed by Taliep Abrahams, coach of the Spesbona *klops*. It describes what happens in a barber shop. The barber, Bother Joe, is a keen observer, and a good listener, in whom customers can confide:

Jy kan jou storie deel met
    Joe Barber
Hy hou vir jou fyn dop
Hy's kwaai, jy moet pas op vir
    Joe Barber

You can share your story with
    Joe Barber
He pays you close attention
He's smart, you need to be careful of
    Joe Barber

His shop is so popular that he even attracts bald men who just come, sit and chat. Brother Joe listens to customers' dreams when they play the lottery or the horses:

Som praat van lotto speel
Daar's die wat perde speel
En ook van die jackpot speel

Some discuss the Lotto
There are those who play the horses
And others the jackpot

Even in the barber shop, the spirit of the festive season can be felt as everyone gets ready to celebrate:

Festive season bly die plek vol	During the festive season the place stays busy
Die queue is so lank jy sal sweer daars 'n jol	The line is so long you'd swear there's a party
Twee speakers by die deur music klop daar deer	Two speakers at the door bellow music violently
Die bergies[14] *dans daar voor deur*	The tramps are dancing at the door

Brother Joe's customers are men. However, explained Taliep Abrahams, they are as talkative and gossipy as women. At the end of the day, the barber is tired, not only from cutting hair, but from listening to the men he attends to:

Boeta Joe se hy's klaar en gedaan	Brother Joe says he's completely exhausted
Hy's moeg van heeldag op sy voete staan	He's tired of being on his feet all day
'n Mens voel somtyds flou	And sometimes one feels like fainting
Daarom moet ta Joe sy voete in warm water hou	That's why he has to soak his feet in warm water

"*Joe Se Barber*" is also interesting from another point of view: it tells about hair. This may sound quite obvious for a song dedicated to a barber, but hair in black, and especially coloured, communities has to do with more than just head pilosity. Hair has been socially constructed as an identity marker with clear connotations. It was used by government officials in charge of classifying South Africans on the basis of the Population Registration Act, 1950, as a feature distinguishing coloureds from black Africans and whites. The "pencil test" consisted of putting a pencil in the hair of someone whose "race" was "uncertain". If the pencil stayed in, the person was declared coloured; if it slipped out, the person was registered white. Having frizzy, coarse hair became a stigma which was internalised, especially among the coloured petty-bourgeoisie. Since the appearance of hair could be changed thanks to various techniques to straighten it, strategies of hair dressing developed. This is why Zimitri Erasmus asserts that hair is both a "cultural construct" and a "site of contestation" (Erasmus 2000: 381). In the musical *Afrikaaps*,[15] which celebrates the glory of coloured Cape Town's culture, Blaqpearl, the only woman in the show, asks: "Women with no straight hair *daais 'n straat meit*, no hair *nou wat is ek dan*?" (Women with no straight hair are but street sluts, [I have] no hair, like this what am I now?). Blaqpearl solved the dilemma of "good" versus "bad" hair by shaving her head (Becker & Oliphant n.d.: 2). There is "sleek" hair and *boesman korrels*

(Bushman's hair, i.e. "grainy") (Erasmus 2001: 13), straight hair and coconut hair; in other words, "good" and "bad" hair, the bad being what identified a coloured person as coloured — distinct from "white" — and connoted disrespectability. To show "good" hair and avoid shame, Zimitri Erasmus tells of the seventeen steps that had to be taken when she was a teenager (Erasmus 2000: 382–383). Therefore, when Taliep Abrahams lists the types of hair that Brother Joe has to sweep on the floor of his parlour, this is not just as a matter of fact; he hints at what characterises his clientele:

Die hare lê daar op die vloer in Joe se Barber	The hair is lying on the floor at Joe Barber's
Dis hare Dis hare	There is hair, there is hair
[Dis] hare al die soorte, Goema Goema hare	All kinds of hair, ghoema ghoema hair
Dis hare Dis hare	There is hair, there is hair
[Die] hare hare lê daar rond in Joe se Barber	Hair, hair lying on the floor at Joe Barber's
Dis hare Dis hare	There is hair, there is hair
Hare klapper hare le daar op die vloer	Hair coconut hair lies on the floor

"*Ghoema* hair" refers to the drum but also carries an innuendo; the composer explained:

> We call it "Goema hare", it is not pretty hair like your [Armelle Gaulier's straight] hair [...] This hair [ghoema hair, that is frizzy hair], in other words I can say it is a third grade types of hair. Like, you've got the long strings [showing Armelle Gaulier's hair], you've got the girls' hair that can swing around with all the new types of [...] shampoos and things that they used and [...] And I've got the ghoema hair it is tied together like steel wool, you saw steel wool? You know sometimes your hair is like steel wool. Now that is the word "Goema hare" [...] In other words it is like third grade types of hair.[16]

"*Klapper hare*" (coconut hair) also designates frizzy hair, hair in which the infamous pencil would get trapped. Although he is talking of men, who attach less importance to their hair than women, Taliep Abrahams suggests that Brother Joe's barber shop is patronised by coloured males, most probably working class individuals. The *moppie* therefore tells of a place where ordinary people socialise.

"*Die Lied Vannie Hawker-Boy*",[17] by Anwar Gambeno, features a character that used to roam the streets of Cape Town, usually on a horse-driven cart, selling fruits and vegetables, and advertising his wares by shouting or blowing a seaweed horn.[18] The song also suggests that his customers are living in difficult situations: they not only want to be sure that his produce is fresh, they try to hide from him when he comes to collect what they owe him. That is compensated for by the very special quality of the fruits and vegetables he sells:

Daar's piesangs virrie brood	There are bananas for the sandwiches
En sy wortel is so groot	And the carrots are so big
Avekarepere maak jou hare mere	Avocadoes make your hair grow
En sy skwassies gee die meisiekinners pere	And his squashes make the girls' breasts grow

Beyond incidents of everyday life, *moppies* also hint at more general aspects of social and political life. This is the case with *"Die Toyi Toyi/Ons Hoor"*. As we saw in the previous chapter, it paints South African society as it could be perceived through the media, just before the first general elections by universal suffrage. Originally written by Adam Samodien, a new verse was added by Anwar Gambeno at the end of the song to pay tribute to Nelson Mandela, South Africa's first black African president:

Mense, mense, toyi toyi ons almal saam	People, people, we all toyi-toyi together
Toyi ons almal saam	We all toyi-toyi together

Anwar Gambeno's final stanza:

Viva Madiba,[19] *(ya) viva Madiba,*	Viva Madiba, (ya) viva Madiba,
(ya) viva Madiba, viva Suid-Afrika	(ya) viva Madiba, viva South Africa
Viva Madiba, (ya) viva Madiba,	Viva Madiba, (ya) viva Madiba,
(ya) viva Madiba,	(ya) viva Madiba,
Ons almal sê nou vaarwel (x3)	We all now say farewell (x3)
Madiba	Madiba

Anwar Gambeno explained why he decided to complement the song in this way:

> I think that Madiba is the man that has […] He was the role model, he has so much to do with our freedom, he has so much to do with what the people was feeling at that time and the people were toyi-toying because of him […] Yes it is a homage to him. And also to make it [the song] more my own, because I didn't write it.[20]

When his choir performs in concert, singers usually raise a clenched fist when pronouncing the final "Madiba". Again, what is to be noted here is the association of *"Ons almal"* (all of us), Madiba and *"Viva Suid-Afrika"* (Viva South Africa). Adam Samodien's *"Die Toi-Toi vir 12%"*[21] also emphasises togetherness: the unity of all who are struggling and need a salary increase. When they march and protest in front of Parliament, in Cape Town, there are "whites, blacks and coloureds, all mixed together". They sing the liberation hymn that has become part of the national anthem, "*Nkosi Sikelel' iAfrika*" for they have to speak out, they have to *toyi-toyi "almal saam"*, all together.

The tone of "*Die Son*" is quite different. It stages a businessman and a politician who are obviously not treated with the same respect as Nelson Mandela. The song deals with corruption and suspicion ("*Hy is net skuldig as die hof hom nov straf jee*", He is only guilty if the court finds so), but the most important point it makes is probably that it combines corruption – a fact of political life in South Africa – with social problems and the activism it fosters; it highlights the government's inefficiency in fighting drug trafficking, leaving the field open for various organisations suspected of having a hidden agenda.

Ons sien a laaaities staan	We see a youngster standing
Op die hoeke van 'n Kaapse straat	On a street corner of Cape Town
Koerante in sy hand	The newspaper in his hand
Skree hy wat daar in aan gaan	Shouting what's in it
Vertel ons dat die mense march	He is telling us that the people marched
Daar bo in Hanover Straat	From the top of Hanover Street
Tot by die Parlement oor die tik in Tafelsig[22]	To the Parliament about "tik in Tafelsig
Die Pankies hulle was ook daar	PAGAD members were also there
Met koefias[23] *en hul toppe*[24] *aan*	In their koefias and robes
Dit alles kan jy lees in die Son	All that you can read in Die Son
Die skinder koerant (ja)	The gossip newspaper (yes)

Here, *Pankies* refer to members of the People Against Gangsterism And Drugs (PAGAD), a militant group that emerged in the mid-1990s as a grassroots organisation, gathering people of all faiths who wanted to put an end to gangsterism and drug trafficking. PAGAD crowds murdered a notorious drug dealer, Rashaad Staggie, on 4 August 1996 and burned the *bakkie* (van) of another one, known to be a *Klops* captain and carnival organiser. After several incidents, PAGAD's violence alienated a number of its activists. Many thought it was infiltrated by members of Qibla (a marginal but extremely vocal extremist Muslim grouping) and PAGAD members were made responsible for a number of pipe bomb explosions in the Western Cape in 1998. Repression by the police and expensive court cases weakened the organisation to a point where it seems to have become inactive in the 2000s (Baderoon 2014: 107–132; Vahed & Jeppie 2005). "*Die Son*" exemplifies — as do "*Die Toyi Toyi/Ons Hoor*" and "*Die Toi-Toi vir 12%*" — how *moppies* can string together very serious issues and much lighter incidents:

Daar's waarde vir jou geld, jou geld	There's value for your money, your money
As Die Son die storie vertel, vertel	When *Die Son* tells a story, tells a story
Dit is hiervan dit is daarvan	It's about this, it's about that
Van 'n ander vrou se man	About another woman's husband
Hulle sê hy is gay	They say he's gay
Met 'n moffie het hy gevry	He was seen with a moffie
Is it jou man of dit haar man?	Is it your husband or her husband?
Die Son sê hy's gevang (wooo)	*Die Son* says he was caught (ooh)
Lees nou Die Son	Now read *Die Son*
Op page drie is daar ook porn	On page three there's also porn
Daars 'n mooi meit, daars 'n sexy meid[25]	There's a pretty bird, there's a sexy bird
Kyk, jou bek hang op die grond! (wooo)	Look, your mouth will drop to the ground! (ooh)

Moffies

Moffies are a favourite topic of comic songs. They are gently mocked, in the *moppie* spirit, whereby mocking amounts to paying a tribute of sorts. *Moffies* have been honoured for a long time: they were, and still are often, given a position at the head of the troupe when *Klopse* parade in the streets or at stadia. A woman who watched the Coons in the 1940s, Angelina Clark, remembered:

> The troupe invariably was led by a transvestite (Moffie) whose outfit was often far more flamboyant than the rest of the troupe. The Moffie while being accepted as part of the troupe would not be part of the formal activities in terms of songs and the marches, but was allowed to perform on his own. Moffies were not allowed to practice with the rest of the troupe and after gaining the captain's permission to be the "voorloper" [the drum-major, the one who leads the troupe in the parade] would simply show up on the day of the Carnival having provided his own costume and having prepared entirely on his own. (Rahman 2001: 9)

Moffies were similarly treated in 1990s carnivals and later; as in the 1940s, their ambiguity generates ambiguity in the way they are seen. They often sport elaborate and shiny dresses with hats *à la* Carmen Miranda; they draw attention to the *Klops* they lead. They can sing on stage (only with the *Klopse*) and be acclaimed. In "normal" life, they are not ostracised, at least in certain milieus. Vincent Kolbe insisted on their integration in the neighbourhood where they lived:

> If you are part of the underclass culture that [moffies] is part of the family, that's friends. They cook for you, you know, they hang up the

curtains, you love them, you protect them, you treat them like girls, you use to call them by their girl names. There was an acceptance of gays in place where I grew up in District Six. Every street had a moffie [...] they were accepted by the community because they were someone's son, someone's brother, you know, part of the community.[26]

Felicia Lesch drew the same type of picture for a more recent period:

> The moffie is venerated within the moppie. And that is social commentary in itself, on the place of the moffie in the community. I use that term very cautiously, but that's what they call that person. And that person is protected by everybody, gangsters, community members, judge, members, everybody protects that person. They have a special kind of leadership, not a leadership, but they have a special role or place in the community [The moffie] is a homosexual who prefers to dress like a woman. It's a homosexual cross dresser, a transvestite. And you know that kind of person is normally suppressed in society, but in the community in a certain social economic group they are not suppressed, they're allowed to be what they want to be, and when they do parades, they are in front [But] only with the Klopse. They parade in front of the troupes. And it is their time and everybody looks out for them, everybody looks after them, and they have a special role in everyone else's life, a special contribution to make.[27]

These special places and special roles — which should not conceal the reality of various forms of stigmatisation — explain why *moppies* about *moffies* are so numerous. She is made fun of not only because she cross-dresses, but because she tries to be more than a woman and exaggerates all the characteristics of a female: make-up, dress or body language, something that Taliep Abrahams underlined in his "*Queen van die Moffie*",[28] a song quite representative of *moppies* dedicated to *moffies*:

Haar lippies is so rooi jy kan van ver af sien	Her lips are so red you can see from afar
Haar oegies blink soos sterretjies dis glittering	Her eyes glow like little stars, they're glittering
As sy die pad af stap doen sy dit als met 'n beat Oh Ho Ho	When she walks in the street she struts with a beat Oh Ho Ho
Sy dra kort sweaters laat haar naaltjie uit wys	She wears short tops to show her navel
Die vingers is vol ringe sy wil vir almal wys	The fingers are full of rings for all to see
Wil latest skoene dra maar jy kan sien sy loop swaar Oh Ho Ho	[She] will wear the latest shoes but you can see that she walks heavily Oh ho ho

The conclusion of the *moppie* introduced a comment on recent news: the passing by Parliament in November 2006 of the Civil Union Act (17 of 2006), authorising the marriage of same-sex couples. The composer of the *moppie* assumed that from then on *moffies*' seductive strategies could change and advised an imaginary *moffie*: "You don't need to show off in front of the other man, you can do it legally. [...] Now you are legal now". Consequently he wrote:

Moffie kyk wat gaan aan wat gaan aan	Moffie, look what's happening, what's happening
Dis in die skinder koerant, skinder koerant	It's in the gossip paper, gossip paper
Dis wettig nou in ons land	It's legal now in our country
'n man kan trou met 'n nogge man man man man"	A man can marry another man, man, man, man
Hey Moffie hey Moffie	Hey moffie, hey moffie
Jy moet nie vir jou uit kom gee nie	You no longer have to show off
Hey Moffie hey Moffie	Hey moffie, hey moffie
Dis nou jou opportunity	This is now your chance
Dis 'n reality	It's a reality

"Queen van die Moffie" sounds like a little chronicle of South African society's evolution. It tells about a character who occupies a definite place in certain milieus and comments on a new legislation that will profoundly affect her life. In so doing, the song intimates that in the "new" South Africa, all citizens should, from the legal point of view, be treated in the same way, whatever their appearance, their creed or their sexual orientation. "*Wilhemina die Moffie*"[29] by Abduraghman Morris puts the *moffie* in a different light. It illustrates the ambivalence *moffies* generally arouse. She is a "queen", a "star"; even her family is proud of her, because she is "the Drag Queen of the Year". But, however feminine she tries to look, she cannot conceal that she's a man with a fast-growing beard and hair on her legs. Even worse, she is described as very untidy and she herself confesses in the gimmick:

Ek was my vier keur 'n jaar	I wash four times a year
En change net twee keur my bra	And my bra I only change twice
Sies! Die Moffie is 'n wonderlike ding	Urgh! The Moffie is an amazing thing
O die Moffie, o ja die Moffie	Oh the Moffie, Oh the Moffie
Die Moffie is 'n wonderlike ding	The Moffie is an amazing thing
Ek staan op daai hoek	I stand on the street corner
Heena man, ek ruik net soos snoek!	Oh damn, I smell of snoek!
Sies! Die Moffie is 'n wonderlike ding	Urgh! The Moffie is an amazing thing

Snoek (*thyrsites atun*) is a kind of snake mackerel extremely popular in Cape Town, especially among coloured people. It can be prepared in many different, and usually delectable, ways. It may release a strong smell, particularly when it is sold from *bakkies* parked in the sun on the roadsides. Here the idea seems to be that a *moffie* can be accepted by her family, be popular and win awards in Drag Queen competitions, and yet be sloppy and smelly. That's why the *pak* reacts to her self-description by screaming "*Sies!*", an exclamation of deep disgust. The *moffie* is definitely "*'n wonderlike ding*", someone who is at the same time wonderful (she is attractive and is the pride of her family) and amazingly bizarre (a messy mix of male and female).

A message behind the funny

Moppies generally use a particular form of humour, which is pervaded with ambivalence. Behind the comic lies something serious. This confirms Vladimir Jankélévitch's contention that "irony banters, but in the very way it mocks it is possible to read truth as in an open book" (Jankélévitch 1964: 173). Every *moppie* induces at least two interpretations. "*Fiesta Tyd*" (Fiesta Time) manifests the identification with pop stars from overseas and at the same time makes fun of both these stars and those who in Cape Town play their copy-cats. *Boeta* Joe Barber has a male clientele, who is taunted because they behave like women in a beauty salon; however, the description of hair lying on the floor of his shop shows that these men are not ashamed of who they are. The tabloid *Die Son* is scoffed at because it is vulgar and prints gossip, but its exposure of corruption makes its worthwhile reading. "*Die Toyi Toyi*" simultaneously underlines the happiness of a new being-together and the difficulties with which South Africans are confronted. "*Queen van die Moffie*" offers a sprightly portrait of homosexual cross-dressers and implicitly hails a new law on same-sex marriage. "*Die Goema Dans*" celebrates the New Year festivals as a Cape culture, but also notes that they may need to be defended against those who consider them worthless. The above mentioned *moppies* are but a few examples illustrating their essential ambiguity and ambivalence.

The incongruous

The duality of *moppies* is probably the reason why their comicality often escapes outsiders. When talking about *moppies*, the word "comic" acquires a large semantic field, which includes humour as a non-necessary condition. Several techniques can be used to create funniness, one of the most frequent being the introduction of incongruous situations. In "*Ouma*" by Mogamat Meniers,[30] an old woman, a "granny" (*ouma*) wants to look sexy and chat up men when she goes to a party. This pays off for she eventually marries a Mr van Aarde. In *"Die Moffie met die Houte Been"* (The Moffie with a Wooden Leg), Adam Samodien tells of a widower who becomes infatuated with a peg-leg moffie[31]). The insertion of a "spliff" among a list of newly taxed food products in *"Die Toyi Toyi/Ons Hoor"* by Adam Samodien demonstrates how the incongruous works.

This last example shows that the incongruous is often associated with a comic of repetition. In *"Die Moffie"*,[32] another *moppie* dealing with the law on same-sex marriage, Adam Samodien asks:

Wat kan 'n moffie wees? Maar net 'n man	What can a moffie be? But just a man
Wat wil 'n moffie he? Maar net 'n man	What does a moffie want? But just a man
Wat wil 'n moffie trou, maar net 'n man	What will a moffie marry? But just a man
Wie gaan die bruid afhaal, maar net 'n man	How will the bride unveil? But just as a man

"Die Bruilof van die Jaar"[33] (The Wedding of the Year), by Ismail and Gamja Dante, describes the impressive quantity of food displayed on the occasion of a particularly big wedding:

Die tafels was gedek	The tables were laid
Met al die soorte van koeke	With all kinds of cakes
Hier's 'n paar wat ek on'hou	Here's a few I remember
En nog so veel van koeke	There was so much cake
Dis ronde koeke, plat koeke	It's round cakes, flat cakes
Regop koeke, lang koeke	Straight cakes, long cakes
Korte koeke, nat koeke	Short cakes, soaked cakes
Lekker om te kou	So nice to eat
Ronde korsies lang met worse	Long cracker breads with sausage
Lang worse, kort worse	Long sausages, short sausages
Lang worse, tong worse	Long sausages, tongue sausages
Lekker om te bou	So nice to eat

The comical effect of repetition is frequently increased by alliterations. The local name given to a drug that wreaks havoc among underprivileged youth in coloured townships, *tik* (crystal meth) attracts rhymes in "k", which reinforce repetitions of the word in *"Tik"*[34] by Adam Samodien:

Daar's 'n lelike ding wat nou hand uitruk	There is an ugly thing which is getting out of hand
*Dit is die **tik tik** (die **tik tik** die **tik tik**)*	This is the tik tik (the tik tik, the tik tik)
*Ons weet van **kinders** wat hul ouers vernuk*	We know of children who kill their parents
*Om te gaan **tik tik** (gaan **tik tik**, gaan **tik tik**)*	To go tik tik (to go tik tik, to go tik tik)

In the "*Mellie*" variant of "*Die Son*",³⁵ Anwar Gambeno uses the same method, to add zest to a much lighter topic:

*Allie mense staan **nou op (nou op)***	All the people are now rising to their feet (to their feet)
*Hulle was soe **diep geskok (geskok)***	They were so shocked (shocked)
*Ou Mellie skree "**hou nou op**" (**hou op**)*	Old Mellie shouts "stop it!" (stop it!)
*My vrou gat my nou **uitskop (uitskop)***	My wife's gonna kick me out! (kick me out!)
*Toe hy byrie huis **ankom (ankom)***	When he got home (got home)
*Was sy vrou soe **dom vestom (vestom)***	His wife was so dumbfounded (dumbfounded)
*Slaan hom met 'n **biesemstok***	She chased him with a broom
*Ja ou Mellie bly ma **dom***	Yes, old Mellie stays thickheaded!
Dom, dom, dom, dom dom, dom	Stupid, stupid, stupid, stupid, stupid, stupid

"*Die Spoek*" (a spook or ghost),³⁶ provides an instance of comic produced by the combination of alliteration and textual-musical associations. The music consists of an assemblage of several melodic fragments borrowed from international pop hits. Anwar Gambeno recognised, among others, "Hello Mary Lou" by Gene Pitney and Cayet Mangiaracina, popularised by Ricky Nelson in 1961, and a song by Beyoncé.³⁷ The *ghoema* beat cemented the whole. When performed on the stage of the Good Hope Centre in February 2012, the song made listeners roar with laughter. The punchline — "*Sing, sing, sing, wan' die spoek is a lelike ding*" (Sing, sing, sing, for the spook is an ugly thing) — was highlighted by the attitudes of the soloist and the *pak*, inspired by horror films. This *moppie* provides a good example of the way lyricists multiply layers of significations by playing on words and spurring associations of ideas: *lelik* means horrible, ugly, deformed, evil; *ding* means thing, affair and may carry sexual connotations. The repetition of "sing" may refer not only to Louis Prima's composition made famous by Gene Krupa with Benny Goodman's orchestra (1937) and his own combo "Sing sing sing", but also to Sing Sing Correctional Facility, a maximum security prison located in the state of New York. To sing "Sing sing sing" seems to imply that the "spook" is not only ugly and evil, but that he belongs in jail. The original version of "*Die Son*" by Anwar Gambeno was based on the same mechanism: the comicality of the punchline "Shaik Zuma Shaik" aroused a series of association of ideas likely to give the words a plurality of meanings.

In many songs that are meant to make the listener laugh, sexual innuendos are common. The sausages in "*Die Bruilof van die Jaar*" most probably carry such overtones, as do the vegetables trumpeted by Anwar Gambeno's hawker boy ("*Die Lied Vannie Hawker Boy*"[38]) (The Song of the Hawker Boy):

Daar's piesangs vinnie brood	There are bananas for the sandwiches
En sy wortel is so groot	And the carrots are so big
Avekarepere maak jou hare mere	Avocadoes make your hair grow
En sy skwassies gee die meisiekinners pere	And his squashes make the girls' breasts grow

There is no doubt that Galiema's *frikkedels* (minced meatballs) are genuinely aphrodisiac ("*Kaklak Frikkedel*",[39] Cockroach *Frikandel*, by Adam Samodien; another example of alliteration):

Kyk net hoe lekker kry Abdol	Look at the pleasure Abdul has
As Galiema frikkedelle rol	When Galiema rolls frikkedels
Die heel hele nag door deur wil die on ou net	The whole night through the old bloke just wants
Met maar frikkedelle lol	To trifle with her frikkedels

The meaning of a song which the noted banjo player, Mr Mac, was very keen on is much less obvious:

Abassie staan in die winkel	Abassie is in the shop
In die winkel, winkel deur	In the shop, the shop doorway
In die winkel, winkel deur	In the shop, the shop doorway
En hy maak vir Nellie seer	And he's hurting Nellie

According to Mr Mac's son, the guitar player and composer Mac McKenzie, this song dates back to a time when lodgings were overcrowded, making it difficult for men and women to entertain intimate relationships. There were small corners in corridors leading to shops that could shelter surreptitious love. Mac McKenzie's interpretation of the song is that: "It's about a guy quickly telling his girlfriend 'hey, let's do it right here', you know, and people say 'they're busy having a fight', but they're not having a fight, they're having a 'quicky', now and then."[40] This understanding makes fun of an urge to make love when conditions are not favourable; it also suggests a link between violence and sex, something that is quite widespread in Cape Town's impoverished neighbourhoods, and reminds listeners of overpopulation in District Six. A situation very precisely described in *"Almal in Een Kamer"* (Everyone in One Room) by Adam Samodien.[41]

Bitter memories and hopes

There are very few recorded examples of "protest" *moppies*. This does not mean that they did not exist, just that they were not printed in the media, and that memories of songs that were sung in the 1950s, even during the 1960s, have vanished. Journalists writing stories about the New Year festivals for local newspapers during the apartheid era could not or did not want to mention or quote them and collective memories tended to forget them. An exception is *"Almal in Een Kamer"* by Adam Samodien,[42] although the composer denies that he intended to write a protest song. A mere description of living conditions, in which the comic underlines situations that may in fact be rather dramatic, could also be heard as a protest. *"Almal in Een Kamer"* draws a picture of housing conditions in District Six during the 1950s:

Ons woon almal saam, almal in een kamer	We all live together, all in one room
Ons eet almal saam	We all eat together
Ons slaap same in die selfde kamer	We sleep together in the same room
Almal op die grond lê ons rond	All over the floor we lie
Die familie wat daar woon, hulle is so groot	The family who lives there, they are so many
Die skoon ouers woon ook saam	The in-laws also live with them
En die skoondogter met haar kindertjies,	An the daughter-in-law with her kids
Diese man het weer vir haar laatstaan.	Her husband has left her again.
Nou woon ons almal saam in die kamer	Now we all live together in the room
(3x)	(x3)

Adam Samodien explained why he wrote this *moppie*, actually one of his first compositions:

> You write about District Six, how the people used to live. You start off with a mother and father living in a little room, then the family accumulates its children, they're also in that room, then the children get big, they get married, they're also in that room, they get children, they're all in that room, that is the way the life was in District Six. Now in Afrikaans, I call it *"Almal in Een Kamer"*, all in one room. The way they sleep on the floor, on the benches, things like that, but they survived, that was life.[43]

Adam Samodien insisted that with this *moppie* he wanted to make a song about an experience shared by many inhabitants of District Six and not to protest against the causes of such an experience. What he emphasised, beyond the not-so-comic description of a family which has to cram into one single room, was the endurance, the capacity of survival, the resilience of poor people confronted with the housing crisis in District Six. Adam Samodien's observation: "That was life" contains both an element of fatalism and a silent, if not denunciation, then at least an interrogation, as to who was responsible for this state of affairs. And it is far from impossible that many of those who heard the song went a little further than the composer in their answer to this interrogation.

In spite of its overcrowding and the dilapidated state of many buildings, District Six was home to a vibrant social and cultural life and close enough to several places of employment to allow its inhabitants to walk to work. Although it may have been idealised later, it was a neighbourhood to which its inhabitants were strongly attached. When orders to move and bulldozers, charged with razing down houses, reached District Six, when people had to put all their belongings onto a lorry taking them to the Cape Flats, they were filled with anger and sorrow. There are traces of a few *moppies* expressing these feelings. A good instance is "*Boeta Dola*", a *moppie* quoted in one of the first serious articles on the Coon carnival published by Shamil Jeppie in 1990:[44]

> Boeta Dola's out of District
> He was there all the time
> Now he is very angry
> He had to leave his house in District
> He was there all the time
> Now he lives in Mitchells Plain
> There where the sand dunes have fine sand
> He's filled with memories
> There on the Cape Flats

The sand dunes may be "fine", but everyone who has been forcibly moved to the Cape Flats knows full well that the environment is drab and the sandstorms unbearable. This is indeed a form of very sad sarcasm, accentuated by subsequent lines telling: "about subsequent rent increases in Mitchells Plain and the suffering imposed by forced removals" (Jeppie 1990: 23).

The same sentiments were expressed in an indirect way (this time in English) by twisting the meaning of a famous song. In the early 1960s, Joseph Gabriels, who was to become an acclaimed tenor on international opera stages (Martin 2013: 126), taught the Young Stars a version of "Exodus", the theme song of the film by the same title directed by Otto Preminger and released in 1961. It was again sung in 1977 by one of the major troupes of the times, the Great Gatsbys. The lyrics of "Exodus", as rendered by the Great Gatsbys said:

This land is mine
God gave this land to me…
This brave… and ancient land to me…
And when the morning sun
Reveals the hills and plains
Then I see a land
Where children can be free […]
To make this land my home
If I must fight, I'll fight
To make this land my own
Until I die… This land is mine.[45]

On the sheet handed over to Great Gatsbys' members, the verses in bold were handwritten and replaced the original words "With the help of God, I know I can be strong", which were crossed out. In 1977, the intensity of the struggle in South Africa lit a little flame of hope. Freedom was in sight, in spite of the repression, and the rewritten words of "Exodus" seemed to echo Martin Luther King's famous "I have a dream" speech.

In 1994, several *Klopse* and audiences at the stadia sung the popular anti-apartheid song by Eddy Grant "Gimme Hope Jo'Anna", in which Jo'Anna personified Johannesburg. Originally released in 1977, and banned by the South African government, it became nonetheless a favourite with young black South Africans. In 1994, a few months before the first elections by universal suffrage, it became the "the national anthem of Mitchells Plain" and its lyrics were somewhat adapted to the new South African situation. In the *moppie* version of the Woodstock Starlites,[46] they went:

[…] You don't have to be white
to be right (twice)

I say I say
Johanna, Johanna, Johanna, Johanna

Well Johanna she runs a country
She runs in Durban and in whole Transvaal
She makes a few of her people happy
Or she doesn't care about the rest at all

Oh gimme hope Johanna
Hope Johanna

Gimme Hope Johanna
Gimme Hope Johanna (twice)
fore the morning comes.

According to Christine Winberg, an old *ghoemaliedjie* telling of a girl named Johanna, sounded like "a celebration of miscegenation" (Winberg 1992: 85–86). To some Capetonians, the Johanna of "Give me Hope" may have brought back memories of the Johanna of the *ghoemaliedjie*, or the similarity of the two names may only have been a coincidence. Whatever the case, 1994 was definitely a time for hope, in spite of acute anxieties. Another song frequently used by *Klopse* was the theme-song of Walt Disney's Studios *Aladdin*: "A Whole New World". Among others, the Good Hope Entertainers and the Woodstock Starlites sung:[47]

> [...] A whole new world
> A new fantastic point of view
> None to tell us no
> Or where to go
> Or say we're only dreaming.
> A whole new world
> A dazzling place I never knew
> But now from way up here, it's crystal clear
> That now I'm in a whole new world with you.

Here no changes in the words were necessary to convey the expectations of millions of people who had been victims of apartheid: "You don't have to be white to be right...", "None to tell us no...", these words were certainly loaded with meaning in 1994 in Cape Town and could then be uttered without restraint.

Subdued protest and resistance

The last three examples indicate that twisting the words of foreign pop songs could be a means to engage conditions under which people lived; in these cases, the original language of the songs was retained. The few examples of political, or potentially political, *moppies* that we have been able to identify are probably just the tip of the iceberg. They suggest that since *moppies* usually deal with everyday life, politics can never be very far away. But we lack evidence to ascertain it. During apartheid, *moppies* could not openly protest against segregation and oppression. As a matter of fact, the few songs we know of which evoke or just hint at political and social life date from either before the apartheid era or after the end of apartheid. Gamja Dante explained that, in 1948, he wrote a song in support of Jan Smuts who, he thought, was the only solid shield against the threat of DF Malan's *Herenigde Nasionale Party* (Reunited National Party) and its programme of apartheid.[48] Between 1948 and 1994, patriotic *moppies* such as "*Hip Hip Horah Suid-Afrika*" by Adam Samodien[49] and "*Ons Land Suid-Afrika*" (South Africa Our Country) by Ismail and Gamja Dante[50] manifested ambiguous feelings.

They exalted South Africa, but in doing so claimed full belonging to the country. Written in 1972, when another festival was organised to commemorate the arrival of Jan van Riebeeck at the Cape, "*Hip Hip Horah Suid-Afrika*", contains a discreet clue which seems to confirm this interpretation:

Toe ek met my skippie in die Tafelbaai kom	When I sailed into Table Bay with my little boat
Toe kyk ek na die berg en vra toe hoekom	I looked at the mountain and asked why
Die berg so plat is soos die tafel in 'n huis	The mountain was as flat as a table from home
Toe kry ek die antwoord dit kom uit die kombuis	The answer came from the kitchen

Jan van Riebeeck asked a question and the only ones who could answer were the people in the kitchen, slaves and/or Khoikhois, the ancestors of many people who were later classified coloured. Again, on an occasion when the beginnings of European colonisation of southern Africa were celebrated, the songs are a reminder that Khoikhois, slaves and their descendants played a decisive role in the edification and development of Cape Town and South Africa.

Other songs may have intimated derision or criticism of the leaders through plays on words and use of slang that whites could not understand. But there was always a risk that the songs would reach the ears of police informers or government experts able to decipher their meaning.[51] Adam Samodien, a very astute juggler of words, participated in the split that saw a number of choirs leave the CMCB in 1952 to form the SAKR because they refused to participate in the celebration of the tercentenary of Jan van Riebeeck's arrival at the Cape.[52] However, he insists, in the *moppies* he wrote in those times, he wanted first to make his audiences laugh and did not intend in the least to formulate protests. That was the case with "*Almal in Een Kamer*", and also with other songs in which he detailed the hardships endured by people who had been moved to the new townships or, on a more comic note, chronicled the hazards of traveling by taxi from townships to the town centre in "*Die Ontmoeting in die Taxi*" (The Meeting in the Taxi).[53] His argument was: "Don't make a sad situation even sadder, try to laugh about it, that's the purpose of a *moppie*" (Van der Wal 2009: 39). For Anwar Gambeno, there was something more: the possibility to use humour in order to say things that were not supposed to be said:

> I don't know what kind of term you use in music when you talk about hiding the story away, surrounding the story with humour. This is the way I write the *moppie*; I take a story, a serious story, and I try to come across the story with humour, so that I don't have a direct attack on whoever I'm talking about. You understand?

> But this is the way I was taught to write a *moppie*, because if we go back, you will see that a lot of *moppies* were written during the struggle, but because the white man at that time, especially the guys that were in power, the bourgeois, they thought... They promoted the idea of the "jolly hotnot",[54] you remember that term, the "jolly hotnot"? They thought that the coloureds were a bunch of clowns [...] a bunch of clowns, of drunkards, you know what I mean, they live to drink wine. But what they did not know is that in the meantime the coloureds were educating themselves all the time and becoming *au fait* with what is going on in the country. But there were some of the people that went out and blew up the toilets; there were some of the people that went to stand on the Parade and shouted what they wanted to shout and got arrested; but then there was the Minstrels and the Malay Choirs that was very subtle, and we used to write the *moppies* to actually tell these guys what we thought of them, but in humour, in a humorous way, in a humorous way.[55]

If there was "resistance" in *moppies*, it also lay, added Anwar Gambeno, in the very acts of continuing to write and sing *moppies*, and to celebrate the New Year. To perpetuate, in spite of infinite tribulations, a rite of entry into a new cycle of life and to maintain original practices that displayed the historicity and originality of a culture amounted to symbolic gestures, which contradicted stereotypes forged about coloureds to justify their treatment under apartheid (i.e. the "jolly hotnot"). These gestures manifested endurance and resilience that became foremost qualities in the eyes of people whose history had gone from slavery to racism and humiliation.

Anwar Gambeno's emphasis on the political implications of just writing and singing *moppies* tends to confirm that no songs with deeply corrosive political meanings were written during apartheid. This does not preclude the fact that a few texts may have addressed political issues, but contributes to explaining why they were so few and why they have not been collected and have not remained in people's memories. There are, however, scattered clues that lead to thinking that even if *moppies* entered in competitions did not engage head-on with the social and political situation, *moppies* or what could be called the "spirit of *moppies*" inspired songs which were sung in other circumstances. In the streets, words of popular songs could be spontaneously twisted to produce impromptu refrains mocking the authorities. In 1952, when Jan van Riebeeck's arrival at the Cape was officially celebrated, a song appeared — probably modelled on Lionel Hampton's 1946 hit "Hey! Baba Rebop" — whose catchphrase was: "*Hey! Ba-ba-re-ba se ding is vim*" (Hey! Jan van Riebeeck is impotent)[56] (Howard 1994: 73). Later, in the 1960s, children, revelling in their own carnival, adapted Elvis Presley's ballad "It's Now or Never" to coin a prophetic line: "It's now or never, Verwoerd is gonna die".⁵⁷ In the late 1980s, *ghoema* music, that is, the legacy of *ghoemaliedjies* and *moppies*, provided young musicians calling themselves The Genuines (Martin 2013: 236–237) with material upon which they built a jazz-rock repertoire. One of its kingpins, bassist and guitarist Gerald "Mac" McKenzie, was himself the son of a banjo player known as "Mr Mac". "Mac" McKenzie recalled: "We used the *ghoema* rhythm to sing English and ... sharp social comment [...] that is basically the *moppie*. And we always said that we were taking that *moppie* tradition to a political level, and social comment level on another plane."⁵⁸ Naas Botha,⁵⁹ a white icon of South African rugby at the time when it was totally segregated, was one of their targets. The song went:

> It's only a matter of time, till time catches you on the wrong foot.
> Hum hum. Off side, off balance, off side, off balance, off side, Prruit Prruit, Mister Referee, off side, off balance [...] [shouting] Mister Referee,
> When you look at a scrum, you only see a lot of bums,
> Now Bhota is a *naai*,⁶⁰ really, Mister Ref. [referee] and Naas Bhota is a hooligan, check out your percentages, according to the law, [...] it's only a matter of time, till time catches you on the wrong foot,
> Off side, off balance, off side, Prruit Prruit, Mister Referee,
> Off side, when looking at a rugby scrum, you just see a lot of bums,
> This Naas Bhota is a NAAI.⁶¹

This song was recorded but never released.

Moral messages

After 1994, the social and political dimensions of life in the new South Africa could be more openly evoked in *moppies*. In *"Die Toyi Toyi vir 12 %"*,⁶² Adam Samodien told of protesters claiming salary increases and suggested that disenchantment was on the rise. In the same vein, *"Die Toyi Toyi/Ons Hoor"* described, as we have already seen, troubles and anxieties rampant before the 1994 elections. In 2008, Adam Samodien, again, praised Nelson Mandela on the occasion of his 85th birthday with *"Die Party van die Jaar"*.⁶³ However, *moppies* have more of a moral, rather than overtly political, orientation. They tend to expose and convey a message. Although they may be called "comic songs" or "comics", humour does not necessarily pervade their lyrics. They speak of domestic violence, abusive sex,⁶⁴ alcoholism, drug use; evils which plague coloured townships. References to racism are scarce. One exception is *"Fiela se Kind"*⁶⁵ (Fiela's Child) by Adam Samodien, based on a feature film exposing the absurdity of racial categorisation.⁶⁶ Here the distress and the dignity of the coloured woman are not really made funny by her portrayal in the song:

*Sy dra 'n bonte **rok***	She wears a floral dress
*En 'n turban op haar **kop***	And a turban on her head
*Sy is **kort** en **dik soos** 'n vuilnis**blik***	She's short and bulky like a trashcan
*Net **soos** 'n **br**oeis vol**str**uis*	Like a grumpy ostrich
*Sleep sy weg van die **h**uis*	She hits the road leaving her home

There is definitely nothing comic, either in these words or in the rest of the lyrics. Instead, the lyrics suggest a form of unrelenting resolution (signalled by alliterations printed in bold), which once more underlines a capacity to survive and a resolution not to accept things passively.

Today, humour can be used to express a veiled criticism of gangs and drug dealers. It is a well-known fact that some *Klopse* captains are themselves drug dealers and that drugs are sold at some *Klopskamers* during practices. *Moppies* can then be used to send a warning to young troupe members. Anwar Gambeno, who coached teams other than his own, clearly stated:

> You see I teach a team but the owner of the team is a gangster, or the owner of the team is a drug merchant, or the owner of the team is a wine seller, but I teach that team. But I am talking about that guy, the owner, in my song I am talking about him. I am telling him: "Why are you selling drugs to the children?" But I am not using his name. He is also laughing about it, because he is too stupid to realise that I am talking about him [laughing]. I am telling the youngsters: "Listen here you mustn't associate with those kinds of people, these guys are detrimental."[67]

The relationship between *Klopse* and gangs is indeed difficult to investigate; there are rumours and reputations; an observer can sometimes catch glimpses of exchanges between money and a small bag of white substance during a rehearsal; but it is delicate to go beyond that and, of course, to name names. What is obvious is that some *Klopse* are wealthier than others and can afford to hire several specialised coaches and excellent soloists and musicians. Their resources may come from businesses which are perfectly legitimate (a transport company, for instance) or not. Several coaches confessed that they had to work for "funny people" to make ends meet, but they were not ready to mention their names. Anwar Gambeno admitted that he had to coach teams "owned" by such people but, at the same time, considered that it gave him the opportunity to talk to the youth through his *moppies*, even in a form of indirect speech:

> The message, that is the most important [...] I wrote a moppie about the drugs for example, a couple of years ago. The people who sell the drugs used to be the Rastaman, they sold ganja.[68] I wrote a moppie about the Rastaman[69] [...] and in that moppie I am saying

that this guy claims he is a doctor, but he is not a doctor, he sells drugs [...] The weed, the herb that he's selling is drugs. It makes you eat and it makes you laugh. You see, so it is funny, people laugh about it because they recognise it. They acknowledge what you're saying because they know that is an evil in the society. But it is a message to the youngsters you see. For example if I can educate one youngster, I am [...] It is a victory for me. That is what I do.[70]

Musical intertextuality

As we have just seen, the lyrics of "comic songs" need not necessarily be funny. Humour may be found in the way everyday realities are described and in rhetorical and phonetic techniques; however, many texts appear devoid of the faintest drollery. The comic in *moppies* does not only lie in the words, but in the combination of the lyrics with the antics of the soloist[71] (and sometimes of the *pak* as well) and with the music. The music must season the words, according to Adam Samodien: "It's spice for the food, let's take it like that, it is spice, if you use the right amount of spice, then the food will be perfect."[72] It is built upon the *ghoema* beat and generates a mood which colours the story being told.[73]

This combination has to be understood against the backdrop of the social situation in which *moppies* are performed: it is offered to listeners who have the comic within themselves and transform it in laughter because the combination of lyrics-music-gesticulation of the soloist meets their expectations (Jeanson 1950: 87–88). Music composed as potpourris also gives listeners the opportunity to display an outstanding musical expertise. *Moppie* composers possess an incredible musical culture and have in their memory an almost infinite stock of international and South African pop songs, not to mention several European classical "hits". Their audiences' abilities in this field are no less. The feeling of musical humour is stirred up by the capacity to identify in a composition elements coming from another piece and to appreciate the ingenuity of their assembling (Covach 1991). John R Covach studied parodies of songs by the Beatles shown in a film by Eric Idle and Gary Weis: "All You Need is Cash" (The Ruttles).[74] He concluded that the listeners' expertise allowed them to grasp the comic, the incongruous, or the disconcerting that arise from the relationship between the original music and its parody, and between the music and the lyrics (Covach 1991: 122). Vladimir Jankélévitch (1964) highlighted how puzzling aspects of Gabriel Fauré's compositions, and how amazing contrasts in Claude Debussy's produced humorous effects.[75] John Covach and Vladimir Jankélévitch's studies suggest that listeners are endowed with a capacity to navigate the channels of musical intertextuality (Covach 1991: 144), which allows them to reconstruct a dialectical relationship between the congruous and the incongruous (Scruton

1987). This is not only a source of pleasure, but of personal satisfaction, if not of pride.

These mechanisms – pleasure generated by the identification of musical borrowings, by the perception of a dialectic of the congruous and the incongruous, and by feelings of amazing contrasts – are at work when audiences attending Malay Choir competitions watch and listen to *moppies*. Melodic "snatches", appropriated and transformed, spice up the words and hint at something other than their explicit topic, and even sometimes seem to contradict their content. The listener finds pleasure in untangling enmeshed significations. When it comes to the gimmick part of the *moppie*, when borrowings are made even more easily identifiable, the relationship between music and words becomes truly exhilarating. For these mechanisms to operate fully, music must meet the audiences' tastes, which fluctuate according to times and fads. This is why *moppie* composers keep abreast of trends in pop music and especially of evolutions in youth musical preferences. In order for their moral messages about violence, drugs and other social evils to be heard, they have to use tunes that are likely to attract the youth, but at the same time, they cannot totally do away with a "tradition" to which teenagers do not necessarily relate. This is one of the challenges *moppie* composers have to meet. Yet, even when a *moppie* does not contain or suggest a moral message, the ability to identify a musical source and to associate the meanings of the original words with those of the *moppie* lyrics is indeed a source of satisfaction, pleasure and pride. As we have seen above, Waseef Piekaan used in "*Sokkie Bokkie*" fragments of "Baby", the hit that launched the career of Justin Bieber. The superimposition of the words of "Baby" with those of "*Sokkie Bokkie*" is clearly complementary. Waseef Piekaan draws a burlesque and somewhat naughty portrait of the "*bokkie*":[76]

Daar kom my bokkie,	There comes my babe,
Daar kom sy aan	Here she comes
Sy het 'n lekker sexy mini aan	She's wearing a nice sexy mini
Sy vat haar tyd	She takes her time
Sy gee haar uit	She shows off
Sy doen die sokkie terwyl sy die tuin nat spuit.	She does the sokkie while watering the garden.

The melody of "Baby" conjures up an amorous desire which will explicitly surface later in "*Sokkie Bokkie*", because it recalls the words chirped by the juvenile voice of the Canadian singer:

> You know you love me
> I know you care
> Just shout whenever

And I'll be there
You want my love
You want my heart
And we would never, ever, ever be apart[77]

The combination of "*Sokkie Bokkie*" and "Baby" includes young singers and young listeners in a prestigious world of globalisation, mediated by the internet. It illustrates a phenomenon which sociologist Crain Soudien highlighted in a study on Cape Town high school students. Music is a powerful means to extend the borders of the local so that they absorb the international; in so doing, it makes it easier to construct new identities and conveys wishes to belong to a transnational youth community (Soudien 2009: 28).

Self-esteem

The composition and performance of *moppies* are underpinned by composers', singers' and musicians' need to be recognised as talented and creative individuals, and consequently by the will to see the groups to which they belong awarded the same consideration. Michael Abrahams, aged 74 at the time of the interview, played double-bass for the choirs when he was young. He recalled the times of apartheid and the feelings generated by participating in *Klopse* and Malay Choirs:

> You know we never had a chance to do anything, we couldn't even go anywhere. Then we made our own things with the *Klopse*, with the Coons, we made our own things and we created our own songs and our *moppies* were great […] Yeah, there was guys, they were nothing. When they came into the Coons, they learned to sing, they learned to play, they learned to dance and they became stars. Some of them went overseas […] You know now I praise the Coons, because the Coons build me up, everybody know me. And when I got a young man, I started playing in a band and then the big guys came and ask me: "Come and play with us". And I started playing in white night clubs with white people and I made money and I bought my own home. I had nothing but through my bass playing, I've got my own home today. I'm telling you and I can never forget, it really comes from the Coons, from the Coons, I will never forget. Because it's the only place where you were known. Because you couldn't describe what you've got in anywhere else, but in the Coons you can. And there is thousands of people come watch the Coons then they see you and they listen to you, look at Yusuf Williams[78] he was nothing.[79]

Michael Abrahams mentions Yusuf Williams as an example of Cape Town artists who became fully appreciated only after they had left South Africa. In many other interviews the names of Joseph Gabriels,[80] Dollar Brand/Abdullah Ibrahim,[81] Jonathan Butler[82] appear as evidence that talents who could not blossom in South Africa had to go into exile to become recognised as they deserved. As far as Michael Abrahams is concerned, the Coons were a launching pad from which he could reach more prestigious stages as a jazz and dance musician playing for white audiences. The Coons opened the door to a double recognition: within the world of New Year festivals and by music aficionados, without distinction of colour. The sense of pride he got from such an achievement is obvious in the interview.

Years later, in the time of computers, Ismail Bey recounted a similar experience:

> When I started off, computers were just a few years old and I got myself a computer. In fact I never paid for it, the Coons they paid for it. Because like I said, they wanted the music and I needed equipment. So we spoke a deal I said: "You buy me equipment and I'll make the music".[83]

In the 2000s, Ismail Bey owned his own recording studio in Kensington, Cape Town. *Moppie* composers share the pride expressed by musicians and usually emphasise that the music they create is different from European or "white" music, and is actually unique. Anwar Gambeno is a fervent advocate of what he considers the Cape Town tradition:

> This is how this thing was carrying over to generations, it is orally, this is oral tradition. And this is important, don't forget this. Cape Malay who is singing moppies is an oral tradition, the ghoemalidjies is an oral tradition, because it hasn't been written down [...] People do it spontaneously; they feel it, that's what's unique [...] I am talking about the ordinary man in the street that comes from the townships. That the slaves, what did they know about 16 beat to a bar, what did they know about the smaller values? What did they know about the minor notes and the sharps and [...] and major [...] They didn't know these things! But they did it! And this is what makes it unique. What makes me unique? I feel like I am unique. I teach a choir, but I am not [...] musically literate. I can't read a note [...] and it is a very good choir, so that makes me unique.[84]

Anwar Gambeno not only claims his legitimacy as a composer who does not know how to read or write music, he asserts that his particular mode of composition allows him to create songs whose musical characteristics are unique, and cannot be found anywhere else in the world. And that is indeed a source of great satisfaction which nurtures self-esteem in the face of contempt directed at coloured people in general and at the music of *Klopse* and Malay Choirs in particular. Many other musicians articulated similar opinions. Adam Samodien explained: "Myself and so many others we can't write or read music. And I think that is what it make so unique."[85] Ismail Bey insisted that this uniqueness is not only South African, it is a product of the Cape Town situation: "Because let me put it in this way, you won't find this type of music nowhere around the world, not even in Johannesburg, only in Cape Town, that makes it so unique. It is something different."[86] Moreover, the self-esteem derived from the uniqueness of *Klopse* and Malay Choirs music is inextricably linked with an historical consciousness that relates *moppies* to *ghoemaliedjies* and slave songs: it constitutes coloured people as fully-fledged participants in the history of South Africa.

Everyone together

This can also be apprehended from another angle in several songs describing events that happened after the collapse of apartheid; there is a clear emphasis on the unity of all South Africans. "*Ons almal*" (all of us together) embraces every South African citizen, irrespective of the category they were previously put into. This is obvious in "*Die Toyi Toyi/Ons Hoor*", in which "*Almal doen die toyi toyi toyi*" (they are all doing the *toyi-toyi*) is complemented with "*Ons almal sê nou vaarwel Madiba*" (we all say farewell Madiba). The *toyi-toyi*, initially danced by black African activists and protesters, is now performed by all those who participate in protest marches to claim an improvement in their living conditions. In "*Die Toi-Toi vir 12%*" Adam Samodien details who are the people included in "*ons almal*": "*Daar was wittes, swartes and bruines deurmekaar*" (there were whites, blacks and coloureds, all mixed together, the use of *deurmekaar* in a *moppie* suggesting happy to be together); and they all sang "*Nkosi Sikelel' iAfrika*". The same "*ons almal*" participated in 2004 in the "party" celebrating Nelson Mandela's 85th birthday. Among revellers enjoying the "Party of the Year" ("*Die Party van die Jaar*")[87] Adam Samodien noticed people coming from black African townships (Soweto, Khayelitsha, Gugulethu, Langa and Nyanga), as well as "honoured guests from America". The entire ANC was there, including the then President and Deputy-President of the country, Thabo Mbeki and Jacob Zuma. The latter, known for singing and dancing in political meetings, is even said to have played the *ghoema*. Coloured politicians were also there: national or provincial ministers as if the author wanted to stress that in the "new" South Africa, in Nelson Mandela's South Africa, coloureds can access the highest positions of authority. However, the best example of this new conception of a reunited South Africa is probably Terry Hector's "*Vusie van Guguletu*".[88] As we explained in Chapter Two, this tells how a black African from Soweto became a go-between facilitating a fusion of coloured and "highbrow" white cultures. The fable of Vusie intimates that cultures and musics can be fused to create something new and enjoyable: there are no barriers to exchanges, and the meeting of people with different backgrounds stimulates inventiveness and originality.

Comic, identity and survival

Moppies are not always very funny. Why then are they called "comic songs" or "comics"? Because they sometimes are and because they form a repertoire whose main characteristic is to trigger laughter. Most songs performed in competitions attain this goal, yet not always and not necessarily in a spectacular manner. However, these explanations are not sufficient. It is necessary, in order to grasp a full understanding of the meaning of comic in "comic songs", to come back to the notion of a situation organised around the intention to find the songs funny. The very names "comic song" and "comics", applied to a repertoire performed in institutionalised competitions and characterised by a particular combination of unusual musical assemblage, lyrics and gestures, make *moppies* comic. When "comic songs" are seen from that angle, their social functions can be more easily understood.

Whatever the ridicule of the situations or the characters they depict, *moppies* impact upon the identity of those who sing and listen to them. They operate in a way that is not dissimilar to "ethnic jokes": "For those who enjoy the ethnic jokes about the group to which they are linked by ancestry, such jokes are an appropriate response to yet another ambiguous and uncertain situation — that of their ethnic identity itself" (Davies 1990: 311). In other words, wrote Daniel Sibony: "To laugh is to shake one's identity while being certain that it can be recovered, that the jolt is harmless" (Sibony 2010: 19);[89] it amounts to a reconciliation with the world and with oneself. This is what young people targeted by Waseef Piekaan with his "*Sokkie Bokkie*" do: they realise that the situation they live in is not at all disconnected from global cultures and that they have a right, and the possibility, to share in them. With regard to the question of identity, comic, humour and laughter entertain close relationships with feelings of shame, and especially with self-shame or self-hate stirred up by the Other's gaze. In South Africa, as in many countries which have been submitted to colonial and racial domination, persons who were treated as inferior in part internalised the inferiority ascribed to them,[90] while they never ceased to fight against it. They were traversed by a form of ambivalence that intertwined shame and self-esteem, struggle against scorn and efforts to recover dignity. Laughter, in the course of such struggles and efforts, appears, wrote Igor Krichtafovitch[91] (2006), commenting on Thomas Hobbes' conception of laughter, as the antithesis of shame. In the *Leviathan*, the latter wrote:

> Sudden glory is the passion which maketh those grimaces called laughter; and is caused either by some sudden act of their own that pleaseth them; or by the apprehension of some deformed thing in another, by comparison whereof they suddenly applaud themselves. And it is incident most to them that are conscious of the fewest abilities in themselves; who are forced to keep themselves in their own favour by observing the imperfections of other men.[92]

Within the circle of *moppies*, *Klopse* and Malay Choirs aficionados, those who laugh (even if the laughter is reduced to an *in petto* chuckle) discover at the same time their capacity to be and their superior adaptation to life (Ludovici 1932), an epiphany that brings to the fore endurance and resilience. This discovery is supported by a wide musical culture that transcends the borders of townships, formal education and social status. According to Francis Jeanson, laughter testifies to

> a need to discover oneself superior, [to] a type of promethean need to protest in a human manner against a relative and miserable condition, as well as against who is possibly responsible for this condition. [Laughter] is in its most general form a grouchy demurral against the relative, i.e. finally an implicit remonstration addressed by the subject to his own cowardice, because he does not take on his effective role as subject. (Jeanson 1950: 179)[93]

Couched in Sartrian language, Francis Jeanson's suggestion is that laughter is a weapon which can be used to fight shame, but does not totally free the subject from ambivalence. Coming from another philosophical tradition, Vladimir Jankélévitch (1964: 183) pushed the argument a little further when he wrote: "Irony says in its own way that the whole essence of the human being implies becoming, that he has no other possibility of being than to become what he ought to be."[94] Reinserted in Francis Jeanson's line of reasoning, this implies that, in particular in situations of oppression and inferiorisation, this ought-to-be points towards liberation (Jeanson 1950: 179). In *moppies*, the irony that corrodes the Self (a Self that was at least in part ascribed) and what it experiences (an experience that was largely imposed) already gestures towards freedom: it is a movement that carries "beyond". (Jankélévitch 1964: 35)

> Irony, because it mimics false truths compels them to spread out [...] It brings in full light their nonsensical nature, it makes absurdity self-refute itself. In other words, it makes the absurd responsible for furnishing the evidence of its own impossibility. It makes the absurd itself do all it is able to do. (Jankélévitch 1964: 100)[95]

Moppies, weaving fragments of music coming from beyond the walls of apartheid to trumpet, to the *ghoema* beat, words which told of everyday life — sometimes funnily, sometimes not —, exposed the absurdity of apartheid and brought to the limelight apartheid displaying its own absurdity.

The ought-to-be free, reinforced by the evidence of the system's absurdity, does not urge to upset anything or to imagine a decisive fight. It seems to feed a latent demurral that continues to struggle with shame. Francis Jeanson considered that "to persistently remonstrate against someone or something amounts to eluding — by addressing it elsewhere — the reproach of incapacity that one is tempted to direct at oneself. I denounce an outside evil in order to avoid encountering it in my own doing" (Jeanson 1950: 186).[96] Laughter enables one not to mock oppression itself, but to discreetly question the principles on which the law that organises oppression is based. Consequently, it scoffs at oppression to give one the strength to continue enduring it: laughter is a means to play "between open creativity and contained imagination" (Sibony 2010: 31). Laughter does not aim at fostering "resistance" and, adds Daniel Sibony: "the idea that laughter 'subverts' institutions is a stale cliché" (Sibony 2010: 125).

When people are subjected both to contempt and hardships, their priority is to survive. Humour can help people live through such situations. Untouchables in India have used it for a long time; they have displayed, especially women, "an aptitude to self-mockery, to make fun of [their] misfortunes, perhaps because they had no other possibility to react to the harshness of their lot and the callousness of men" (Racine & Racine 1995: 482). Daniel Sibony explains how, in general, humour operates in conditions of oppression: "Humour goes beyond accommodating disorder or integrating the abnormal; it makes them say strange things that denounce order and norms — within which it is nevertheless incorporated. Humour never forgets what is most important: to survive" (Sibony 2010: 182).[97] Humour, he concludes "amounts to consoling oneself of being oneself, given that one cannot do otherwise" (Sibony 2010: 176).[98] To play with words, gestures, music, to be able to circumvent, at least partially, domination, brings consolation. It makes it possible to recover one's self-esteem, a pre-requisite to be able to think about liberation. In some cases, *moppies* have constituted a model for struggle songs. They provided a framework that was symbolically linked to self-assertion, historical consciousness and dignity. The *ghoema* beat was the foundation upon which Cape Jazz was built, a new style that accompanied the emergence of the United Democratic Front (UDF) in the 1980s. In post-apartheid South Africa, characterised by acute and increasing inequalities, some *moppies* continue to convey ethical messages and expose the dangers of alcohol, drugs and violence in the very milieus where they are rampant. *Moppies* — and the New Year festivals as a whole — are replete with symbolic codes that can be used in other creative forms.

The study of *moppies* demonstrates that, as underlined by Daniel Sibony, the idea that comic, humour and derision are systematically subversive is a sterile cliché. This observation invites us to reconsider analyses that pre-suppose that all forms of "popular culture" are forms of resistance. As a matter of fact, one can discern in cultural practices a much wider gamut of reactions to oppression, many of them pervaded with ambivalence. First appears the necessity to survive and, indissolubly, to regain one's self-esteem; it is the condition to be able to think about liberation for, as Georges Balandier stated: "Liberation begins with liberation in the imaginary" (Balandier 1971: 163). On this basis, many different strategies can be devised, ranging from a tactical acceptance of domination to a determination to fight the oppressive system. In between can be identified passive — often discursive and symbolic — rejections of domineering powers and small acts aimed at alleviating certain effects of domination without attempting to completely upset it. South Africa and Cape Town offer many examples of such strategies and contribute to a better understanding of the role humour plays: an indispensable, and at the same time limited, role.

* * *

Cape Town *moppies* illustrate how a social group construes and exhibits its culture. Appropriation and transformation of foreign elements, circulated through the international networks of popular culture, have for a long time furnished the means to overcome and break through the barriers erected by racism and apartheid. They have complemented and enriched "traditions" invented by members of the proletariat, confirming that "traditions" should be understood as "established structures of creativity" (Coplan 2001: 113). Cultural practices can be perpetuated because they are incessantly renewed, thanks to the dialectics of the dynamics from inside and outside (Balandier 1971). *Moppies* maintain and express an imaginary centred on the idea of resilience that is rarely explicitly articulated. This was suggested by the first reactions from Denis-Constant Martin's interlocutors to a prompt he used to start non-directive interviews he conducted in 1994. The question "What do the Coons[99] mean to you?" frequently triggered the answer: "The Coons will never die". This unexpected (at least by the interviewer) answer echoes Pumla Dineo Gqola's proposition that to celebrate a history of survival politically means "to assert, in the words of the old slave song, 'we are here because we are here' and to invite an interrogation of the untidy meanings we attach to survival" (Gqola 2010: 50). This is not a South African particularity, not even a Cape Town specificity; the Guadeloupian writer Maryse Condé recalled an old West Indian saying: "*Un nègre ne meurt jamais*" (a negro never dies) and commented: "Paradoxically, negroes have faith in themselves, in their resistance, in their capacity to survive. 'A negro never dies.' They are the weed none can get rid of. Negroes have survived the middle passage. They have survived strokes, scaffolds, dogs' jaws [...] Hated, scorned, they have nevertheless invaded the islands; they have nevertheless shaped the whites to their semblance, before giving West Indian civilisations their idiosyncratic figure" (Condé 1978: 32).[100] *Moppies*' brand of humour affirms the same conviction: it is imperative to survive, whatever the burden of oppression; it is imperative to demonstrate the historical rootedness of coloured people and to show that this rootedness fuelled a creative energy that underpinned resilience and still nourishes reactions to a situation where many people feel they are: "Not White Enough, Not Black Enough" (Adhikari 2005). *Moppies* perpetuate a system whereby elements likely to enrich local imaginaries are borrowed from outside, are transformed and become an integral part of the local culture. In the process, they are re-signified (Manuel 1994: 274) and contribute to a constant *aggiornamento* of forms and contents that makes them contribute to coping with endlessly changing situations.

Notes

1. Van der Wal 2009, "Appendix 2": 12.
2. See: The Tulips 2002. "*Die Oxford*" is a very fine example of a song probably composed in the 1940s, which includes fragments of a much older song, probably dating back to the mid-19th century; the lyrics are included in Part Three Appendix: "*Moppie* Lyrics".
3. Ismail and Gamja Dante, interview with Denis-Constant Martin, Hanover Park, 20 October 2011; the lyrics are included in Part Three Appendix: "*Moppie* Lyrics".
4. Van der Wal 2009, "Appendix 2": 22.
5. The lyrics are included in Part Three Appendix: "*Moppie* Lyrics".
6. *Deurmekaar* rhymes with *Nuwe Jaar* (New Year), just as Carnival rhymes with Bacchanal in Trinidad; similarly *musiek* rhymes with *tariek*.
7. Ismail Dante, interview with Armelle Gaulier, Mitchells Plain, 31 August 2006.
8. Shawn Pettersen, interview with Armelle Gaulier, Cape Town, 3 October 2006.
9. As mentioned by Ismail Dante in "*Fiesta Tyd*": rumba, samba, breakdance.
10. It has not been possible to trace with certainty the date when this song was composed. According to Melvyn Matthews, it was probably during apartheid for it includes words, such as "*peraare*", which are no longer used in today's Afrikaans.
11. "Une dépassante imprévisible".
12. Van der Wal 2009, "Appendix 2": 9.
13. The character, or his name, may have been inspired by *Joe Barber*, a popular South African stage play and television series by Oscar Petersen and David Isaacs; the lyrics are included in Part Three Appendix: "*Moppie* Lyrics".
14. *Bergies*: from *berg*, mountain; originally vagrant individuals living on the slopes of Table Mountain in Cape Town; it has acquired the general meaning of homeless people, tramps, outcast, waifs.
15. *Afrikaaps* is a musical play that was performed on stage in Amsterdam in 2009, at the Klein Karoo Nasionale Kunstefees in Oudtshoorn, then at the Cape Town Baxter Theatre in 2010. Written by Dylan Valley and Khalid Shamis, it glorifies Cape Town's coloured cultures and language. It featured several renowned Cape Town artists, such as pianist and composer Kyle Shepherd, poet Jethro Louw and rapper Emile XY? Jansen. The show has been made into a documentary film directed by Dylan Valley: *Afrikaaps*, Cape Town: Plexus Films, 2010. Available at https://afrikaaps.wordpress.com/ [accessed 2 October 2015].
16. Taliep Abrahams, interview with Armelle Gaulier, Mitchells Plain, 18 September 2006.
17. The lyrics are included in Part Three Appendix: "*Moppie* Lyrics".
18. One of the strongest *Klops* is named the Cape Town Hawkers; it used to comprise a majority of hawkers.
19. *Madiba* is the name of the Xhosa clan to which Nelson Mandela belonged. It underlines the fact that his ancestry goes back to a chief who ruled the Thembu kingdom in the 18th century, before the British conquest. Using "*Madiba*" connotes both respect and affection.
20. Anwar Gambeno, interview with Armelle Gaulier, Mitchells Plain, 31 August 2006.
21. The lyrics are included in Part Three Appendix: "*Moppie* Lyrics".
22. A neighbourhood in the coloured township of Mitchells Plain developed by the apartheid government in the mid-1970s. It soon gained a reputation for gang violence and illicit drug and alcohol trading.
23. From Arabic *kūfiyyah* (كوفية, from the city of Kufa) and Kiswahili *kofia*: a small cap, frequently embroidered, worn by Muslim men.
24. Thawb or thobe (ثوب), a Muslim garment men usually wear when going to mosque.

25. On page three, *Die Son* prints the picture of a scantily clad woman; it can hardly be considered "porn" but may be shocking to some.
26. Vincent Kolbe, interview with Armelle Gaulier, Plumstead, 11 October 2006.
27. Felicia Lesch, interview with Denis-Constant Martin, Stellenbosch, 7 October 2011.
28. The lyrics are included in Part Three Appendix: "*Moppie* Lyrics".
29. The lyrics are included in Part Three Appendix: "*Moppie* Lyrics".
30. Van der Wal 2009, "Appendix 2": 26.
31. Van der Wal 2009, "Appendix 2": 54.
32. Van der Wal 2009, "Appendix 2": 49–50.
33. Ismail and Gamja Dante, interview with Denis-Constant Martin, Hanover Park, 20 October 2011; the lyrics are included in Part Three Appendix: "*Moppie* Lyrics".
34. Van der Wal 2009, "Appendix 2": 46–47.
35. Anwar Gambeno, in Anwar Gambeno and Muneeb Gambeno, interview with Denis-Constant Martin, Mitchells Plain, 2 May 2015.
36. A song by Taliep Abrahams, composed circa 1975. Interpreted by the Young Tulips Sangkoor in the CMCB 2012 competition; its lyrics are included in Part Three Appendix: "*Moppie* Lyrics".
37. Anwar Gambeno, interview with Denis-Constant Martin, Mitchells Plain, 11 October 2011.
38. Anwar Gambeno, interview with Denis-Constant Martin, Mitchells Plain, 11 October 2011; the lyrics are included in Part Three Appendix: "*Moppie* Lyrics".
39. Van der Wal 2009, "Appendix 2": 36.
40. Mac McKenzie, interview with Denis-Constant Martin, Bridgetown, 4 October 2011.
41. Van der Wal 2009, "Appendix 2": 35-36.
42. Van der Wal 2009, "Appendix 2": 31.
43. Adam Samodien, in Adam Samodien and Rashaad Malick, interview with Denis-Constant Martin, Woodstock, 12 October 2011.
44. Jeppie, 1990; the Afrikaans words are not quoted; Shamil Jeppie only gave the following translation.
45. Reproduced from a sheet given to Great Gatsbys' singers, kindly lent by Gerald L Stone. The late Gerald L Stone was a psychotherapist and linguist; he did pioneering research on the Afrikaans spoken by working class coloureds in Cape Town and on the gang lingo; he was among the first, if not the first, to undertake serious research on the *Klopse* (Stone 1971, 1991, 1995). Denis-Constant Martin is extremely grateful to Gerald L Stone for the support he granted him when he began his research in Cape Town and for the documents he lent him.
46. Recorded by Denis-Constant Martin during the 1994 *Klopse* carnival.
47. Recorded by Denis-Constant Martin during the 1994 *Klopse* carnival.
48. "*Generaal Smuts*" by Gamja Dante; Van der Wal 2009, "Appendix 2": 5.
49. Rashaad Malick and Adam Samodien, interview with Denis-Constant Martin, Woodstock, 12 October 2011; the lyrics are included in Part Three Appendix: "*Moppie* Lyrics".
50. Ismail and Gamja Dante, interview with Denis-Constant Martin, Hanover Park, 20 October 2011; the lyrics are included in Part Three Appendix: "*Moppie* Lyrics".
51. Rashaad Malick, in Rashaad Malick and Adam Samodien, interview with Denis-Constant Martin, Woodstock, 12 October 2011.
52. Johan Anthoniszoon "Jan" van Riebeeck (1619–1677) was a Dutch administrator who came to the Cape in 1652 to establish a supply station for the Dutch East Indies Company's ships sailing between Holland and Batavia; the colonisation of South Africa developed from this station.
53. Van der Wal 2009, "Appendix 2": 42–43.
54. "Hotnot", a deformation of hottentot, is an offensive term used to designate coloured people; the phrase "jolly hotnot" suggested that coloured people were happy and satisfied under racist regimes.

55. Anwar Gambeno, interview with Denis-Constant Martin, Mitchells Plain, 11 October 2011.
56. *Ba-ba-re-ba* could be a deformation of "Baby Riebeeck"; the translation of "*se ding is vim*" is provided by Colin Howard.
57. Melvyn Matthews, in Gamja Dante and Melvyn Matthews, interview with Denis-Constant Martin, Victoria and Alfred Waterfront, 17 October 2011. Hendrik Verwoerd was Prime Minister from 1956 to 1968; he was stabbed in Parliament on 6 September 1966. The song "It's Now or Never", with lyrics by Aaron Schroeder and Wally Gold, was released in 1960. Its tune was based on a well-known Italian ditty: "*O sole mio*".
58. "Mac" McKenzie, interview with Denis-Constant Martin, Bridgetown, 4 October 2011.
59. Available at http://en.wikipedia.org/wiki/Naas_Botha#The_1981_tour_and_sporting_bans [accessed 21 October 2015].
60. *Naai* is an Afrikaans word which literally means: stitch or sew; it also has a slangy signification: to fuck, have (hot) sex. It can be used as a strong insult to belittle someone (see: http://www.urbandictionary.com/define.php?term=naai [accessed 14 August 2012]).
61. "Mac" McKenzie, interview with Denis-Constant Martin, Bridgetown, 4 October 2011.
62. Rashaad Malick and Adam Samodien, interview with Denis-Constant Martin, Woodstock, 12 October 2011; the lyrics are included in Part Three Appendix: "*Moppie* Lyrics".
63. Rashaad Malick and Adam Samodien, interview with Denis-Constant Martin, Woodstock, 12 October 2011; the lyrics are included in Part Three Appendix: "*Moppie* Lyrics".
64. A bad boy who impregnates his fiancée ("*Gamad Salie*" by Adam Samodien (Van der Wal 2009, "Appendix 2": 38)); an adulterous relationship ("*Ou Tiefie en sy Houmeit*" [Old Tiefie and his mistress or "tart"] — *houmeit* conveys the idea of a kept girl; it means, in a derogatory way, an illicit lover—by Adam Samodien (Van der Wal 2009, "Appendix 2": 35)).
65. Van der Wal 2009, "Appendix 2": 40.
66. Van der Wal 2009, "Appendix 2": 40. *Fiela se Kind* was the title of a 1988 film by Katinka Heyns, produced by Sonneblom Films (South Africa), based on a novel by Dalene Matthee (Cape Town, Tafelberg, 1985). It told the story of Fiela Komoetie, a coloured woman who found a white boy on her doorstep and decided to adopt him. Several years later, she was ordered to give the boy "back" to a white couple who pretended they were his biological parents.
67. Anwar Gambeno, interview with Armelle Gaulier, Mitchells Plain, 31 August 2006.
68. The word *ganja* comes from the Sanskrit *gañjā*; it designates *cannabis sativa* and is used in Jamaica, in particular among adepts of the Rastafarian cult. It is commonly called *dagga* in South Africa.
69. "*Charlie Die Rasta-man*"; the lyrics are included in Part Three Appendix: "*Moppie* Lyrics".
70. Anwar Gambeno, interview with Armelle Gaulier, Mitchells Plain, 31 August 2006.
71. The body language of the *Voorsinger* sometimes appears as an illustration of Henri Bergson's theory that the comic "superimposes the mechanical on the living", which otherwise is not really applicable to *moppies* (Bergson 2011: 55, 61).
72. Adam Samodien, in Rashaad Malick and Adam Samodien, interview with Denis-Constant Martin, Woodstock, 12 October 2011.
73. Waseef Piekaan, interview with Denis-Constant Martin, Mitchells Plain, 25 October 2011.
74. Above Average Productions Inc., Broadway Video, Rutle Corp., 1978.
75. "*Clair de lune*", Op. 46 No. 2, on a poem by Paul Verlaine, by Gabriel Fauré (Jankélévitch 1964: 77); "Jimbo's Lullaby", second piece of *Children's CornerI*, by Claude Debussy (Jankélévitch 1964: 79).
76. Waseef Piekaan, interview with Denis-Constant Martin, Mitchells Plain, 25 October 2011.
77. Available at http://www.youtube.com/watch?v=N08Cw4RDuJg [accessed 23 April 2012].
78. Yusuf Williams, a.k.a. Joe Curtis, is a singer who started with the *Klopse* when still a child. He took singing lessons with the Eoan Group and became an acclaimed interpreter of

operas, operettas and pop songs. He toured Europe with the Golden City Dixies and settled in Sweden in 1959, from where he pursued a successful career as a jazz singer and entertainer, appearing at various casinos and on cruise ships around the world (Yusuf Williams *The Voice from South Africa Live: Music was my First Love.* Nimshuscheid [Germany]: Audimur, CD 02290902).

79. Michael Abrahams, in Michael Abrahams, Ronald Fisher and Eddie Matthews, interview with Armelle Gaulier, Mitchells Plain, 11 October 2006.
80. The late Joseph Gabriels indeed illustrates the difficulties "non-white" individuals were confronted with in apartheid South Africa when they wanted to enhance their artistic capabilities. Joseph Gabriels was born in Cape Town in 1937. He started singing with the *Klopse* and the Malay Choirs. In 1957 Joseph Manca, who regularly adjudicated *Klopse* competitions, heard him and asked him to join the Eoan Group which had organised a troupe of amateur coloured opera singers (Eoan History Project 2013). Joseph Manca trained him, and helped him to memorise his parts, since he could not read music. Joseph Gabriels appeared in the 1958 production of *Rigoletto*. In 1967, he was offered a bursary by the Schneier family of Johannesburg to study in Milan. Two years later, he won a prestigious singing competition in Busseto, the birthplace of Giuseppe Verdi. From 1969 onwards, he was invited to sing at some of the most renowned opera houses in the world: La Scala de Milano, the Metropolitan Opera in New York, where he made his debut on 5 February 1971 as Canio in *I Pagliacci* (he was the first South African to perform there); the opera houses of Dusseldorf and Duisburg (Joseph Gabriels, interview with Denis-Constant Martin, Groote Schuur Hospital, Cape Town, 18 October 1994; Martin 2013: 126).
81. Born Dollar Brand, pianist, composer and band leader, Abdullah Ibrahim, sang as a child in his grandmother's and mother's church choirs. He started playing with dance and jazz bands in the late 1940s and also performed with the *Klopse*. During the 1950s he became one of the foremost exponents of modern jazz in South Africa. He developed an original piano style, influenced by Duke Ellington and Thelonius Monk, and pervaded with influences from *Klopse* and Malay Choirs repertoires. He left South Africa in 1962 and became a respected jazz musician, participating in a musical movement called "free jazz", while he continued to refine his own style imbued with memories of Cape Town (Lucia 2002; Mason 2007; Rasmussen 2000).
82. Jonathan Butler is a guitarist, singer and composer whose South African debuts were quite successful: he was the first black artist to have one of his recordings played by white radio stations. He joined the popular jazz-rock group Pacific Express in the late 1970s and decided to move to Great Britain in the early 1980s. He then met with great success in Europe and the United States, thanks to a personal brand of jazz-fusion and inspirational music.
83. Ismail Bey, interview with Armelle Gaulier, Kensington, 19 September 2006.
84. Anwar Gambeno, interview with Armelle Gaulier, Mitchells Plain, 31 August 2006.
85. Adam Samodien, interview with Armelle Gaulier, Woodstock, 10 August 2006.
86. Ismail Bey, interview with Armelle Gaulier, Kensington, 19 September 2006.
87. The lyrics are included in Part Three Appendix: "*Moppie* Lyrics".
88. The lyrics are included in Part Three Appendix: "*Moppie* Lyrics".
89. "Rire, c'est se secouer l'identité en étant sûr qu'on peut la récupérer, que la secousse est sans danger."
90. James O'Toole considered that, in the late 1960s, self-deprecation was rampant among coloured people (O'Toole 1973: 11).
91. A soviet engineer, also known as a satirical poet, who migrated to the United States in 1994.
92. Hobbes, Thomas (1651) Introduction. In: Thomas Hobbes *Léviathan*. Available at http://oregonstate.edu/instruct/phl302/texts/hobbes/leviathan-a.html [accessed 23 February 2015].

93. Un "besoin de se découvrir supérieur, et [d'une] sorte de besoin prométhéen, de protestation humaine contre une condition misérable et relative, et contre le Responsable éventuel de cette condition [...] constitue sous sa forme la plus générale une récrimination contre le relatif, c'est-à-dire finalement une récrimination implicite du sujet contre sa propre lâcheté à ne point assumer son rôle effectif de sujet".
94. "l'ironie dit à sa manière que toute l'essence de l'être est de devenir, qu'il n'y a pas d'autre manière d'être que de devoir-être [...]".
95. "l'ironie, mimant les fausses vérités, les oblige à se déployer [...] elle fait éclater leur non-sens, elle induit l'absurdité en auto-réfutation, c'est-à-dire qu'elle charge l'absurde d'administrer lui-même la preuve de son impossibilité ; elle fait faire par l'absurde tout ce que l'absurde peut faire lui-même".
96. "si l'on récrimine toujours contre quelqu'un ou contre quelque chose, c'est fondamentalement pour éluder, en le reportant à l'extérieur, le reproche de carence que l'on serait tenté de s'adresser à soi-même. Je dénonce le mal au dehors pour ne point risquer de le rencontrer dans mes propres actes".
97. "l'humour fait mieux qu'accueillir le désordre ou intégrer l'anormal ; il leur fait dire des choses étranges qui dénoncent l'ordre et la norme — où pourtant il s'intègre. L'humour n'oublie jamais l'essentiel: survivre".
98. "l'humour c'est se consoler d'être soi vu qu'on ne peut pas faire autrement [...]".
99. That is, members of the *Klopse*, *Klopse* and New Year festivals as a whole.
100. "Paradoxalement, c'est en eux-mêmes que les nègres ont foi, en leur résistance, en leur capacité de survie. "Un nègre ne meurt jamais." Telle est la mauvaise plante dont on ne peut venir à bout, les nègres ont survécu aux vaisseaux négriers. Ils ont survécu aux coups, aux quatre-piquets, aux crocs [...] Haïs, méprisés, ils n'en envahissent pas moins les îles; ils n'en modèlent pas moins les blancs à leur image, avant de donner en fin de compte à la civilisation antillaise son visage particulier."

Brothers Ismail & Gamja Dante, at Ismail's place, Hanover Park, October 2011

CONCLUSION

Memory, resilience, identity and creolisation

Musicological descriptions of *nederlandsliedjies* and comic songs, complemented with information provided by singers, coaches and experts establish irrefutably that songs belonging to these repertoires are works of art. The particularities of their form, the technical mastery and the finesse required for their interpretation show that they are definitely *works*, demanding effort and talent, which aim to produce a form of *art* combining pleasure and beauty. Beauty, here, should be understood according to Édouard Glissant's conception: "Beauty is not the splendour of the true; it is and it reveals in a work or in a given *the strength of differences which, in the same time, come about and already foretell their relation to other differences*" (Glissant 2006: 45).[1] In other words, the beauty of a work of art lies as much in its intrinsic aesthetic qualities as in the capacity of these unique qualities to relate (to give an account of) and relate to (to establish two-way connections with) other, different, specificities. The "effusions of art" embrace spirit and affect, knowledge and sharing, truth and doubt, memories and mandatory filiations (Glissant 2006: 41); therefore they make works of art into "effective points of reference in and for the examination of the real" (Glissant 2006: 67), a real criss-crossed by networks linking differences and facilitating their interaction. Nathalie Heinich insists on the idea that art results from production processes and does something in the world where it is received: art is done and does (Heinich 1998: 37–38). In Édouard Glissant's vocabulary, it is part of the Relation that "links (relays), relates" (Glissant 1990: 187)[2]; art relates the real from which it emerges and links it to other realities, which will in turn relay it to even more realities. These premises invite us to consider that art — as lived by those who make it, along with the representations they build of it — can be the object of sociological studies (Heinich 1998). These studies should focus on "an analysis of the operations of production and reception, and of the representations of these operations by their agents. The aim of these analyses should be not to tell what art is, but what it 'represents' for the agents" (Heinich 1998: 24).

This is what we have attempted to do in this volume. The particularities of Malay Choirs and *Klopse*'s artistic productions, as discussed by the people who are involved in them, point towards several themes which underpin the configurations and reconfigurations of coloured identities: memory, resilience and community.

Memories

Nederlandsliedjies, *moppies* and their precursors, *ghoemaliedjies*, nurture an imaginary of the past which (re)creates a strong link with the times of slavery; they give choral practices — and the New Year festivals as a whole — a historical depth which in the contemporary period counterbalances whatever shame may have been attached to memories of servitude. Pumla Dineo Gqola — elaborating on a paper by writer Zoë Wicomb (Wicomb 1998), in which she dealt with the burden of shame in coloured people's history — proposed that: "The effect of this shame is forgetting, since it is the past, and awareness of this past, which inscribes these subjects with what is seen as shameful [...] The shame is therefore a response to a series of degrading periods in the past [...] it is a collective self-protection from the trauma of slavery and successful colonisation and dispossession" (Gqola 2007: 28). From another point of view, historian Alan Mountain wrote that: "Slave history is an unsung history" (Mountain 2004: 133). He considered that: "Contributions slaves made to the Cape have been largely ignored or unrecognised by the descendants of both slave owners and slaves. For personal and national reconciliation to be complete, this ignorance has to be addressed so that the contributions slaves made to Cape society can be acknowledged and celebrated in a spirit of respect, compassion and understanding" (Mountain 2004: 83). A better knowledge of *nederlandsliedjies* and *moppies* may contribute to such an acknowledgement; the more so since they probably sing a little bit more about slavery than Alan Mountain assumed. As a matter of fact, one should not only look for individual songs dealing, implicitly or explicitly, with slavery and oppression, but take into account the significance of perpetuating musical practices, which may have been initiated during slavery and which memories tie to the slavery period. Songs and singing do represent an important part of the archives stored in "the stubborn memories of people" (Gabeba Baderoon quoted in Gqola 2007: 37). The link they create with the very first episodes of the colonisation of South Africa is construed as evidence — along with architecture, the aesthetics of home decoration and furniture making, agricultural expansion, the formation of Afrikaans — of not only a founding presence, but a decisive role in the construction and development of South Africa. This link affirms that, contrary to what white racist or patronising ideologues contended, slaves and all those who were put in the coloured category were not an "appendage to the whites", as Jan Christiaan Smuts bluntly said (Lewis 1987: 210), but, in spite of their social situation, proved active and innovating participants in the edification of the country that was to be called South Africa. Thanks to these repertoires, the "stubborn memories of people" have archived a history of survival and resilience that can illuminate today's life. In her masters dissertation, Channel Oliphant recounts the story of *"Waalendorp"*, a song composed by the late Herbie van der Schyf in 1996 and sung by the Evergreens, then by the Young Ideas Malay Choirs and eventually by the Las Vegas *Klops*. It told of slavery in Cape Town and "how cultures grew from it, through people, through music and musical instruments" (Oliphant 2013: 82).[3] One of the singers explained "that to them 'Waalendorp' is about the story of slavery and that through singing it they are able to carry it over to the next generations [...] he felt happy and sad at the same time because although the slaves had it really bad yet still they rejoiced" (Oliphant 2013: 82). Singing that song made choir members aware of the history; it allowed them to tell their side of the story and articulate the inescapable conclusion: "Yet we still stand here" (Oliphant 2013: 82).

Songs and singing help overcome the feeling of shame that may be associated with a history of slavery and "racial" oppression because they testify to a protracted spirit of resilience and inventiveness. According to Adam Samodien, composing, coaching and singing amounts to "showing the roots, where we come from".[4] Humour in *moppies* hardly engages oppression head-on, but it contributes to providing the strength needed to survive because it subverts with creativity and imagination the very principles according to which domination is perpetrated (Sibony 2010: 31). *Nederlands* and *moppies* crossed through trials and tribulations, giving a comfort of sort to those who endured them; they kept a little ditty of hope audible. This is probably why musician Michael Abrahams could affirm that "the people never die".[5] Anthropologist Michel Agier, at the end of a transversal study of urban cultures, including South African townships, concluded more generally that festivals keep being celebrated whatever the circumstances because: "It is the force of hope, and not of despair, that feeds social and cultural creations, the capacity to go beyond one's limits and the calling into question of borders, the borders of real and false ghettos" (Agier 1999: 160).[6] As we have seen, songs of survival and resilience encapsulate potential models for more openly political creations: the forms of *nederlands* and *moppies*, fashioned by history, and the irony of *moppies* may be "recycled" to give birth to protest songs and music accompanying defiance actions.

Resilience

Resilience is a concept that was originally used by psychologists to describe processes of "successful adaptation to stressful events, oppressive systems, and other challenges of living" (Sonn & Fisher 1998: 458). Its semantic field has been extended to cover collective reactions and the role culture may play in adaptive processes. Susan Healey proposed the following definition, endorsed by John Fleming and Robert J Ledogar (2008): "Cultural resilience is defined here as the capacity of a distinct cultural system to absorb disturbance and reorganize while undergoing change so as to retain key elements of structure and identity that preserve its distinctness" (Healey 2006: 12). The human collective that animates the cultural system must be structured and organised in order to be able to adapt to change and to overcome traumas, without losing its cohesion and breaking its relationships with the rest of the world. The collective must develop an open and flexible mental model, which fosters an ability to innovate.[7] Communal resilience is therefore a process, not a trait (Fleming & Ledogar 2008); it generates dynamics that fuel changing and adapting, while the group maintains its cohesion. This implies a sense of belonging together, solid enough to put up with internal differences and divergences, as well as possibilities to entertain multiple identifications. Christopher C Sonn & Adrian T Fisher, citing many other authors, suggest that mediating structures and activity settings may "moderate the impact of oppressive systems and provide contexts for resilience and consciousness raising" (Sonn & Fisher 1998: 460). School, religious and sports groups, for instance, provide these structures and create opportunities of activities; Malay Choirs and *Klopse* have obviously similar effects. An important dimension of communal resilience underlined by the same authors (inspired by Vicki M Mays' research on African-American experiences)[8] is the existence of a gamut of attitudes generated by processes of resilience among oppressed people:

> At a surface level, communities show signs of capitulation and assimilation, while at a deeper, internal level they manage to protect core community narratives and identities. That is, they acquire the skills, competencies, and behaviours that are functional in the dominant group context; thus, they become bicultural, or they pass and external indicator suggest [sic] the loss of primary community identity. To an outside observer, this might be indicative of loss or compromise of cultural identities. However, this does not necessarily mean the complete loss of their primary community and cultural identities. (Sonn & Fisher 1998: 464)

The notion of "biculturalism" ought to be specified in the light of the type of creativity nurtured by mixing and blending, which the study of *nederlandsliedjies* and *moppies* revealed. This observation points nevertheless towards two interlocked phenomena. On the one hand, the ability to reconstruct, away from the oppressor's gaze, self-definitions of the group of belonging; these self-definitions are built on a recovered self-esteem, in which the awareness of one's creativeness is decisive; they may remain concealed, but may also be expressed in symbolic ways which make them difficult to decipher for outsiders (Bruinders 2012: 218–219). On the other hand, reconstructed self-definitions cannot totally wipe away the internalisation of negative stereotypes and the shame (Wicomb 1998) that remains attached to them; thence the presence of ambiguities and ambivalences, such as those which we discerned in discourses about *nederlands*. Agents of the New Year festivals participated actively in these processes of identity rehabilitation. The *Klopse* carnival and the Malay Choirs competitions have often been interpreted by whites and also by "élite" coloureds[9] as manifestations of subservience, while they symbolically manifested self-assertion, rootedness in history underpinning an inventive culture, and all that was denied by racist stereotypes. Cultural practices and their outcomes are one of the engines of resilience, understood as the capacity to confront the traumas of oppression and to circumvent their consequences by resorting to multiple strategies, from apparent submission to open opposition. They reinforce the cohesion of a subjugated group and give its members a sense of historical continuity. But in every case, the "group" has to be qualified. In the case of the participants in the New Year festivals, we have seen that they come in their majority from a particular socio-economic stratum: workers, employed or not, and artisans. They belong to a proletariat that, in addition to racism, has been a victim of the contempt of better educated and better-off coloured people.

Finally, this short discussion of the notion of resilience suggests that the gap between resilience and resistance should not be analytically bridged too promptly. As a matter of fact, it seems to show that there is not really any gap between the two, but rather a continuum, along which resilience generates many forms of actions and non-actions: apathy, deliberate acquiescence, strategic adaptation, silent disagreement, symbolic mockery, open contestation, to mention a few. Anwar Gambeno situated *moppies* somewhere in the middle of this continuum when he said that composers and singers aimed at telling with subtlety what they thought of the perpetrators of apartheid.[10] Globally, the obduracy displayed in celebrating the New Year, in spite of the multiplication of tragedies — an attitude that was sometimes interpreted as a show of insensibility to dramas endured by innumerable families, if not as an act of support for the authorities — should be reinterpreted in that perspective: what was foremost was the continued affirmation of a capacity to endure and survive; the uninterrupted demonstration of a creativeness rooted in history.

Community

Resilience is both an engine of creativity and one of its outcomes. People treated as subhuman or despised as inferior creatures have first to convince themselves that they are full-fledged human beings; then they can endeavour to persuade others, including those who look down upon them and oppress them, that they are their equals. Creation is one of the means they use to achieve both these ends. Although they do not always articulate it explicitly, human beings construe their capacity to invent something new, original and different, as evidence of their humanness (Cassirer 1979). Their innovations in the fields of social organisation, language, religion and culture render them special in their own eyes and give them strength to bear domination and, when the possibility arises, to confront it. The fact that creations contributed to slaves' and oppressed people's ability to survive was demonstrated in the Americas and the West Indies; the history of South Africa is not different in that respect. Music is indeed one of the privileged domains where creation can blossom. For it requires only a human body: a mouth to sing or whistle, hands to clap, feet to stomp and a chest to strike; these are amply sufficient to make music. The body can move to its own music and may be supported, when circumstances allow, with instruments. The symbolic importance of the body, and of its magnification through music and dance, cannot be underestimated, since bodily characteristics were frequently used as markers of a servile position. Individuals can find solace in making music by themselves, as shepherds often do; but the social effects of music are much stronger when several people join forces, especially when they form a group.

Musicologist, Bernard Lortat-Jacob, studied collective singing in various contexts, from which he concluded that: "Singing is first and foremost an experience shared by people who know themselves well and live the same story together every day. Every song, in its own way, relates a moment of that story within a particular timeframe" (Lortat-Jacob 2004: 100)[11]. Musicologist and conductor, Karen Ahlquist, links choirs to communities: "A chorus is not one thing, but an adaptable idea of community that places serious attention to matters artistic at the centre of its world" (Ahlquist 2006: 10). A choir is, according to ethnomusicologist Gregory Barz: "The musical performance of [a] community" (Barz 2006: 19). "Artistic matters" cement communities that can evolve according to changing contexts. This is confirmed in the Cape situation by Sylvia Bruinders' investigations:

> My research is based on the premise that music and dance create a sense of belonging and group consciousness in this extremely diverse community. Certain cultural practices, particularly the music and dance styles mentioned above [langarm (social ballroom) dances, "jazz" dancing, Cape Jazz music, Christmas Bands, Malay Choirs, and the Minstrel Carnival], are viewed as unique to the colored community by other South Africans, and colored people, specifically those belonging to lower socio-economic classes, pride themselves on this cultural difference. These practices are particularly important for them at significant annual and life-cycle events that are focal points for community maintenance and revitalization. Moreover, these practices appear to have gained in importance for creating community, identity, and solidarity amongst the lower socio-economic classes in the postapartheid era. (Bruinders 2012: 25)

The idea of a choir being a community that represents a larger community is indeed central to *Klopse* and Malay Choirs. The Fabulous Woodstock Starlites, for instance, are "actively involved in the Woodstock community";[12] the statement of mission posted on their website mentions among their aims: "To work towards a social upliftment of our under-privileged communities [...] To co-operate with others who pursue similar aims and objectives [...] and Generally to engage in any activities and means that may appropriately advance the interest of the FABULOUS WOODSTOCK STARLITES".[13]

Tape Jacobs, the captain of the Beystars *Klops*, developed the idea of the Coons as a community belonging to a community:

> The Coons belong to the community and it belongs actually to the poorest people. People that can't afford to have a holiday, so if they spend that 4 or 3 days Coon then it was like they have been overseas. Because when you have the Coon uniform you can go everywhere [laughing], just get into the bus, and the bus take you anywhere, right? But I mean not individually he is taking the troupe, the troupe must go from Mitchell's plain out of Cape Town, the troupe must be there. I mean you wouldn't be able to afford to go there yourself, if you have a uniform on so you can go. So I analyse this thing that the Coons is for the poor and what a Coons really is to me this is another mixture, right? It is the mixture of the Christmas Choir, and it is a mixture of the Malay Choir, and it's the man on the street.[14]

Community is a word which, in the discourse of people involved with the *Klopse* and the Malay Choirs, has acquired various nested acceptations; it designates human groups to which the speaker can relate, according to context and circumstances: family, inhabitants of a neighbourhood, coloureds, citizens of the Cape conurbation or of the Western Cape. "Community" enables the expression of feelings of belonging which are multiple; it defies assignment to a single group and, consequently, stereotypes attributed to this group. In the past, it was frequently combined with attachment to a territory. It used to be District Six, the Bo-Kaap or smaller areas, such as Harfield Village in Claremont. The relationship between memories of District Six, feelings of belonging to a territory and configuration of identities is particularly strong. Forced relocations, following the implementation of the 1950 Group Areas Act, undermined the territorial bases of *Klopse* and Malay Choirs and replaced them with networks of friendship and support that span long distances. In discourses formulated after the destruction of this neighbourhood, an idea of the District was developed which put forward at least two main themes: community and solidarity. These attributes were encapsulated in one of the affectionate names given to District Six: *Kanaladorp*, the village of *kanala*,[15] of give and take, of sharing, of helping each other (McCormick 2002: 48; Schoeman 1994); "an intense will to survive", a tenacity that makes people manage "against all odds" (Soudien 2001: 119). After its inhabitants were removed, District Six became: "a site for the production of a South African identity [...] District Six as a signifier is understood to embody the qualities of tolerance, mutual respect, and respect for difference which, by contrast, 'South Africa', as a counter-signifier, was, and might still be, presumed to be without. 'District Six' was, therefore, in this way of looking, the opposite of 'South Africa'"(Soudien 2001: 115).[16]

Forced relocations to distant townships indeed caused a very severe trauma. Yet, it did not annihilate the sense of solidarity and the will to survive that were associated with District Six. It might even be supposed that the way memories of District Six were elaborated served to maintain these attitudes in the new situations. They probably helped rebuilding a "psychological sense of community", the feeling of being part of a group criss-crossed by affective attachments and shared values. Such a sense facilitates investment in the community and in sub-groups to which individuals can identify (Sonn & Fisher 1996: 418). The continued celebration of the New Year festivals, including the *Klopse* carnival and the Malay Choirs competitions, seems to confirm the validity of that supposition. Marches and parades were one of the means of building new feelings of belongings and of reclaiming lost territories. After Green Point was declared a "white area" in 1968, making parades in the Central Business District impossible, and later, following the Soweto upheavals in 1976, when all marches were forbidden by virtue of the 1956 Riotous Assemblies Act, carnival organisers fought an incessant battle to recover the right to parade in the town centre; that is, to show that their existence was tied by unbreakable historical and cultural links to the "Mother City" and that they consequently had a right to be there, a right that was eventually granted back in 1989 (Martin 2005). Simultaneously, the townships were appropriated; social life was reorganised and the inhabitants gave a personality to the spaces where they had to continue living: Hanover Park, Lentegeur, Bonteheuwel, Manenberg, Mitchells Plain became alive, even though life was rough and violence was rife. Having conducted participant observation on the carnival as a member of the Las Vegas *Klops*, Channel Oliphant suggested that: "These marches through the streets [*voorsmaakie*, preview marches] demonstrate a making of the Cape Flats home through the marching carnival body" (Oliphant 2013: 3), and that "through marching through the different areas and streets on the Cape Flats a sense of belonging is performed" (Oliphant 2013: 94). The leaders of many *Klopse* and Malay Choirs consider that their efforts are not exclusively musical, but that, through music and entertainment, they contribute to educating young people and to bringing a form of development to the community. The Bishop Lavis Development Youth specifically targets children and adolescents. "Regular" troupes or choirs, such as the Young Tulips Sangkoor associate youths' social and cultural upliftment with the perpetuation of traditions. According to their constitution, the aims of the choir are:
1. "To foster *Nederlands* and Afrikaans *Liedere*.
2. The advancement of the interest of the youth, is singing of the Traditional *Liedere*.

3. The preservation of the Traditional Liedere as part of the Malay Culture in the Cape."[17]

Many captains and coaches emphasise their determination to attract youth in order to keep them off the streets and remove them from the influence of drug dealers and gangs. Anwar Gambeno extends the role of his choir and conceives of it as an educational and developmental institution:

> We try to teach the youngsters the oral tradition of Cape Malay singing and we work with the most disadvantaged youngsters in Cape Town, in the townships; we try to teach them discipline in singing, discipline in their life through the medium of music [...] this youngster when he goes home he has got problems and this is very important because when he goes home he takes that little bit of discipline and that little bit of happiness with him.[18]

Eventually:

> It's quite a number of youngsters who were taught here as well, they're coaching their choirs now themselves, other choirs. So things are [...] Tulips [...] I still say Tulips is a development institution because they come here when they know nothing, then they get taught here and when they leave, they can play the banjo, and they can coach a choir. Obviously, they go further, they get taught further wherever they go, but the basics, the basis they get here.[19]

Elaine Salo demonstrated that before and after 1994, coloured men, especially in the most deprived townships, fell victim to a process of "social and economic emasculation" which consisted in "a progressive cycle of gendered, economic and racial denigration". This started with forced removals in the 1960s and has continued in the post-apartheid period, since the high rate of unemployment and the lack of adequate training has prevented men from fulfilling what is supposed to be their economic role. Gangs — and the myths that surround them, nowadays mixed with prestigious images from movies or American "gangsta" rap — give young men the possibility to reconstruct and assert their masculinity, and therefore their personhood (Salo 2005b). In such conditions, *Klopse* and choirs cannot simply be seen as an alternative to gangs; however, they do offer men another way — which may be associated with membership in a gang, but may also deter from it — to display masculinity and have it recognised positively. In this perspective, *Klopse* and Malay Choirs appear as organisations likely to (re)kindle self-esteem; hence the importance of participating in a winning outfit, which makes members proud of their team and proud of themselves.

Identity

Étienne Wenger, a Swiss educational theorist showed how common practices foster communities: "Practice, even under circumstances of utter control and mandates, is the production of a community through participation. This local production implies a notion of agency in the negotiation of meaning, which even the most effective power cannot fully subsume. It is a small opening, a crack that represents a limitation to the application of power: the creation of a practice takes place in response to power, not as an outcome of it" (Wenger 2012: 9). This theoretical proposition seems to be fully relevant to the South African case. *Klopse* and Malay Choirs illustrate how participation contributes to building communities, within which the participants' agency generates new meanings regarding society at large and the position of the group they belong to within that society. The notion of remembering as "doing something" (Ricœur 2006: 100), as well as the practice of appropriation leading to transformation and creation, which both underlie *nederlandsliedjies* and *moppies*, invites a consideration of social meanings developed around the practices of *Klopse* and Malay Choirs as related to notions of identity. Étienne Wenger (2012: 5–6), in agreement with several scholars who studied identity configurations (Brubaker & Cooper 2000; Brubaker et al. 2006; Erasmus 2001; Martin 2010), underlined three characteristics of identity:

> **Identity is a trajectory.** Over time, it reflects our journeying within some communities as well as transitions across communities [...].
>
> **Identity is a nexus of multimembership.** Identity also comes to reflect the multiplicity of locations of identification that constitute it. Multimembership is sequential as we travel through the landscape and carry our identity across contexts. It is also simultaneous as we belong to multiple communities at any given time [...].
>
> **Identity is multi-scale.** Our identities are constituted at multiple levels of scale all at once [...] through the combination of engagement, imagination, and alignment many levels of scale do enter into the constitution of identity.

Regarding South African identities, a group of sociologists reached conclusions which are in line with Étienne Wenger's propositions: "It is probable that South Africans are developing for themselves multiple identities, some of which may be based neither on historically inherited labels nor on national sentiments. It may be that local place and local culture, language, and minority status are being employed to construct a new shared form of identification which is able to transcend other identities in many domains of daily life" (Bekker et al.

2000: 222). Within this framework, "coloured identities formations" appear ambiguous and fluid, but not passive; they are "part of the shifting texture of a broader black experience" (Erasmus 2001: 14). Zoë Wicomb specified the notion of identity formation by explaining that it could aggregate multiple identities: "Instead of denying history and fabricating a totalizing colouredness, 'multiple belongings' could be seen as an alternative way of viewing a culture where participation in a number of coloured micro-communities whose interests conflict and overlap could become a rehearsal for cultural life in the larger South African community where we learn to perform the same kind of negotiation in terms of identity within a lived culture characterized by difference" (Wicomb 1998: 105). This can explain the instability of coloured identities and shifts in their assertion (Gqola 2010: 24).

The study of *nederlandsliedjies* and *moppies* brings a few additional precisions to the ideas of coloured identity configurations (or "formations") as multiple, flexible and dynamic. Individuals who are part of the "New Year festivals world" (to use Howard S Becker's terminology) can be considered as constituting one of the micro-communities postulated by Zoë Wicomb; a community of practice largely gathered within a community of social status essentially composed of regularly employed workers, precarious workers, unemployed workers, artisans and members of the underworld. The community of the New Year festivals overlaps with other communities centred on religion, occupation, neighbourhood, political inclinations; this community or "micro-community" is included in the group called coloured, a self-referential label as much as an outside categorisation. The practices developed by participants in the "New Year festivals world" produce meanings, relative not only to their "world", but also to the whole coloured group and the situation of this group within the larger South African society. Meanings relative to various social levels, or "communities", are obviously nested and evolutive. *Nederlandsliedjies* and *moppies* are rooted in history and are said to embody "tradition"; yet they have continuously changed and have adapted to social and political circumstances, as well as to musical fashions. They have not only been proof of coloured people's creativity, but have demonstrated that their creativity is an on-going process.

The fluidity and adaptability of these repertoires appear as symbols of coloured identities. With specific means, *Klopse* and Malay Choirs denied and fought against derogatory stereotypes assigned to people classified coloured. By seeking inspiration in Europe (*nederlands*), in American and globalised popular musics (*moppies*), they blew up the walls of racial categorisation and township imprisonment that successive South African governments erected. Consequently, they contributed to setting up within coloured identities an unswerving openness to the world. Musically, this translated in the practice of appropriation, central to *moppies* but also present in *nederlands*' styles of interpretation, a practice which can also be understood as an expression of identifications. In this respect, the eagerness with which musical material from the United States has been integrated and transformed since the first minstrel songs' scores reached Cape Town illustrates the intensity of identification with a mythical land of freedom and opportunities for people of colour; this confirms the role of identifications in configuring identities. The diversity of musics which have been appropriated and the diversity of the identifications they reveal underpin the multiplicity, fluidity, and variability of coloured identities. They also shed light on conceptions of coloured identity configurations as a mix.

Discussions on *nederlandsliedjies* revolve around the question of blending and mixing between largely imaginary representations of the "East" and the "West", be it when their origins are debated or when contemporary styles of interpretation are assessed. *Moppies* also set in motion processes of mixing, since they necessitate the combination of several melodic snatches and their homogenisation in one song, which must display its own character and coherence. If the Klopse and Malay Choirs' repertoires are considered as emblems of what is called by their practitioners a "culture", then they suggest that the basis of the identity of those who are the agents and the carriers of this "culture" is mixing. Whatever change occurs in the configuration of their identity results from reorganising and rebalancing elements present in the mix and/or introducing new elements. Musical creativity, as applied to *nederlands* and *moppies*, consisted in identifying ingredients that could be used to manifest a people's specificity, in transforming them, and in inventing new expressive means from their transformation. This brings us back to Pope's contention that creativity is: "the capacity to make, do or become something fresh and valuable, with respect to others as well as ourselves" (Pope 2005: xvi). It exemplifies Michel Foucault's definition of creators as "establishers of discursiveness", who "not only made possible certain analogies, they have made possible certain differences" (Foucault 1994: 805).

These differences — the compositional and interpretive characteristics of *nederlands* and *moppies* which do not permit confusion with other repertoires — assert the specificity of the human group who performs them; at the same time, these differences, being rooted in relations tied by appropriation and identification, are bridges connecting this group to other human groups: "micro-communities" to larger communities; participants in the New Year festivals world to coloured people, to the Western Cape, to South Africa, and to the world. This is, as posited by Édouard Glissant, why these repertoires are considered in the situations where they are magnified, as beautiful and moving (Glissant 2006: 45).

Creolisation

Agency geared towards creation in a situation of oppression and contempt can be subsumed in processes of creolisation. It does not only result from *métissage*, for according to Édouard Glissant: "If we posit *métissage* as, generally speaking, the meeting and synthesis of two differences, creolization seems to be a limitless *métissage*, its elements diffracted and its consequences unforeseeable" (Glissant 1990: 46).[20] Unforeseeableness clearly results from creation; the unforeseeable nature of creation taking place as part of processes[21] of creolisation derives from "the coming into contact of several cultures, or at least several elements of distinct cultures, in one particular place of the world, which results in a new phenomenon, totally unpredictable in relationship with the sum or only the synthesis of these elements" (Glissant 1997: 37). These processes are not limited to circumscribed areas, but affect the whole world:

> Creolisation does not limit its workings only to the Archipelagos' creoles realities, or to their budding languages. The world is creolising, it does not become creole, it is becoming this inextricable and unpredictable [reality] which every creolisation process bears in itself and which is neither propped up nor legitimated by any model.[22] (Glissant 2005: 75)

In this perspective, South Africa and its musics can be considered as creolising (Martin 2013: chap.2). Based on Robin Cohen and Paola Toninato's introduction to their creolisation reader, it seems possible to consider that it is the whole of South Africa, and not one segment of its population, which is engulfed in a process of creolisation:

> From a social scientist's perspective the process of cultural creolization testifies to human resilience and creativity under extreme conditions, such as those encountered in colonial societies. The use of the notion of creolization highlights the fact that even when cultural contact occurs as a result of enslavement, colonization or forced exile, as in the case of New World plantation societies, it remains a highly dialogical process that affects and involves — indeed may be constitutive of — both colonizers and colonized, or, more generally, dominant and minority groups […] In broad terms, creolization in social sciences can be used to understand complexity, overlaps, human inventiveness and the emergence of convergent cultures, often forged under adverse circumstances with highly asymmetric power relations. (Cohen & Toninato 2010: 12–13)

Violence, domination, hierarchisation and inequality provide the circumstances from which creolisation processes set off.[23] These processes entangle various forms of control, adaptation and resistance (Cohen & Toninato 2010: 29–31) and, as underlined by Zimitri Erasmus, they generate "histories not only of loss, rupture, transportation, dislocation and discontinuity, but also of cultural creation and contestation in contexts of forced human and cultural heterogeneity and colonial dominance [...]" (Erasmus 2011: 639). From these premises, K*aapse Klopse* and Malay Choirs' repertoires may be conceived as products of creolisation processes; that is, of unceasing entanglements, generating creations which bear testimony to the resilience of the human beings who have been involved in their invention. Looking at *nederlandsliedjies* and *moppies* in this light brings forward the association of entanglement, creation and resilience. It consequently rules out any notion of one closed, immutable coloured identity, but makes the existence of combined, nested and evolving feelings of belonging understandable.

To be continued...

The combination of musical analysis with the study of discourses about stylistic change appears particularly fruitful for research aiming at understanding the social significations of music. In the present case, focusing on music allowed a better comprehension of electoral behaviour in the Western Cape, going deeper than the mere surface of polemics. In addition to that, focusing on music also led to discrediting unequivocal notions of what would be one single coloured identity. It disclosed that social representations of mixing and blending, which bear on human beings and their practices, are deeply pervaded with hesitations, uncertainties and anxieties. The uneasiness that ensues relates to balances within mixes, as well as to the place and the acceptance of mixing in South Africa. It impacts upon the very idea of "coloured identity" and confirms that, under that common-sense notion, the reality is made of an entanglement of diverse conceptions of coloured identity, distinguished by many nuances, both related and differentiated by protracted experiences within interlocked micro-communities and communities. Such an interpretation of the social meaning of an ensemble of musical practices — embracing repertoires and styles of interpretation — can only be considered as valid if the music is carefully described, with reference to the concepts and words of its practitioners, for musical practices carry symbols likely to reveal the complexity of social mutations which are not always easily observable. Music can be considered as one of the "social revealers" theorised by Georges Balandier to "detect the streams of change under the dead waters of continuity" (Balandier 1971: 86).[24]

In this book, we have attempted to apply a combination of musicological and sociological analysis to two choral repertoires, which are considered by practitioners and audiences as the most emblematic of a series of cultural practices constituting Cape Town's New Year festivals. In spite of the number of pages it contains, the present volume should be considered as a first step on a path which remains largely unexplored. Our hope is that it will encourage other investigators to continue studying the musical creativity which blossoms in *nederlandsliedjies* and *moppies*. The mechanisms of *moppie* com-position, the subtleties of *nederlands' aan gee* and *karienkel*, the ingenuity of arranging and coaching, especially when neither coach nor singers are musically literate, and many other aspects of the conception and interpretation of these repertoires, deserve more attention. A better understanding of what they mean in terms of a sense of history, of relationships with non-New Year festival worlds, of identifications and identity configurations, calls for further in-depth research in the description of their musical specificities and in the analysis of the discourses they prompt. In this respect, a multidisciplinary exploration of the musicians' cognitive mechanisms at work when composing *moppies* and interpreting *nederlandsliedjies*, such as the one conducted by Aurélie Helmlinger in her study of Trinidadian steel bands (Helmlinger 2012) would indubitably be enlightening. Although it can generally be considered that outsiders shed a different (hopefully stimulating) light on what they observe, we are fully aware of the limitations of research conducted by two foreigners. In the present instance, it appears that refined analyses could result from research undertaken by people — preferably teams associating musicologists and sociologists, possibly also historians and political scientists — who live, or can spend long periods of time, in Cape Town and speak Afrikaans and Afrikaaps. Our own investigations could then be seen as initiating a much broader conversation about the New Year festivals and their social significations. As indicated by the studies conducted by Glen Holtzman, Stigue Nel, Chanell Oliphant, Zarin Rahman and Tazneem Wentzel, it has, to some extent, already begun. However, such a conversation will only develop if universities and research institutions recognise that topics such as the *Kaapse Klopse* and the Malay Choirs, and their repertoires, are academically legitimate and fecund, and if departments of music, sociology, anthropology and political science invite students to write masters or doctoral dissertation on such topics.[25]

Notes

1. "la beauté n'est pas la splendeur du vrai, elle est et elle révèle dans une œuvre ou un donné *la force des différences qui dans le même temps s'accomplissent et déjà prédisent leur relation à d'autres différences*" (italics in the original).
2. "La Relation relie (relaie), relate". Relation is a key concept in Glissant's theorisation of the "Whole-World" (Tout-Monde). Relation is constituted by the weft of relationships that criss-cross the human universe and on the threads of which innumerable possibilities of interactions, exchanges and blending run. Relation is the "actual quantity" of all the differences and places existing in the world; it differs from the universal in that it encompasses passages between these differences and places, while preserving their particularities (Glissant 2006: 186–187). This is why Relation links and also relates; at the same time it allows people or human phenomena to relate and be related to each other and tells about these phenomena and the relationships they entertain (Glissant 1990: 187).
3. A history that is remarkably exhibited at the Music van de Caab Centre of the Solms Delta wine farm in Franschhoek. Available at http://www.solms-delta.co.za/music-van-de-caab-centre/ [accessed 27 January 2016].
4. Adam Samodien, interview with Armelle Gaulier, Woodstock, 29 January 2008.
5. Michael Abrahams, in Michael Abrahams, Ronald Fisher and Eddie Matthews, interview with Armelle Gaulier, Mitchells Plain, 11 October 2006.
6. "C'est l'énergie de l'espoir, et non du désespoir, qui alimente les créations sociales et culturelles, les dépassements de soi et la remise en cause des frontières, celles des vrais ou faux ghettos."
7. These ideas are developed in an anonymous article published in the French *Wikipedia* under the title: "Résilience communautaire"; no English translation was available at the time of writing. Available at https://fr.wikipedia.org/wiki/R%C3%A9silience_communautaire [accessed 1 February 2016].
8. Mays, VM (1986) Identity development of Black Americans: The role of history and the importance of ethnicity. *American Journal of Psychotherapy* 40: 582–593.
9. A recent example of the misinterpretation of the New Year festivals by some educated coloureds is given in Christopher C Sonn and Adrian T Fisher's article titled "Psychological sense of community in a politically constructed group" (Sonn & Fisher 1996). The sample selected for their survey was composed of "twenty-three people who had been classified as Cape or other Coloured in South Africa were 16 years old or older when they left South Africa, now residing in Melbourne, Australia" (ibid.: 420) and the senior author (Christopher C Sonn) was of "a similar background as the participants" (ibid.: 421). When asked to discuss common symbol systems and cultural traits specific to the coloured group "a number of participants mentioned that 'the minstrels' (a choir group) was perhaps a 'visible reflection of (Coloured) culture'. Others suggested that they did not identify with the minstrels at all and that it did not represent the group's culture"(ibid.: 423). Although no information is given on the socio-economic background of the interviewees, one may assume that people who migrated to Australia were probably not among the most underprivileged; the definition of "the minstrels" as a "choir group" shows at least a lack of familiarity with *Klopse* and Malay Choirs on the part of the "senior author". Finally the whole discussion, assuming the existence of the group's culture, does not take into account internal differences, although in a subsequent paper the same authors acknowledged that the "community" was not homogeneous (Sonn & Fisher 1998: 468).
10. Anwar Gambeno, interview with Denis-Constant Martin, Mitchells Plain, 11 October 2011.
11. "Le chant est d'abord et avant tout une expérience concernant des hommes qui se connaissent

12. bien et partagent tous les jours la même histoire. Chaque chant, à sa façon, rend compte d'un moment de cette histoire à l'intérieur d'un temps calibré " (see also: Lortat-Jacob (2006), in English).
12. Armstrong, Aubrena (2014, 7 February) Passion keeps Woodstock Klopse going. *Woodstocklife*. Available at http://woodstocklife.weebly.com/download-woodstocklife.html [accessed 6 January 2016].
13. Available at http://fabulouswoodstockstarlites.yolasite.com/mission.php [accessed 6 January 2016].
14. Tape Jacobs, interview with Armelle Gaulier, Mitchells Plain, 9 August 2006.
15. *Kanala* is a word supposed to come from Malay languages; it is used as an equivalent of "please" when asking for something. However, its semantic field is larger than "please" and connotes a moral obligation to help and support.
16. This is marvellously illustrated in some of Richard Rive's writings, especially in the novel: *"Buckingham Palace", District Six*. Cape Town: David Philip, 1986.
17. The Young Tulips Sangkoor Constitution, mimeographed loose sheet, kindly communicated by Anwar Gambeno.
18. Anwar Gambeno, intervention at the Round Table "What is Cape Town Music?", Stellenbosch Institute of Advanced Studies, 12 November 2007.
19. Anwar Gambeno, interview with Denis-Constant Martin, Mitchells Plain, 13 April 2015.
20. "Si nous posons le métissage comme en général une rencontre et une synthèse entre deux différents, la créolisation nous apparaît comme le métissage sans limites, dont les éléments sont démultipliés, les résultantes imprévisibles"; given here in Betsy Wing's (1997) translation: *Poetics of Relation*. Ann Arbor: University of Michigan Press. p 34.
21. "La créolisation, qui est un des modes de l'emmêlement — et non pas seulement une résultante linguistique — n'a d'exemplaire que ses processus et certainement pas les 'contenus' à partir desquels ils fonctionneraient" (Glissant 1990: 103); "Creolization, one of the ways of forming a complex mix — and not merely a linguistic result — is only exemplified by its processes and certainly not by the 'contents' on which these operate" Betsy Wing's translation (ibid.: 89). "*Emmêlement*" could also be translated by entangledness, and "*n'a d'exemplaire que ses processus*" by "is only made exemplary (in the sense of serving as a model or pattern) by its processes".
22. "La créolisation ne limite pas son œuvre aux seules réalités créoles des Archipels ni à leurs langages naissants. Le monde se créolise, il ne devient pas créole, il devient cet inextricable et cet imprédictible que tout processus de créolisation porte en lui et qui ne se soutient ni ne s'autorise d'aucun modèle."
23. Zimitri Erasmus emphasises that "sociopolitical and cultural innovations" under conditions of trauma, oppression and dehumanisation distinguish creolisation from hybridity (Erasmus 2011: 640). For critiques of the use of hybridity in the social sciences, see: Cohen, Robin & Toninato, Paola (2010) Introduction to Part Four: Kindred concepts. In: Robin Cohen & Paola Toninato (eds) *The Creolization Reader: Studies in Mixed Identities and Cultures*. London: Routledge. pp. 243–246 and Sabine Mabardi: Hybridity in cultural theory, encounters of a heterogeneous kind (ibid.: 247–256).
24. "détecter les courants du changement sous les eaux mortes de la continuité".
25. Denis-Constant Martin has donated the research material he has gathered since 1994, including recordings of interviews he conducted and their transcriptions, to DOMUS (Documentation Centre for Music, Music Library, Stellenbosch University, South Africa). In order to obtain information on the "Denis-Constant Martin Collection" and how it can be accessed, interested readers should contact DOMUS at: Tel: +27 (0)21 808 2597; Fax: +27 (0)21 808 2340; E-mail: santiedj@sun.ac.za or bgl@sun.ac.za

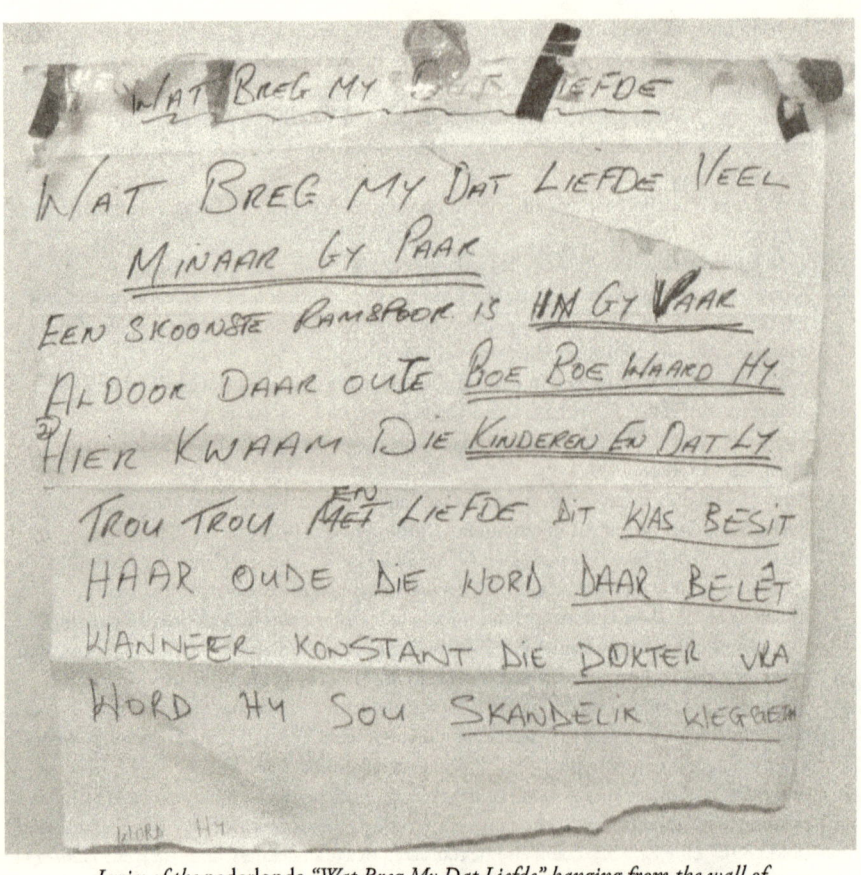

Lyrics of the nederlands *"Wat Breg My Dat Liefde"* hanging from the wall of the Parkdales' klopskamer, *2008 (Armelle Gaulier)*

APPENDIX 1

Nederlandsliedjies *lyrics*

Lyrics included in this annex reproduce texts given to Armelle Gaulier by coaches and strictly respect their wording and spelling. As explained in Chapters 3 and 4, no attempt has been made at translating these texts. The presentation aims at illustrating the interplay between the *voorsinger* and the *pak*, as well as the extent of the soloist's *karienkeling*. These songs were tape-recorded during rehearsals and unfortunately cannot be made available to the public due to poor technical and acoustic conditions and problems of copyright. A fairly representative sample of video clips of choirs singing *nederlandsliedjies* and *moppies* in competition can be found at the following internet addresses:

NEDERLANDSLIEDJIES
Jonge Studente : *"Wees Ewig Lustig"* https://www.youtube.com/watch?v=AeoZAB_6IhM&list=PL1IcPRQmXbmh5V8AI7JoviAF1u3cU33Tx
Jonge Studente : *"Groot Vogelen"* https://www.youtube.com/watch?v=zemUxV_nlW8&index=10&list=PL1IcPRQmXbmh5V8AI7JoviAF1u3cU33Tx
Ottomans Sporting Club : *"Vriende wilt gij mijn aanhooren"* https://www.youtube.com/watch?v=bmo2VDVRbeE&list=PL1IcPRQmXbmh5V8AI7JoviAF1u3cU33Tx&index=6
Primrose MVC: *"Blom en Blaar"* https://www.youtube.com/watch?v=1FUOgiOP_ho
Young Men Sporting Club : *"Die Klok Slaan Acht"* https://www.youtube.com/watch?v=kLwPbMj_6J8&list=PL1IcPRQmXbmh5V8AI7JoviAF1u3cU33Tx&index=9
Young Men Sporting Club : *"Die Orkaane"* https://www.youtube.com/watch?v=ynritZr15u0&index=11&list=PL1IcPRQmXbmh5V8AI7JoviAF1u3cU33Tx
MOPPIES
Calypso Singkoor: *"Paris Hilton Vanie Kaap"* https://www.youtube.com/watch?v=v6uo5AyKRDU
Coronation Singkoor: *"Sokkie Dans"* https://www.youtube.com/watch?v=wVNmWMleWZA

Coronations: "*Sarah SE frikkedella*" https://www.youtube.com/watch?v=vK4ZloPlZsY
Ottomans Sporting Club: "*Gertie*" https://www.youtube.com/watch?v=GJV3KzXiD4s
Young Men Sporting Club: "*Koor Kompetisie in 7nde Laan*" https://www.youtube.com/watch?v=o2-CGcBC1fE
Young Men Sporting Club: "*Wilhemina die Moffie*" https://www.youtube.com/watch?v=2CFa3dLXVN8
A comprehensive list of Malay Choir performances can be found at: https://www.youtube.com/results?search_query=cape+malay+choirs

<u>Underlined</u> passages in the songs below indicate interventions by the pak; passages in **bold** indicate when the soloist *karienkels*.

"Die Loods"

Recorded on 8 January 2008
Sung by the Young Men; soloist: Abrahams Salieg
Tempo = ± 72 quarter-note beats per minute

    Waar die **orkaa**nen (die) dond**eren**-<u>Loeien</u>.

    Het wolks gy-<u>Vaar</u> ons <u>vliegend</u> <u>tart</u>.

    Angst en schrik de ziets **kragt <u>boeien</u>** <u>waakt</u> **een zee-**zeemans
        moe**dig** <u>hart</u>.

    Thans is **hy daar-**<u>is hy daar hy wyst gebiedend</u>.

    Op **den**-<u>branden golven</u> **zieden**,

    Mannen <u>roept</u> hy, **<u>hier</u>** is **gyvaar** ek **bens loods,** god **<u>roept</u>** <u>my daar</u>.

    Het **sal verbry**zelen **hoort-**<u>kra</u> **krasssen** die **beman** mannen
        wa<u>g**tend** dood</u>.

    Schenk my **den kraght** <u>my den kraght</u> **om hem** te **na**deren.

    Valders-<u>hart valt niet te</u> **breuken, redder** steun **en,** dit **doods
        gyvaar waare hel,** god **wagt u daar.**

    <u>Redder</u> steun **en,** dit **doods gyvaar** waare hel, god **wagt wagt** u **daar.**

"Jager Uitgaande"

Recorded on 26 February 2008
Sung by the Morning Glories; soloist: Ismail Morris
Tempo = ± 69 quarter-note beats per minute

Ek sou daar een **Jager Uitgaan**

Ek sou **daar** een **Jager Uit** Gaanen

Wat vond ek **niks te Ja-Jager**

Meer daar is **drie** oefen **skone** Jongy **Ma-Mager**

Die **jongste van dat** Drie dit hep **ek** Lief

Die jongste **van dat Drie dat** hep **ek** Drie

Ek **ging by** haar en **ek Spraak haar** aan

Soetse Liewe **mager** wil Gy **al** met my gaan

Ek sal haar niet so **ver** gaan **Mis**lei-**lei**den

Langens veldskyn en met **bosskyn** groene **Bo-Bo**men

Hier **omtrent waar die** Jager bloem en stond

Hier omtrent **waar die Jager** bloem en **stond**

Hier **omtrent** waar die **Jager** bloem en stond

"Nembenoom"

Recorded in February 2008
Sung by the Villagers; soloist: Adnaan Mustapha
Tempo = ± 69 quarter-note beats per minute

>Nembenoem **hief haar naam <u>naam-naam</u> dit <u>was nooit-
nooit geneom</u>**

>**Haar lip en lis beniet voor <u>die-die laa</u>**-laaste **di**-die<u>rbaar word</u>

>Van **dag tot <u>dag seg mens-mens</u> tot** <u>myn</u>

>Ver**bonde <u>van-van voor</u>** driet

>**Maar skoon laat sy** een **grimelik <u>heid en dit-dit vergeet-geet
my</u>** niet.

>Van **dag tot <u>dag seg mens-mens</u>** tot **<u>myn</u>**

>**Verbonde <u>van-van voor</u>** driet

>**Maar skoon laat** sy een **grimelik** <u>heid **en dit**-dit **vergeet** dit **vergeet
grimelik** my **niet vergeet vergeet vergeet** grimelik **heid** en dit
ver-ver**geet** vergeet</u>

"*Treade Jongsman*"

Recorded on 8 January 2008
Sung by the Tulips; soloist: Ismail
Tempo ± 72 quarter-note beats per minute

Treade jongs**man** en kom **luister** <u>na **myn** klag</u>

Treade **jongsman** (en) **kom luister na myn** klag

Myn gen**iese** dit was aldoor **hoar** <u>vriese</u>

(Een) ander life **meisie** sy **stond in** <u>myn **gy**dagt</u>

O**preg** dat **liefde** doet myn **hart Soebe** <u>vriese</u>

Sy was maar **pas** <u>a**gtien** jaar</u>

Nou gaan hy **diese** <u>maager maa be**min**de</u>

Spraak hy die **woord van** <u>trou akoord</u>

Spraak hy die woord **van trou** <u>akoord</u>

Als dat hy vir **haar nooit** <u>sal mis**lei**den mis**lei**den (sal)</u>

<u>Want **hy moes**-moes diens **alles een soldaat**</u>

<u>**Na sy** diens</u>

als dat hy vir **haar,** mooit sal mis**leiden**

Want <u>hy</u> moes diens **alles** <u>een **soldaat**</u>

<u>**Na sy** diens alles een **soldaat** een **soldaat** Na **sy** diens</u>

"Wat Breg My Dat Liefde"

Recorded on 18 February 2008
Sung by the Parkdales; soloist: Ibrahim Hendricks
Tempo ± 66 quarter-note beats per minute
(?) = words not included in the original written text

    Wat **breg** my dat **liefde viel** (?) **minnaar gy** paar

    Een (?) **ramspoor is** hy een (?) gy vaar

    Aldoor haar **dutjie boe waard** hy

    Hier **kwaam die kin**deren en **dat** ly

    Hier **kwaam die kin-kinderen en-en dat** ly

    (Hier) **kwaam** die kinderen en **dat ly**

    Kwaam die kin-kin**deren en-en dat** ly

"*U Gydagte*"

Recorded on 14 January 2008
Sung by the Starlites; soloist: Faeez
Tempo ± 76 quarter-note beats per minute

    U gyda-**dagte**, <u>stel-stel maar ein-einde</u>

    Sy't gydink-**dink tog**, <u>aan-aan-**aan u** min-minde</u>

    Maar **sy't gydink tog**, <u>aan die **afen** ston-stoned</u>

    Op diede**rin** tyd-**tyd toen**, <u>sy haar gaan verbon-bonde</u>

    Gyn**oeg lat** hy-**hy haar**, <u>gaan ver-**vergee**-geefen</u>

    En voor, <u>u allien-ien maar allien</u>

    En voor, <u>u allien maar allien</u>

    En (voor u) **al-**<u>lien maar allien</u>

    hy haar <u>gaan ver-vergee-geefen</u>

"En Ek Hep Daar Op Diese Dag"

Recorded on 24 January 2008
Sung by the Woodstock Royals; soloist: Ikeraam Leeman
Tempo ± between 63 and 66 quarter-note beats per minute

En ek **hep daarop** <u>die-**op**</u> <u>die</u>se <u>dag</u>

Soetste liewe <u>meisie diet</u> <u>myn-myn</u> **kom** <u>vraag</u>

En sy <u>seg sy is</u> weg

Mog haar <u>wise **voor**</u> my

En **sy** <u>wou daar **een an-abder nooit-nooit gy**</u>vra

Maar (al) **sy** <u>dan wie**deren aan**</u> kwaam

Dan gaan **sy diese paasjie** met saal-saal **en** toem

Haar twee bloufen (oegies) **leg** klaar **met** haar **swar**te krilje haar

En **oe** <u>verder **gy** noeg **en hoe duidelik** skyn **diet**</u> maan

Maar <u>al sy dan **wiederen kwaame** dan (gaan) al sy diese paadjie met saal en toem</u>

Maar al sy dan **wiederen** aan **kwaam**

Dan gaan sy diese <u>paasjie met saal-saal **en toem**</u>

Diese paadjie met <u>saal-saal **en** toem</u>

"Gaaf Maria"

Recorded on 21 January 2008
Sung by The Continental Male Choir; soloist: Mohammad Ashraf
Tempo ± 76 quarter-note beats per minute

Gaaf Maria <u>haar trou tot</u> (??)

En wat **ging** sy door **dit <u>Karet</u> <u>door</u> dit** <u>straat</u>

En wat **wond sy** <u>haar waar</u> **sinde**

<u>**Skink voor** my een **gla**sie</u>

<u>**Al voor my** jongste vroufie</u>

<u>**nie** (nie) sy is **myn** deer</u>

En wat wond **sy** <u>haar waar</u> **sin**de

<u>Skink voor my een **gla**sie</u>

<u>Al **voor** my jongste **vroufie** nie</u>

<u>(Nie) sy is **myn** deer</u>

En wat **wond** sy <u>haar waar</u> **sin**de

<u>Skink **voor** my een **gla**sie</u>

<u>**Al voor**-voor my jongste **vrou**fie nie</u>

APPENDIX 2

Cape Malay Choir Board adjudication reports

These reports were made available by Shafick April, president of the CMCB, or by the teams' coaches. We would like to thank Shafick April, Ahmed Ismail and Abduraghman Morris for allowing us to photograph them.

a) Young Men, 2007

First column = percentage; second column = note

CAPE MALAY CHOIR COMPETITION 2007

NAME OF CHOIR: Young Men **DATE:** 17-Mar-07
COMPETITION: TOP 8 - GOOD HOPE CENTER **ITEM:** NEDERLANDS LIED
NAME OF SONG: Ek Neem Dit Van Myn Jongskap Af

#	Category	%	Note
1.	Rhythm / Tempo	10	8
2.	Music	10	9
3.	Lead Singer	10	8.5
4.	Harmony	20	8.5
5.	Variation	15	13
6.	Overall Intonation	20	16.4
7.	General Presentation	10	8.6
8.	Outstanding Performance	15	12.7
	TOTAL	100	84.7

PERCENTAGE %: 84.70%

REMARKS

It was pleasurable to have listened to this well trained choir and cognisance should be taken of the following:

The lead singer did was required of him and must be commended in the manner he blended in and inspired his choir. His diction must improve but it must be mentioned that he rendered an outstanding performance and did his choir proud.

The melody of the lied was well projected and the choir maintained good balance and support throughout but harmonically, it varied. This could be attributed to the lack of tenor voices. Whilst the second voice could have contributed more, the bass singers must be commended.

The tempo seemed a fraction too fast for the lied and the guitarist must refrain from hammering their guitars.

ADJUDICATOR'S SIGNATURE:

ADJUDICATOR'S SIGNATURE:

ADJUDICATOR'S SIGNATURE:

b) Shoprite Jonge Studente, 2011

First column = percentage; second column = note

CAPE MALAY CHOIR COMPETITION 2011

NAME OF CHOIR:	Shoprite Jonge Studente	DATE:	
COMPETITION:	******* - GOOD HOPE CENTRE	ITEM:	NEDERLANDS LIED
NAME OF SONG:	Koningzoon		

1.	Rhythm / Tempo	10	8.33
2.	Music	10	8.167
3.	Lead Singer	10	7.833
4.	Variation	15	13
5.	Harmony	15	13
6.	Overall Intonation	15	11.83
7.	Balancing	15	12.33
8.	General Presentation / Outstanding Performance	15	12.7
		100	72.7

PERCENTAGE %	
	82.67%

REMARKS

The lead singer had a shaky start with the result that the "aangee" in the first couple of lines "was not spot -on". He should learn to carry on with "karinkel" singing when the choir breaths and not breath with them.

It must be mentioned that the choir was very subdued up to the "wip draai". It was evident that the choir struggled with the "skondeer" in the first couple of lines but all credit should go to them for holding their composure and made a remarkable recovery. Harmonically the choir was very good with outstanding variation coming to the fore.

The tempo was not consistent band also increased after the "wip draai".

The choir should try and sing the lied in the "G" key at their practice as it can bring a better sound out of the choir. If it is too high, they should revert back to the "F" key.

ADJUDICATOR'S SIGNATURE: ....

ADJUDICATOR'S SIGNATURE: ....

ADJUDICATOR'S SIGNATURE: ....

c) **Young Zinnias, 2013**

Cape Malay Choir Board

NEDERLANDS

NAME OF CHOIR: Young Zinnias

Adhere to rules regarding	YES	YES
Instruments		
Accompaniment		
Language		
Duration of TOTAL PERFORMANCE		

	Max	Score	Comment
Rhythm / Tempo	10	8	Steady tempo. Nice and steady.
Music	10	8	Steady, no variation. Banjo het darm so bietjie ingekleur teen die einde. Beautiful accompaniment.
Lead Singer	15	13	Changes smoth; karinkels well-shaped and classy. Very moving performance. Karinkels have a spiritual quality to them. Beautiful karinkel singing.
Harmony	15	12	Strong skondeer. Well co-ordinated.
Variation	10	8	Wipdraai cleverly brough song back to original time. Nice variation at the end. Complexities of harmonies and rhythmic changes very effective.
Balancing	10	8	Good balance between LS and choir. As the song progressed, the choir become louder. Chorus a bit to loud from the start.
Overall Intonation	15	12	Secure. Pragtig gehou deur acapella!
General Presentation	15	12	Good mic technique of the LS. Be careful of too many harmonics due to too loud singing from chorus otherwise very moving performance. Goed afgeronde vertolking. Dankie vir 'n genotvolle uitvoering.
TOTAL	100	81	

Adjudicator: _[signature]_

Date: 16/03/2013

Appendices

d) Young Men, 2015

Cape Malay Choir Board

NEDERLANDS

NAME OF CHOIR: Young Men

Adhere to rules regarding	YES	YES
Instruments	✓	
Accompaniment	✓	
Language		
Duration of TOTAL PERFORMANCE	38:30	

	Max	Score	Comment
Rhythm / Tempo	10	10	Good balance between lead singer & choir. Lead singer sometimes breathless. Good karinkel singing
Music	10	12	Good harmonies
Lead Singer	15	12	Accurate
Harmony	15	6½	Variation could have been used more throughout the lied
Variation	10	8	Good balance between voice parts
Balancing	10	9	Good rhythmic tempo. Good controlled accompaniment
Overall Intonation	15	7	Diction not too clear. Consonants need emphasizing
General Presentation	15	8	A good performance.
TOTAL	100	78%	

Adjudicator: N. B. Hoape

Date: 07 February 2015

The Woodstock Starlites practise the moppie *"Die Party van die Jaar", 2004*

APPENDIX 3

Moppie *lyrics*

Texts reproduced in this appendix were collected by Armelle Gaulier and Denis-Constant Martin in various circumstances. Some have been noted from carton boards hanging on the wall at *klopskamers*; others have been quoted in the course of interviews and transcribed. In a few cases, composers were able to give us sheets on which lyrics were printed or handwritten; occasionally the words were transcribed from recordings. In every case, in spite of many difficulties, we did our best to provide an accurate transcription and an adequate translation of the songs.[1] This could not have been done without the kind assistance of several friends and interlocutors. Apart from a few exceptions, the translations proposed here generally result from a compromise between two or three renderings of the Afrikaans texts; when this is not the case, the name of the translator(s) is given in brackets. We have to thank several composers, who took time to explain to us the meanings they wanted to convey. We are extremely grateful to Melvyn Matthews, who assisted in translating some of the songs, and to Paul Sedres, who translated and revised many songs in our collection, and also provided explanations pertaining to the musical sources of the melodies, as well as to allusions, innuendos and double-entendres that could lie behind the words. In a few cases, when we thought that explanations given in Chapters 5 and 6 were not sufficient, we have inserted a few additional comments before the text of the *moppie*. We have chosen to reproduce *moppies* that were quoted during interviews we conducted. They do not constitute a "representative sample" of styles and themes addressed in *moppies*, but we hope that they provide interesting examples of the material we examined in the two previous chapters; this sample complements the collection proposed at the end of Anne Marieke van der Wal's study (2009).

Taliep ABRAHAMS: *"Die Spoek"*

Oh-ho-ho-ho…Oh-ho-ho-ho-ho ho-Oh-ho-ho-ho-ho-hooooo…
  oh-ho-ho-ho-ho-hoooooo…
O' die spoek
En hy vat my hier, vat my daar, vat my deurmekaar (x2)
Sing, sing, sing, ja die spoek is 'n lelike ding (x2)
Die spoek hy loep so sag dat niemand hom kan hoor
Hy loep so sag in die nag jy sal hom nooit nie hoor
Daar kom hy aan (x2)
Hy loep so sag in die nag jy sal hom nooit nie hoor
Vang hom-vang hom-vang hom-vang hom
Die spoek is dom
Tra-la-la-la hoole – ha (x3)
Kyk hoe lyk Amina sy's die lekke sister van Fatima
Sy's getroud met Abassie, hy's daai ou hy't lank nie gewas
Die doekoem sê sy't swaar gesamba, daarom lyk haa gesig soes 'n mamba

Haar bek is skeef en haar oë dop om
Nou lyk sy nes 'n verlepte blom
Tra-la-la-la hole-ha (x3)
Kyk hoe lyk Amina nou
O die spoek hy maak my bang, hy maak my bang want hy lyk soos 'n doring slang
Hy laat my huk en skrik alles tesaame
En hy vat my hier, vat my daar, vat my deurmekaar (x2)
Sing, sing, sing, ja die spoek is 'n lelike ding (x2)
Die spoek hy loep so sag dat niemand hom kan hoor
Hy loep so sag in die nag jy sal hom nooit nie hoor
Daar kom hy aan (x2)
Hy loep so sag in die nag jy sal hom nooit nie hoor
En dit was op een aand toe dit donker raak loep Abassie en Amina lekker lank
In a coma, hulle is in a coma
En die spoek het sy dinge met Amina probeer en Abassie het probeer om die spoek te keer soes 'n gekke, hy is mos 'n gekke

"The Ghost" (translation: Anwar and Muneeb Gambeno)

Oh-ho-ho-ho…Oh-ho-ho-ho-ho ho-Oh-ho-ho-ho-ho-hooooo…
  oh-ho-ho-ho-ho-hoooooo…
Oh the ghost
Oh he grabbed me here, grabbed me there, grabbed me everywhere (x2)
Sing, sing, sing, oh a ghost is an ugly thing (x2)
The ghost walks with stealth and nobody can detect it
It walks with stealth at night you will never detect it
He is approaching (x2)
He walks with stealth at night and you will never detect him
Catch him-catch him-catch him-catch him
The ghost is stupid
Tra-la-la-la hoole – ha (x3)
Look at Amina she's the sexy sister of Fatima
She's married to Abassie, the guy who seldom bathes
The witchdoctor says she had a heavy fit now her face looks like that of a
  mamba [an African snake]
Her mouth is skew and her eyes are bulgy
Now she looks like a faded flower
Tra-la-la-la hole-ha (x3)
Look at Amina now
Oh the ghost scares me, he scares me because he looks like a thorny snake
He frightens and shocks and scares me altogether
Oh he grabbed me here, grabbed me there, grabbed me everywhere (x2)
Sing, sing, sing, oh a ghost is an ugly thing (x2)
The ghost walks with stealth so that nobody can detect him
He walks with stealth at night and so that you will never detect him
He is approaching (x2)
It walks with stealth at night you will never detect him
It was during one long evening walk of Abassie and Amina
In a coma, they were in a coma
The ghost approached Amina with malicious intent but Abassie tried to stop
  the ghost like a crazy man, he (Abassie) is a crazy man

Taliep ABRAHAMS: *"Joe Se Barber"*

Joe-se-Bar-ber [spoken]

Wat gaan daar aan
Waat gaan daar aan
Kyk wat gaan daar by Boeta Joe se Barber aan

Baie manne sny hare by Joe Barber *la la la la la la la la la la la*
Som gaan weer sit daar sonder hare *la la la la la la la la la la la*
Som praat van lotto speel
Daar's die wat perde speel
En ook van die jackpot speel
Jy kan jou storie deel met Joe Barber / *la la la la*
Hy hou vir jou fyn dop
Hy's kwaai jy moet pas op vir Joe Barber

Die hare lê daar op die vloer in Joe se Barber / Dis hare Dis hare
[Dis] hare al die soorte Goema Goema hare / Dis hare Dis hare
[Die] hare hare lê daar rond in Joe se Barber / Dis hare Dis hare
Hare klapper hare le daar op die vloer
Nou voort hy jou hare gaan sny

Hang hy 'n lappie om jou nek, lappie om jou nek
Sy tools lê daar in 'n rakkie als in 'n plek, als in 'n plek
Nou hy druk die hare machine dwaars deur jou hare
Jy kry 'n gril toe trek hy jou koppie weer nare

Joe barber / oo oo oo dis Hy / oo oo oo
Joe barber / oo oo oo kan kwaai hare sny / oo oo oo

Hy vra vir jou baie mooi
Watte style hy dit moet sny
Moet hy dit bai kort sny
Als af of 'n kyffie laat bly wo

As die rastaman daar kom
Dan se Boeta Joe vir hom
Jy maak al my skêrre stom
Joe is al dik van hom

Dis geel touwentjies en groen blommetjies
Hang aan sy hare daar
As jy hom van ver af sien lyk sy kop

Nes 'n bossie blomme verlepte bossie blomme
Sy hare bly deurmekaar
Rasta jy's 'n groot las
Jou kop sal in my tuin pas
Jy't lank laas hare gewas

Festive season bly die plek vol
Die queue is so lank jy sal sweer daars 'n jol
Twee speakers by die deur music klop daar deer
Die bergies dans daar voor deur

As jy se dat jy nou pension kry
Sal hy jou hare vir half prys sny
Jou baart skeur hy verniet
Maar [war] jy net moet wiet
Jou pension boekie moet hy sien

Boeta Joe se hy's klaar en gedaan
Hy's moeg van heeldag op sy voete staan
'n mens voel somtyds flou
Daarom moet ta Joe sy voete in warm water hou

Die hare hare lê daa rond in Joe se barber / dis hare dis hare
Hare klappe hare lê daar op die vloer
Hare lê daar hare lê daa-daa in Joe se Barber (x4)

Daa
Boeta Joe se barber daa
Dis hare

"Brother Joe, the Barber"

Joe-se-bar-ber [spoken]

  What's going on in there
  What's going on in there
  Look what's going on at Brother Joe's

  Many men have their hair cut by Joe Barber la la la la la la la la la la
  Some bald men sit there too la la la la la la la la la la
  Some discuss the Lotto
  There are those who play the horses
  And others the jackpot
  You can share your story with Joe Barber la la la
  He pays you close attention
  He's smart, you need to be careful of Joe Barber

  The hair is lying on the floor at Joe Barber's, hair, hair
  All kinds of hair, *ghoema ghoema* hair
  Hair is lying all over Joe Barber's, hair, hair
  Hair, coconut hair, is lying on the floor
  Now before he cuts your hair

  He hangs a towel around your neck, towel around your neck
  His tools is on a rack everything at its place, at its place
  Now he pushes the hair clipper through your hair
  It gives you a thrill then he pulls your head nearer

  Joe Barber oo oo oo that's him oo oo oo
  Joe Barber oo oo oo is a good hair dresser oo oo oo

  He asks you nicely
  What style he must cut
  Must he cut it very short,
  Everything off or a small piece in front

  When the Rastafarian comes,
  Then Joe Barber tells him
  You make my scissors blunt
  Joe is no longer happy with him

Yellow strings and green flowers
Hang in his hair
If you look at him from a distance

His head looks like a bunch of wild flowers, a bunch of wild flowers
His hair stays untidy
Rasta you're quite a burden
Your head would fit in my garden
Your hair has not been washed for long

During the Festive Season the place stays busy
The line is so long you'd swear there's a party
Two speakers at the door bellow music violently
The tramps are dancing at the door

If you say you get a pension
He will cut your hair half price
Your beard he shaves for you
But what you should know
Your pension book he must see

Brother Joe says he's completely exhausted
He's tired of being on his feet all day
And the man sometimes feels like he's going to faint
That's why he has to soak his feet in warm water

Hair lies scattered all over the floor at Joe's barbershop
Hair, hair
Hair, hair all over Joe's barbershop
Hair, coconut hair is lying on the floor
Hair is lying there, lying theeere at Joe Barber's

There
At Joe Barber's
Hair

Taliep ABRAHAMS: *"Queen van die Moffie"*

Luister nou hier
Hier na die storie

Daa kom die *Moffie* aan oooo oooo daa kom se aan
Daa kom die *Moffie* aan daa kom se
Daa kom die *Moffie*
Die queen van die *Moffie*s
Die mooiste in die Kaap

Moffie jy moet onthou
Jy is 'n man wat jou lyf vrou wil hou
Sy is die *Moffie* die queen van die *Moffie*s
Die mooiste in die kaap

Van soggens vroeg tot in die aande laat wooo
Dwaal sy in die kaap wooo
En almal ken haar naam op die parade
Sy gee haar uit sy gee haar lelik uit
Klop aan by elke man
Soek net aandag waar sy kan

Maar sy bly in die speel gaan kyk
Want sy wil soos Madonna lyk
En as sy haar lyf swaai
Sien jy koppe draai

Van haar hare is sy bewus
Maar ons almal weet dat dit is
'n Wig wat sy dra
Ons lag Wa Ga Ga

Wat maak jy as die wind so sterk daar waai
Wat maak jy as die wind jou wig af waai
Ek se jy tel jou hare op
Sit dit op jou kop
Jy moet net pasop
Sit dit net reg op
As die wind weer waai

En jou wig afwaai
Dan lyk jy nets 'n Guy

Haar lippies is so rooi jy kan van ver af sien
Haar oegies blink soos sterretjies dis glittering
As sy die pad af stap doen sy dit als met 'n beat Oh Ho Ho
Sy dra kort sweaters laat haar naaltjie uit wys
Die vingers is vol ringe sy wil vir almal wys
Wil latest skoene dra maar jy kan sien sy loop swaar Oh Ho Ho

La la la la

Moffie kyk wat gaan aan wat gaan aan
Dis in die skinder koerant skinder koerant
Dis wettig nou in ons land
'n man kan trou met 'n nogge man man man man

Hey *Moffie* lalalalalala hey *Moffie* lalalalalala
Jy moet nie vir jou lalalalalala uit kom gee nie lalalalalala
Hey *Moffie* lalalalalala hey *Moffie* lalalalalala
Dis nou jou opportunity lalalalalala
Dis 'n reality lalalalalala

Hey *Moffie* lalalalalala hey *Moffie* lalalalalala
Jy moet nie vir jou uit lalalalalala kom gee nie lalalalalala
Hey *Moffie* lalalalalala hey *Moffie* lalalalalala
Dis nou jou opportunity lalalalalala
Dis 'n reality lalalalalala

Wat maak jy as die wind so sterk daar waai
Wat maak jy as die wind jou wig af waai
Ek se jy tel jou hare op
Sit dit op jou kop
Jy moet net pasop
Sit dit net reg op
As die wind weer waai
En jou wig afwaai
Dan lyk jy nets 'n Guy

Dan lyk, dans lyk jy nets 'n Guy
Moffie jy nets 'n Guy

"Queen of the Moffies"

Now listen here
Listen to the story

There comes the *Moffie* ooo ooo there she comes
There comes the *Moffie*, there she comes
There comes the *Moffie*
The Queen of the *Moffies*
The most beautiful in the Cape

Moffie you need to remember
You're a man who keeps a woman's body
She is the *Moffie*, the queen of the *Moffies*
The most beautiful in the Cape

From early morning till late at night wooo
She wanders in the Cape
And everyone knows her name on the Parade
She is flaunting herself, she is flaunting terribly
She hits on every man
Seeks attention where she can

But she is continuously looking in the mirror
Because she wants to look like Madonna
And if she sways her body
To see heads turn

She is aware of her hair
But everyone knows it's
A wig that she's wearing
We're laughing wa ghaah ghaah

What do you do when the wind blows so strong
What do you do when the wind blows your wig off
I say you pick up your hair
Put it on your head
You need to be careful
Put it on right
If the wind blows again

And blows your wig off
Then you look like a Guy

Her lips are so red you can see from afar
Her eyes glow like little stars, they're glittering
When she walks in the street she struts with a beat Oh Ho Ho
She wears short tops to show her navel
The fingers are full of rings for all to see
[She] will wear the latest shoes but you can see that she walks heavily Oh ho ho

La la la la

Moffie, look what's happening, what's happening
It's in the gossip paper, gossip paper
It's legal now in our country
A man can marry another man, man, man, man

Hey *Moffie* lalalalalala hey *Moffie* lalalalalala
You no longer lalalalalala have to show off lalalalalala
Hey *Moffie* lalalalalala hey *Moffie* lalalalalala
This is now your chance lalalalalala
It's a reality lalalalalala

Hey *Moffie* lalalalalala hey *Moffie* lalalalalala
You must stop doing this lalalalalala stop doing this lalalalalala
Hey *Moffie* lalalalalala hey *Moffie* lalalalalala
It's your opportunity lalalalalala
Now it is reality lalalalalala

What do you do when the wind blows so strong
What do you do when the wind blows your wig off
I say you pick up your hair
Put it on your head
You need to be careful
Put it on right
If the wind blows again
And blows your wig off
Then you look like a Guy

You look, you look just like a Guy
Moffie, you're just a Guy

Ismail DANTE: *"Fiesta Tyd"*

Fiesta, al die mense hou daar van
Fiesta, al die mense sing en dans
Fiesta, dis die tyd van plesierigheid
Kyk daar vir Dollie en vir Pieter en die kinders
Hul almal is soe vrolik
Die musiek speel die fiesta melody

Dans die samba dat die ding so speel
Dans die samba dat die luidjies klink
Doen die breakdans en ruk jou reg, nou soe en soe

Kyk wie kom nou hier aan
Dis nou Dolly Parton met haar headlights aan
Kyk wie bring sy saam?
Dis ou Tony van *Who's the Boss*
Dis hier en daar, so raak ons deurmekaar

Dis ou Tony van *Who's the Boss*
Dis Peter Tosh en sy hare hang los
Dis Michael Jackson met sy aksin
Tra la la la, tra la la la
Tra la la la la la

Hier's ons nou weer almal te same
Dans en sing hier oppie Peraare
Dit gaan lekker hier
So maak die manne plesier
Dis 'n ruk en 'n pluk
Oo, die ding soek geluk
Dis van die en van daai
Ooh la la, daa' maak ons Dollie 'n draai
Tra la la bamba
Die ding begin
Hier kom Dollie en sy doen haar ding
Hie kom Pieter en sy voete stink

La, la, la, la, la, la Bamba
Laat die dans begin

Daar kom Dolly en sy doen haar ding
Hier kom Peter, oe sy voete sting
La, la, Bamba, la, la Bamba, la, la, Bamba
Laa Bamba

"Fiesta Time"

Fiesta, everyone is there
Fiesta, all the people sing and dance
Fiesta, it's the time for merriment
Look, there's Dollie and Peter and the kids
They are all so happy
The music plays the fiesta melody

Dance the rumba that is played
Dance the samba played by powerful musicians
Do the breakdance and get fit, now so, and so

Look who's coming
It's Dolly Parton with her headlights on
Look who she's coming with to this evening's dance, hou laa?
It's old Tony from *Who's the Boss*
Here and there, we become entranced

There's old Tony from *Who's the Boss*
There's Peter Tosh with his hair hanging loose
There's Michael Jackson with his action
Tra-la-la, la, tra, la, la, la.
Tra-la, la, la, tra, la, la, la, laa, la, laa

Here we are again, all together
We dance and sing here on the Parade
It is going very well here
This is the way they enjoy themselves
It's showing and pushing,
O the thing is trying its luck
It's about this and that oh la la
There old Dolly makes her gyration
Tra la la bamba
Let the dance begin
There comes Dolly and she does her thing
Here comes Peter with his stinky feet

La, la, la, la, la, la Bamba
Let the dance begin

There comes Dolly and she does her thing
Here comes Peter with his stinky feet
La, la, Bamba, la, la Bamba, la, la, Bamba
Laa Bamba

Ismail and Gamja DANTE: *"Die Bruilof van die Jaar"*

[The words of this song were recorded during an interview taped by Denis-Constant Martin with Ismail and Gamja Dante in Hanover Park, on 20 October 2011; because of the poor quality of the tape, some passages could not be transcribed.]

[…] moet ek uit ga' vra
Kyk om, da' staan die bruidegom
Ou Langie kom so brom brom brom

Dam-dam-dam-dam-wa
wo-wo-wo-wo-wowa
ah-ha-ha-ha-haha
Net 'n bietjie liefde

Kyk hoe jol Tant Ravie
dam-dam-dam-dam
Sy's die idol van die jaar
wo-wo-wo-wo-wowo
Sy gaa' mos trou van jaar
Met ou Kokkie, die wiewenaar

Daa' kom Tant Evie
Daa' kom ou Koos
Daa' staan Oom Abel
Hannie en Tant Lee
Net 'n bietjie liefde

Daa' staan Oom Abel
Hannie en Tant Lee
Net 'n bietjie liefde
Nou is dit 'n hele […]
Want Lee, sy is mos die skinnerbek

Tra-lalalala
Tra-la la-la-lala
Tra-la-la lala-lala

Kom, kom gaa' saam
Na die bruilof, die bruilof van die jaar

Dis rooi tapytte en groot geskenke
Die bruid is in die Good Hope Centre
Wow [...]

Die tafels was gedek
Met al die soorte van koeke
Hier's 'n paar wat ek on'hou
En nog so veel van koeke

Dis ronde koeke, plat koeke
Regop koeke, lang koeke
Korte koeke, nat koeke
Lekker om te kou

Ronde korsies lang met worse
Lang worse, kort worse
Lang worse, tong wors
Lekker om te bou

Nou dis 'n [...] ding
Kleine ding, grote ding
Kleine ding, dooie ding
Hannie en Tant Lee
Net 'n bietjie liefde

Tant Ravie het geluk gevind
[...]
Die hele ding is verby
Dit was mos die bruilof, die bruilof van die jaar
Die bruilof van die jaar

"The Wedding of the Year"

[…] I have to ask
Turn around, there's the bridegroom
Old Langie comes charging along

Dam-dam-dam-dam-wa
wo-wo-wo-wo-wowa
ah-ha-ha-ha-haha
Just a little love

Look how Aunt Ravie is happy
dam-dam-dam-dam
She's the idol of the year
wo-wo-wo-wo-wowo
She's getting married this year
To old Kokie, the widower

Here comes Aunt Evie
Here comes old Koos
There's Uncle Abel
Hannie and Auntie Lee
Just a little love

There's Uncle Abel
Hannie and Aunty Lee
Just a little love
Now it's the entire […]
Because Lee, she's a gossiper

Tra-lalalala
Tra-la la-la-lala
Tra-la-la lala-lala

Come, come along
To the wedding, wedding of the year
The red carpet and many presents
The wedding is taking place at the Good Hope Centre
Wow […]

The tables were decked
With all kinds of cakes
Here's a few I remember
There was so much cake

It's round cakes, flat cakes
Straight cakes, long cakes
Short cakes, soaked cakes
All very tasty

Cracker bread with sausage
Long sausage, short sausage
Long sausage, tongue sausage
All very tasty
That's a thing
Little things, grand things
Little things, dead things
Old things
Hannie and Aunty Lee
Just a little love

Aunty Ravie has found some luck
[…]
The wedding is over
That was the wedding of the year, the wedding of the year
The wedding of the year

Ismail and Gamja DANTE: *"Ons Land Suid-Afrika"*

Ons land Suid-Afrika
Ons land van prag en praal
Met liefde en met vrede
Kan ons ons land verbeter
Volk van ons land
Staan hand aan hand
O, ons sing 'n lied
Die lied van ons mooi land
Wat moet daar nog groei
Oor velde en dit bring'n mooie geur
Lank soos mooi riviere
Die wind waai so saggies
Voor jy sit en sing
Die melodie so saggies en so […]
Soos die son sak oor die land
Skyn die maan nog op die sëe
Stewig staan ons Tafelberg
En eiland op die sëe
Dit is ons land, ons land Suid-Afrika
Ons mooie land van mooiheid en plesier
Nou breek daar 'n tyd aan
Van hartseer en swaarheid
Kom ons help ons jeug
En stop die trane wat ons ouers stort
Met liefde, troosheid
Ons land Suid-Afrika
Die mooiste land wêreld deur

"Our Country South Africa"

Our country South Africa
Our country of beauty and magnificence
With love and peace
We can heal our land
People of our land
Stand hand in hand
Oh, sing our song
The song of our beautiful country
What must still grow
On fields, and it brings a sweet smell
Long as beautiful rivers
The wind whispers
As you sit down to sing
The melody, so soft and so [...]
As the sun sets on the horizon
The moon lights the sea
Steady remains our Table Mountain
And island on the sea
That is our country, our country South Africa
Our beautiful country of beauty and pleasure
Now's the time
Of pain and hardship
Come let's help our youth
And stop the tears of our parents
With love, care
Our country South Africa
The most beautiful country in the world

Abbassie DRAMAT: *"Die Goema Dans"*

Hies ons weer ons sing nou voor jom deur (alwee)
Wat mekeer kom jol jy nog 'n keer (ja)

Ons sing 'n goema pop musiek
Dit laat my voete jeuk en dit gee my skoons tariek (ja)

Oe ja

Mense luister hierse goema ding
Wat toeriste na die kaap toe bring
Hoor die ritme wat soe lekke klink
Klopse spring hier kom 'n ding

Nou hoor net para para para papdap

Kom staan maar nare (stand maar nare)
Op die kaap se vlak hier op die strare (ek se vir jou)
Die ritme vloei soe deur my aare
Ek doen dit weer nog 'n keer

Vorige jare (vorige jaar)
Het ons saam gekom op die peraare (op Nuwe Jaar)
En plek gevat voor al die skare
Dis 'n goema ding loat ons bring

Dis 'n Kaapse kultuur en dis hoe ons mense vuur
Hou plesier tot in die oggend uur
Dis grebring oor die see en gemeng met die ritme hier
So was die goema gevier

Bokkie (het die *Moffie* gesing) paraa paa
Bokkie (het soes 'n vlieg gespring) paraa paa
Bokkie (het ons 'n jol gebring)
En dit laat vir my terug dink

Goema (was Boeta Pang se ding) paraa paa
Vra maar (wiet die wind gebring) paraa paa
Goema (het ons die jol gebring)
En dit laat vir my terug dink

Local is mos lekker vir wat wil jy nog stry
Gaan vra jou ma waar het sy jou gekry
Vertel die skinder bekke die goema gat hier bly
Die klopskamer is waar jy my sal kry

Nou wys vir my die goema dans
Sit jou in 'n trans
Give one man a chance
Ons doen nou die goema dans

Jy lyk verniet soe skaam
Bly sê is geraam
Jol maar net met Kenfac saam
Ons doen die goema dans
Sit jou in 'n trans
Ons doen nou die goema dans ja

So was die goema gevier
Goema dans

"The *Ghoema* Dance"

Here we are again singing at your door (altogether)
What's wrong? Come dance one more time

We sing a *ghoema* pop music
It leaves my feet itching and puts my shoes in a trance (yes)

Oh yes

People hear this, it's a *ghoema* thing
That brings tourist to the Cape
Hear the rhythms that sound so nice
Klopse jump, there's something coming

Now just listen para para para papdap

Come stand nearer (stand nearer)
On the Cape Flats here in the street (I'm telling you)
The rhythms flow through my veins
I do it again and again.

Years ago (years ago)
We gathered at the Parade (on New Year)
And found a spot before the crowd
It's this ghoema thing we bring

It is a Cape culture and this is how our people get on fire
Have fun until the morning hour
It was brought from across the sea and mixed with the local rhythm
That's how the *ghoema* was celebrated

Bokkie (the *Moffie* sang)
Bokkie (jumped like a fly)
Bokkie (brought us a *jol*)
And it lets me think back

Ghoema (was Boeta Pangs' thing)
Just ask (who brought the wind)
Ghoema (brought the *jol*)
And lets me think back

Local is very nice why would we argue
Go ask your mother where she got you
Tell the gossip mongers the *ghoema* is here to stay
The *klopskamer* is where you'll find me

Now show me the *ghoema* dance
Puts you in a trance
Give one man a chance
We are doing the *ghoema* dance

You don't have to be ashamed
It's a sin
Dance with the Kenfac
We are doing the *ghoema* dance
It puts you in a trance
We are doing the *ghoema* dance

That's how the *ghoema* was celebrated
Ghoema dance

Anwar GAMBENO: *"Charlie die Rasta-man"*

Hê djy, wies djy?!
Waar-verdaan kom djy, Charlie?
Charlie, die Rasta-man
Hy maak die kinders bang
Hy was soo min
Sy voete stink
Rook krye maak hom so versin
Charlie, die rasta-man
Sy motjie dra 'n sak-rok
Kyk hoe lyk sy nou
Haar hare is soos toue
Jy kan karre daarmeen tou

Daar kom hy nou, daai vuil Rasta-ou
Sy oë's vlou, hy rook hom aanhou blou
As jy hom vra wat dink hy, wat sy naam is
Dan sê hy gou
Hy's daai Rasta-ou
Hy het sy naam vergeet
In sy oë kan jy sien daar's net verdriet
Hy het nog lank nie gewas
Sy hare is so swart soos giet
Hy is so maar soos 'n riet
Die ruik van sy voete maak jou baie siek
Dit laat jou huk en snuk
Dit maak jou naar, o sies!
Sy naam is Boeta Charlie-bum
Hy's vannie skwatte kamp
Hy willie was nie
Hy stink, hy stink, hy stink

"Charlie the Rastaman"

Hey you! Who are you?!
Where do you come from, Charlie?
Charlie the Rastaman
He scares the children
He seldom takes a bath
His feet smell
Smokes herbs that leave him all drugged
Charlie, the Rastaman
His girlfriend wears a bag as a skirt
Look at her
Her hair is like ropes
You can tow cars with it

Here he comes, the soiled Rastaman
His eyes are murky, he's forever smoking
If you ask him what he thinks, what his name is
His quick reply is
He's that Rastaman
He's forgotten his name
His eyes are filled with despair
He's not washed for long
His hair is pitch black
He's as thin as a rake
The stench of his feet is nauseating
It makes one run away
It makes you really sick, oh yuck!
His name is Brother Charlie-bum
He's from the squatter camp
He refuses to bath
He stinks, he stinks, he stinks

Anwar GAMBENO: *"Die Lied vannie Hawker-boy"*

Voor die son opkom
En jy hoor daar's ysterwiele wat draai
Hoe sal jy nou weet dis die Hawker-boy se perdewa daai
Hoor net hoe sing hy
Sing hy sy lied nou daar
Sal jy dan weet ja
Dis die Hawker-boy daar

Hawker-boy, wat maak jy daar?
Is jou vrugte, jou groente vars vandag?
Die mense kla
Is dit nou waar
Jou attepels loop jou vooruit, ja

Van deur tot deur loop hy
Geen huis loop hy verby
Met sy mandjie aan sy sy sing hy
Hy hoor die kinners skree
Maar kyk die hawker is hier
Hoor net hoe sing hy weer sy lied
Hy gee sy goed vir almal wie hom vra
O ja, dis waar
Hy gee op skuld, ja
Maar Vrydagaand het hy sy geld kom vra
Dan sê jou ma sy issie daar

Hy't alles op sy wa
Net wat die mense vra
Daar's piesangs virrie brood
En sy wortel is so groot
Avekarepere maak jou hare mere
En sy skwassies gee die meisiekinners pere
As jy mooi vra dan gee hy jou mere
Dis die lied wat hy sing van sy wa
Hier innie Kaapse strate

O ja, hy's nou ons hawker
Die lied wat hy sing is vol smaak

"The Hawker-boy's Song"

Before sunrise
And the sound of iron wheels turning
How will you know if it's the Hawker-boy's carriage?
Just listen to him sing
He sings his song
That's how you'll know
That it's the hawker-boy who's coming

Hawker-boy, what are you doing?
Are your fruit and vegetables fresh today?
The people complain
Can it be true
That your potatoes precede you, yes?

Door to door he goes
No home he skips
With his basket by his side he sings
He hears the children call
Look, the hawker is here!
Just hear him sing his song
He shows his goods to all who ask
Oh yes, it's true
He sells on credit, yes
But Friday night he comes asking for his money
Then your mother hides herself

He's got everything on his wagon
Just what the people want
There are bananas for the sandwiches
And the carrots are so big
Avocadoes make your hair grow
And his squashes make the girls' breasts grow
If you ask nicely he'll give you more
It's the song he sings from his wagon
Here in the streets of Cape Town

Oh yes, he's our hawker
The song he sings is so tasteful

Anwar GAMBENO: *"Die Son"*

Ons sien a laaaities staan
Op die hoeke van 'n Kaapse straat
Koerante in sy hand skree hy wat daarin aan gaan
Vertel ons dat die mense march
Daar bo in Hanover Straat
Tot by die Parlement oor die tik in Tafelsig
Die Pankies hulle was ook daar
Met koefias en hul toppe aan
Dit alles kan jy lees in *Die Son*, die skinder koerant

Ons sien 'n laatie op die hoek stan en rook
Hy is die laatie wat die koerante verkoep
Hy skree, *Die Son*, die skinder koerant
Ja, jy kan jou mind opmaak
Die Son sien nou alles raak
Dis laat die mense praat
Die Son, *Die Son*, die skinder koerant
Hier, hier in die Kaap, verskyn *Die Son* elke dag
Deur storm wind en reën verskyn *Die Son* hier in die Kaap
Daar's waarde vir jou geld, jou geld
As *Die Son* die storie vertel, vertel
Dit is hiervan dit is daarvan van 'n ander vrou se man
Hulle sê hy is gay, met 'n *Moffie* het hy gevry

Is it jou man of dit haar man
Die Son sê hy's gevang (wooo)
Lees nou *Die Son*, op page drie is daar ook porn,
Daars 'n mooi meit, daars 'n sexy meit
Kyk, jou bek hang op die grond (wooo)

Original words

Ou Shaik is daai ou, hy sê hy's van die ANC
(Shaik Zuma Shaik Shaik Zuma)
Die Son vra Mo vir wie het hy die brood gegee
(Shaik Zuma Shaik Shaik Zuma)
Hy sê hyt 'n vriend maar hy het geen antwood nie

Zuma sê Shaik het hom niks gegee
(Shaik Zuma Shaik Shaik Zuma)
Hy is net skuldig as die hof hom nov straf jee
(Shaik Zuma Shaik Shaik Zuma)
Maar hy's nie meer in onse Parlement nie
En ons sê, Shaik Zuma Shaik
Shaik Zuma, maar hy's nie meer in onse Parlement nie

Mellie variant

Ou boeta Mellie wat het jy gemaak (x3)
Die Son het jou gevang is jy dan vaak

Allie mense staan nou op (nou op)
Hulle was soe diep geskok (geskok)
Ou Mellie skree "hou nou op" (hou op)
My vrou gat my nou uitskop (uitskop)

Toe hy byrie huis ankom (ankom)
Was sy vrou soe dom vestom (vestom)
Slaan hom met 'n biesemstock
Ja ou Mellie bly ma dom

Dom, dom, dom, Dom dom, dom

Daar was 'n hele skelery
(kyk hoe haloep Mellie, kyk hoe haloep Mellie)
Toe Mellie op die frontpage daar veskyn
(kyk hoe haloep Mellie, kyk hoe haloep Mellie)
Hulle het hom in die Main road nous sien ry
Toe sê *Die Son* hy het met a *Moffie* gevry

Ja daar's 'n nuwe koerant op die straat nou
En jou secret is nie meer 'n luxury
As jy 'n losmyt in die Main Road optel
Sal *Die Son* die hele Kaap daarvan sê O-o-o-o-o-o
[Lees nou] *Die Son*, die koerant maak die mense vol
Van daai losser meid, en Hou daai *Moffie* lyk
Ons lees nou van jou slegtigheid

In *Die Son*
Die skinder koerant

"The Sun"

We see a youngster standing
On a street corner of Cape Town
The newspaper in his hand shouting what's in it
He is telling us that the people marched
From the top of Hanover Street
To the Parliament about "tik" in Tafelsig
PAGAD members were also there in their koefias and robes
All that you can read in *Die Son*, the gossip newspaper

We see a youngster standing smoking at the corner
He is the youngster that sells the newspaper
He shouts *Die Son*, the gossip newspaper
Yes you can make up your mind
Die Son now sees everything
It makes the people talk
Die Son, *Die Son*, the gossip newspaper
Here, here in Cape Town
You'll see *Die Son* everyday
Through storms and rain *Die Son* will still shine, here at the Cape
There's value for your money, your money
When *Die Son* tells a story, tells a story
It's about this, it's about that, about another woman's husband
They say he's gay, he was seen with a *Moffie*

Is it your husband or her husband?
Die Son says he was caught (ooh)
Now read *Die Son*, on page three there's also porn
There's a pretty bird, there's a sexy bird
Look, your mouth will drop to the ground! (ooh)
His mouth is open on the ground (ooh)

Original words

Old Shaik is a big shot, he says he's from the ANC
(Shaik Zuma Shaik, Shaik Zuma Shaik)
Die Son asks Mo who he gave the dough to
(Shaik Zuma Shaik, Shaik Zuma Shaik)

He says he's got a friend but he's got no answer
(Shaik Zuma Shaik, Shaik Zuma Shaik)
Zuma says Shaik gave him nothing
(Shaik Zuma Shaik, Shaik Zuma Shaik)
He is only guilty if the court court finds so
(Shaik Zuma Shaik, Shaik Zuma Shaik)
But he is no longer in our Parliament
And we say Shaik Zuma shaik
Shaik Zuma but he is no longer in our Parliament

Mellie variant

Brother Mellie, what have you done
Die Son has caught you, were you asleep

All the people are now rising to their feet (to their feet)
They were so shocked (shocked)
Old Mellie shouts "stop it!" (stop it!)
My wife's gonna kick me out (kick me out)

When he got home (got home)
His wife was so dumbfounded (dumbfounded)
She chased him with a broom
Yes, old Mellie stays thickheaded

Stupid, stupid, stupid, stupid, stupid, stupid

There was a big argument
(see how Mellie runs, see how Mellie runs)
When Mellie appeared on the front page
(see how Mellie runs, see how Mellie runs)
They saw him driving along Main Road
So *Die Son* said he had been making love to a *Moffie*

Yes there is a new newspaper on the street now
And your secret is no longer a luxury
If you pick up a street girl in Main Road
Die Son will tell the whole of Cape Town
Read *Die Son* now, the newspaper tells everybody everything
About your slut, and how the *Moffie* looks
We'll read about your feebleness in *Die Son*

In *Die Son*
The gossip newspaper

Terry HECTOR: *"Vusie van Guguletu"*

Vusie van Guguletu
Was gebore in Suwetu
Hy kom een dag daar
Om vir ons te vra
Oh hy saam met ons kan sing
Hy's lief om te Pavarotti koppie
En hy dink hy's Pavarotti
Hy was duidelik
En hy het 'n plak
Toe leer ons hom die moppie

Ah ha die ou was nogal kwaai
Ah ha toe ons die ou uit try
Ah ha hy't 'n lekker style
Ah ha ah ha ah ha ah ha
Ah ha hy kan lekker sing
Ah ha en hy doen sy sing
Ah ha ja hy het 'n plak
Ah ha ah ha ah ha ah ha
La la la la – la la la la

Keer hom keer hom ky wat ma [...]

Hy daar
Hy choke haar vrek
Lyk die ou is tatie
Want hy choke haar vrek

Vusie het gou geleer
Niks kan vis Vusie keer
Nou kan hy saam sing
En ons doen ons ding
Wat soek 'n man nog meer

Hy's lief om af te koppie
En hy sing glad nie vroinie
Hy is duidelik en hy het n plak

Nou sing ons saam die moppie
Nou sing hy saam met ons
En ons sing opera
Dis die opera moppie van die jaar

"Vusie from Gugulethu"

Vusie from Gugulethu
Was born in Soweto
One day he came there
To ask us
If he could sing with us
He loves to copy Pavarotti
And he thinks he's Pavarotti
He was cool
And he put himself out
To learn the *moppie* from us

Ah ha the guy was cool enough
Ah ha for us to try him out
Ah ha he's got a nice style
Ah ha ah ha ah ha ah ha
Ah ha he can sing nicely
Ah ha and he's doing his thing
Ah ha yes he is dedicated
Ah ha ah ha ah ha ah ha

La la la la – la la la la

Stop him stop him what is he doing
He there
He chokes her to death
The guy looks crazy
He wants to choke her to death

Vusie learned quickly
Nothing can stop Vusie
Now he can sing with us
And we're doing our thing
What more does a man look for

He likes to copy
And does not sing like before
He is nice and dedicated

Now we sing the *moppie* together
Now he sings with us
And we sing opera
This is the opera *moppie* of the year

Kaparie JANUARY: *"Die Oxford"*

[*According to Anwar Gambeno: "'Die Oxford' was written by a man called Boeta Kaparie and his surname was January. I think he died in 1984, I think he was about 80 years old when he died and he wrote this song. The Oxford was a fashionable trouser in the 1940s, it was a 3/4 trousers with a cord that you could pull tight at the bottom, a sort of knickerbocker. The Oxford was a wide pant that they used at Oxford University in England and that time it was also the fashion to smoke and there was a link between the smoke and the Oxford University. It was made in checkered material. It is a very traditional* moppie *that was written in the early 1940s." Another song was interpolated in the "Oxford", possibly a refrain sung on the occasion of the cushion dance, recalling intercourses that may have taken place during the Great Trek. Anwar Gambeno explained: "The cushion dance was a dance of the Cape malays in the old days. This dance was done with pillows. Now there are two reasons for the pillow. We don't know which is the true reason because the people who used to do this dance they don't want to talk about it. The girls used to be on the one side and the guys used to be on the other side, in a circle, and they used to pass the pillow. The one school of thought says that the pillow represented a baby and the one guy used to pass it to the other guy. You know: 'this is not mine this is yours' type of thing. The other school thought the pillow was there to prevent the touching of the women and the men, which is against the religion: unmarried people shouldn't touch. So I don't know which is the true history." Anwar Gambeno, interview with Denis-Constant Martin, Mitchells Plain 3 October 1994*]

    Ma ek wil die Oxford dra (bis)
    Want die broekie is so kort
    En sy pype hang daar
    Sy dra in kort mini
    Is die fashion van die jaar
    Ma ek wil die Oxford dra

    O la ma di, wie se kind is die?
    Sala Wiesa sê saam met die wa
    Saam met die wa hier
    Japie my, die wind waar deur my sy
    Laat staan sulle dinge laat staan
    Jy's dorung in my sy
    Boegoeberg se dam is in doodlekker dam
    Daar wat die volkies hulle tone lekker stamp

Liedjies word gesung as hul vaaljape drunk
Boegoeberg se dam is in doodlekker dam
Ek jol nie met in loskop dolla nie

Die traue die rol oor jou bokkie
Die traue die rol oor my bokkie
Dis daar waar die son en die maan ondergan
Bokka jy moet huis toe gaan
Nee, nee, nee, my dolla nee
Ek jol nie met in loskop dolla nie

Ma ek wil die Oxford dra

"The Oxford"

Mom I want to wear an Oxford
Because the trouser is short
And the legs hang wide
My sister wears a short mini
It is the fashion of the year
Mom I want to wear an Oxford

Oh Ma, whose child is this?
Antie Sala Wisa says that she was with the ox wagon
With the ox wagon when it happened
Japie my, the wind blows through your jacket
Please stop you silly things, please stop
You are a thorn in my side
Boegoeberg dam is a very nice dam
This is the place where people dance all night
Songs get sung and they drink *vaaljapie* [homebrew, type of brandy]
Boegoeberg dam is a very nice dam
The tears will roll over your girl
The tears will roll over my girl
It will happen when the moon goes down
Then your girl will have to go home
No, no, no, not my girl
I do not dance with a loose girl, no

Mother I would like to wear an Oxford

Abduraghman MORRIS: *"Wilhemina die Moffie"*

[This comic song was performed by the Young Men in the Top 8 2015 *moppie* competition of the CMCB and won first prize.]

Daar kom die Moffie
Daar kom die Moffie
Daar kom sy
Daar kom sy
Daar kom die Moffie
Ons sien die Moffie elke Saterdagaand
In die Sea Point op die Main Road staan
Ons sien die kar stop
(Ah! ah!)
Om by haar aan te klop
Sy gaan na die jol vanaand

Om die ou het sy haar lyffie
En sy loop te nuit te styf nie (x 4)

Hier kom 'n ding, 'n lekker ding
'n Moffie ding
Hello julle
My naam is Wilhemina
Ek is so sexy en ek maak die ouens mal

Sy is so sexy
Sy maak die ouens mal
Laat ons julle vertel
Hoe die Moffies in die Main Road staan
Is 'it jou man of is 'it my man
Wat vir haar will optel?

Julle wiet mos van my
Ek is sexy, ek is great
Sy hou om van die ouens te kry
Want sy vry om lekker te kry

Sy sê haar naam is Wilhemina
Kyk hoe doen sy die Macarena

Haar naam is Wilhemina
Sy's die Moffie van Hanover Park

Vanaand kom al die Moffies bymekaar
(ooh-la-lala, ooh-la-lala)
Dis die Drag Queen Competition van die jaar
(ooh-la-lala, ooh-la-lala lala)
Sy's Wilhemina

Haar kop is so rooi van die hienna
Sy kan so lekker Macarena
Sy's die ster
Sy's die ster vanaand

Die Moffies shock
O ja, die Moffies shock
As Wilhemina die stage vat in haar mini rok
Sies, sy stink! Sies, sy stink! Sies, sy stink!
Oh, wow! She's a teaser
Die Moffies skree: Wilhemina, moet jou tog nie so uitgee nie!
Haar hare's ge-gel maar haar bene is geswel en vol hare
Hare
Sy't vir oggend geskee (shaved)
Maar haar bies baard die grooi al weer

Sy draai en sy swaai dat haar hare so waai soos 'n…
Die mense staan
Hulle's woes geslaan
Haar mamma en haar pappa en haar niggies en haar aunties
Is so proud
Want sy is mos die Drag Queen van die Jaar

O die Moffie, ja die Moffie
Die Moffie is 'n wonderlike ding

Ek was my vier keur 'n jaar
En change net twee keur my bra
Sies! Die Moffie is 'n wonderlike ding
O die Moffie, o ja die Moffie
Die Moffie is 'n wonderlike ding
Ek staan op daai hoek

Heena man, ek ruik net soos snoek!
Sies! Die Moffie is 'n wonderlike ding

Al die Moffies jol nou lekker te saam
Dans sy lekker lekker
Oo, so baie lekker

Sy's die ster
Al die Moffies hou nou lekker te saam
Dit is a raarde tyd en almal celebrate
Want sy's die ster vanaand
Vanaand kom die Moffies – vanaand kom die Moffies – aan!
Sy's die Moffie van die jaar

Ek is die Moffie

"Wilhemina the *Moffie*"

There comes the *Moffie*
There comes the *Moffie*
There she comes
There she comes
There comes the *Moffie*
Every Saturday night we see the *Moffie*
In Sea Point on Main Road
We see the car stop
(Ah ha!)
To hustle her
She's going to have fun tonight

On her arm she has her man
And she struts like a peacock

Here comes something, a pleasant thing
A *Moffie* thing
Hey you!
My name's Wilhemina
I'm so sexy and I drive the guys crazy

She's so sexy
She drives the guys crazy
Let me tell you
How the *Moffie* stands in the Main Road
Is that your man or is it my man
Who will pick her up?

You know about me
I am sexy, I am great
She likes to chase the men
Because she's free to have a nice time

She says her name is Wilhemina
Look how she does the Macarena
Her name is Wilhemina
She's the *Moffie* from Hanover Park

Tonight the *Moffie*s all gather
(ooh-la-lala, ooh-la-lala)
It's the Drag Queen Competition of the Year
(ooh-la-lala, ooh-la-lala lala)
She's Wilhemina

Her hair's all red with henna
She can do the Macarena nicely
She's the star
She's the star tonight

The *Moffie*s are shocked
Oh yes, the *Moffie*s are shocked!
When Wilhemina takes to the stage in her mini dress
Urgh, she stinks! Urgh, she stinks! Urgh, she stinks!
Oh, wow! She's a teaser
The *Moffie*s call out: Wilhemina, stop showing off
Her hair is gelled, but her legs are swelled and covered in hair
Hair
She shaved this morning
But her stubble beard has grown again

She twists and turns so that her hair flutters like…
The people can see
They're shocked
Her mother and her father and her nieces and her aunts
Are so proud
Because she is the Drag Queen of the Year

Oh the *Moffie*, yes the *Moffie*
The *Moffie* is an amazing thing

I wash four times a year
And my bra I only change twice

Urgh! The *Moffie* is an amazing thing
Oh the *Moffie*, Oh the *Moffie*
The *Moffie* is an amazing thing

I stand on the street corner
Oh damn, I smell of *snoek*!

Urgh!
The *Moffie* is an amazing thing

All the *Moffie*s are nicely dancing together
They dance pleasantly, pleasantly
Oh, yes, so nicely

She's the star
All the *Moffie*s enjoy being together
It is a rare occasion and every one is celebrating
Because she's the star tonight
Tonight the *Moffie*s come – tonight the *Moffie*s come
She's the *Moffie* of the Year

I am the *Moffie*

Waseef PIEKAAN: *"Sokkie Bokkie"*

Daar kom my bokkie,
Daar kom sy aan
Sy het 'n lekker sexy mini aan.

Sy vat haar tyd,
Sy gee haar uit.
Sy doen die sokkie terwyl sy die tuin nat spuit.

Ja, ek het rollers in my hare.
Sy doen die sokkie tussen in die blare
Ek hou van sing (sing, sing)
Ek hou van dans (dans, dans)
Sexy bokkie, gee vir my 'n kans.

Ons almal wil dans,
Ag bokkie, kom ons almal doen die sokkiedans.
Sy kan my neem
Gee my nog net een kans
Oe, ja, my bokkie, ek will sokkie
Met jou vanaand (x3)

Oh, ja, daar onder by die disco baan
Doen sy nou die sokkie met haar rokkie aan

Sy se vir my sy is soe lief vir my (x2)
Sy doen it (x4)
Sy jol

Bokkie, ek lyk jou soos jy is.
My hart klop chocolates as jy naby is
Ja, bokkie, kom ons doenie sokkie dans

Kaptein, spaanie seile,
My bokkie, sy is myne
Sy doen die sokkie dans
Daa by die disco baan vinaand

Sy dans, sy sing, my bokkie doenie
Sokkie dans op 'n Sater'ag aand
Sy doen it soe (x12)
Soe en soe en soe en soe

Hoe ja, sy dans en doen die sokkie,
Sing en doen die sokkie dans
Sy spring en doen die sokkie dans vanaand

Hoe ja, sy dans and doen doe sokkie dans
Sing en doen die sokkie dans
Sy spring en doen die sokkie dans vanaand

Hand op, sit die hande op
My bokkie doenie sokkie met 'n hop en 'n skop
Hande op, hande op, sit die hande op
My bokkie doenie sokkie met 'n hop en 'n skop, ja!
Sy sokkiedans hier vanaand oppie vloer (x3)
Want sy is mos to-do,
Sy kan dit mos roer, woo-hooh!

Hande op, almal saam terwylie klop
kom en dans met my
Ja, soe doen ons mos nou die sokkiedans.

"Dancing Darling"

There goes my babe,
Here she comes
She's wearing a sexy mini

She takes her time
She shows off
She does the *sokkie* while watering the garden.

Yes, I'm styling my hair with rollers
She does the *sokkie* among the leaves
I love to sing (sing, sing)
I love to dance (dance, dance)
My sexy babe, just give me a chance.

We all want to dance
Oh, babe, let's all do the *sokkie* dance
You can have me
Just give me one more chance
Oh, yes, my babe, I want to *sokkie* with you tonight.

Oh, yes, there at the disco
She does the *sokkie* in her mini dress

She tells me she loves me so much,
She's doing it,
She's flirting.

My babe, I love you just the way you are
My heart beats chocolates each time you're near
Yes, babe, let's do the *sokkie* dance.

Captain, set sail!
My babe, she's mine
She does the *sokkie* dance
Down at the disco scene tonight

She dances, she sings,
My babe does the *sokkie* dance on a Saturday night

She does it so,
So and so, and so and so

Oh, yes, she's dancing, doing the *sokkie*
Singing and doing the *sokkie* dance
She hopping and doing the *sokkie* dance tonight

Oh, yes, she's dancing, doing the *sokkie*
Singing and doing the *sokkie* dance
She hopping and doing the *sokkie* dance tonight

Hands up, hands up!
My babe's doing the *sokkie* with a hop and a skip
Hands up, hands, hands up!
My babe's doing the *sokkie* with a hop and a skip, yesss!

She's doing the *sokkie* dance here on the floor tonight
'Cause she's so chic
And she can shake it! woo-hoo!

Hands up, all together while I clap
Come dance with me
Yes, that's how we do the *sokkie* dance!

Adam SAMODIEN: *"Die Party van die Jaar"*

[*This* moppie *was written in 2004 on the occasion of the celebration of Nelson Mandela's 85th birthday (Van der Wal 2009, "Appendix 2": 48). At the time, Thabo Mbeki was President of South Africa; Jacob Zuma was Deputy-President; Geraldine Fraser-Moleketi was Minister of Public Service and Administration in the national government; Ebrahim Rasool was the ANC Premier of the Western Cape province; and Patrick McKenzie, who crossed from the New National Party to the ANC in 1999, was Minister of Community Safety in the Western Cape provincial government. "Pata Pata" is a song written by Dorothy Masuka which became famous worldwide when Miriam Makeba recorded it in 1957. Usually accompanied by specific body movements, it became one of the symbols of black African music and culture.*]

Dit was so lekker, ja so lekker
By die party van die jaar
Dit was so lekker, ja so lekker
Mandela het verjaar
Dit was so lekker, ja so lekker
En ons almal was daar

Toe sing ons
Hip hop hoorah
Madiba Mandela
Hip hop hoorah
Madiba Mandela

Ja, daar was mense van Soweto, Khayelitsha en Gugulethu
Daar was van Langa en Nyanga en ere gaste van Amerika
Want dit was Nelson Madiba Mandela se neentigste jaar

Ooh, dit was lekker daar (lekker daar)
Want Thabo Mbeki en Moleketi het die pata-pata gedans
Ons weet dat Mugabe was nie in die Kaap nie en Zuma het die goema geslaan

Nou jol almal saam
En doen die Madiba dans
Nou jol almal saam
En doen die Madiba dans

En sy sê, en sy sê
Doen die Madiba *kwela*, Madiba *kwela*
En sy sê, ja sy sê
Doen die Mandela kwela

Nelson Mandela, ja hy kan nog *kwela*, ja
Doen die Madiba kwela, Madiba *kwela*
Wie sê hy's oud, ja hy's alweer getroud, ja
Doen die Madiba *kwela*
Hy het geveg vir onse reg

Doen die Madiba *kwela*, Madiba *kwela*
Ons sal onthou, ja, hy is mos daai ou, ja
Doen die Madiba *kwela*

Rasool was daar, MacKenzie was daar
Mbeki en die hele ANC was daar
Nou sê vir ons, was jule ook daar
By die party van doe jaar?

(Nelson) Mandela
(Nelson) Madiba Mandela
Nou wens ons veëls geluk, Madiba Mandela
En ons sal onthou, hy is daai ou, hy is daai ou

"The Party of the Year"

It was so nice, yes so nice
At the party of the year
It was so nice, yes so nice
Mandela had his birthday
It was so nice, yes so nice
And all of us were there

Then we sang
Hip hop hooray
Madiba Mandela
Hip hop hoorah
Madiba Mandela

Yes, there were people from Soweto, Khayelitsha and Gugulethu
They came from Langa and Nyanga and honoured guests from America
Because it was Nelson Madiba Mandela's ninetieth birthday.

Ooh, there it was so nice (so nice there)
Because Thabo Mbeki and Moleketi did the *pata-pata* dance
We know Mugabe was not in the Cape and Zuma beat the *ghoema* drum

Now everybody is dancing together
Doing the Madiba dance
Now everybody is dancing together
And doing the Madiba dance

And she says, and she says
Do the Madiba *kwela*, Madiba *kwela*
And she says, yes, she says
Do the Mandela *kwela*

Nelson Mandela, yes he can still do the *kwela*, yes
Do the Madiba *kwela*, Madiba *kwela*
Who says he's old, yes he's married again, yes
Do the Madiba *kwela*
He fought for our rights

Do the Madiba *kwela*, Madiba *kwela*
We'll remember, yes, after all he is that elder, yes
Do the Madiba *kwela*

Rasool was there, McKenzie was there
Mbeki and the entire ANC were there
Now tell us, were you also there
At the party of the year?

(Nelson) Mandela
(Nelson) Madiba Mandela

Now we congratulate Madiba Mandela
And we shall remember: he is that elder, he is that elder

Adam SAMODIEN: *"Die Toi-Toi vir 12%"*

[*This* moppie *was composed in 2007 in response to the mass strike for higher wages organised by COSATU. It speaks of some events in Cape Town during a major public service sector national protest for better wages. The protesters toyi-toyied in the hope of persuading the government to meet their demand for a 12% increase. In the end the protesters only got 7.5% and the toyi-toying for that year ended. The* moppie *depicts a few characters involved in the Cape Town protests, in particular Geraldine Fraser-Moleketi who was Minister of Public Service and Administration from June 1999 to September 2008. "Motjie" is a term of endearment for female Muslims in the Cape. Most often the female would be a mature person, often a mother or grandmother; here motjie Garatie probably refers to a leader or an activist of the trade union COSATU (Paul Sedres, personal communication to Denis-Constant Martin).*]

Ons almal was daar by die toi toi van die jaar, ja
Om te gaan kla ons almal kry baie swaar ja
Almal het gestrike voor die Parlement
Al wat ons vra is 12%
Daar was wittes, swartes and bruines deurmekaar

Hoor hoe skel motjie Garatie
Wat gaan met ons gebeur as ons nie praat nie
12% is wat ons wil hê, en dit is wat die mense sê
Vandag doen ons die toi toi almal saam

En hoor hoe sing hulle
Nkosi Sikilele Afrika
Ek en jy ons woon almal daar
Die mense skel met Moleketi
Cosatu se ons moenie werk nie
12% is wat ons wil hê, en dit is wat die mense sê

Hop Moleketi, hop Moleketi, hop Moleketi deurmekaar
Hop Moleketi, hop Moleketi, ons toyi-toyi aanmekaar

Nou's dit weer toyi-toyi en klipgooi
Bande brand oor die hele land
Van die Kaap tot in Soweto
Toyi-toyi almal saam

Kyk hoe lekker, hoe lekker, hoe lekker jol Galiema
En boeta Salie agterna met sy rooi koefieya
Boeta Mylie jol met 'n vlag in die hand
Boeta Salie jol met 'n klip in die hand
Deur die strate tot op die Parade toi toi almal saam

Boeta Salie gooi vir Dullah met 'n klip teen die kop
Dullah draai om en tel die klip weer op
Gooi vir Boeta Salie dat koefiya waai
Dat Boeta Salie soos 'n tol om Rukieya draai

Hoor hoe skel motjie Garatie
Wat gaan met ons gebeur as ons nie praat nie
12% is wat ons wil hê, en dit is wat die mense sê
Vandag doen ons die toi toi almal saam

"The Toyi-Toyi for 12%"

We were all there at the *toyi-toyi* of the year, yes
To complain as we are all struggling a lot, yes
Everybody protested in front of Parliament
All we are asking for is 12%
There were whites, blacks and coloureds, all mixed together

Hear how *motjie* Garatie scolds
What will happen to us if we do not speak out?
12% is all we ask for, and that's what people are saying
Today we all do the *toyi-toyi* together

They are singing
Nkosi Sikilel' iAfrika
You and I we all live there
The people are reprimanding Moleketi
Cosatu says we should not be working
12% is all we ask for, and that is what people are saying

Hop Moleketi, hop Moleketi, hop Moleketi, all mixed up
Hop Moleketi, hop Moleketi, we *toyi-toyi* on and on

Now it's time again to *toyi-toyi* and to stone
Burn tyres across the entire country
From Cape Town to Soweto
We all *toyi-toyi* together

Look how much fun Galiema is having
And Boeta Salie behind in red keffiyah
Boeta Mylie is dancing with a flag in hand
And Boeta Salie comes with a stone in hand
Along the streets up to the Parade we all *toyi-toyi* together

Boeta Salie strikes a stone on Dullah's head
Dullah turns back to pick up the stone
Throws it back at Boeta Salie, and his keffiyah goes flying
Boeta Salie spins like a top around Rukieya

Hear how *motjie* Garatie scolds
What will happen to us if we do not speak out?
12% is all we ask for, and that's what people are saying
Today we all do the *toyi-toyi* together

Adam SAMODIEN: *"Die Toyi Toyi/Ons Hoor"*

(with additional lyrics by Anwar Gambeno)

Hi, hi hier kom hulle aan,
Ya hi, hi hier kom hulle aan
Ya hi, hi hier kom hulle aan
Almal doen die *toyi toyi toyi*, ja
Ons hoor (ja hi), ons hoor (ja hi), ons hoor (hi)
Almal doen die *toyi toyi toyi*

Daar's onrus in Nyanga, Khayelitsha en Langa
Orals in Suid-Afrika, *toyi* ons almal saam
Ons lees in die koerante
Die Kaap is aan die brand
Ons sien op die TV
Hoe brand die squatter kamp
Die riot squad was daar
Om hulle uitmekaar te jaa'
Oe lalala, oe lalala laa

Eers het ons nie geworrie nie,
Toe was alles tax free
Maar toe kom die GST
Maar nou is dit die VAT

Daar's VAT op koffie, VAT op tea
Daar's VAT op vleis en reis
Maar niks op 'n stompie nie

Hulle het uit die werk gebly vir die twee dae stayaway
COSATU het gesê dat hulle almal vol sal pay
Die een loop voor met die flag in die hand
Die anders kom almal agter aan
In die straat op die parade *toyi toyi* ons almal saam

Mense, mense, *toyi toyi* ons almal saam
Toyi ons almal saam

Original final stanza by Adam Samodien

Viva hier en daar, viva aan mekaar, viva deurmekaar
Viva in Suid-Afrika
Ons hoor, ons hoor, ons hoor
Hulle almal doen die *toyi toyi toyi*
En viva

Anwar Gambeno's final stanza

Viva Madiba, (ya) viva Madiba, (ya) viva Madiba, viva Suid-Afrika
Viva Madiba, (ya) viva Madiba, (ya) viva Madiba
Ons almal sê nou vaarwel
Madiba

"The Toyi Toyi/We Hear"

Hee, hee, here they come
Ya, hee, hee here they come
Ya, hee, hee here they come
They are all doing the *toyi-toyi*, yes

We hear (ya-hee), we hear (ya-hee), we hear (ya-hee)
Everybody does the *toyi-toyi*

There's unrest in Nyanga, Khayelitsha and Langa
All over South Africa we all do the *toyi-toyi* together
We read in the newspaper
The Cape is on fire
We see on TV
The squatter camps are burning
The riot squad was there
To disperse them all
Oo-la-la, oo-la-la

Before, we did not worry
Then everything was tax free
But then came the GST
Now it's the VAT
VAT on coffee, VAT on tea
There's VAT on meat and rice
But nothing on spliffs

The people did not go to work for a two days stay-away
COSATU said all workers would get full pay
One leads with flag in hand
All the others follow after him
On the streets, on the Parade, we *toyi-toyi* all together
Guys, guys, we all *toyi-toyi* together
We all *toyi-toyi* together

Original final stanza by Adam Samodien

Viva here and there, viva one and the other, viva bewilderment
Viva South Africa
We hear, we hear, we hear
They are all doing the *toyi-toyi*
And viva

Anwar Gambeno's final stanza

Viva Madiba, (ya) viva Madiba, (ya) viva Madiba, viva South Africa
Viva Madiba, (ya) viva Madiba, (ya) viva Madiba,
We all say farewell
Madiba

Adam SAMODIEN: *"Hip Hip Horah Suid-Afrika"*

[*Adam Samodien said he composed this* moppie *for the Van Riebeeck Festival of 1972, 30 years after he refused to participate in the Van Riebeck tercentenary. This song is a commentary on the celebration of the arrival of Jan van Riebeeck on Cape shores in 1652 to establish a Dutch halfway house on behalf of the Dutch East India Company. It signaled the start of white settlement in southern Africa. The author takes liberties regarding some historical events depicted in the above* moppie:
1. *Van Riebeeck commandeered three ships, not one, in his convoy when they landed at the Cape;*
2. *Johannesburg was only founded in 1886, many years after the Dutch first arrived;*
3. *The first and most popularly accepted European rounding of the Cape was by Portuguese explorer Bartolomeu Dias in 1488 who named it the Cape of Storms. The Dutch later named it Cape of Good Hope, its name bearing no relation to the discovery of gold and diamonds further into the interior.*

"Hip Hip Horah Suid-Afrika" also celebrates in an indirect way the role slaves played in the creation of Cape Town: they were in the kitchen and knew some answers to questions asked by Jan van Riebeeck. The melody of the first verse is taken from a 1970s Afrikaans country ballad by Lance James called "Dankie" (Thank You): http://www.youtube.com/watch?v=v_6sOaDOXIE (Paul Sedres, personal communication to Denis-Constant Martin).]

Hip hip horah Suid-Afrika
Hip hip horah Suid-Afrika
Dankie sê ons Jan van Riebeeck
Ons sal vir jou nooit vergeet
Dankie 1652 net vir hierdie dag

Toe ek met my skippie in die Tafelbaai kom
Toe kyk ek na die berg en vra toe hoekom
Die berg so plat is soos die tafel in 'n huis
Toe kry ek die antwoord dit kom uit die kombuis

In 1652 het die wind gewaai
Toe kom hy met sy skippie in die Tafelbaai
De wind het so gewaai hulle was almal op 'n klomp
En toe gee hy die naam die Kaap van Storm

Toe gaan hy na Johannesburg net om te kyk
Hoe die land in die binnekant lyk
Goud en diamante was daar gevind
En so het Kaap die Goeie Hoop begin

'n Beeld van hom is toe geplant
Daar onder by die punt van Tafelbaai strand
Dit is nou soveel jare waarvan ek praat
Maar tog staan ek nog in Adderley Straat

Horah Suid-Afrika. Horah Suid-Afrika
Suid-Afrika Horah

"Hip hip hooray, South Africa"

Hip hip hooray, South Africa
We say thank you, Jan van Riebeeck
We will never forget you
Thank you 1652, just for this day

When I sailed into Table Bay with my little boat
I looked at the mountain and asked why
The mountain was as flat as a table from home
The answer came from the kitchen

In 1652 the wind was blowing
When he sailed into Table Bay with his little boat
It was gusting so much they were all huddled together
Then he gave it the name: the Cape of Storms

Then he travelled to Johannesburg just to see
How the country looks on the inside
Gold and diamonds were found there
And so the Cape of Good Hope began

A statue of him was erected
Down there at the edge of Table Bay beach
I'm speaking of many years ago now
But I still stand on Adderley Street

Hooray, South Africa! Hooray, South Africa!
South Africa, hooray!

Notes

1. Once again we would like to emphasise that more research is needed to compile a collection of songs that could be read as a people's social history of Cape Town and South Africa. See: Martin, Denis-Constant (2005) Social history through the Moppies, calling for research. *IFAS-Research Newsletter* 3 July. Available at http://www.ifas.org.za/research/pdf/lesedi3-eng.pdf

References

Adhikari, Mohamed (1992) The sons of Ham: Slavery and the making of coloured identity. *South African Historical Journal* 27(1): 95–112
Adhikari, Mohamed (1993) *'Let us Live for Our Children': The Teachers' League of South Africa, 1913–1940*. Cape Town: Buchu Books
Adhikari, Mohamed (2005) *Not White Enough, Not Black Enough: Racial Identity in the South African Community*. Athens: Ohio University Press
Agier, Michel (1999) *L'Invention de la ville. Banlieue, township, invasions et favelas*. Paris: Éditions des Archives contemporaines
Ahlquist, Karen (2006) Introduction. In: Karen Ahlquist (ed.) *Chorus and Community*. Urbana: University of Illinois Press. pp. 1–15
Aigrain, Philippe (2010) Le contexte politique et culturel des droits intellectuels. *Gradhiva* 12: 159–174
al Fārūqī, Lois (1987) Qur'ān Reciters in competition in Kuala Lumpur. *Ethnomusicology* 31(2): 221–228
Allen, Lara (1999) Kwela: The structure and sound of pennywhistle music. In: Malcolm Floyd (ed.) *Composing the Music of Africa: Composition, Interpretation and Realisation*. Ashgate: Aldershot & Brookfield. pp. 227–263
Ampene, Kwasi (2005) *Female Song Tradition and the Akan of Ghana: The Creative Process in Nnwonkoro*. Aldershot: Ashgate
Amselle, Jean-Loup (1990) *Logiques métisses: anthropologie de l'identité en Afrique et ailleurs*. Paris: Payot. [English translation: Royal, Claudia (1998) *Mestizo Logics: Anthropology of Identity in Africa and Elsewhere*. Stanford: Stanford University Press]
Amselle, Jean-Loup (2001) *Branchements, anthropologie de l'universalité des cultures*. Paris: Flammarion
Arom, Simha & Martin, Denis-Constant (2011) Combining sounds to reinvent the world: World music, sociology, and musical analysis. In: Michael Tenzer & John Roeder (eds) *Analytical and Cross-Cultural Studies in World Music*. Oxford & New York: Oxford University Press. pp. 388–413
Arom, Simha & Martin, Denis-Constant (2015) *L'enquête en ethnomusicologie: préparation, terrain, analyse*. Paris: Vrin
Averill Gage (2003) *Four Parts, No Waiting: A Social History of American Barbershop Harmony*. New York: Oxford University Press
Avorgbedor, Daniel (2001) Competition and conflict as a framework for understanding performance culture among the urban Anlo-Ewe. *Ethnomusicology* 45(2): 260–282
Baderoon, Gabeba (2002) Everybody's mother was a good cook: Meanings of food in Muslim cooking. *Agenda: Empowering Women for Gender Equity* 51: 4–15
Baderoon, Gabeba (2014) *Regarding Muslims: From Slavery to Post-Apartheid*. Johannesburg: Wits University Press

Balandier, Georges (1951) La situation coloniale, approche théorique. *Cahiers internationaux de sociologie* 11(51): 44–79. [English translation: Wagoner, Robert A (1951) The colonial situation: A theoretical approach. In: Immanuel Wallerstein (ed.) *Social Change: The Colonial Situation*. New York: John Wiley & Sons. pp. 34–61]

Balandier, Georges (1971) *Sens et puissance, les dynamiques sociales*. Paris: Presses universitaires de France

Balandier, Georges (1988) *Le désordre: éloge du mouvement*. Paris: Fayard

Ballantine, Christopher (2012) *Marabi Nights: Jazz, "Race" and Society in Early Apartheid South Africa*. Scottsville: University of KwaZulu-Natal Press

Bangstad, Sindre (2006) Diasporic consciousness as a strategic resource: A case-study from a Cape Muslim community. In: Leif O Manger & A Assal Munzoul (eds) *Diasporas Within and Without Africa: Dynamism, Heterogeneity, Variation*. Uppsala: Nordic Africa Institute. pp. 32–60

Barthes, Roland (1984) [1968] La mort de l'auteur. In: *Le bruissement de la langue: essais critiques IV*. Paris: Le Seuil: 63–69. [English translation: Howard, Richard (1984) The Death of the Author]. Available at http://www.tbook.constantvzw.org/wp-content/death_authorbarthes.pdf [accessed 4 November 2015]

Barz, Gregory F (2000) Politics of remembering: Performing history(ies) in youth Kwaya competitions in Dar es Salaam, Tanzania. In: Frank Gunderson & Gregory F Barz (eds) *Mashindano! Competitive Music Performance in East Africa*. Dar es Salaam: Mkuki na Nyota Publishers. pp. 379–405

Barz, Gregory F (2006) 'We are from different ethnic groups, but we live here as one family': The musical performance of community in a Tanzanian *Kwaya*. In: Karen Ahlquist (ed.) *Chorus and Community*. Urbana: University of Illinois Press. pp. 19–44

Bastide, Roger (1972) *African Civilizations in the New World*. Translated by P Green. London: C Hurst & Co Publishers

Bastide, Roger (2006) [1998] Acculturation. *Encyclopaedia Universalis* (CD Rom Version 2006). Paris: Encyclopaedia Universalis France

Baxter, Lisa (1996) History, identity and meaning: Cape Town's Coon Carnival in the 1960s and 1970s. MA thesis, History Department, University of Cape Town, Cape Town

Becker, Heike & Oliphant, Chanell (n.d.) A hip-hopera in Cape Town: Performance, aesthetics, and the everyday of re-proclaiming Afrikaans. Unpublished paper, Department of Anthropology and Sociology, University of the Western Cape, Bellville. Available at http://www.health.uct.ac.za/sites/default/files/image_tool/images/2/HipHopera2014.pdf [accessed 9 April 2015]

Becker, Howard S (1982) *Art Worlds*. Berkeley: University of California Press

Becker, Judith (1975) Kroncong: Indonesian popular music. *Asian Music* 7(1): 14–19

Bekker, Simon, Leildé, Anne, Cornelissen, Scarlett & Horstmeier, Steffen (2000) The emergence of new identities in the Western Cape. *Politikon* 27(2): 221–237

Bergson, Henri (2011) *Le rire, essai sur la signification du comique*. Paris: Payot. [English translation: Cloudesley Brereton & Fred Rothwell (2008) *Laughter: An Essay on the Meaning of the Comic*. Mineola: Dover Publications]

Besteman, Catherine (2008) *Transforming Cape Town*. Berkeley: University of California Press

Bickford-Smith, Vivian (1994) Meanings of freedom, social position and identity among ex-slaves and their descendants in Cape Town, 1875–1910. In: Nigel Worden & Clifton C Crais (eds) *Breaking the Chains: Slavery and its Legacy in the Nineteenth Century Cape Colony*. Johannesburg: Witwatersrand University Press. pp. 289–312

Bickford-Smith, Vivian (1995) *Ethnic Pride and Racial Prejudice in Victorian Cape Town*. Johannesburg: Witwatersrand University Press

Bickford-Smith, Vivian (1996) Aspects of leisure and social identity in Cape Town, Cape Colony, ca. 1838–1910. Paper presented at the Third International Urban History Conference, Budapest, August
Brubaker, Rogers & Cooper, Frederick (2000) Beyond 'identity'. *Theory and Society* 29(1): 1–47
Brubaker, Rogers, Feischmidt, Margit, Fox, Jon & Grancea, Liana (2006) *Nationalist Politics and Everyday Ethnicity in a Transylvanian Town*. Princeton: Princeton University Press
Bruinders, Sylvia (2006/2007) 'This is our sport!': Christmas Band competitions and the enactment of an ideal community. *South African Music Studies* 26/27: 109–126
Bruinders, Sylvia (2012) Parading respectability: An ethnography of the Christmas Bands Movement in the Western Cape, South Africa. Dissertation submitted in partial fulfillment of the requirements for the degree of Doctor of Philosophy in Musicology, University of Illinois at Urbana-Champaign, Urbana. Available at https://www.ideals.illinois.edu/handle/2142/30896 [accessed 17 September 2012]
Burkholder, J Peter (1994) The uses of existing music: Musical borrowing as a field. *Notes* 50(3): 851–870
Caïn, Jacques & Caïn, Anne, (1982) Freud 'absolument pas musicien'. In: Jacques Caïn, Anne Caïn, Guy Rosolato, Jacqueline Rousseau Dujardin, Pierre Schaeffer, Jacques-Gabriel Trilling et al. *Psychanalyse et musique*. Paris: Les belles lettres. pp. 91–137
Cape Malay Choir Board (2004) *65th Anniversary Souvenir Brochure*. Cape Town: Cape Malay Choir Board
Casey, Edward S (1987) *Remembering: A Phenomenological Study*. Bloomington: Indiana University Press
Cassirer, Ernst (1979) *Symbol, Myth and Culture: Essays and Lectures of Ernst Cassirer, 1935–1945*. Edited by Donald Phillip Verene. New Haven: Yale University Press
Chartier, Roger (2011) *Cardenio, entre Cervantès et Shakespeare: histoire d'une pièce perdue*. Paris: Gallimard [English translation: Lloyd, Janet (2013) *Cardenio Between Cervantes and Shakespeare: The Story of a Lost Play*. Cambridge: Polity]
Chaumont, Jean-Michel (1997) *La concurrence des victimes: génocide, identité, reconnaissance*. Paris: La Découverte
Christopher, Anthony J (2002) 'To define the indefinable': Population classification and the census in South Africa. *Area* 34(4): 401–408. Available at http://onlinelibrary.wiley.com/doi/10.1111/1475-4762.00097/epdf [accessed 22 April 2015]
Christopher, Anthony J (2009) Delineating the nation: South African censuses 1865–2007. *Political Geography* 28: 101–109. Available at http://ac.els-cdn.com/S0962629809000067/1-s2.0-S0962629809000067-main.pdf?_tid=30a951a0-e8bf-11e4-a5ff-00000aacb361&acdnat=1429687038_b4a64c3f607040559657dea91880f1af[accessed 22 April 2015]
Cockrell, Dale (1997) *Demons of Disorder: Early Blackface Minstrels and their World*. Cambridge: Cambridge University Press
Cohen, Robin & Toninato, Paola (eds) (2010) *The Creolization Reader: Studies in Mixed Identities and Cultures*. London: Routledge
Collins, John (1989) The early history of West African highlife music. *Popular Music* 8(3): 221–230
Collins, John (1996) *Highlife Time*. Accra: Anansesem Press
Condé, Maryse (1978) *La civilisation du bossale*. Paris: L'Harmattan
Coplan, David B (2001) Sounds of the 'Third Way': Identity and the African Renaissance in contemporary South African popular traditional music. *Black Music Research Journal* 21(1): 107–124
Cornelissen, Scarlett & Horstmeier, Steffen (2002) The social and political construction of

identities in the new South Africa: An analysis of the Western Cape Province. *The Journal of Modern African Studies* 40(1): 55–58

Côté, Gérald (1998) *Processus de création et musique populaire: un exemple de métissage à la québécoise.* Paris: L'Harmattan

Cotten, Jean-Pierre (1982) Appropriation. In: Georges Labica & Gérard Bensussan (dir.) *Dictionnaire critique du marxisme.* Paris: Presses universitaires de France. pp. 56–59

Couzens, Tim (1982) 'Moralizing leisure time': The transatlantic connection and black Johannesburg, 1918–1936. In: Shula Marks & Richard Rathbone (eds) *Industrialisation and Social Change in South Africa: African Class Formation, Culture and Consciousness.* London: Longman. pp. 314–337

Covach, John R (1991) The rutles and the use of specific models in musical satire. *Indiana Theory Review* 11: 119–144. Available at https://scholarworks.iu.edu/dspace/bitstream/handle/2022/3529/CovachTheRuttlesV11.pdf?sequence=1 [accessed 23 April 2012]

Dangor, Suleman (2014) *Shaykh Yusuf Of Macassar: Scholar, Sufi and Freedom Fighter.* Saarbrücken: Lambert Academic Publishing

Darbon, Dominique (1996) La Truth and Réconciliation Commission: le miracle Sud-africain en question. *Revue française de science politique* 48(6): 707–724

Darracq, Vincent (2010) La question raciale à l'African National Congress (ANC) post-apartheid: production de discours, régulation et changement dans un parti politique. Thèse pour le doctorat en Science politique, Université Montesquieu-Bordeaux IV / Sciences Po Bordeaux, Pessac

Davids, Achmat (1980) *The Mosques of Bo-Kaap: A Social History of Islam at the Cape.* Athlone: South African Institute of Arabic and Islamic Research

Davids, Achmat (1985) Music and Islam. In: *5th Symposium on Ethnomusicology*, 30 August to 1 September 1984. Grahamstown: International Library of African Music. pp. 36–38

Davids, Achmat (1994a) 'My religion is superior to the law': The survival of Islam at the Cape of Good Hope. In: Yusuf Da Costa & Achmat Davids *Pages from Cape Muslim History.* Pietermaritzburg: Shuter & Shooter. pp. 57–70

Davids, Achmat (1994b) Alternative education: Tuan Guru and the formation of the Cape Muslim Community. In: Yusuf da Costa & Achmat Davids (eds) *Pages from Cape Muslim History.* Pietermaritzburg: Shuter & Shooter. pp. 47–56

Davids, Achmat (2011) *The Afrikaans of the Cape Muslims.* Cape Town: Protea

Davies, Christie (1990) *Ethnic Humor Around the World: A Comparative Analysis.* Bloomington: Indiana University Press

De Andrade, Oswald (1995) *A Utopia antropofágica.* São Paulo: Globo

De Andrade, Oswald (2015) *Manifesto Antropófago* [Cannibalist Manifesto]. In: *Enciclopédia Itaú Cultural de Arte e Cultura Brasileiras.* São Paulo: Itaú Cultural. Available at http://enciclopedia.itaucultural.org.br/termo4110/manifesto-antropofago-cannibalist-manifesto [accessed 2 November 2015]. [English translation available at https://events.ccc.de/congress/2009/Fahrplan/attachments/1386_cannibalmanifesto1928.pdf]

De Mijolla, Alain (1982) En guise d'ouverture. In: Jacques Caïn, Anne Caïn, Guy Rosolato, Jacqueline Rousseau Dujardin, Pierre Schaeffer, Jacques-Gabriel Trilling et al. *Psychanalyse et musique.* Paris: Les belles lettres: 7–17

Depestre, René (1980) *Bonjour et adieu à la négritude suivi de Travaux d'identité.* Paris: Robert Laffont

Desai, Desmond (1983) An investigation into the influence of the 'Cape Malay' child's cultural heritage upon his taste in appreciating music, with a proposed adaptation of the music curriculum in South African schools to reflect a possible application of 'Cape Malay' music therein. Unpublished M.Mus dissertation, University of Cape Town, Cape Town

Desai, Desmond (1986) Islamic music in South Africa: An investigation into Cape Muslim and Indian Muslim practices, both past and present. Unpublished thesis, University of Cape Town, Cape Town

Desai, Desmond (1993) The Ratiep art form of South African Muslims. PhD thesis, University of Natal, Durban

Desai, Desmond (1995) The musical context of the *Ratiep* performance in relation to South African Islamic and Cape Malay Music. In: Carol Muller (ed.) *Music in Southern Africa. Eleventh Symposium on Ethnomusicology, 23-25 August 1993.* Grahamstown: International Library of African Music. pp. 16–31

Desai, Desmond (2004) Adjusted performance requirements in musico-stylistic conservation strategies for the Cape Malay Nederlandslied: online. Stellenbosch, 26 August 2004. Available at http://www.eduprop.co.za/DUTCH.htm [accessed 25 February 2016]

Desai, Desmond (2005) Cape Malay music. In: Christine Lucia (ed.) *The World of South African Music: A Reader.* Newcastle: Cambridge Scholars Press. pp. 199–206

Dor, George Worlasi Kwasi (2004) Communal creativity and song ownership in Anlo Ewe musical practice: The case of Havolu. *Ethnomusicology* 48(1): 26–51

Drewett, Michael (2008) Packaging desires, album covers and the presentation of apartheid. In: Grant Olwage (ed.) *Composing Apartheid: Music for and Against Apartheid.* Johannesburg: Wits University Press. pp. 115–135

Du Plessis, Izak David (1935) *Die Bydrae von die Kaapse Maleier tot die Afrikaanse Volkslied.* Kaapstaad: Nasionale Press

Ebr.-Vally, Rehana (2001) *Kala Pani: Caste and Colour in South Africa.* Cape Town: Kwela Books

Eldridge, Matt & Seekings, Jeremy (1996) Mandela's lost province: The African National Congress and the Western Cape electorate in the1994 South African elections. *Journal of Southern African Studies* 22(4): 517–540

Eoan History Project (2013) *Eoan: Our History.* Johannesburg: Fourthwall Books

Erasmus, Zimitri (2000) Hair politics. In: Sarah Nuttal & Cheryl-Ann Michael (eds) *Senses of Culture: South African Culture Studies.* Oxford: Oxford University Press. pp. 380–392

Erasmus, Zimitri (2001) Re-imagining coloured identities in post-apartheid South Africa. In: Zimitri Erasmus (ed.) *Coloured by History, Shaped by Place.* Cape Town: Kwela Books. pp. 13–28

Erasmus, Zimitri (2008) Race. In: Nick Shepherd & Steven Robins (eds) *New South African Keywords.* Johannesburg: Jacana. pp. 169–181

Erasmus, Zimitri (2011) Creolization, colonial citizenship(s) and degeneracy: A critique of selected histories of Sierra Leone and South Africa. *Current Sociology* 59(5): 635–654

Erasmus, Zimitri & Pieterse, Edgar (1999) Conceptualising coloured identities in the Western Cape province of South Africa. In: Mai Palmberg (ed.) *National Identity and Democracy in Africa.* Uppsala: Nordic Africa Institute. pp. 167–187

Erlmann, Veit (1991) *African Stars: Studies in Black South African Performance.* Chicago: The University of Chicago Press

Erlmann, Veit (1996) *Nightsong, Performance, Power and Practice in South Africa.* Chicago: The University of Chicago Press

Erlmann, Veit (1997) 'God's Own country': African-American and black South African inventions of modernity. Paper presented at the Workshop on Les pratiques du panafricanisme, interactions culturelles et projets politiques, Bordeaux, Institut d'études politiques de Bordeaux, 22-24 mai

Escusa, Elodie (2015) À la recherche d'une identité sociale post-apartheid, l'Afrique du Sud du " milieu ", espace social stratégique de la Transformation. Thèse pour le Doctorat en Science politique, Pessac, Sciences Po Bordeaux. Available at https://tel.archives-ouvertes.fr/tel-01251990 [accessed 25 February 2016]

Evans, David (ed.) (2009) *Appropriation.* Cambridge: The MIT Press

Feld, Steven (1996) Pygmy POP: A genealogy of schizophonic mimesis. *Yearbook for Traditional Music* 28: 1–35

Feld, Steven (2000) A sweet lullaby for world music. *Public Culture* 12(1): 145–171

Feld, Steven & Kirkegaard, Annemette (2010) Entangled complicities in the prehistory of 'World Music': Poul Rovsing Olsen and Jean Jenkins encounter Brian Eno and David Byrne in the Bush of Ghosts. *Popular Musicology:* online. Available at http://www.popular-musicology-online.com/issues/04/feld.html [accessed 30 October 2015]

Fernando, Nathalie (2007) La construction paramétrique de l'identité musicale. *Cahiers d'ethnomusicologie* 20: 39–66

Fleming, John & Ledogar, Robert J (2008) Resilience, an evolving concept: A review of literature relevant to aboriginal research. *Pimatisiwin* 6(2): 7–23. Available at http://www.ncbi.nlm.nih.gov/pmc/articles/PMC2956753/ [accessed 1 February 2016]

Foucault, Michel (1994) Qu'est-ce qu'un auteur? In: *Dits et écrits 1954–1988, Tome 1, 1954–1969.* Édition établie sous la direction de Daniel Defert et François Ewald, avec la collaboration de Jacques Lagrange. Paris: Gallimard: 789–821 [English translation: Donald F Bouchard, Donald F & Sherry Simon (1977) What is an Author? In: Donald F Bouchard (ed.) *Language, Counter-Memory, Practice.* Ithaca: Cornell University Press. pp. 124–127]

Gassiep, A (1942) *Nederlandse Volksliedjies Soos Deur Maleiers Gesing.* Johannesburg: Ivan Joffee

Gendrel, Bernard & Moran, Patrick. n.d.(a) Atelier de théorie littéraire: humour, panorama de la notion. *Fabula, la recherche en littérature.* Available at http://www.fabula.org/atelier.php?Humour%3A_panorama_de_la_notion [accessed 23 November 2011]

Gendrel, Bernard & Moran, Patrick. n.d.(b) Atelier de théorie littéraire : humour, comique, ironie. *Fabula, la recherche en littérature.* Available at http://www.fabula.org/atelier.php?Humour%2C_comique%2C_ironie [accessed 23 November 2011]

Gensburger, Sarah & Lavabre, Marie-Claire (2005) Entre 'devoir de mémoire' et 'abus de mémoire': la sociologie de la mémoire comme tierce position. In: Bertrand Müller (ed.) *L'histoire entre mémoire, épistémologie: autour de Paul Ricœur.* Paris: Payot. pp. 75–96

Glissant, Édouard (1990) *Poétique de la Relation: Poétique III.* Paris: Gallimard [English translation: Wing, Betsy (1997) *Poetics of Relation.* Ann Arbor: University of Michigan Press]

Glissant, Édouard (1997) [1969] *L'intention poétique: Poétique II.* Paris: Gallimard

Glissant, Édouard (1997) *Traité du Tout-Monde: Poétique IV.* Paris: Gallimard

Glissant, Édouard (2005) *La cohée du Lamentin: Poétique V.* Paris: Gallimard

Glissant, Édouard (2006) *Une nouvelle région du monde: Esthétique I.* Paris: Gallimard

Glissant, Édouard (2007) *Mémoires des esclavages: La fondation d'un Centre national pour la mémoire des esclavages et de leurs abolitions.* Paris: Gallimard/La documentation française

Gqola, Pumla Dineo (2007) "Like three tongues in one mouth": Tracing the elusive lives of slave women in (slavocratic) South Africa. In: Nombonisa Gasa (ed.) *Women in South African History: Basus'iimbokodo, Bawel'imilambo/They Remove Boulders and Cross Rivers.* Cape Town: HSRC Press. pp. 21–41. Available at http://www.hsrcpress.ac.za/product.php?productid=2186&freedownload=1 [accessed 25 February 2016]

Gqola, Pumla Dineo (2010). *What is Slavery to Me? Postcolonial/Slave Memory in Post-Apartheid South Africa.* Johannesburg: Wits University Press

Green, Lawrence (1951) *Grow Lovely, Grow Old: The Story of Cape Town's Three Centuries.* Cape Town: Howard Timmins

Gruzinski, Serge (1996) Découverte, conquête et communication dans l'Amérique ibérique: avant les mots, au-delà des mots. In: Laurier Turgeon, Denis Delâge & Réal Ouellet (eds)

Transferts culturels et métissages Amérique / Europe, XVIème – XXème siècle. Québec: Presses de l'Université Laval. pp. 141–154

Gruzinski, Serge (1999) *La pensée métisse.* Paris: Fayard. [English translation: Dusinberre, Deke (2002) *The Mestizo Mind: The Intellectual Dynamics of Colonization and Globalization.* New York: Routledge]

Guillebaud, Christine (2010) Nimbuda ou la carrière d'un citron amer: musiques régionales et industrie cinématographique en Inde. *Gradhiva* 12: 57–79

Guillebaud, Christine, Mallet, Julien & Stoichita, Victor A (2010) La musique n'a pas d'auteur: ethnographies du copyright. *Gradhiva* 12: 5–19

Gunderson, Frank (2000) Kifungua Kinywa, or 'Opening the contest with chai'. In: Frank Gunderson & Gregory F Barz (eds) *Mashindano! Competitive Music Performance in East Africa.* Dar es Salaam: Mkuki na Nyota Publishers. pp. 7–17

Halbwachs, Maurice (1992) *On Collective Memory* (translated by Lewis A Coser). Chicago: University of Chicago Press

Hamm, Charles (1991) 'The constant companion of man': Separate development, Radio Bantu and music. *Popular Music* 10(2): 147–173

Haron, Muhammed (2001) Conflict of identities: The case of South Africa's Cape Malays. Paper presented at the Malay World Conference, Kuala Lumpur, 12–14 October. Available at http://phuakl.tripod.com/eTHOUGHT/capemalays.htm [accessed 8 May 2015]

Healey, Susan (2006) Cultural resilience, identity and the restructuring of political power in Bolivia. Paper submitted for the 11th Biennial Conference of the International Association for the Study of Common Property, Bali, Indonesia 19–23 June. Available at http://dlc.dlib.indiana.edu/dlc/handle/10535/1488 [accessed 02 February 2016]

Heinich, Nathalie (1998) *Ce que l'art fait à la sociologie.* Paris: Éditions de Minuit

Heins, Ernst (1976) Kroncong and Tanjidor: Two cases of urban folk music in Jakarta. *Asian Music* 7(1): 20–32

Helmlinger, Aurélie (2008) Les steelbands de Trinidad et Tobago : Ethnomusicologie cognitive d'une mémoire d'orchestre. *Intellectica* 1(48): 81–101. Available at http://hal.inria.fr/docs/00/55/70/37/PDF/2008_Intellectica_Helmlinger.pdf [accessed 4 October 2008]

Helmlinger, Aurélie (2011) La virtuosité comme arme de guerre psychologique. *Ateliers d'anthropologie*: online. Available at http://ateliers.revues.org/8798 [accessed 27 August 2013]

Helmlinger, Aurélie (2012) *Pan Jumbie: Mémoire sociale et musicale dans les steelbands (Trinidad et Tobago).* Nanterre: Société d'ethnologie

Hendriks, Cheryl (2005) Debating coloured identity in the Western Cape. *African Security Review* 14(4): 117–119

Hennion, Antoine (2010) Soli deo gloria. Bach était-il un compositeur? *Gradhiva* 12: 41–55

Henry, Edward O (1989) Institutions for the promotion of indigenous music: The case for Ireland's Comhaltas Ceoltoiri Eireann. *Ethnomusicology* 33(1): 67–95

Hobsbawm, Eric & Ranger, Terence (eds) (2012) *The Invention of Tradition.* Cambridge: Cambridge University Press

Holtzman, Glen G (2006) A treatise on Langarm in Cape Town. Dissertation for the B Mus, South African College of Music, University of Cape Town, Cape Town

Houssay-Holzschuch, Myriam (1999) *Le Cap, ville sud-africaine, ville blanche, vies noires.* Paris: L'Harmattan

Howard, Colin (1994) The 'No-Persons': An investigation into aspects of secular popular music in Cape Town. Submitted in partial fulfilment of the M.Mus degree in Ethnomusicology, Goldsmiths' College, University of London, London

Inglese, Francesca (2014) Choreographing Cape Town through goema music and dance. *African Music Journal* 9(4): 123–145

Jankélévitch, Vladimir (1964) *L'ironie*. Paris: Flammarion
Jankélévitch, Vladimir (1983) *La musique et l'ineffable* Paris: Le Seuil
Jappie, Saarah (2011) From the madrasah to the museums: The social life of the 'Kietaabs' of Cape Town. *History in Africa* 38: 369–399
Jeanson, Francis (1950) *Signification humaine du rire*. Paris: Le Seuil
Jenkins, Henry (1992) *Textual Poachers: Television Fans and Participatory Culture*. New York: Routledge, Chapman & Hall
Jeppie, Shamil (1987) Historical process and the constitution of subjects: I.D. du Plessis and the reinvention of the Malay. BA Honours thesis, University of Cape Town, Cape Town
Jeppie, Shamil (1990) Coon Carnival. *ADA (Art, Design, Architecture)* 8 (1st and 2nd quarters): 23
Jeppie, Shamil (1996a) Leadership and loyalties: The Imams of nineteenth century colonial Cape Town. *Journal of Religion in Africa* 26(2): 139–162
Jeppie, Shamil (1996b) Commemorations and identities: The 1994 tercentenary of Islam in South Africa. In: Tamara Sonn (ed.) *Islam and the Question of Minorities*. Atlanta: Scholars Press. pp. 73–90
Jeppie, Shamil (2001) Re-classifications: Coloured, Malay, Muslim. In: Zimitri Erasmus (ed.) *Coloured by History, Shaped by Place*. Cape Town: Kwela Books. pp. 80–96
Jeppie, Shamil & Soudien, Crain (eds) (1990) *The Struggle for District Six: Past and Present*. Cape Town: Buchu Books
Joyner, Charles (1975) A model for the analysis of folklore performance in historical context. *Journal of American Folklore* 88: 254–265
Jules-Rosette, Bennetta (1984) *The Messages of Tourist Art: An African Semiotic System in Comparative Perspective*. New York: Plenum Press
Keep the Dream Male Choir Board (2013) *A Member of Keep The Dream Malay Choir Forum Presents The Heritage Cup, Malay Choir Competitions*. Cape Town: Keep the Dream Male Choir Board
Kornhauser, Bronia (1978) In defence of Kroncong. In: Margaret Kartomi (ed.) *Studies in Indonesian Music*. Monash Papers on Southeast Asia 7. Victoria (Australia): Monash University, Centre of Southeast Asian Studies. pp. 104–183
Kosmicki, Guillaume (2010) Musique techno, *mix*, *sample*: un défi à la notion de propriété. *Gradhiva* 12: 99–115
Krichtafovitch, Igor (2006) *Humor Theory: Formula of Laughter*. Denver: Outskirts Press
Krog, Antjie (1998) *Country of My Skull*. Johannesburg: Random House
Lavabre, Marie-Claire (1994) Usages du passé, usages de la mémoire. *Revue française de science politique* 44(3): 480–493
Lavabre, Marie-Claire (1995) Entre histoire et mémoire: à la recherche d'une méthode. In: Jean-Claude Martin (ed.) *La guerre civile entre histoire et mémoire*. Nantes: Ouest Éditions. pp. 39–47
Lewis, Gavin (1987) *Between the Wire and the Wall: A History of South African 'Coloured' Politics*. Cape Town: David Philip
Lodge, Tom (1981) The destruction of Sophiatown. *The Journal of Modern African Studies* 19(1): 107–132
Lortat-Jacob, Bernard (1998) *Chants de passion, au cœur d'une confrérie de Sardaigne*. Paris: Les éditions du Cerf
Lortat-Jacob, Bernard (2004) Ce que chanter veut dire. Étude de pragmatique (Castelsardo, Sardaigne). *L'Homme* 171/172: 83–101
Lortat-Jacob, Bernard (2006) Concord and discord: Singing together in a Sardinian brotherhood. In: Karen Ahlquist (ed.) *Chorus and Community*. Urbana: University of Illinois Press. pp. 87–110

Lucia, Christine (2002) Abdullah Ibrahim and the uses of memory. *British Journal of Ethnomusicology* 11(2): 125–143
Ludovici, Anthony (1932) *The Secret of Laughter*. London: Constable. Available at http://www.anthonymludovici.com/sl_03.htm [accessed 11 October 2012]
Malan, Rian (2000) Where does the lion sleep tonight? *Rolling Stone*, May 25. Available at http://www.3rdearmusic.com/forum/mbube2.html [accessed 3 November 2015]
Mallet, Julien & Samson, Guillaume (2010) Droits d'auteur, bien commun et création: tensions et recompositions à Madagascar et à La Réunion. *Gradhiva* 12: 117–137
Mangolte, Pierre-André (2010) Copyright et propriété intellectuelle, retour sur un vieux débat, l'exemple américain. *Gradhiva* 12: 21–37
Manuel, Peter (1993) *Cassette Culture: Popular Music and Technology in North India*. Chicago: The University of Chicago Press
Manuel, Peter (1994) Puerto Rican music and cultural identity: Creative appropriation of Cuban sources from Danza to Salsa. *Ethnomusicology* 38(2): 249–280
Martin, Denis-Constant (1998) *Le gospel afro-américain: des spirituals au rap religieux*. Arles: Cité de la musique/Actes Sud
Martin, Denis-Constant (1999) *Coon Carnival: New Year in Cape Town, Past and Present*. Cape Town: David Philip
Martin, Denis-Constant (2000) The burden of the name: Classifications and constructions of identity. The case of the 'Coloureds' in Cape Town (South Africa). *African Philosophy* 13(2): 99–124
Martin, Denis-Constant (2001) What's in the name 'Coloured'? In: Abebe Zegeye (ed.) *Social Identities in the New South Africa: After Apartheid*. Volume 1. Cape Town: Kwela Books. pp. 249–267
Martin, Denis-Constant (2005) Musique dans la rue et contrôle de l'espace urbain, Le Cap (Afrique du Sud). *Cahiers internationaux de sociologie* 119: 247–265
Martin, Denis-Constant (2008) Our kind of jazz: Musique et identité en Afrique du Sud. *Critique internationale* 38: 90–110. Available at [http://www.sciencespo.fr/ceri/sites/sciencespo.fr.ceri/files/critique_add/ci38_martin.pdf]
Martin, Denis-Constant (ed.) (2010) *L'identité en jeux. Pouvoirs, identifications, mobilisations*. Paris: CERI/Karthala
Martin, Denis-Constant (2013) *Sounding the Cape: Music, Identity and Politics in South Africa*. Somerset West: African Minds
Martin, Denis-Constant & Roueff, Olivier (2002) *La France du jazz: musique, modernité et identité dans la première moitié du XXe siècle*. Marseille: Parenthèses
Mason, John Edwin (1999) 'Some religion he must have': Slaves, Sufism, and conversion to Islam at the Cape. South Eastern Regional Seminar in African Studies, Fall Conference, Savannah, GA, October 15-16. Available at http://www.ecu.edu/african/sersas/MasonSERSASF99.htm [accessed 15 March 2011]
Mason, John Edwin (2002) 'A faith for ourselves': Slavery, Sufism, and conversion to Islam at the Cape. *South African Historical Journal* 46(1): 3–24
Mason, John Edwin (2007) 'Mannenberg': Notes on the making of an icon and anthem. *African Studies Quarterly* 9(4): 25–46. Available at http://www.africa.ufl.edu/asq/v9/v9i4a3.htm [accessed 12 January 2011]
Mattos, Hebe Maria (2003) Citoyenneté, mémoire de la captivité et identité noire dans le Brésil contemporain. *Cahiers du Brésil contemporain* 53/54: 115–147
Mbeki, Thabo (1998) *Africa: The Time has Come*. Cape Town/Johannesburg: Tafelberg/Mafube
McCormick, Kay (2002) *Language in Cape Town's District Six*. Oxford: Oxford University Press

Mellet, Patric Tariq (2010) *Lenses on Cape Identities: Exploring Roots in South Africa.* Cape Town: Dibanisa Publishing

Mellor, David A (2009) Media-haunted humans: Cindy Sherman, Richard Prince, John Stezaker (1998). In: David Evans (ed.) *Appropriation.* Cambridge: MIT Press. pp. 99–103

Mills, Sherylle (1996) Indigenous music and the law: An analysis of national and international legislation. *Yearbook for Traditional Music* 28: 57–86

Molino, Jean (2007) Du plaisir à l'esthétique: les multiples formes de l'expérience musicale. In: Jean-Jacques Nattiez (ed.) *Musiques: une encyclopédie pour le XXIe siècle, 5: L'unité de la musique.* Arles: Actes Sud/Cité de la Musique. pp. 1154–1196

Molino, Jean (2009) *Le singe musicien: sémiologie et anthropologie de la musique;* précédé de: 'Introduction à l'œuvre musicologique de Jean Molino', par Jean-Jacques Nattiez. Paris: Actes Sud/INA

Motala, Tasnim (2013) Muslim residential patterns in Cape Town: An examination of the changes and continuities in the Cape Town Muslim community. A dissertation submitted in fulfillment of the requirements for the award of the degree of Masters in Sociology, Faculty of the Humanities, University of Cape Town, Cape Town. Available at https://open.uct.ac.za/handle/11427/6830?show=full [accessed 29 June 2015]

Mountain, Alan (2004) *An Unsung Heritage: Perspectives on Slavery.* Claremont, Cape Town: David Philip

Moussali, Bernard (1999) Sufi chants from Cairo. In: Delia Morris (trans.) *Egypt, La Châdhiliyya, Sufi Chants from Cairo.* Paris: Institut du monde arabe (CD 321023)

Nattiez, Jean-Jacques (1990) *Music and Discourse: Toward a Semiology of Music.* Translated by Carolyn Abbate. Princeton: Princeton University Press

Nattiez, Jean-Jacques (1997) Faits et interprétations en musicologie. *Horizons Philosophiques* 7(2): 33–42

Nattiez, Jean-Jacques (2009) Introduction à l'œuvre musicologique de Jean Molino. In: Jean Molino (ed.) *Le singe musicien, sémiologie et anthropologie de la musique.* Paris: Actes Sud/INA. pp. 13–69

Nel, Stigue (2012) The repertoire of Nederlandse liedjies of the Cape Malay Choirs: A comparison of contemporary performances of these compositions to published transcriptions of seventeenth and eighteenth century Dutch folk songs. A minor dissertation submitted in partial fulfillment of the requirements for the award of the degree of M.Mus, Faculty of the Humanities, University of Cape Town, Cape Town

Nketia, Kwabena (2005) Ethnomusicology and African music: Collected papers. Volume 1: *Modes of Inquiry and Interpretation.* Accra: Afram Publications

Noiriel, Gérard (1997) Représentation nationale et catégories sociales, l'exemple des réfugiés politiques. *Genèses* 26: 25–54

Oliphant, Chanell (2013) The changing faces of the Klopse: Performing the Rainbow Nation during the Cape Town Carnival. Dissertation presented in partial fulfilment of the degree of Master of Arts in Anthropology, Department of Anthropology and Sociology, University of the Western Cape, Belleville. Available at http://etd.uwc.ac.za/xmlui/handle/11394/3969 [accessed 20 October 2015]

O'Toole, James (1973) *Watts and Woodstock: Identity and Culture in the United States and South Africa.* New York: Holt, Rinehart & Winston

Parker, Martin (1991) Reading the charts: Making sense with the hit parade. *Popular Music* 10(2): 205–217

Pettan, Svanibor (1992) 'Lambada' in Kosovo: A case study in gipsy creativity. *Journal of the Gipsy Lore Society* 2(2): 117–130

Pope, Rob (2005) *Creativity, Theory, History, Practice.* Oxon: Routledge

Posel, Deborah (2001) Race as common sense: Racial classification in twentieth-century South Africa. *African Studies Review* 44(2): 87–113

Prince, Richard (1977) Practicing without a license: online. Available at http://www.richardprince.com/writings/practicing-without-a-license-1977/ [accessed 2 November 2015]

Racine, Josiane & Racine, Jean-Luc (1995) La bouche d'ombre ou comment est né ce livre et ce qu'il nous dit. In: Viramma, Josiane Racine & Jean-Luc Racine (eds) *Une vie de paria, le rire des asservis, Pays tamoul, Inde du Sud.* Paris: Plon/Éditions UNESCO. pp. 433–508

Radano, Ronald (2003) *Lying a Nation: Race and Black Music.* Chicago: University of Chicago Press

Rahman, Zarin (2001) The Coon Carnival in the 1940's: An expression of culture within a changing political and economic environment. MA dissertation, Department of Historical Studies, University of Cape Town, Cape Town. Avaialable at https://open.uct.ac.za/bitstream/handle/11427/7894/thesis_hum_2001_rahman_z.pdf?sequence=1 [accessed 26 January 2015]

Ramello, Giovanni B (2004) *Private Appropriability and Sharing of Knowledge: Convergence or Contradiction ? The Opposite Tragedy of the Creative Commons.* Available at http://papers.ssrn.com/sol3/papers.cfm?abstract_id=639102 [accessed 5 November 2015]

Rasmussen, Lars (2000) *Abdullah Ibrahim: A Discography.* Copenhagen: The Booktrader

Ricœur, Paul (1969a) Existence et herméneutique. In: Paul Ricœur (ed.) *Le conflit des interprétations: essais d'herméneutique.* Paris: Le Seuil. pp. 7–28

Ricœur, Paul (1969b) Herméneutique des symboles et réflexion philosophique (II).In: Paul Ricœur (ed.) *Le conflit des interprétations: essais d'herméneutique.* Paris: Le Seuil. pp. 311–329

Ricœur, Paul (1990) *Soi-même comme un autre.* Paris: Le Seuil. [English translation: Blamey, Kathleen (1990) *Oneself as Another.* Chicago: University of Chicago Press]

Ricœur, Paul (2006) *Memory, History, Forgetting.* Translated by Kathleen Blamey & David Pellauer. Chicago: The University of Chicago Press (Kindle edition)

Ridd, Rosemary (1994) *Creating ethnicity in the British colonial Cape: Coloured and Malay contrasted.* Collected Seminar Papers 48: 51–61. London: Institute of Commonwealth Studies. Available at http://sas-space.sas.ac.uk/4251/ [accessed 26 May 2015]

Rohlehr, Gordon (1985) 'Man talking to man': Calypso and social confrontation in Trinidad 1970 to 1984. *Caribbean Quarterly* 31(2): 1–13

Roseberry, William (1994) Hegemony and the language of contention. In: Gilbert M Joseph & Daniel Nugent (eds) *Everyday Forms of State Formation: Revolution and the Negotiation of Rule in Modern Mexico.* Durham: Duke University Press. pp. 355–366

Rosolato, Guy (1982) L'écoute musicale comme méditation. In: Jacques Caïn, Anne Caïn, Guy Rosolato, Jacqueline Rousseau Dujardin, Pierre Schaeffer, Jacques-Gabriel Trilling et al. *Psychanalyse et musique.* Paris: Les belles lettres: 139–151

Ross, Lloyd & Malan, Rian (2010) *The Silver Fez.* A feature documentary. Johannesburg: Shifty Records (87', SHIFT DVD 003)

Roubertie, Lorraine (2012) La transmission du jazz en Afrique du Sud depuis la chute du régime d'apartheid, enseignement, action culturelle et sociale, l'exemple de la région du Cap Occidental. Unpublished dissertation for the PhD in Musicology, Université de Paris 8-Saint Denis, Saint Denis

Salo, Elaine (2004) Respectable mothers, tough men and good daughters. Making persons in Manenberg township, South Africa. Doctoral dissertation submitted to the Anthropology Department, Emory University, Atlanta

Salo, Elaine (2005a) Negotiating gender and personhood in the new South Africa: Adolescent women and gangsters in Manenberg township on the Cape Flats. In: Steven L Robins (ed.)

Limits to Liberation After Apartheid: Citizenship, Governance and Culture. Cape Town: James Currey/David Philip. pp. 173–189

Salo, Elaine (2005b) Mans is ma soe: Ganging practices in Manenberg, South Africa and the ideologies of a masculinity, gender and generational relations. Paper presented at the Conference on A New Decade of Criminal Justice in South Africa – Consolidating Transformation, Villa Via Hotel, Gordon's Bay, Western Cape, 7–8 February. Available at http://www.csvr.org.za/wits/confpaps/salo.htm [accessed 22 September 2016]

Sayer, Derek (1994) Everyday forms of state formation: Some dissident remarks on 'Hegemony'. In: Gilbert M Joseph & Daniel Nugent (eds) *Everyday Forms of State Formation: Revolution and the Negotiation of Rule in Modern Mexico*. Durham: Duke University Press. pp. 367–377

Scales, Christopher (2007) Powwows, intertribalism, and the value of competition. *Ethnomusicology* 51(1): 1–29

Schlanger, Judith (1995) Tradition et nouveauté. In: Vincent Dehoux et al. (eds) *Ndroje Balendro, Musiques, terrains et disciplines: textes offerts à Simha Arom*. Louvain: Peeters. pp. 179–185

Schoeman, Chris (1994) *District Six: The Spirit of Kanala*. Cape Town: Human and Rousseau

Scruton, Roger (1987) Laughter. In: John Morreall (ed.) *The Philosophy of Laughter and Humor*. Albany, New York: State University of New York Press. pp. 156–171

Seeger, Anthony (1996) Ethnomusicologists, archives, professional organizations, and the shifting ethics of intellectual property. *Yearbook for Traditional Music* 28: 87–105

Seeger, Anthony (1997) Ethnomusicology and music law. In: Bruce Ziff & Pratima V Rao (eds) *Borrowed Power: Essays on Cultural Appropriation*. New Brunswick: Rutgers University Press. pp. 52–67

Seekings, Jeremy (2000) *The UDF: A History of the United Democratic Front in South Africa, 1983–1991*. Cape Town: David Philip

Serfaty-Garzon, Perla (2003) L'Appropriation. In: *Dictionnaire de l'habitat et du logement*. Paris: Armand Colin. pp. 27–30. Available at http://www.perlaserfaty.net/texte4.htm [accessed 3 November 2015]

Shain, Richard M (2002) Roots in reverse: *Cubanismo* in twentieth century Senegalese music. *International Journal of African Historical Studies* 35(1): 83–101

Shain, Richard M (2009) The Re(public) of Salsa: Afro-Cuban music in fin de siècle Dakar. *Africa* 79(2): 186–206

Shell, Robert CH (1994) *Children of Bondage: A Social History of the Slave Society at the Cape of Good Hope, 1652–1838*. Johannesburg: Witwatersrand University Press

Shell, Robert CH (2006) Madresahs and Moravians. Muslim educational institutions in the Cape Colony, 1792 to 1910. *New Contree: A Journal of Historical and Human Sciences for Southern Africa* 51: 101–113

Shepherd, Nick (2008) Heritage. In: Nick Shepherd & Steven Robins (eds) *New South African Keywords*. Johannesburg: Jacana. pp. 116–128

Sibony, Daniel (2010) *Le sens du rire et de l'humour*. Paris: Odile Jacob

Sonn, Christopher C & Fisher, Adrian T (1996) Psychological sense of community in a politically constructed group. *Journal of Community Psychology* 24(4): 417–430

Sonn, Christopher C & Fisher, Adrian T (1998) Sense of community: Community resilient responses to oppression and change. *Journal of Community Psychology* 26(5): 457–472

Soudien, Crain (2001) District Six and its uses in the discussion about non-racialism. In: Zimitri Erasmus (ed.) *Coloured by History: Shaped by Place*. Cape Town: Kwela Books. pp. 114–130

Soudien, Crain (2009) *Youth Identity in Contemporary South Africa: Race, Culture and Schooling*. Claremont, Cape Town: New Africa Books

Statistics South Africa (1998) *The People of South Africa: Population Census 1996, the Count and*

How It was Done (Report No. 03-01-17(1996)). Pretoria: Statistics South Africa. Available at https://apps.statssa.gov.za/census01/Census96/HTML/Metadata/Docs/count/chapter_1.htm [accessed 21 December 2015]

Stillman, Amy Ku'Uleialoha (1996) Hawaiian hula competitions: Event, repertoire, performance, tradition. *The Journal of American Folklore* 109/434: 357–380

Stone, Gerald L (1971) The Coon Carnival. Mimeographed unpublished paper. University of Cape Town: Abe Bailey Institute of Interracial Studies

Stone, Gerald L (1991) An ethnographic and socio-semantic analysis of lexis among working class Afrikaans-speaking coloured adolescent and young adult males in the Cape Peninsula. 1963–1990. MA thesis, University of Cape Town, Cape Town

Stone, Gerald L (1995) The lexikon and sociolinguistic codes of the working class Afrikaans-speaking Cape Peninsula coloured community. In: Rajend Meshtrie (ed.) *Language and Social History: Studies in South African Sociolinguistics.* Cape Town: David Philip. pp. 277–290

Stuempfle, Steven (1995) *The Steelband Movement: The Forging of a National Art in Trinidad and Tobago.* Philadelphia: University of Pennsylvania Press

Taguieff, Pierre-André (2001) *Force of Prejudice: On Racism and Its Doubles (Contradictions of Modernity).* Translated and edited by Hassan Melehy. Minneapolis: University of Minnesota Press

Taguieff, Pierre-André (2010) *Le racisme.* Paris: Archives Karéline/Bookollegium

Thomas, Wyndham (1998) Composing, arranging and editing: A historical survey. In: Thomas Wyndham (ed.) *Composition, Performance, Reception: Studies in the Creative Process in Music.* Aldershot: Ashgate. pp. 35–52

Trébinjac, Sabine (1997) Une utilisation insolite de la musique de l'autre. In: François Borel et al. (eds) *Pom, Pom, Pom, Pom: musiques et caetera.* Neuchâtel: GHK/Musée d'ethnographie. pp. 227–241

Turgeon, Laurier (1996) Échange d'objet et conquête de l'Autre en nouvelle France au XVIème siècle. In: Laurier Turgeon, Denis Delâge & Réal Ouellet (eds) *Transferts culturels et métissages Amérique/Europe, XVIème – XXème siècle.* Québec: Presses de l'Université Laval. pp. 155–168

Turgeon, Laurier. (2003) *Patrimoines métissés, contextes coloniaux et post-coloniaux.* Paris: Éditions de la Maison des sciences de l'homme/Québec: Presses de l'Université Laval

Vahed, Goolam & Jeppie, Shamil (2005) Multiple communities: Muslims in post-apartheid South Africa. In: John Daniel, Roger Southall & Jessica Lutchman (eds) *State of the Nation, South Africa, 2004-2005.* Cape Town: HSRC Press. pp. 252–286

Van der Merwe, Schalk Daniël (2015) The dynamics of the interaction between music and society in recorded popular Afrikaans music, 1900–2015. Thesis presented in fulfilment of the requirements for the degree of Doctor of Philosophy, History, Faculty of Arts and Social Sciences, Stellenbosch University, Stellenbosch

Van der Wal, Anne Marieke (2009) '*Dis 'n Kaapse Kultur'. The Cape Malay Choir Board and their Moppies: Governing a Culture and Community.* Leiden: African Studies Centre. Available at http://www.asclibrary.nl/docs/327/520/327520221-01.pdf [accessed 3 October 2011]

Vovelle, Michel (1992) *Idéologies et mentalités.* Paris: Gallimard

Wale, Kim (2013) Confronting exclusion: Time for radical reconciliation. *Reconciliation Barometer 2013.* Cape Town: Institute for Justice and Reconciliation. Available at http://reconciliationbarometer.org/wp-content/uploads/2013/12/IJR-Barometer-Report-2013-22Nov1635.pdf [accessed 18 November 2015]

Wale, Kim (2014) Reflecting on reconciliation: Lessons from the past, prospects for the future. *Reconciliation Barometer 2014.* Cape Town: Institute for Justice and Reconciliation. Available at http://reconciliationbarometer.org/wp-content/uploads/2014/12/IJR-SA-Reconciliation-Barometer-Report-2014.pdf [accessed 18 November 2015]

Ward, Kerry (1995). The '300 years: The making of Cape muslim culture' exhibition, Cape Town, April 1994: Liberating the castle? *Social Dynamics* 21(1): 96–131

Waterman, Christopher A (1990) *Jùjú: A Social History and Ethnography of an African Popular Music*. Chicago: University of Chicago Press

Waterman, Christopher A (2000) Race music: Bo Chatmon, 'Corrine Corrina', and the excluded middle. In: Ronald Radano & Philip V Bohlman (eds) *Music and the Racial Imagination*. Chicago: University of Chicago Press. pp. 167–205

Weintraub, Andrew N (2001) Contest-ing culture: Sundanese Wayang Golek Purwa competitions in New Order Indonesia. *Asian Theatre Journal* 18(1): 87–104

Wenger, Étienne (2012) *Communities of Practice and Social Learning Systems: The Career of a Concept*. Available at http://wenger-trayner.com/wp-content/uploads/2012/01/09-10-27-CoPs-and-systems-v2.01.pdf [accessed 9 July 2015]

Wentzel, Tazneem (2011) The city with soul and carnival. Unpublished paper presented at the New Social Forms Seminar, Department of Sociology and Social Anthropology, University of Stellenbosch, Stellenbosch

White, Bob W (2008) *Rumba Rules: The Politics of Dance Music in Mobutu's Zaire*. Durham: Duke University Press

Wicomb, Zoë (1998) Shame and identity: The case of the coloured in South Africa. In: Derek Attridge & Rosemary Jolly (eds) *Writing South Africa: Literature, Apartheid, and Democracy 1970–1995*. Cambridge: Cambridge University Press. pp. 91–107

Williams, Patrick (1991) L'histoire drôle comme instrument de connaissance. In: Éliane Daphy & Diana Rey-Hulmann (eds) *Paroles à rire*. Paris: INALCO (Colloques Langues'O). pp. 77–87

Williams, Patrick (2010) Standards et standardisation: sur un aspect du répertoire des musiciens de jazz. In: Jean Jamin & Patrick Williams *Une anthropologie du jazz*. Paris: CNRS éditions. pp. 147–202

Winberg, Christine (1992) Satire, slavery and the ghoemaliedjies of the Cape Muslims. *New Contrast* 19(4): 78–96

Yampolsky, Philip (2010) Kroncong revisited: New evidence from old sources. *Archipel* 79: 7–56

Zemp, Hugo (1996) The/An ethnomusicologist and the record business. *Yearbook for Traditional Music* 28: 36–56

Ziff, Bruce & Rao, Pratima V (1997) Introduction to cultural appropriation: A framework for analysis. In: Bruce Ziff & Pratima V Rao (eds) *Borrowed Power: Essays on Cultural Appropriation*. New Brunswick: Rutgers University Press. pp. 1–27

Interviews with musicians, judges and experts[1]

Armelle Gaulier

1. Michael ABRAHAMS, musician, Ronald FISHER, musician, and Eddie MATTHEWS, former Klops captain, Mitchells Plain, 11 October 2006.
2. Taliep ABRAHAMS, composer, coach, Spesbona (*Klops*), Mitchells Plain, 18 September and 21 September 2006.
3. Ismail BEY, backtrack composer, Mitchells Plain, 19 September and 23 September 2006.
4. Mujait BOOYSEN, *moppie* soloist, The Kenfac Entertainers, Kensington, 11 October 2006.
5. Gamja and Ismail (†) DANTE, Malay Choir musicians, composers and coaches, Mitchells Plain, 17 January 2008.
6. Ismail DANTE (†), musician, coach and composer, Mitchells Plain, 31 August and 7 September 2006.
7. "Kaatje" Abubakar DAVIDS, coach, the Continentals Male Choir, Athlone, 22 January 2008.
8. Anwar GAMBENO, coach and composer, the Young Tulips Sangkor; captain, The All Stars, Mitchells Plain, 31 August 2006 and 11 October 2006; 19 January 2008.
9. Frank HENDRICKS, Department of Afrikaans and Nederlands, University of the Western Cape, 20 February 2008.
10. Ibrahim HENDRICKS, *nederlands* soloist, the Parkdales, Parkwood, 18 February 2008.
11. Tape JACOBS, captain of the Beystars (*Klops*), Mitchells Plain, 9 August 2006.
12. Vincent KOLBE (†), former librarian; expert on Cape Town musics, Plumstead, 11 October 2006.
13. Ikeraam LEEMAN, *nederlands* soloist, the Woodstock Royals Malay Choir, Woodstock, 28 January 2008.
14. Ismail LEEMAN, coach, the Parkdales Malay Choir, Kensington, 5 March 2008.
15. Mariam LEEMAN, school teacher and amateur singer, Bridgetown, 12 February 2008.
16. Melvyn MATTHEWS, former Klops captain, Mitchells Plain, 11 October 2006.
17. Abduraghman "Maan" MORRIS, coach, the Young Men Sporting Club, Mitchells Plain, 9 and 17 January 2008.
18. Ismail MORRIS, adjudicator for the *nederlandsliedjies*, *Suid-Afrikaanse Koorraad*, Athlone 26 February 2008.
19. Shawn PETTERSEN, coach, the Kenfac Entertainers (*Klops*), Cape Town, 3 October 2006.
20. Mr SALIE, coach, the Continentals Malay Choir, Athlone, 14 January 2008.
21. Adam "Aram" SAMODIEN (†), *moppie* composer; former coach, the Woodstock Royals Malay Choir; former president, *Suid-Afrikaanse Koorraad*, Woodstock, 10 August and 6 September2006; 24 and 29 January 2008.
22. Robert CH SHELL (†), historian, University of Cape Town, Cape Town, 19 February 2008.

23. Wim van ZANTEN, ethnomusicologist, Institute for Social and Cultural Studies, Leiden University, the Netherlands, Paris, 17 June 2008.
24. Wium van ZYL, Department of Afrikaans and Nederlands, University of the Western Cape, 8 February 2008.

Denis-Constant Martin

1. Sallie ACHMAT, former *nederlands* solo singer; coach, The Starlites Malay Choir; former chief adjudicator, Keep the Dream Malay Choir Forum, Landsdowne, 20 May 2013.
2. Shafiek APRIL, president, Cape Malay Choir Board, Hanover Park, 20 May 2013.
3. Gamja DANTE, musician, coach and composer, and Melvyn MATTHEWS, former Klops captain and chief executive officer, Kaapse Klopse Karnaval Association, Victoria and Alfred Waterfront, Cape Town, 17 October 2011.
4. Ismail (†) and Gamja DANTE, musicians, coaches and composers, Hanover Park, 20 October 2011.
5. Shamiel DOMINGO, former *nederlands* solo singer; former chief adjudicator for the *nederlandsliedjies*, Cape Malay Choir Board, Wynberg, 15 October 2011 and 22 May 2013.
6. Rushdien DRAMAT, *nederlands* solo singer; coach for several Malay Choirs, Athlone, 17 October 2011.
7. Joseph GABRIELS (†), opera singer, Groote Schuur Hospital, Cape Town, 18 October 1994.
8. Anwar GAMBENO, coach and composer, the Young Tulips Sangkoor; captain, the Nokia All Stars; president, Keep the Dream Malay Choir Board, Mitchells Plain, 3 October 1994; 4 December 2001; 11 October 2011; 15 May 2013; 13 April 2015.
9. Anwar GAMBENO, coach and composer, the Young Tulips Sangkoor; captain, the Nokia All Stars; president, Keep the Dream Malay Choir Board, and Muneeb GAMBENO, businessman, lawyer; director of the Kaapse Klopse Karnaval Association, Mitchells Plain, 2 May 2015.
10. Ahmed ISMAIL, chairperson, the Shoprite Jonge Studente, Landsdowne, 13 October 2011; Mitchells Plain, 22 April 2015.
11. Felicia LESCH, Certificate Programme Co-ordinator, Outreach Co-ordinator, Department of Music, University of Stellenbosch; adjudicator, Cape Malay Choir Board, Stellenbosch, 7 October 2011 and 15 May 2013.
12. Achmat Hadji LEVY, tailor; former carnival organiser, Lentegeur, 28 January 1994.
13. Mac McKENZIE, guitarist, composer, Bridgetown, 4 October 2011.
14. Abdullah "Hajji" MAGED, coach, the Primroses Malay Choir, Landsdowne, 13 October 2011.
15. Melvyn MATTHEWS, former Klops captain; chief executive officer, Kaapse Klopse Karnaval Association, Kensington, 22 April 2015.
16. Melvyn MATTHEWS, then *Klops* captain, the Penny Pinchers All Stars and Sakie "van Die Star"(†), former usher, The Star bioscope (District Six), Woodstock, 17 January 1994.
17. Abduraghman "Maan" MORRIS, president and coach, the Young Men Sporting Club, Colorado Park, 21 April 2015.
18. Adnaan MORRIS and Abduraghman "Maan" MORRIS, respectively coach and president, the Young Men Sporting Club, Primrose Park, 21 May 2013.
19. Taliep PETERSEN (†), composer; singer; coach, Athlone, 15 January 1994.
20. Waseef PIEKAAN, *moppie* composer; solo singer; comedian; coach, the Kenfac Entertainers, Mitchells Plain, 25 October 2011.

21. Adam "Aram" SAMODIEN (†), composer; former coach, the Woodstock Royals Malay Choir; former president, *Suid-Afrikaanse Koorraad*; and Magdie LUCKIE, Omar PETERSEN and Anwar LOSPER, Malay Choirs experts, Woodstock, 19 January 1994.
22. Adam "Aram" SAMODIEN (†) and Rashaad MALICK, respectively, composer; former coach, the Woodstock Royals Malay Choir; former president, *Suid-Afrikaanse Koorraad*, and musician, Woodstock, 12 October 2011.

Note

1. Affiliations of captains, coaches and singers with particular choirs are indicated as they were at the time of the interviews.

Cover of the CMCB programme for the Top 8 and Grand Finale of the 2011 competitions

Keep the Dream Malay Choir Forum Coat of Arms

www.ingramcontent.com/pod-product-compliance
Lightning Source LLC
Chambersburg PA
CBHW021931290426
44108CB00012B/804